The Unmaking
of a President

HERBERT Y. SCHANDLER

☆☆

The Unmaking of a President

Lyndon Johnson and Vietnam

PRINCETON UNIVERSITY PRESS
PRINCETON, NEW JERSEY

Copyright © 1977 by Princeton University Press
Published by Princeton University Press
Princeton, New Jersey
In the United Kingdom: Princeton University Press
Guildford, Surrey

Library of Congress Cataloging in Publication Data
will be found on the last printed page of this book

Printed in the United States of America
by Princeton University Press
Princeton, New Jersey

DEDICATED TO

THE BRAVE YOUNG AMERICANS WHO
GAVE THEIR LIVES FOR THEIR
COUNTRY'S OBJECTIVES IN VIETNAM

CONTENTS

☆ ☆

vii

1968

JANUARY

SUN	MON	TUES	WED	THURS	FRI	SAT
	1	2	3	4	5	6
7	8	9	10	11	12	13
14	15	16	17	18	19	20
21	22	23	24	25	26	27
28	29	30	31			

FEBRUARY

SUN	MON	TUES	WED	THURS	FRI	SAT
				1	2	3
4	5	6	7	8	9	10
11	12	13	14	15	16	17
18	19	20	21	22	23	24
25	26	27	28	29		

MARCH

SUN	MON	TUES	WED	THURS	FRI	SAT
					1	2
3	4	5	6	7	8	9
10	11	12	13	14	15	16
17	18	19	20	21	22	23
24	25	26	27	28	29	30
31						

INTRODUCTION

THE Tet offensive of 1968 was one of the great events of the Vietnam war, a high point in the military action, and, in all likelihood, the only battle of the war that will be long remembered. It has been seen by many as an historic turning point that swung the United States to a new course of action in Vietnam and led directly to the end of American military intervention in that nation. In any case, it certainly caused the United States government to undergo a massive, soul-searching reevaluation of its purposes and objectives in Vietnam. Decisions made on the basis of that reevaluation changed the American domestic political scene dramatically, led to placing limits on American participation, and set the stage for the withdrawal of American troops from Vietnam. The decisions made in March of 1968 involved elements not just of military strategy, but of public and congressional opinion, the nature and technology of news gathering, national psychology, and the personalities within the decision-making machinery, both at and on the periphery of the highest levels of government. Also involved were the programs of the Great Society, the stability of the American dollar, and the fate of the Democratic party. The episode offers perhaps a unique opportunity to examine the complexities of decision making at the highest levels of government as influenced by all these factors.

The divisions and disagreements over American participation in the Vietnam war are still fresh in memory, and the perils of "instant history," especially when the writer aspires to description as well as explanation, have been demonstrated often and convincingly.[1] Some would argue that all efforts to

[1] Barbara Tuchman, "History by the Ounce"; C. V. Wedgewood, *The Sense of the Past*; Henry Stuart Hughes, *History As Art and Science*; Barbara Tuchman, "The Historian's Opportunity," p. 29.

grasp the inner meaning of a recent event can be nothing but high-order journalism at best. This can be true for many reasons. The documentation is often highly incomplete or defective, some of it possibly remaining classified. The passions, biases, reputations, and opinions of the actors are immediately involved, and those who participated in the events know both too much of their own part in the decisions made and too little of the part that others played.[2] It is extremely difficult to be objective about one's own past performance, views, and influence.

There are obvious answers to these arguments against the rigorous study of recent events. All historical documentation has built-in limitations. The historian only rarely finds himself possessed of all the relevant information. Much of what he does find has been seriously altered by war or the effects of time. Thus, it should not be concluded that it is necessary to postpone the writing of history until all the facts are known, all the relevant material assembled.[3] Indeed, a participant in the events can bring some special insights to bear. For one thing, he is more aware of the constraints imposed by operational and bureaucratic difficulties in framing and executing policies and programs at the top policy-making level. In addition, no writing takes place in an intellectual vacuum, and every investigator approaches his task with his own philosophical assumptions and preconceptions derived in large measure from his own experience, culture, and times. In this sense, all history must in some way be a reflection of the times in which it is written.[4]

The study and analysis of recent events, systematically conducted and with the full understanding and awareness of the implicit and explicit assumptions of the participants, has a larger relevance in that it may affect the course of future policy precisely because it deals with the existing problems

[2] John P. Roche, "The Jigsaw Puzzle of History."
[3] Henri Pirenne, "What Are Historians Trying To Do?"
[4] Hans Meyerhoff, ed., *The Philosophy of History In Our Time*, pp. 21, 212; Barbara Tuchman, "Can History Be Served Up Hot?" p. 28.

of the "real world." As one scholar has stated: "I would urge that the ultimate justification of the study of contemporary affairs at the university is not very different from the justification of historic studies. Such studies involve intellectual issues—vital not only to the solution of current issues but to larger, more durable concerns . . . . It is indeed precisely this relevance to the larger, more enduring intellectual issues that ultimately justifies the study of the emerging present within the walls of the academy."[5]

Precisely because the events in Vietnam are so fresh in memory and the lessons learned from our involvement there may be relevant to current and future policy it becomes even more important that the study of this great tragedy not be left to the journalists and commentators. A rigorous examination of the available evidence to see what lessons can be derived from the U.S. involvement in Vietnam must not await the distant future.

The decisions of March 1968, have already become a controversial episode in modern history. They have been described from different vantage points and with different heroes and villains. The participants have made varying efforts to describe and justify their individual roles. By April 1971, some ten books had been published that covered in one way or another the making of the post-Tet decisions.[6] All these books tell a common story, that the decisions marked a turnabout of American policy toward Vietnam and were the result of a major bureaucratic battle within the highest

[5] Benjamin I. Schwartz, *Communism and China: Ideology in Flux*, pp. 3–4.

[6] Townsend Hoopes, *The Limits of Intervention*; Don Oberdorfer, *Tet*; Marvin Kalb and Elie Abel, *Roots of Involvement: The United States in Asia 1784–1971*; Henry Brandon, *Anatomy of Error: The Inside Story of the War on the Potomac 1954–69*; Theodore H. White, *The Making of the President, 1968*; Chester L. Cooper, *The Lost Crusade: America in Vietnam*; David Kraslow and Stuart H. Loory, *The Secret Search for Peace in Vietnam*; Henry F. Graff, *The Tuesday Cabinet: Deliberation and Decision on Peace and War under Lyndon B. Johnson*; Sam Houston Johnson, *My Brother, Lyndon*; Phil G. Goulding, *Confirm or Deny: Informing the People on National Security*.

levels of government between those who advocated a continuation of our Vietnam policies and those who favored a negotiated settlement to end the war.

All these accounts state that this change in strategy, this turnabout of policy, was advocated, fought for, and directly, indeed overwhelmingly, influenced by Clark Clifford, the president's longtime friend and newly appointed secretary of defense. Influenced by his civilian associates, both within and outside the government, Clifford, it is stated, became convinced that the direction the nation was pursuing in Vietnam could not lead to victory. He convinced the president that a new approach was needed, one that would limit American effort in the war and would actively seek a negotiated settlement. Some of these accounts also stress the impact of public opinion on the president's decisions, especially because it was a presidential election year.

In April 1971, an undergraduate honors thesis presented at Harvard College by John B. Henry attempted to refute this theory. Henry, through a series of interviews with the participants, divided the president's advisors into "hawks" and "doves." In this original, thorough, but somewhat over-simplified version, Henry maintained that, since the hawks, who wanted to continue our policies as before, outnumbered and had more influence with the president than the doves, who advocated a change in policy, the hawks predominated. The decisions of March 1968, then, as seen by Henry, "stand in retrospect, not as a major Vietnam policy turnabout, but as the threshold of the Johnson administration's commitment to a protracted and costly conflict of still uncertain outcome."[7]

Several presidential advisors, including Clifford, General Maxwell Taylor, Walt W. Rostow, George Christian, Harry McPherson, Jr., and, more recently, Jack Valenti and General William C. Westmoreland, have also published their ac-

[7] John B. Henry, "March 1968: Continuity or Change?," unpublished honors thesis, Harvard College, p. 186. Portions of this thesis have been published under the title "February, 1968," in *Foreign Policy*.

counts of the events of January through March 1968.[8] Many of these personal memoirs question in some part the popular version of this period, which had become current through the publication of the numerous secondhand interpretations. Clifford, while indicating that his views toward the war in Vietnam had undergone a substantial transformation during this period, modestly admits that "to reach a conclusion and to implement it are not the same, especially when one does not have the ultimate power of decision."[9] McPherson also felt that "something more than Clifford's style and contacts must have caused men like Dean Rusk and Walt Rostow— staunch believers in the justice and necessity of war—to acquiesce."[10]

In addition, two dramatic and unusual publishing events shed even more light on the decision-making process as it functioned in Washington during the post-Tet period of 1968. On Sunday, June 13, 1971, the *New York Times* began publication of a series of articles concerning the decision-making process in the United States government during the course of the Vietnam war.[11] These analyses were based

[8] Clark M. Clifford, "A Vietnam Reappraisal: The Personal History of One Man's View and How It Evolved"; General Maxwell D. Taylor, *Swords and Plowshares*; Walt W. Rostow, *The Diffusion of Power: An Essay in Recent History*; Harry C. McPherson, Jr., *A Political Education*; George Christian, *The President Steps Down: A Personal Memoir of the Transfer of Power*; Jack Valenti, *A Very Human President*; General William C. Westmoreland, *A Soldier Reports*. See also Admiral U.S.G. Sharp, USN, *Report on the War in Vietnam: Section I, Report on Air and Naval Campaigns Against North Vietnam and Pacific Command-Wide Support of the War, June 1964–July 1968* and General William C. Westmoreland, USA, *Report on the War in Vietnam: Section II, Report on Operations in South Vietnam, January 1964–June 1968*. Also Hubert H. Humphrey, *The Education of a Public Man: My Life and Politics*; Doris Kearns, *Lyndon Johnson and the American Dream*.

[9] Clifford, "A Vietnam Reappraisal," p. 613.

[10] McPherson, *A Political Education*, p. 435.

[11] Neil Sheehan, Hedrick Smith, E. W. Kenworthy, and Fox Butterworth, eds., *The Pentagon Papers as Published by the New York Times*. For an account of the writing of the papers and the legal and political controversy concerning their publication, see Sanford J. Ungar, *The Papers and the Papers; An Account of the Legal and Po-*

on a highly classified documentary history of the war prepared by a Pentagon task force at the instigation and direction of Secretary of Defense Robert McNamara. The publication of these documents, which became known as the Pentagon Papers, was by any standard a major event in journalism. The Pentagon study disclosed the functioning of a major segment of the decision-making machinery in government on a single issue over a twenty-year period. The series of articles led to the declassification of the study, which was subsequently published by the government in twelve volumes and entitled *United States-Vietnam Relations, 1945–1967.*[12] The Defense Department study is one of the richest documentary lodes ever made available to students of American foreign policy and sheds new light on decision making at the highest levels of government following the Tet offensive, especially as it involved the Defense Department. Indeed, the volumes covering the post-Tet period have been characterized as being "among the best in the entire history, at least in the level of sophistication with which the authors [sic] treat their documents."[13]

---

litical Battle Over the Pentagon Papers and "The First Amendment on Trial." For Congressional reaction to the publication of the papers, see Patricia A. Krause, ed., *Anatomy of an Undeclared War: Congressional Conference on the Pentagon Papers.*

[12] U. S., Department of Defense, *United States-Vietnam Relations, 1945–1967* (hereafter cited as *U.S.-Vietnam Relations*). Another edition, containing some material excised from the government version, is contained in Senator Mike Gravel, ed., *The Senator Gravel Edition: The Pentagon Papers.* According to Major General Robert N. Ginsburgh, military assistant to Walt W. Rostow, the White House was not consulted by McNamara as to the preparation of this study. "I took the initiative in offering White House assistance on an informal basis, but this wasn't taken advantage of by the Defense Department. I told Rostow this study was being conducted and expressed concern that it would be construed as a policy document possibly undercutting the president. The Defense Department prohibited outside review of the study. A copy was finally delivered to the White House around January 19–20, 1969." Personal interview with Major General Robert N. Ginsburgh, August 25, 1975.

[13] Ernest R. May, Samuel R. Williamson, Jr., and Alexander B. Woodside, "The Pentagon Papers: An Assessment," paper presented before the American Historical Association, p. 6. See also Richard H. Ullman, "The Pentagon's History as 'History' "; Noam Chomsky,

The second major publishing event was the publication of *The Vantage Point* by Lyndon B. Johnson, a memoir of how the president saw the issues "from my vantage point."[14] The chapter in this volume covering the post-Tet period of 1968 is particulary detailed. Accepting at face value a president's statement of his motives and rationale for a policy decision is not necessarily a reliable historical method, of course, especially when that president shows everyone agreeing with each other and agreeing with him. But these remembrances become more reliable when they can be checked against the memories of other participants in the decision-making process and against the documentation contained in the Pentagon Papers.[15]

In addition, the president's book offers a wealth of heretofore unknown facts, quotes, paraphrases, and accounts of White House meetings and conversations. Although the presidential papers of this period are still classified, and although what has been left out may prove to be as interesting as what was included, "every fact in the book can be backed up by documentary evidence."[16] Furthermore, the publication of these official documents and personal reminiscences has made other participants in the decision-making process more willing to share their personal recollections of that period.

Thus, it appears that sufficient material may now be avail-

"The Pentagon Papers as Propaganda and as History," pp. 179–197; George McT. Kahin, "The Pentagon Papers: A Critical Evaluation"; H. Bradford Westerfield, "What Use Are Three Versions of the Pentagon Papers?"

[14] Lyndon B. Johnson, *The Vantage Point: Perspectives of the Presidency, 1963–1969.*

[15] Leslie H. Gelb, "The Pentagon Papers and *The Vantage Point*," pp. 30-31.

[16] Personal interview with Walt W. Rostow, December 4, 1972. Even so open a president as Harry Truman prefaced his published memoirs with the statement: "I have omitted certain material. Some of this material cannot be made available for many years, perhaps for many generations." Truman, *Memoirs*, vol. 1, p. x. For a version of the classification of the papers contained in President Johnson's book, see David Wise, *The Politics of Lying: Government Deception, Secrecy and Power*, pp. 88–97.

able to attempt a more rigorous and detailed analysis of both the "how" and the "why" of the decisions that were made during the exciting and controversial period of January through March 1968. This analysis would attempt to shed some light on the process of decision making at a period of intensive debate and discussion, both inside and outside the government, about the proper course of United States policy. The intentions of the actors must also be examined and, indeed, may be crucially important to an evaluation of the ultimate effects on subsequent United States policy and politics of the decisions announced by President Johnson on March 31, 1968.

The examination of intentions, however, is the most difficult task of all. Even the principal actors may themselves have been unaware of or unclear as to their ultimate intentions. The danger also arises that, in hindsight, intentions are ascribed to one's self that did not actually exist at the time. John F. Kennedy aptly described these difficulties: "There will always be the dark and tangled stretches in the decision-making process—mysterious even to those who may be most intimately involved . . . . And it is mysterious because the essence of ultimate decision remains impenetrable to the observer—often, indeed, to the decider himself."[17]

Nonetheless, the effort must be made. The warped perspective caused by time, individual pride, and faulty memory can be overcome insofar as possible by documentation and by matching up the accumulated recollections of all the actors, to arrive at some common perspective of the decision-making process—how it worked and how it was seen through the eyes of those who had a major part in it.

Most of this volume was prepared while the author was on a six-month leave of absence from the Office of the Chief of Staff of the Army. For providing that time, I am grateful to General William C. Westmoreland, Major General Warren K. Bennett, and the late Colonel James K. Patchell.

---

[17] Theodore Sorensen, *Decision-Making in the White House*, Foreword by John F. Kennedy, pp. xiii, xi. For a similar view see Truman, *Memoirs*, vol. 1, p. ix.

I am also grateful to Congressman Tom Foley and his wife and assistant, Heather, for making space available for my use in the Library of Congress during that six-month period. I am also indebted to Colonel James Cannon for support in transcribing tapes, to Carolyn Newlin, my friend and loyal secretary, who graciously typed the initial manuscript, to Patricia A. Gress for her efficient research and typing assistance, to Annette Lovecchio for typing assistance, and to Sharron Kimble for advice, encouragement, and assistance.

The complete and well-organized files of newspaper clippings of the period maintained by the Research and Analysis Division, Office of the Secretary of the Air Force, were also extremely useful, and I am grateful to Harry Zubkoff and his staff for assisting my access to and use of those files.

In addition to the works already cited, sources for this volume included newspapers and periodicals of the period, government documents, and interviews with the principal participants in the decision-making process. A word concerning the source, availability, content, and accuracy of these documents and interviews may be helpful.

As indicated, the largest single source of official documents was, of course, the official twelve-volume *United States–Vietnam Relations, 1945–1967*, known as the Pentagon Papers. The sections of these volumes that deal with the Tet offensive, sections IVC6(b) and IVC6(c), were published by the government with all footnote citations omitted. At the author's request, and for purposes of this study, the Department of Defense released those footnote citations. Documents referred to in those footnotes have been cited, as appropriate, in this work.

While assigned to the Office of the Assistant Secretary of Defense, International Security Affairs (OASD/ISA) in 1968–69, the author was the principal compiler of the two sections of the Pentagon Papers that dealt with the Tet period. The author has supplemented research done on that project with study of additional materials not then available, in particular the valuable MACV *Command History, 1968* and voluminous communications between the chairman of the

Joint Chiefs of Staff (General Wheeler) and the military commander in Vietnam (General Westmoreland) and the cables between the American embassy, Saigon, and the Department of State.

For the *Command History* and various miscellaneous documents in the archives of the U.S. Army Center of Military History, I am indebted to Colonel Reamer W. Argo, Jr., Charles B. MacDonald, and Vincent H. Demma. For the Wheeler-Westmoreland communications and embassy cables, I am indebted to General Westmoreland and to a former member of his staff, Lieutenant Colonel Paul Miles. In the interests of scholarship and historical accuracy, these documents have been cited as appropriate, and because many are still classified, the manuscript has been submitted to the Department of the Army for official clearance. Such clearance for the release of these documents, as used in the context of this work, has been granted. Portions of the *Command History, 1968* had been previously declassified and used by Admiral Sharp and General Westmoreland in their *Report on the War in Vietnam*.

Documents in the Lyndon Baines Johnson Library concerning foreign affairs during the Johnson administration remain unavailable to scholars pending formal compilation and declassification procedures. Similarly, all copies of drafts of the president's speech of March 31, 1968 were subsequently returned to the president, along with the working notes of participants in the White House meetings. However, these documents were used in the preparation of President Johnson's book, *The Vantage Point*.

The files of the State Department are extremely scanty. Very few planning papers were done in the department during the gestation period of the president's decisions of March 31. Knowledge of what was being discussed was held extremely closely and was provided by Secretary Rusk only to Undersecretary Katzenbach, Assistant Secretary Bundy, and Philip Habib.

The documents, clippings, and other written materials used in this work were supplemented by a series of interviews and personal correspondence with most of the principal actors involved in the decision-making process described. Their names and roles are listed in the bibliography. I am indebted to them all for the time, interest, courtesy, and assistance they offered as I intruded into their busy schedules.

Subsequent to these interviews, the completed draft manuscript was submitted to many of them in order to insure both the accuracy and the proper context of the quotations ascribed to them. This manuscript, in draft form, has been read by the following individuals who have agreed to the accuracy of the quotes ascribed to them: Clark Clifford, Dean Rusk, Walt W. Rostow, William Bundy, and Generals Maxwell D. Taylor, William C. Westmoreland, and Robert N. Ginsburgh. I am especially grateful to Clark Clifford, Walt W. Rostow, and Generals William C. Westmoreland and Robert N. Ginsburgh for their guidance, advice, and suggestions which went far beyond merely insuring the accuracy of their words. I am also indebted to Robert W. Komer, Henry Fairlie, Timothy Dickinson, and Colonel George K. Osborne, III, who read the manuscript and offered helpful suggestions.

This manuscript was originally written as a Ph.D. dissertation at Harvard University. Professors Samuel P. Huntington and Graham T. Allison of that institution read the manuscript and provided wise counsel and helpful guidance, for which I am grateful. I am grateful to Ellen Munson, also at Harvard, who was instrumental in steering the manuscript through the administrative process incident to the awarding of a degree. Sanford G. Thatcher and Barbara Westergaard of the Princeton University Press were helpful in insisting that what was perfectly clear to me should also be made reasonably clear to the reader.

I alone, of course, am responsible for the views and judgments expressed and for all errors and omissions.

HERBERT Y. SCHANDLER

Washington, D.C.
January 1976

ABBREVIATIONS

☆☆☆

AID	Agency for International Development
ARVN	Army of the Republic of (South) Vietnam
CHICOM	Chinese Communist
CINCPAC	Commander in chief, United States Forces Pacific
CJCS	Chairman, Joint Chiefs of Staff
COMUS-MACV	Commander, United States Military Assistance Command, Vietnam
CONUS	Continental United States
CTZ	Corps Tactical Zone
DMZ	Demilitarized Zone
DRV	Democratic Republic of (North) Vietnam
FY	Fiscal Year
GVN	Government of (South) Vietnam
ISA	International Security Affairs (Assistant Secretary of Defense)
JCS	Joint Chiefs of Staff (United States)
KIA	Killed in Action
LOC	Line(s) of Communication
MACV	Military Assistance Command, Vietnam
NLF	National Liberation Front (Viet Cong)
NSC	National Security Council
NVA	North Vietnamese Army
NVN	North Vietnam
RD	Revolutionary Development (Pacification)
RVNAF	Republic of (South) Vietnam Armed Forces
SVN	South Vietnam
SEA	Southeast Asia
VC	Viet Cong

The Unmaking
of a President

SOUTH VIET-NAM
ADMINISTRATIVE DIVISIONS
AND MILITARY REGIONS

_____ Province boundary

▨▨▨▨▨ Military corps boundary

✳ Province capital

DA LAT Autonomous municipality

ONE

☆☆

The Decision to Intervene, 1964–1965

"IT WAS almost imperceptible, the way we got in. There was no one move that you could call decisive, or irreversible, not even very many actions that you could argue against in isolation. Yet when you put it all together, there we were in a war on the Asian mainland, with nobody really putting up much of a squawk while we were doing it."[1]

The year 1965 saw major and historic decisions concerning the level of U.S. effort in South Vietnam that transformed the character of the war and the U.S. role in it. These decisions foreshadowed a dramatic increase in the U.S. commitment and led eventually to a virtual American takeover of the war. From 1965 on, U.S. involvement grew in slow stages, with each step preceded by an agonizing policy review at the highest levels of government. Throughout the course of this involvement, however, none of the policy makers involved in these reviews and decisions seemed capable of looking ahead to the long term, of developing an overall, coherent, long-range strategy for the achievement of specific U.S. objectives.

From the time of the overthrow of the Diem government in November 1963, to the end of the winter in February and March of 1964, it became increasingly clear to the American leadership, as it had not been clear before, that the situation in Vietnam was deteriorating so badly that the kind of American effort invested thus far could not reverse the trend. It also became clear during this period that previous optimistic reports of progress in the war had been overstated and that, despite significant American aid, the South Vietnamese had

[1] Philip L. Geyelin, *Lyndon B. Johnson and the World*, pp. 213–214.

3

not been able to achieve political stability. Concern in Washington grew over American inability to arrest the imminent collapse of the government of South Vietnam. As the realization grew that an ally on whose behalf the United States had steadily increased its commitment was in a state of political and military collapse, the president undertook a determined policy reassessment of the future American role in the war.

On March 8, 1964, President Johnson sent Secretary of Defense Robert S. McNamara and chairman of the Joint Chiefs of Staff General Maxwell D. Taylor to Vietnam for a firsthand assessment of the situation there. Their report was presented to the president on March 16, 1964, and was approved the following day. The program contained in this document, labeled NSAM (National Security Action Memorandum) 288, called for enlarging the U.S. commitment of aid to South Vietnam considerably. The major emphases of the program were on strengthening the South Vietnamese armed forces by providing them with increased quantities of new equipment so that they could add 50,000 men to the armed forces, and providing American budgetary and political support to the South Vietnamese government.

The McNamara-Taylor report of March 1964, however, specifically rejected the following options: (1) accepting a neutralized South Vietnam by withholding additional support; (2) placing military pressure on North Vietnam; (3) furnishing troops to secure Saigon; and (4) fully taking over the South Vietnamese military command. McNamara did, however, recommend that plans be developed to allow the initiation of graduated U.S. military pressure against North Vietnam should this prove necessary in the future.[2]

The Joint Chiefs of Staff (other than General Taylor) expressed doubt that these rather limited measures of support would be adequate to reverse the situation and recommended to the president immediate U.S. military measures against North Vietnam. In rejecting the advice of his military leaders,

[2] Johnson, *The Vantage Point*, pp. 62–66; Taylor, *Swords and Plowshares*, pp. 308–311; *U.S.–Vietnam Relations*, IVC(1), pp. 1–55.

President Johnson specified his two principal objections to such a course: (1) the political and military base in the South was too fragile to invite increased enemy action by direct U.S. participation, and (2) striking the North might lead to retaliation by the Soviets, the Chinese, or both.[3]

From the beginning, however, it seemed evident that this limited program would not be enough. Almost uninterrupted political upheaval in Saigon was reflected in progressive military demoralization in the countryside. Throughout the late spring and into July, as the U.S. program was put into effect, the Buddhist-Catholic quarrel intensified. The civil administration in South Vietnam continued in a state of disarray and ineffectiveness. Military forces were becoming more and more defensive and demoralized. Desertions increased, and combat operations ground to a near standstill. At the same time, the Communists were visibly strengthening their support base in Laos, stepping up their infiltration of men and supplies into South Vietnam, and initiating larger, more frequent, and more aggressive attacks against government outposts. Outside the urban population centers and areas of traditional local religious power, the country was slipping, to a great extent by default, to the Viet Cong.[4]

The controversial Tonkin Gulf incident on August 4-5, 1964, precipitated the first U.S. reprisal against North Vietnam and provided the president with a broad congressional resolution of support.[5] The swift reprisal and the nearly unanimous congressional support demonstrated in dramatic fashion the U.S. commitment to South Vietnam, a commitment undertaken with little domestic criticism or questioning. In addition, the precedent for U.S. military action against North Vietnam had been established.

[3] Johnson, *The Vantage Point*, pp. 66–67.
[4] Taylor, *Swords and Plowshares*, p. 311; *U.S.–Vietnam Relations*, IVC(2)(b), pp. 23–24; IVC(1), pp. 93–98.
[5] Eugene G. Windchy, *Tonkin Gulf*, p. 317; Joseph C. Goulden, *Truth is the First Casualty—The Gulf of Tonkin Affair; Illusion and Reality*, pp. 37, 48–79. U.S., Congress, Senate, Committee on Foreign Relations, *The Gulf of Tonkin, the 1964 Incidents*.

Encouraged by this reprisal and dismayed by the continued political turmoil in South Vietnam and the apparent ineffectiveness of U.S. programs, several officials and agencies within the administration argued that continued military action against the North would have to be conducted at an increasingly faster tempo to have any lasting effect in arresting the deteriorating situation. The president and the secretary of state, however, continued to feel that such moves were not worth the risk of Chinese or Soviet retaliation and that they could not be effective without a degree of government stability in the South.[6]

These continuing pressures for further action, however, culminated in a series of strategy meetings of administration officials in Washington early in September 1964. Proposals by the Air Force and Navy chiefs for an immediate bombing campaign against the North were rejected by the president. He did approve, however, preparations for retaliatory action against North Vietnam on a tit-for-tat basis in the event of any further attacks on U.S. forces or installations. The consensus seemed to be that emphasis at this time should be placed on further strengthening the structure of the South Vietnamese government.[7]

But there was rather general agreement among these close advisors to the president that after the political stability of the South Vietnamese government improved, it would be necessary to subject North Vietnam to overt U.S. military pressure, that without direct pressure it would not be possible to stop North Vietnamese sponsorship of the insurgency in the South. This anticipation of the eventual need to use —

[6] Johnson, *The Vantage Point*, p. 119; *U.S.–Vietnam Relations*, IVC(2)(b), pp. 19–24.

[7] Johnson, *The Vantage Point*, p. 120; Taylor, *Swords and Plowshares*, p. 321; *U.S.–Vietnam Relations*, IVC(1), p. 97; IVC(2)(b), p. 32. Present at the Washington meetings were Secretaries Rusk and McNamara, chairman of the Joint Chiefs of Staff General Earle Wheeler, CIA Director McCone, Assistant Secretaries of State William P. Bundy and Robert J. Manning, Assistant Secretary of Defense John T. McNaughton, and General Maxwell D. Taylor, who had been appointed U.S. ambassador to Saigon in July 1964.

American force was reinforced during the remainder of 1964 by the continued deterioration of the political structure in South Vietnam, by evidence of increased levels of North Vietnamese troop infiltration into South Vietnam, and by the actions of North Vietnamese and Viet Cong forces in the South.

However, the United States refrained from direct military action for the time being. President Johnson was engaged in an election campaign in which he was presenting himself as the candidate of reason and restraint as opposed to the warlike, unpredictable, and irresponsible Barry Goldwater. Throughout the campaign, Johnson had made plain his disinclination to lead the United States into a wider war on the Asian continent. Speaking in Manchester, New Hampshire in late September, he had reiterated, "I have not thought that we were ready for American boys to do the fighting for Asian boys. What I have been trying to do was to get the boys in Vietnam to do their own fighting—we are not going north and drop bombs at this stage of the game."[8] Thus, hard decisions on subsequent American actions in Vietnam were not allowed to intrude upon the campaign.

Twice before the year 1964 was over, recommendations were made to begin retaliatory raids against North Vietnam. On November 1, the American air base at Bien Hoa was attacked by the Viet Cong. There were numerous American casualties and widespread destruction of aircraft. This singling out of the major American air base in South Vietnam as the target for a damaging attack was the most spectacular and deliberate anti-American incident in the conflict to date. The Joint Chiefs of Staff along with General

[8] Jack Shepherd and Christopher S. Wren, *Quotations From Chairman LBJ*, p. 66; "President Wary of GI's Fighting China's Millions." For other accounts of the Vietnam issue in the 1964 election, see Theodore H. White, *The Making of the President, 1964*, pp. 132–133, 443–445; Geyelin, *Lyndon B. Johnson and the World*, pp. 193–198; Milton C. Cummings, Jr., ed., *The National Election of 1964*; Stephen C. Shadegg, *What Happened to Goldwater? The Inside Story of the 1964 Republican Campaign*, pp. 124–125; Westmoreland, *A Soldier Reports*, pp. 113–114.

Maxwell Taylor, now United States ambassador to South Vietnam, felt that this attack warranted the immediate retaliation against North Vietnam that had been contemplated at the September conference, and they so recommended. But this attack was an unwelcome reality on the very eve of the presidential election, and the recommendations were rejected.

Similarly, the bombing of an American billet in Saigon on Christmas eve evoked the same recommendation and the same response from the president.[9] Even though the idea of increasing military pressure against North Vietnam had been generally agreed to in September, the president was still reluctant to order the war to be extended in this manner without some greater degree of political stability in South Vietnam. In addition, President Johnson, as was his custom, was not going to make this difficult decision until all available alternatives could be carefully and thoroughly reexamined.

Therefore, subsequent to the Bien Hoa bombing but before the election, the president appointed a working group to conduct another thorough review of U.S. Vietnam policy and to present him with alternatives and recommendations for future action in Vietnam. After almost a full month of deliberation, the advisors failed to come up with promising alternatives, and at a December 1 meeting with the president, could only repeat old recommendations, now divided into two phases. Phase I would merely comprise a continuation of current actions, tit-for-tat reprisals against North Vietnam for attacks on U.S. forces in the South, and increased efforts to reform and strengthen the South Vietnamese government. When this had been accomplished or was well underway, Phase II, a campaign of gradually increasing air strikes against North Vietnam to dissuade it from further support of the war in the South would be undertaken. These were not new proposals, and no prospect was held out for speedy results. Again, the president emphasized the need to strength-

[9] Johnson, *The Vantage Point*, p. 121; Taylor, *Swords and Plowshares*, pp. 323–325, 332–333; *U.S.–Vietnam Relations*, IVC(2)(c), pp. 3–5, 72–73; IVC(3), pp. 4, 9.

en the Saigon government before beginning any military action against the North. He approved Phase I and gave assent, at least in principle, to Phase II. It is clear, however, that the president did not make any commitment at that point to expand the war through future military operations against North Vietnam.[10]

The alternative of withdrawing American support from a Saigon government demonstrably incapable of pulling itself together and organizing a stable government in its own defense was briefly considered in this policy review. However, the Joint Staff representatives objected forcefully to this alternative, and their objections were effective in downgrading it, so that it was not presented to the president. Johnson had previously considered this alternative, however, and at the September policy review had asked whether any of his advisors doubted that "Vietnam was worth all this effort." All had agreed that the loss of South Vietnam would be followed, in time, by the loss of all of Southeast Asia.[11] And Ambassador Taylor admits that it never crossed his mind to recommend withdrawal, rather disingenuously placing the blame on Congress for the American commitment to South Vietnam: "Had not the Congress declared with only two dissenting votes that 'The U.S. regards as vital to its national interest and to world peace the maintenance of international peace and security in Southeast Asia?' With this authoritative confirmation of the essentiality of our mission, no senior officer could in conscience harbor thoughts of retreat."[12]

Although the president's advisors had reached the consensus by the end of 1964 that increased military pressure against North Vietnam would be necessary, this consensus reflected neither a precisely defined strategy as to the subsequent course of American military action in Vietnam nor any commonly held expectation as to the result to be gained by military pressure. Generally speaking, the military leaders

---

[10] *U.S.–Vietnam Relations*, IVC(2)(c), pp. 5–58; IVC(3), pp. 4–6.
[11] Johnson, *The Vantage Point*, p. 120.
[12] Taylor, *Swords and Plowshares*, p. 327.

favored strong action, a dramatic and forceful application of military power, as the only means to apply significant pressure on North Vietnam. This military action, it was stated, would interdict infiltration routes to the South, destroy the overall capacity of the North to provide support to the insurgency there, destroy North Vietnam's will to continue support of the Viet Cong guerrillas, encourage the South Vietnamese government and people, and, finally, punish the North Vietnamese government for its actions in the South.

State Department officials and many of the civilian officials of the Defense Department favored a more gradual, restrained approach, "progressively mounting in scope and intensity," in which the prospect of greater pressure to come would be at least as important as the actual damage inflicted. The State Department, as would be expected, was also concerned with the international political implications of these military measures. These officials saw increased military pressure against North Vietnam as providing the United States with bargaining points in subsequent negotiations and as signalling to the North Vietnamese, to other Communist countries, and to our allies, U.S. resolve to meet its commitments in combatting externally supported aggression. It was this "signal" of American resolve, as opposed to any damage actually to be inflicted on North Vietnam, that was stressed by the civilian leaders.

In any case, there was no dearth of reasons, once the U.S. commitment to South Vietnam was affirmed, for striking North Vietnam. The decision to use military power against the North, in the end, seems to have resulted as much from a lack of alternative proposals as from any compelling logic advanced in its favor. Getting North Vietnam to remove its support and direction of the insurgency in the South was the basic objective, but there was no general agreement as to the likelihood of that result or of a strategy to attain it. And the president's reluctance to approve these actions was based upon a hope that the South Vietnamese government would be able to make itself more effective and thus preclude the need for additional American military commitment and action.

But the hoped for improvement in South Vietnamese governmental stability failed to materialize. The continuing struggle for political power in Saigon clearly was impeding military operations, as large elements of the best units of the South Vietnamese army were maintained on constant "coup alert" in or near Saigon. A highly visible setback occurred during the period of December 26, 1964–January 2, 1965 when the Viet Cong virtually destroyed two South Vietnamese battalions at Binh Gia.[13] This was the first time that enemy forces had chosen to remain on the battlefield and meet government forces in sustained combat.

As the new year began, the administration was beset by frustration and considerable anguish over the threat of the imminent collapse of the government of South Vietnam. The debate continued in Washington over ways and means of generating more intensive military measures against the enemy—and most notably over the desirability and likely effectiveness of Phase II reprisal strikes against the North. But enthusiasm for these operations, although increasing, was far from boundless. The intelligence community continued to express little confidence that these military pressures would have much impact on Hanoi's policies or actions.[14]

The long months of planning, hesitation, and agonized study and debate reached a sudden climax at 2:00 A.M. on February 7, 1965, when the Viet Cong conducted well-coordinated and highly destructive raids upon U.S. advisors' barracks and an American helicopter base near Pleiku in South Vietnam. Eight American soldiers died in the two attacks, and losses of equipment were characterized as severe. This was the heaviest Communist attack up to that time

[13] Westmoreland, *Report on the War in Vietnam*, p. 95. For accounts of the political turmoil in South Vietnam during this period, see Dennis J. Duncanson, *Government and Revolution in Vietnam*, pp. 342–351; Robert Shaplen, *The Lost Revolution*, pp. 266–322; Westmoreland, *A Soldier Reports*, pp. 62–65, 71–74, 77–81, 90–98.
[14] *U.S.–Vietnam Relations*, IVC(2)(c), pp. 8–9.

against American military installations in South Vietnam, and the attack had come at the very beginning of a visit to Hanoi by Soviet Premier Kosygin, a visit that the administration felt presaged increased Soviet aid to Hanoi.[15]

Presidential Assistant McGeorge Bundy was in South Vietnam at this time. Telephoning from General Westmoreland's command post in Saigon, he recommended to the president, through Deputy Secretary of Defense Cyrus Vance who answered the phone in the Situation Room, that, in addition to immediate retaliatory strikes against the North, the United States should initiate Phase II of the previously planned military measures against North Vietnam.[16]

This time the president showed the same decisiveness he had displayed six months earlier during the Gulf of Tonkin incident. The decision to retaliate against North Vietnam was reached in a seventy-five-minute meeting in the Cabinet Room of the White House on the evening of February 6 (Washington time), with Senate Majority Leader Mike Mansfield and House Speaker John McCormick present. George Ball, the senior State Department representative present, indicated to the president that all were in accord that action must be taken.[17]

Retaliatory air strikes were conducted by U.S. naval aircraft against North Vietnamese barracks and staging areas at Dong Hoi, just north of the Demilitarized Zone (DMZ), within fourteen hours. This dramatic action, long on the U.S. planners' drawing boards, precipitated a rapidly moving sequence of events that transformed the nature of the Vietnam war and the U.S. role in it. It also became the opening move in what soon developed into an entirely new phase of that

---

[15] Johnson, *The Vantage Point*, pp. 123–124; see also Shaplen, *The Lost Revolution*, p. 305.

[16] Johnson, *The Vantage Point*, p. 124; Taylor, *Swords and Plowshares*, p. 335; *U.S.–Vietnam Relations*, IVC(1), p. vi; IVC(3), p. 23; Westmoreland, *A Soldier Reports*, pp. 115–116.

[17] Others present were Secretary of Defense Robert McNamara, Deputy Secretary of Defense Cyrus Vance, General Earle Wheeler, Llewellyn Thomson, William Bundy, Treasury Secretary Douglas Dillon, Carl Rowan from the USIA, and Marshall Carter from the CIA. Johnson, *The Vantage Point*, p. 124.

war, the sustained U.S. bombing effort against North Vietnam. As Ambassador Taylor expressed it, "The inhibitions which had restrained the use of our air power against the enemy homeland were broken, and a new phase of the war had begun."[18]

Events began to move more swiftly in Washington. Upon his return from Vietnam on February 8, McGeorge Bundy presented to the president the conclusions his group had reached concerning the situation in South Vietnam. The report stated, "The situation in Vietnam is deteriorating, and without new U.S. action, defeat appears inevitable—probably not in a matter of weeks or perhaps even months, but within the next year or so."[19] Bundy saw no way of "unloading the burden on the Vietnamese" or "negotiating ourselves out of Vietnam." He therefore indicated that the development and execution of a policy of sustained reprisal against North Vietnam was the most promising course of action open to the United States. "That judgment," he added, "is shared by all who accompanied me from Washington and I think by all members of the Country Team."[20]

[18] Taylor, *Swords and Plowshares*, p. 335. The strike against Dong Hoi was something of a fizzle, at least militarily. When the execution order was given, only one of three U.S. aircraft carriers was on station. The other two were en route elsewhere. They were urgently recalled to participate in the attack, which was delayed until they returned to points from which their aircraft could reach the assigned targets. Even then, however, adverse weather precluded atttacks on two targets, and only one was struck in force. In order to stiffen this reprisal and make it a joint U.S.–South Vietnamese response, the target (Dong Hoi) was struck again the following day (February 8) by the U.S. carrier aircraft that had failed to reach their targets the previous day, and a South Vietnamese air strike was carried out against the Vu Con barracks in the same area. *U.S.–Vietnam Relations*, IVC(3), p. 23.

[19] Johnson, *The Vantage Point*, p. 126; *U.S.–Vietnam Relations*, IVC(3), p. 31. Members of Bundy's party included John McNaughton, assistant secretary of defense; Leonard Unger, deputy assistant secretary of state; General Andrew J. Goodpaster, assistant to the chairman of the Joint Chiefs; and Chester Cooper of the National Security Council staff.

[20] Johnson, *The Vantage Point*, pp. 126–127; the text of the Bundy report is in *U.S.–Vietnam Relations*, IVC(3), pp. 31–39. For an opinion as to what Bundy might have recommended had not the Pleiku attack occurred, see Chester Cooper, "Fateful Day in Vietnam—10 Years Ago."

Of the president's advisors in Washington, only Vice President Humphrey voiced concern over the implementation of the principal recommendation of the Bundy report, namely, a program of sustained air reprisals against North Vietnam. Humphrey's objections were based primarily upon domestic political considerations, and he took the unusual step of detailing his thoughts in a memorandum to the president.[21]

Although there was near unanimous support among the president's advisors, there were again differences of opinion as to the pace and scope of these reprisals. Bundy and Ambassador Taylor saw the program as a flexible one, with a controlled sequence of actions in response to and justified by the level of Viet Cong violence and terror in the South. The military pressure against the North could be decreased if Viet Cong terror visibly decreased in the South. The objective would not be to "win" an air war against Hanoi, but to influence the course of the struggle in the South. The military, on the other hand, insisted that the program would have to be a very forceful one, a program of "graduated pressures" rather than "graduated reprisals," with the connotation of steady, relentless movement toward convincing Hanoi of "the prohibitive cost . . . of their program of subversion, insurgency and aggression in Southeast Asia." The need to justify the raids as retaliation would progressively diminish as the intensity of the air strikes increased.[22]

The president's decision was made somewhat easier for him by the enemy. In what was regarded by some as a calculated act of defiance, the Viet Cong staged another dramatic raid against a U.S. enlisted men's barracks in Qui Nhon, South Vietnam, on February 10, 1965, inflicting the single heaviest loss of American life to date (twenty-three U.S. servicemen were killed). Within twenty-four hours, U.S. and South Vietnamese aircraft executed the largest

[21] Humphrey, *The Education of a Public Man*, pp. 318–324. Also Laurence Stern, "Humphrey Early Critic of Viet War."

[22] *U.S.–Vietnam Relations*, IVC(3), pp. 39–47; Westmoreland, *A Soldier Reports*, pp. 112-113.

retaliatory strike against North Vietnam to date.[23] The president's thinking at this time was reflected in the press release from the White House on February 11 that announced the air retaliation. This time, significantly, the air attacks were not characterized as a reprisal for the immediate incident but as a more generalized response to a long series of "continued acts of aggression" which had occurred since February 8 and which had been considered normal features of the war in the South.[24] This change in terminology, from "reprisal" to "response to continued aggression" was clearly deliberate and reflected the president's conscious though unannounced decision to broaden the reprisal concept as his advisors were urging, and to do so as gradually and as imperceptibly as possible. Thus, although the February 11 air strikes set the stage for the sustained and continuing bombing program that was now to be launched, the Viet Cong attack allowed this change in policy to be instituted with a minimum of drama so as to make it appear as almost a logical sequence of unavoidable steps in response to enemy provocations.

On February 13, President Johnson formally approved a program for American action in Vietnam that included "measured and limited" air action against selected military targets in North Vietnam. Details of these air actions, which were to be conducted jointly with the South Vietnamese, were sketchy, indicating that the president still wished to preserve as much flexibility as possible concerning the scope and character of this activity.[25]

Although the first air strike under the new program, dubbed ROLLING THUNDER, was scheduled for February 20, 1965, political turbulence in South Vietnam prevented

---

[23] *U.S.–Vietnam Relations*, IVC(3), p. 27.

[24] U.S. Department of State, *Department of State Bulletin*, vol. 52, pp. 290–291; see also Geyelin, *Lyndon B. Johnson and the World*, pp. 214, 219–220; Henry L. Trewhitt, *McNamara: His Ordeal in the Pentagon*, pp. 217–218.

[25] Johnson, *The Vantage Point*, p. 130; Taylor, *Swords and Plowshares*, p. 337; *U.S.–Vietnam Relations*, IVC(3), pp. 48–51.

obtaining clearance from the South Vietnamese government, and the strikes had to be continuously postponed. The turmoil in South Vietnam was not the only reason for delaying the air action, however. A diplomatic initiative from the Soviet Union to reactivate the cochairmen of the 1954 Geneva Accords on Vietnam to consider the current Vietnam crisis led Washington to delay the air strikes so as not to sabotage that effort.

This initiative finally came to naught, the South Vietnamese government was stabilized to some extent, and the first ROLLING THUNDER air strikes were executed against North Vietnam on March 2, 1965.[26] The next strike occurred eleven days later, and the program became a series of limited, measured, and spaced air attacks against the North occurring about once a week. The pattern adopted was designed to preserve the president's options to proceed or not, to increase the tempo or not, depending on North Vietnam's reaction. The carrot of stopping the bombing was deemed as important as the stick of continuing it. All-out bombing, the president apparently continued to feel, would pose far greater risks of widening the war, would transmit signals to Hanoi and the rest of the world out of all proportion to the limited objectives and intentions of the United States in Southeast Asia, might carry unacceptable internal political penalties, might foreclose the possibility of achieving U.S. goals at a relatively low level of violence, and would not be more likely to get North Vietnam to decrease or call off its support of the insurgency in the South.

Almost immediately after the initiation of the ROLLING THUNDER air strikes, however, efforts began within the administration to make the program more forceful and continuous. Secretary of Defense McNamara expressed his dissatisfaction with the military damage caused by the raids, and Ambassador Taylor voiced his annoyance over what he considered to be an unnecessarily timid approach to these

[26] *U.S.–Vietnam Relations*, IVC(3), pp. 52–59.

increase intensity of Rolling Thunder

air operations, the long delays between strikes, and their marginal effectiveness. He recommended that they be increased in intensity and in tempo.[27] The Army Chief of Staff, General Harold K. Johnson, returning on March 14 from a presidential survey mission to see what more could be done in South Vietnam, also recommended increasing the scope and tempo of the air strikes and removing self-imposed restrictions that had limited their effectiveness. "To date," General Johnson reported, "the tempo of punitive air strikes has been inadequate to convey a clear sense of U.S. purpose to the DRV." The president accepted most of General Johnson's program, and on March 15, 1965, the ROLLING THUNDER program against the North was transformed from a sporadic, halting effort into a regular, continuing, and militarily significant effort.[28]

Nonetheless, the president and the secretary of defense continued to keep this air effort under strict and careful control. The attacks were carried out only by fighter-bombers utilizing low altitude, precision bombing tactics. Final target determinations were made in Washington, and population centers were scrupulously avoided. The secretary of defense set a ceiling on the number of missions, prescribed the areas within which they could be flown, and defined the types of targets to be hit. The use of B-52 bombers in the North was considered but not accepted. Extended bombing programs, which might permit greater latitude in the field, were not approved. Bombing proposals from the Joint Chiefs of Staff were approved only in weekly target packages. Each target package, moreover, had to pass through a chain of approvals in the Department of Defense, the Department of State, and the White House; this chain often included the president and the two secretaries. Within this framework of political control, the ROLLING THUNDER program was allowed to grow in intensity, in geographic coverage, and in assortment of targets. By mid-1965 the number of strikes had increased

[27] Ibid., pp. 64–69.   [28] Ibid., pp. 69–73.

from one or two per week to ten or twelve per week, and the number of sorties to about 900 per week, four or five times what they had been at the outset.[29]

During the closing days of February and throughout March, the administration undertook publicly and privately to defend its rationale for air strikes against North Vietnam. Official and public reaction to the strikes was fairly predictable. Much of the American press initially regarded the air strikes as necessary and justifiable, but many admitted either to confusion or to serious doubt as to just what U.S. policy in Vietnam was and where this policy was heading. The president spent much time with members of Congress, talking to many of them in his office, reiterating the continuity of his policy with that of his predecessors, and emphasizing the restraint and patience he was showing.[30] But despite the full use of his powers of persuasion, the president could not stop a rising tide of criticism. Condemnation of the bombing spread to the campuses and to a widening circle of congressmen.

In addition, despite official hopes that the ROLLING THUNDER bombing campaign would rapidly convince Hanoi that it should agree to negotiate a settlement to the war in the South, or that it should cease to support the insurgency in the South in exchange for a halt in the bombing, these hopes were not realized. After a month of continued and regular bombing with no response from the North Vietnamese, official optimism began to wane. Although enemy military activity in the South had been reduced, the North Vietnamese showed signs of adjusting to the limited bombing campaign and preparing for a long siege while they continued to support the Viet Cong in South Vietnam. The North Vietnamese further indicated their intractability by rejecting President Johnson's proposals for peace made in an address

29 Ibid., p. 79; IVC(7)(a), pp. 1–2. Also Kearns, *Lyndon Johnson and the American Dream*, pp. 269–272.
30 U.S., President, *Public Papers of the Presidents of the United States: Lyndon B. Johnson, 1965*, I, p. 278 (hereafter cited as *Public Papers of Lyndon Johnson*).

at Johns Hopkins University on April 7, and by failing to respond meaningfully to overtures made during a week-long pause in the bombing from May 12 to May 18.[31] Thus, by the middle of April 1965, it was generally recognized that in order to bring Hanoi to the bargaining table, some evidence that the Viet Cong could not win in the South would also be necessary.

But the administration's attention had already shifted from the air war to U.S. actions in South Vietnam. At approximately nine o'clock on the morning of March 8, 1965, a United States Marine Corps battalion landing team splashed ashore at Da Nang in South Vietnam. A companion battalion landed by air later the same day. Although there were already over 20,000 American servicemen in South Vietnam, this was the first time that an organized ground combat unit had been committed. The mission assigned these two battalions was to secure the airfield and U.S. supporting installations and facilities. The orders clearly stated, "The U.S. Marine Force will not, repeat will not, engage in day to day actions against the Viet Cong."[32]

The landing and the mission assigned these forces had been recommended by General Westmoreland on February 22, 1965. He was concerned about the ability of the South Vietnamese to protect the base, from which American aircraft were conducting air strikes against the North and providing air support missions in the South. Although Ambassador Taylor supported Westmoreland's request for the Marines at Da Nang, he also voiced grave reservations as to the wisdom of this course. He saw other bases as equally in need of security and foresaw that, once it became evident that U.S. forces would assume this mission, other tasks for these ground combat units would soon follow. Despite these reservations, the ambassador was informed on February 26 that the Marines were on the way.[33]

[31] *U.S.–Vietnam Relations*, IVC(3), pp. 95–98, 106–130.
[32] Ibid., IVC(4), p. 1.
[33] Ibid., pp. 2–6; Westmoreland, *A Soldier Reports*, pp. 123–124.

The landing of U.S. ground combat units in South Vietnam represented a watershed event in the history of the U.S. involvement in Vietnam. It was a major decision made without much fanfare, deliberation, or planning. Whereas the decision to bomb North Vietnam was the product of a year's discussion, this decision to introduce the Marines apparently was made with little discussion at the highest levels of the administration.

As Ambassador Taylor had predicted, the policy of using these forces only for base security was short-lived. The Marines hardly had their feet dry when several proposals were brought forward to get U.S. troops actively engaged in the ground war. The first of these came from Army Chief of Staff General Harold K. Johnson, following his trip to Vietnam from March 5 to March 12. The purpose of his trip was to examine what more could be done within South Vietnam, and General Johnson proposed the deployment of a full U.S. division for security of various bases. On March 17 General Westmoreland sought an additional Marine battalion to secure Phu Bai, a base north of Da Nang. In forwarding Westmoreland's request, the JCS also recommended that an additional battalion be deployed to Da Nang. In addition, on March 20 the Joint Chiefs proposed a plan that called for the deployment of a three-division force, two American and one Korean.[34]

The president met with his advisors on April 1 and 2, 1965, to review the whole panoply of military and non-military measures that might be undertaken in both South and North Vietnam. But the main focus of the discussions was clearly on action within South Vietnam, and the principal concern of the policy makers was the prospect of additional deployments of U.S. ground forces to South Vietnam and the mission to be assigned to these forces. Ambassador Taylor, while agreeing to the introduction of the additional Marines, opposed the introduction of a full U.S. division

[34] *U.S.–Vietnam Relations*, IVC(5), pp. 56–59.

without further examination of the probable effectiveness of such a unit and of the missions it should be assigned. Other advisors, according to President Johnson, who left them unidentified, opposed any significant involvement in the ground war.[35]

The president's decisions were published as National Security Action Memorandum (NSAM) 328 on April 6, 1965. Approval was given for the deployment of two additional Marine battalions, one to Phu Bai and one to Da Nang, and for an 18,000–20,000-man increase in U.S. logistical and support forces. Of perhaps more significance, however, NSAM 328 sanctioned a change in mission for U.S. ground forces in Vietnam, although in very cautious language: "The President approved a change of mission for all Marine battalions deployed to Vietnam to permit their more active use under conditions to be established and approved by the Secretary of Defense in consultation with the Secretary of State."[36]

This decision, although it did not clearly define the new mission, was a pivotal one. It marked the president's acceptance of the concept that U.S. troops would engage in offensive ground operations against an Asian foe. To be sure, the language indicated a desire to proceed slowly and carefully. But missing from NSAM 328 was any concept of a unified, coherent strategy for the use of American ground forces. Ambassador Taylor, among others, had raised the question as to whether Western troops could fight effectively in Vietnam. The president apparently agreed that before devising a strategy for the use of these forces, it would be necessary to experiment to see how they would perform in this new environment.

But again, efforts were made to make the change as imperceptible as possible to the American public. The memo-

[35] Johnson, *The Vantage Point*, pp. 139–141; *U.S.–Vietnam Relations*, IVC.(3), pp. 85–93; IVC(5), pp. 56–62.

[36] *U.S.–Vietnam Relations*, IVC(5), pp. 68–69, 124–126; Johnson, *The Vantage Point*, pp. 140–141.

randum, signed by McGeorge Bundy, stated that the president wished to avoid premature publicity for these decisions and that "the actions themselves should be taken as rapidly as practicable, but in ways that should minimize any appearance of sudden changes in policy. . . . The President's desire is that these movements and changes should be understood as being gradual and wholly consistent with existing policy."[37] Thus, the change in mission, an important step toward involving American ground forces in combat in South Vietnam, was kept from the American people. It crept out almost by accident two months later, in a State Department press release on June 8 to the effect that "American forces would be available for combat support together with Vietnamese forces when and if necessary."[38] Editorial comment the next day saw the significance in this seemingly innocuous statement: "The American people were told by a minor State Department official yesterday that, in effect, they were in a land war on the continent of Asia. . . . There is still no official explanation for a move that fundamentally alters the character of the American involvement in Vietnam. . . . It [the country] has been taken into a ground war by Presidential decision when there is no emergency that would seem to rule out Congressional debate."[39] But the same day, the White House blandly denied that such a decision had been made. George B. Reedy, press secretary to the president, read the following statement at a press conference: "There has been no change in the mission of U.S. ground combat units in Viet-Nam in recent days or weeks. The President has issued no order of any kind in this regard to General Westmoreland recently or at any other time."[40]

The president's decisions of April 6, 1965, did not cause the pressures for an increased buildup of American forces to

[37] *U.S.–Vietnam Relations*, IVC(5), p. 126.
[38] Ibid., p. 81.
[39] "Ground War in Asia."
[40] U.S., Department of State, *Department of State Bulletin*, vol. 52, p. 1,041; Taylor, *Swords and Plowshares*, pp. 344–345; Westmoreland, *A Soldier Reports*, pp. 135–136, 138–139.

abate. From April 8 on, Ambassador Taylor was bombarded with messages and instructions from Washington testifying to an eagerness to speed up the introduction to Vietnam of U.S. ground combat forces far beyond anything that had been authorized in NSAM 328. Ambassador Taylor's annoyance at these mounting pressures was transmitted to Washington. He forced into abeyance a decision, to which he was not privy, to deploy the 173rd Airborne Brigade from Okinawa to South Vietnam. But communications between Washington and Saigon became more strained, and Ambassador Taylor's annoyance changed to anger and open protest when, on April 15, he received another instruction, allegedly with the sanction of "the highest authority," which proposed, among other things:

(1) Experimental encadrement of U.S. troops into RVNAF either through the assignment of 50 U.S. soldiers to each of 10 ARVN battalions or through the "brigading" of ARVN and US battalions for operations;

(2) The introduction of a brigade force into Bien Hoa/Vung Tau for security of installations and later expansion into counter-insurgency operations . . . ;

(3) The introduction of several battalions into coastal enclaves;[41]

Faced with this rapidly changing picture of Washington's desires, Ambassador Taylor indicated his need to have a clearer statement of U.S. purposes and objectives before he could present the case for these deployments to the South Vietnamese government. In his cable to Washington, the ambassador stated: "Before I can present our case to GVN I have to know what the case is and why. It is not going to be easy to get ready concurrence for the large scale introduction of foreign troops unless the need is clear and explicit."[42]

[41] *U.S.–Vietnam Relations*, IVC(5), p. 70; IVC(3), p. 99.
[42] Taylor, *Swords and Plowshares*, pp. 341–342; *U.S.–Vietnam Relations*, IVC(5), p. 74.

In order to smooth ruffled feathers and to restore some sense of common purpose, a conference was hurriedly convened in Honolulu on April 20, bringing together most of the key personalities responsible for policy in Vietnam: chairman of the JCS General Wheeler, Secretary of Defense McNamara, General Westmoreland, Admiral Sharp, Ambassador Taylor, and Assistant Secretaries William Bundy and John McNaughton. Ambassador Taylor's resistance to a buildup of U.S. forces was overcome at this conference. An increase of U.S. forces to a total of thirteen battalions and 82,000 men was agreed upon. Honolulu also marked the relative downgrading of air pressure against North Vietnam in favor of more intense activity in the South. The president's advisors agreed that henceforth targets in South Vietnam would have first call on air assets. The key to success, it was now stated, was not to put unacceptable pressure upon the enemy, but to frustrate his strategy—"to break the will of the DRV/VC by denying them victory."[43]

The Honolulu conference recommendations in effect postulated an enclave strategy—that is, operations centered on coastal areas with the purpose of protecting the population and denying the resources of these areas to the enemy. This strategy, first proposed by General Harold K. Johnson in March, was tenaciously advocated by Ambassador Taylor throughout this period. Taylor saw many advantages to it:

> The . . . role which has been suggested for U.S. ground forces is the occupation and defense of key enclaves along the coast such as Quang Ngai, Qui Nhon, Tuy Hoa and Nha Trang. Such a disposition would have the advantage of placing our forces in areas of easy access and egress with minimum logistic problems associated with supply and maintenance. The presence of our troops would assure the defense of these important key areas and would relieve some GVN forces for employment elsewhere. The troops would not be called upon to engage in counter-

---

[43] *U.S.–Vietnam Relations*, IVC(3), pp. 99–101; IVC(5), pp. 71–79; Taylor, *Swords and Plowshares*, pp. 342–343.

insurgency operations except in their own local defense and hence would be exposed to minimum losses.[44]

Thus, the enclave strategy envisaged denying the enemy victory because he would be unable to seize decisive areas held by U.S. forces, despite whatever successes he might enjoy throughout the rest of the country. Realizing his inability to gain a final victory, the enemy would be moved to a negotiated settlement of the conflict. Also, U.S. forces would be limited in number, could be brought in and supplied with ease over sea lines of communications controlled entirely by the U.S. Navy, and could be withdrawn with equal ease should the situation so dictate. Beyond the enclaves, the South Vietnamese army would be expected to continue to prosecute the war against the enemy's main forces.

But as Ambassador Taylor had also pointed out, the enclave strategy was "a rather inglorious static defensive mission unappealing to them [U.S. forces] and unimpressive in the eyes of the Vietnamese."[45] It was perceived by the military commanders as a negative strategy, yielding the initiative to the enemy and designed to frustrate rather than to defeat him.

Although security was no longer the only authorized mission of U.S. units, it remained their primary one, and they consolidated and developed their coastal base areas. Patrol perimeters were pushed out, and an active defense was conducted, although failure to solve knotty problems concerning control and coordination between U.S. and Vietnamese forces prevented offensive operations in support of the Vietnamese for some months.

The relative quiet in the war in the South ended in May. Before the month was over, the South Vietnamese were decimated in a series of battles at Ba Gia, near Quang Ngai city. In early June, two Viet Cong regiments again defeated the South Vietnamese at Dong Xoai, inflicting heavy casual-

---

[44] *U.S.–Vietnam Relations*, IVC(3), p. 57.
[45] Ibid., p. 58; Westmoreland, *A Soldier Reports*, pp. 129–130.

ties.[46] Although U.S. troops were nearby in both cases, they were not committed to prevent the South Vietnamese defeats.

On June 7, 1965, shortly after the defeat at Ba Gia, General Westmoreland forwarded to the U.S. Commander in Chief, Pacific (CINCPAC) "a broad review of force requirements . . . in light of the changing situation in Southeast Asia and within RVN." Describing the South Vietnamese army as near collapse, reluctant to assume the offensive, with desertion rates inordinately high, and with its steadfastness under fire coming into doubt, Westmoreland saw "no course of action open to us except to reinforce our efforts in SVN with additional U.S. or Third Country forces as rapidly as is practicable during the critical weeks ahead." In addition, he added, even greater forces should be prepared for deployment, if required "to attain our objectives or counter enemy initiatives." These forces would not be involved in a security or an enclave strategy, however. As General Westmoreland saw it: "I am convinced that U.S. troops with their energy, mobility, and firepower can successfully take the fight to the VC. The basic purpose of the additional deployments . . . is to give us a substantial and hard hitting offensive capability on the ground."[47] In his cable, Westmoreland requested a buildup to a total of thirty-five maneuver battalions, with a further nine battalions to be prepared for deployment if needed at a later date.

In subsequent communications, the U.S. commander spelled out his concept for employing these forces. Sweeping away the last vestiges of the enclave strategy, Westmoreland described his plans for assuming the offensive and defeating the enemy. He saw the war developing in three distinct phases as follows:

 Phase I. Commitment of U.S. (and other Free World) forces necessary to halt the losing trend by the end of 1965.

[46] Westmoreland, *Report on the War in Vietnam*, p. 109.
[47] MACV 19118, 070335Z June 1965, MACV to CINCPAC.

Phase II. U.S. and Allied forces mount major offensive actions to seize the initiative to destroy guerrilla and organized enemy forces. This phase would be concluded when the enemy had been worn down, thrown on the defensive, and driven back from the major populated areas.

Phase III. If the enemy persisted, a period of a year to a year and a half following Phase II would be required for the final destruction of enemy forces remaining in remote base areas.[48]

General Westmoreland's recommendations to the president stirred up a hornet's nest in Washington. His request for reinforcements on a large scale, accompanied by a desire to put the troops on the offensive throughout the country, did not contain any of the comfortable restrictions that had been part of the strategies debated up until that time and, in fact, presaged a virtual American take-over of the war. The spectre of major U.S. military forces engaged in ground combat on the Asian mainland had indeed become a possibility. The implications for the United States in terms of lives and money could not be ignored.

General Westmoreland was first given authority on June 26 to commit U S. ground forces anywhere in the country when, in his judgment, they were needed to strengthen South Vietnamese forces. Thus liberated from the restrictions of the coastal enclaves, the first major operation by U.S. forces under this new authority was conducted on June 27 in War Zone D northwest of Saigon.[49]

Before making any decision to deploy more forces, however, President Johnson again wanted to examine all the options. Secretary McNamara was dispatched to Saigon on July 16 to examine the alternatives and to determine the force requirements for the immediate future and for 1966. General

[48] Westmoreland, *Report on the War in Vietnam*, p. 100; *U.S.–Vietnam Relations*, IVC(5), pp. 118–119.

[49] *U.S.–Vietnam Relations*, IVC(5), p. 7; Westmoreland, *A Soldier Reports*, p. 141.

Westmoreland indicated to McNamara that a buildup to forty-four battalions (now dubbed Phase I forces and totalling 175,000 men) would be needed in South Vietnam by the end of 1965. However, he also made it clear that this force and the new offensive strategy would only prevent defeat long enough to prepare the way for additional forces to allow him to seize the initiative from the Viet Cong in 1966. He foresaw the necessity of some twenty-four additional combat battalions, plus associated combat support and support units by the end of 1966 (Phase II forces totalling 100,000 men). This force would enable him to take the offensive that year and with "appropriate" but unstated additional reinforcements (Phase III), to have defeated the enemy by the end of 1967.[50]

McNamara reported these requirements to the president on July 20. He recommended that Westmoreland's Phase I request be met, with the understanding that additional troops would be needed in 1966, and also recommended asking Congress for authority to call up 235,000 reservists. McNamara's report engendered perhaps the only full-scale examination of U.S. objectives and strategy for Vietnam at the highest levels of the administration until the Tet offensive of 1968. President Johnson met with various advisors and congressional leaders almost continuously during the period July 21 to July 27, 1965.[51] The president's advisors were divided and for the first time expressed their concerns. Ambassador Taylor and his deputy, U. Alexis Johnson, while recognizing the seriousness of the situation, were less than sanguine about the prospects for success if large numbers of U.S. troops were brought in. Both men were concerned with the effect of the proposed buildup on the Vietnamese. Though not directly opposed to the use of U.S. forces to assist the South Vietnamese, they wanted to proceed

[50] *U.S.–Vietnam Relations,* IVC(6)(a), pp. 8–10; IVC(5), pp. 117–119; Taylor, *Swords and Plowshares,* pp. 348–349.

[51] Johnson, *The Vantage Point,* pp. 145–152; Cooper, *The Lost Crusade,* pp. 284–286; Valenti, *A Very Human President,* pp. 318–363.

slowly to prevent the loss of Vietnamese authority and control in the conduct of the war.[52]

Undersecretary of State George Ball, both in meetings with the president and in memoranda that he submitted, directly opposed the buildup. In his view, there was absolutely no assurance that the United States could attain its political objectives in Vietnam by providing additional ground forces. He saw the risk of a struggle of unknown outcome with high but indeterminate costs and felt the United States should not embark on such a course.[53]

Secretary of State Dean Rusk disagreed strongly with the views expressed by his undersecretary. In a rare written memorandum to the president, and later during discussions on this issue, he indicated that he felt it absolutely necessary for the United States to live up to its commitments in South Vietnam. "The integrity of the U.S. commitment is the principal pillar of peace throughout the world. If that commitment becomes unreliable, the communist world would draw conclusions that would lead to our ruin and almost certainly to a catastrophic war. So long as the South Vietnamese are prepared to fight for themselves, we cannot abandon them without disaster to peace and to our interests throughout the world."[54]

Others, such as Assistant Secretary of State William Bundy and Clark Clifford, fell somewhere in between. They wanted to deploy just enough additional forces to prevent defeat so that it would be possible to work toward a diplomatic solution.[55]

Of the congressional leaders consulted, only Senator Mike Mansfield expressed any opposition. As the majority leader

[52] *U.S.–Vietnam Relations*, IVC(5), pp. 104–105; Taylor, *Swords and Plowshares*, p. 349.

[53] *U.S.–Vietnam Relations*, IVC(5), p. 105; IVC(7)(a), pp. 6–8; Johnson, *The Vantage Point*, p. 147; Valenti, *A Very Human President*, pp. 327–330, 333–337.

[54] *U.S.–Vietnam Relations*, IVC(7)(a), p. 8; Johnson, *The Vantage Point*, p. 147.

[55] *U.S.–Vietnam Relations*, IVC(7)(a), p. 106.

saw it: "Whatever pledge we had was to assist South Vietnam in its own defense. Since then there has been no government of legitimacy. We owe this government nothing, no pledge of any kind. We are going deeper into war. . . . We cannot expect our people to support a war for three-to-five years. What we are about to get is an anti-Communist crusade, on and on. Remember, escalation begets escalation."[56]

President Johnson in the end agreed with and accepted the arguments of his secretary of state. As he later indicated:

> If we ran out on Southeast Asia, I could see trouble ahead in every part of the globe—not just in Asia but in the Middle East and in Europe, in Africa and in Latin America. I was convinced that our retreat from this challenge would open the path to World War III. . . . I knew our people well enough to realize that if we walked away from Vietnam and let Southeast Asia fall, there would follow a divisive and destructive debate within our country. . . . A divisive debate over "who lost Vietnam" would be, in my judgment, even more destructive to our national life than the argument over China had been. It would inevitably increase isolationist pressures from the right and from the left and cause a pulling back from our commitments in Europe and the Middle East as well as in Asia.[57]

President Johnson, on July 28, 1965, approved the deployment to South Vietnam of the Phase I forces totalling 175,-000 troops (later raised to 219,000). He refused to call up the reserves and made no decision about the deployment of Phase II forces (no decision was required at the time). In announcing these increases in U.S. forces to South Vietnam, the president stressed the continuity of the U.S. commitment to the defense of South Vietnam and indicated that he foresaw no quick solution to the problem there.[58]

[56] Quoted in Valenti, *A Very Human President*, pp. 354–355.

[57] Johnson, *The Vantage Point*, pp. 148, 151–152. See also Kearns, *Lyndon Johnson and the American Dream*, pp. 252–253.

[58] *Public Papers of Lyndon Johnson, 1965*, II, pp. 794–799.

Whatever they may have thought personally of the wisdom of this momentous decision of July 1965, all the participants realized that a major threshold had been crossed. A new course had been taken, the end of which was not in sight. As General Westmoreland understood: "Explicit in my forty-four battalion proposal and President Johnson's approval of it was a proviso for free maneuver of American and allied units throughout South Vietnam. Thus the restrictive enclave strategy with which I had disagreed from the first was finally rejected."[59] And as Johnson later stated, "Now we were committed to major combat in Vietnam."[60]

Accompanying this change from enclave defense to offensive "search-and-destroy" operations, as they came to be called, was also a subtle, but extremely significant, change in emphasis. Instead of the limited objective of simply denying the enemy victory and convincing him that he could not win, the thrust of U.S. policy was now directed toward providing sufficient forces to defeat the enemy in the South.

The decision to build up U.S. forces and to use them in an offensive strategy left the U.S. commitment to the defense of South Vietnam open-ended. The amount of force required to defeat the enemy depended entirely on the enemy's response to the U.S. buildup and his willingness to increase his own commitment to the struggle. Thus, the force approved by President Johnson in July 1965 was recognized as sufficient only to prevent the collapse of South Vietnam while the stage was being set for further U.S. troop deployments. But the acceptance of the goal of defeating the enemy rather than merely denying him victory opened the door, as George Ball had pointed out, to an indeterminate amount of additional force. Although U.S. forces could maintain the tactical initiative in South Vietnam through their great mobility and firepower, the enemy maintained the strategic initiative throughout by his willingness to increase his commitment of forces to the struggle. Thus, the pace and level of

[59] Westmoreland, *A Soldier Reports,* pp. 144, 146–152.
[60] Johnson, *The Vantage Point,* p. 153.

the fighting would be dictated by the enemy and not by the United States.

Finally, the acceptance of the buildup of U.S. forces and their use in an offensive role throughout Vietnam was an explicit expression of a total loss of confidence in the South Vietnamese Armed Forces (RVNAF) and a concomitant willingness on the part of U.S. commanders to take over the major part of the war effort. The paradox arose of the Americans fighting on behalf of an army (and a government) that they treated with disdain, even contempt. The South Vietnamese, on whose behalf the United States had entered a land war in Asia, were dealt with as if they really weren't worth saving. Thus, there grew a naked contradiction between the political objectives of the war and the actual situation of virtually ignoring the South Vietnamese government and army in the formulation of American strategy.

U.S. involvement in an Asian ground war was a reality. No further proof of the monumental implications of the decisions made in the summer of 1965 is required beyond the fact that, by the end of 1967, the time General Westmoreland estimated was required to defeat the enemy, the United States had 107 battalions and a total of 525,000 men in Vietnam without a victory in sight.

TWO

The Search for a Strategic Concept, 1965–1967

ALTHOUGH General Westmoreland had proposed a tactical concept of operations for the forces that were to be deployed to South Vietnam, an overall strategic plan was required to clarify the national purposes and objectives these additional forces were meant to serve. President Johnson, in his message to the American people announcing the deployments, had indicated that these forces were to resist aggression in South Vietnam and to "convince the Communists that we cannot be defeated by force of arms or by superior power." General Westmoreland, as has been mentioned, had a more ambitious objective, to defeat and destroy enemy forces in South Vietnam.

Therefore, in order to establish a basis for future force requirements and for overall conduct of the ground war, the military chiefs set out to develop a strategic concept for U.S. military operations in Southeast Asia. By the end of August 1965, they had developed a concept that contained their basic assumptions and goals, and they pressed this concept on the civilian leadership with single-minded intensity in the years to come.

The Joint Chiefs saw three equally important military tasks to be accomplished in Vietnam:

(1) To cause the DRV to cease its direction and support of the Viet Cong insurgency;

(2) To defeat the Viet Cong and to extend GVN control over all of South Vietnam;

33

(3) To deter Communist China from direct intervention and to defeat such intervention if it should occur.[1]

This third objective, deterring Communist China from direct intervention, was a thread that had run through the debate over bombing North Vietnam in 1965. The Joint Chiefs of Staff consistently mentioned the possibility of direct Chinese intervention as an additional justification for troop deployments and as an important reason for a reserve call-up to reconstitute the U.S. strategic reserve as these deployments proceeded. The president and his civilian advisors consistently used this possibility to limit military action against North Vietnam. National intelligence estimates just as consistently discounted the probability of such intervention.

The military tasks recommended by the Joint Chiefs to achieve their self-imposed objectives were extremely ambitious and went far beyond anything recommended by General Westmoreland. Aggressive and sustained military action, the military chiefs stated, would allow the United States to hold the initiative in both North and South Vietnam. North Vietnam's war-supporting power would be progressively destroyed and the Viet Cong defeated. To achieve this, they visualized that the following military actions would be required:

> . . . to intensify military pressure on the DRV by air and naval power; to destroy significant DRV military targets; to interdict supporting LOCs in the DRV; to interdict the infiltration and supply routes into the RVN; to improve the combat effectiveness of the RVNAF; to build and protect bases; to reduce enemy reinforcements; to defeat the Viet Cong. . . . The physical capability of the DRV to move men and supplies through the Lao corridor, down the coastline, across the DMZ, and through Cambodia

[1] JCSM 652–65, August 27, 1965, Subject: *Concept for Vietnam*, quoted in *U.S.–Vietnam Relations*, IVC(6)(a), p. 14.

must be reduced . . . by land, naval and air actions. . . . Finally . . . a buildup in Thailand to ensure attainment of the proper U.S.-Thai posture to deter CHICOM aggression and to faciliate placing U.S. forces in an advantageous logistical position if such aggression occurs.[2]

The secretary of defense, of course, did not approve this ambitious program which raised such controversial and far-reaching policy issues as blockading North Vietnam, involving U.S. ground forces in Laos and Cambodia, and building up U.S. forces in Thailand. But he did not reject it either. Indicating that an overall approval was not required at that time, the secretary merely agreed that "recommendations for future operations in Southeast Asia should be formulated" as the occasion necessitated.[3]

Left with no other guidance from their civilian superiors, the Joint Chiefs of Staff continued to formulate recommendations for future operations along the same lines. Throughout the war their recommendations continued to take the form of requests for additional American troops in South Vietnam and for expanded operational authority outside South Vietnam. Since Secretary McNamara, or higher civilian authority, had failed to provide them with any national objectives, missions, or strategic concepts other than the very general ones of "resisting aggression" or "insuring a non-Communist South Vietnam," the military leaders virtually were forced to adopt their own concept for conducting the war and to continue to press for its approval.

By November 1965, the infiltration of units from North Vietnam had increased substantially and had outpaced the buildup of American forces. Moreover, with its augmented forces, the enemy was showing an increasing willingness to stand and fight in large-scale engagements. The implications of this enemy buildup for the future were made abundantly

[2] Ibid.
[3] *U.S.–Vietnam Relations,* IVC(6)(a), p. 15.

clear to newly arrived U.S. forces. There was bloody fighting in the Ia Drang Valley in mid-November in which over 300 U.S. soldiers were killed.[4]

General Westmoreland pointed out to Washington on November 22, 1965 that the enemy buildup rate was double that planned for American forces in Phase II. He requested forces in addition to those already planned as being "essential to meet the immediate threat," and indicated that even the forces he was now requesting (which would raise Phase II forces to approximately 154,000 and bring total U.S. troop strength in Vietnam to nearly 375,000 by mid-1967) would not match the enemy buildup. To reach the level of force required to take the offensive, General Westmoreland indicated, "will ultimately require much larger deployments."[5]

Thus, the cost of the policy the administration had adopted in July 1965 were made apparent by the North Vietnamese in November. Willing to match or exceed the American buildup, the North Vietnamese clearly demonstrated to American leaders the open-ended nature of the troop commitment to South Vietnam that the United States had made by its entry into the ground war.

Faced with this dilemma, the president sent Secretary of Defense McNamara to Saigon to study the situation. McNamara spent two days in Saigon, November 28–30, 1965, and returned to report his grim findings to the president. He stated that present plans for deployment of Phase I and Phase II forces would not be enough. In order to "provide what it takes in men and materiel . . . to stick with our stated objectives," McNamara recommended additional troop deployments which would bring total U.S. maneuver battalions to seventy-four, and total U.S. personnel in Vietnam to approximately 400,000 by the end of 1966, with the possible need for an additional 200,000 in 1967.[6] Even these deployments,

[4] *Command History, 1965,* quoted in *U.S.–Vietnam Relations,* IVC(6)(a), pp. 18–19.

[5] *U.S.–Vietnam Relations,* IVC(6)(a), pp. 21–22; Westmoreland, *Report on the War in Vietnam,* p. 100.

[6] *U.S.–Vietnam Relations,* IVC(6)(a), pp. 24–25.

the secretary of defense warned, "would not guarantee success." Instead, he foresaw that "even with the recommended deployments, we will be faced in early 1967 with a military standoff at a much higher level, with pacification still stalled, and with any prospect of military success marred by the chance of an active Chinese intervention."[7]

The prospect that now faced the president was not a pleasant one. Before approving such a large commitment of American forces, Johnson again sought other alternatives. As has been mentioned, by the summer of 1965 the bombing of North Vietnam had been relegated to a secondary role in U.S. military strategy. From the time of the president's decision in July to send substantial numbers of American troops to engage in combat in South Vietnam, the ROLLING THUNDER campaign in the North was seen as useful and necessary, but as a supplement to, rather than a substitute for, action in South Vietnam. But the bombing was also seen as a negotiating option for the United States, a bargaining chip that could be given up in return for a reduction or cessation of North Vietnam's military efforts in the South. There had been a five-day bombing pause in May 1965 to see if the North Vietnamese government would respond with a gesture of its own. But that pause had been hastily arranged and was not widely publicized before its initiation, so that no adequate diplomatic preparation had been made. In addition, its brief span (May 13–May 18) precluded a meaningful response.

McNamara had suggested to the president in July that, subsequent to the deployment of the U.S. forces contemplated in Phase I, another longer bombing pause might be appropriate. Now McNamara brought the issue up again, indicating that a three- or four-week pause might be useful before any great increase in troop deployments to Vietnam.[8]

President Johnson was at first deeply skeptical of the value of such an initiative, and this skepticism was shared by Dean Rusk, McGeorge Bundy, Ambassador Lodge (who had re-

[7] Ibid., p. 25.
[8] Ibid., IVC(7)(a), pp. 20–21.

placed Taylor in July), and the military commanders. However, with the prospect of heavy new troop deployments, the weight of opinion slowly changed in favor of a bombing pause as "worth the risk."[9] The bombing pause that occurred —for thirty-seven days, from December 25, 1965 until January 31, 1966—was accompanied by a widespread American diplomatic campaign to persuade Hanoi to reciprocate by making some gesture toward peace. But the bombing pause had another, unannounced objective, that of creating a public impression of U.S. willingness to take extraordinary measures in a search for a peaceful solution in South Vietnam before increasing the military commitment there. As Secretary of State Rusk frankly stated in a cable to Ambassador Lodge: "The prospect of large-scale reinforcement in men and defense budget increases of some twenty billions for the next eighteen month period requires solid preparation of the American public. A crucial element will be clear demonstration that we have explored fully every alternative but that aggressor has left us no choice."[10]

The American diplomatic initiatives, however, met with no success, and Hanoi used the bombing pause to rush men and supplies into South Vietnam. The president, on January 31, ordered the bombing resumed.

The decision on additional major U.S. troop deployments to Vietnam now had to be faced. While his military advisors refined their troop requirements, President Johnson met with the top Vietnamese leadership for the first time in Honolulu on February 7–8, 1966. Here the discussions focused primarily on pacification and the nonmilitary measures that could be pursued in South Vietnam. President Johnson indicated that he expected to see results from these programs—to see "coonskins on the wall."[11]

At first the buildup of American forces was limited by the

[9] Johnson, *The Vantage Point*, pp. 233–237, 582; also *U.S.–Vietnam Relations*, IVC(7)(a), pp. 20–57.
[10] *U.S.–Vietnam Relations*, IVC(7)(a), p. 30.
[11] Westmoreland, *A Soldier Reports*, pp. 159–160.

speed with which units could be gotten ready to move and the availability in Vietnam of facilities to receive and support them. Once these problems had been surmounted, as they were by early 1966,[12] the barrier then became either the level at which reserve forces would have to be called up or the time it took to form and train new units. The need for new units became pressing as General Westmoreland's requests for numbers of men and rates of deployment began to exceed the capabilities of the services to provide them from existing forces. But President Johnson, anxious to preserve the facade of normality and reluctant to put the country on a war footing, resisted a reserve call-up. This issue, then, became a major concern of military and political leaders during the next two years of American involvement in Vietnam.

After the conference at Honolulu, a planning process was begun that was designed to refine U.S. troop requirements so as to provide the forces necessary without having to mobilize the reserves. This planning process was followed in all subsequent consideration of U.S. troop deployments and has been described by General Westmoreland as follows:

I customarily developed plans for the troops that I thought were needed based upon my projection of the situation. This was normally done on a calendar-year basis. This request was studied, analyzed, and costed by the Department of Defense, JCS, and the services. After this process had taken place, there was always a personal conference between Secretary McNamara and me, at which time we discussed the matter in detail, examined all alternatives, and came to an agreement on the troops that should be organized and prepared for deployment. The matter would then be discussed by us with the president, who would make a decision.[13]

[12] For details of the logistical buildup, see Lieutenant General Joseph M. Heiser, Jr., *Vietnam Studies: Logistic Support*, pp. 8–34.

[13] Personal interview with General William C. Westmoreland, September 16, 1973.

This planning and refining process continued throughout much of the remainder of the year, with the most important issue being the capability to support deployments without calling up reserves. By April 10, 1966, President Johnson had approved a plan for the subsequent buildup of U.S. forces that did not require a reserve call-up; it projected U.S. strength in South Vietnam at the end of 1966 to be seventy battalions and 383,500 men. By the end of June 1967 total U.S. strength in South Vietnam was scheduled to be 425,000. During the next three months, adjustments in these deployment capabilities raised the totals to seventy-nine maneuver battalions by the end of 1966 and eighty-two battalions by June of 1967.[14] Even this ambitious plan, called Program 3 (not to be confused with Phase III), nevertheless involved fewer men than General Westmoreland's original recommendations.

Even before these figures had been published by the Department of Defense, the military commanders (on August 5, 1966) submitted new troop requirements for 1967. They considered the additional forces to be "rounding out forces" to give a balanced additional capability. If the request was approved, troop strength in Vietnam would be raised to ninety maneuver battalions and 542,588 men by the end of 1967.[15]

Again, the planning and refining process began. Secretary McNamara did not question these new requirements. He gave the following guidance to the Joint Chiefs of Staff: "As you know, it is our policy to provide the troops, weapons, and supplies requested by General Westmoreland at the times he desires them, to the greatest possible degree. The latest revised CINCPAC requirements . . . are to be accorded the same consideration: valid requirements for SVN . . . will be deployed on a schedule as close as possible to CINCPAC/ COMUSMACV's requests. Nevertheless, I desire and expect detailed line-by-line analysis of these requirements to deter-

[14] *U.S.–Vietnam Relations,* IVC(6)(a), pp. 46–50.
[15] Ibid., pp. 52–53.

mine that each is truly essential to the carrying out of our war plan."[16]

By "our war plan," of course, McNamara meant the war plan developed by the Joint Chiefs of Staff and the military commanders in the Pacific. It was these military officials who, in the absence of direction from higher authority, were developing U.S. strategy in Vietnam and setting force requirements. The secretary of defense had limited his role and that of his department to merely examining these requests of the military commanders to make sure they were not excessive and could be supported without a reserve call-up. Up to that time, the civilian Defense officials had largely abnegated any role in the strategic or policy direction of the war and had, in fact, turned it over to the military commanders to win according to their own definition of winning, limited only by certain geographic constraints imposed to prevent involving China or the Soviet Union.

But now other considerations began to intrude that would soon cause the secretary of defense and his advisors to look more closely at these force requests and to begin to question the U.S. war plan in Vietnam, or at least the force requirements for carrying out that plan. U.S. expenditures in South Vietnam had, by the fall of 1966, caused a major inflation in that country. During fiscal year 1966, the embassy reported, the Saigon working-class cost-of-living index had risen by 92 percent. A devaluation of the currency had stabilized the situation, but Ambassador Lodge indicated that projected expenditures by the United States in South Vietnam through 1967 would upset the stabilization effort and "would cause an acceleration of inflation which would jeopardize our political and military progress."[17]

To solve this problem, Ambassador Lodge proposed a ceiling on U.S. military expenditures in SVN through 1967. This recommendation was to have an important impact on the decision about troop deployments in 1967. As Gen-

[16] Ibid., pp. 53–54.　　　　[17] Ibid., p. 71.

eral Westmoreland pointed out in protesting Lodge's recommendation, approval of this expenditure ceiling would have meant that U.S. Program 3 troop deployments to South Vietnam would have to be stopped about mid-December 1966.[18]

Another factor that affected U.S. strategy was the perennial problem of whether reserve forces should be called up to support proposed U.S. deployments and, just as importantly in the eyes of the Joint Chiefs, to reconstitute a strategic reserve that had been seriously depleted by the Vietnam buildup. The military chiefs, in their review of the 1967 force requirements, provided the secretary of defense with their analysis of the U.S. worldwide military posture in the light of these force requirements. Assuming that there would be no call-up of reserve forces and no change in rotation policy (a one-year tour for U.S. personnel), and that resources for the proposed deployments would be taken from the active force structure, the impact of meeting the 1967 requirements would be devastating. Without a reserve call-up, the Joint Chiefs of Staff indicated, the services could not fully respond to the stated force requirements on the time schedule prescribed. Providing these forces on a delayed schedule, in fact, would "further impair the U.S. military posture and capability to maintain forward deployments to deter aggression worldwide. It would further reduce the capability to reinforce NATO rapidly, to provide forces for other contingencies, and to maintain a sufficient rotation and training base. . . . Of particular note in the case of the Army, equipment withdrawals from the Reserve components have substantially weakened the Army's reserve structure."[19] It seemed that now, at last, the Joint Chiefs were telling the secretary of defense that it would no longer be possible to carry on the war in Vietnam in accordance with their strategy without a concurrent call-up of large numbers of reserves.

With all of these facts and recommendations in hand,

[18] Ibid., p. 76.   [19] Ibid., pp. 80–81.

Secretary McNamara again departed for Saigon to confer with the field commander and get a better feel for what was really needed. Upon his return, on August 10, 1966, McNamara revealed with striking clarity that many of the premises under which the United States had committed major combat forces were, in his mind, becoming questionable. In his report to the president, the secretary of defense agreed that the military situation had gotten somewhat better in 1966, but he saw little cause for optimism in the long run. In fact, McNamara seemed somewhat disheartened as he noted that he could "see no reasonable way to bring the war to an end soon."[20]

Based upon these observations, the secretary now recommended changing the emphasis of U.S. strategy. Rather than defeating the enemy by offensive action as had been consistently recommended by the military commanders, McNamara's solution was to return to a rather defensive posture, "by getting ourselves into a military posture that we credibly would maintain indefinitely—a posture that makes trying to 'wait us out' less attractive" to the North Vietnamese/Viet Cong. To achieve this, the secretary recommended a five-part program far different from the war plan envisaged by his military commanders:

(1) Barring a dramatic change in the war, we should . . . level off at the total of 470,000 [U.S. ground forces].

(2) An infiltration barrier should be constructed across the neck of South Vietnam near the 17th parallel and across the infiltration trails in Laos.

(3) Stabilize the ROLLING THUNDER program against the North at present levels.

(4) Pursue a vigorous pacification program.

(5) Increase the prospects for a negotiated settlement of the war [McNamara here suggested several possible actions].[21]

20 Ibid., p. 81.   21 Ibid., pp. 83–88.

Even if these steps were taken, however, McNamara foresaw no great probability of success in the near future. The solution, as he saw it at that time, was to prepare openly for a longer war in order to "give clear evidence that the continuing costs and risks to the American people are acceptably limited, that the formula for success has been found, and that the end of the war is merely a matter of time."[22]

This remarkably somber and pessimistic document gave an answer, finally, to the demands of the military chiefs for an approved strategic concept for U.S. operations in Vietnam. That answer, however, was a clear "no" to their proposals to defeat North Vietnamese forces through major increases in U.S. forces in South Vietnam and expanded bombing in the North. But more than just a "no," McNamara's concept provided an alternative strategy and criteria for success, as well as new assumptions about the meaning of "winning," against which future military recommendations would be measured.

With this posing of alternatives, the planning and refining process continued on a new basis. The JCS, as could be expected, disagreed with McNamara's strategic alternative. They reiterated their previously developed, but unapproved, strategic concept of maximum pressure on the enemy at all points free of most political restraints, in order to achieve U.S. objectives in the shortest possible time and at the least cost in men.[23] They made a twofold case for calling up the reserves: one, that we could not meet Vietnam force requirements and simultaneously fulfill our commitments to NATO and other threatened areas without mobilization; and two, that the achievement of U.S. war objectives "in the shortest time with the least cost" could not be done without mobilization.

President Johnson, with the spectre of reserve mobilization constantly on his mind, was not enchanted with the prospect of a costly major force increase. After a series of conferences with the president, McNamara informed the JCS formally,

[22] Ibid., p. 93.   [23] Ibid., pp. 93–100.

on November 11, 1966, that a new deployment program, Program 4, had been approved with an end strength of U.S. military personnel of 470,000 to be reached by June 1968 (as opposed to the original request for some 542,000 by the end of 1967).

In explaining the reasoning behind the Program 4 decisions, McNamara posed the strategic dilemma and seemed to resolve it finally:

> We now face a choice of two approaches to the threat of the regular VC/NVA forces. The first approach would be to continue in 1967 to increase friendly forces as rapidly as possible, and without limit, and employ them primarily in large scale "seek out and destroy" operations to destroy the main force VC/NVA units. . . .

> The second approach is to follow a similarly aggressive strategy of "seek out and destroy," but to build friendly forces only to that level required to neutralize the large enemy units and prevent them from interfering with the pacification program. It is essential to this approach that such a level be consistent with a stable economy in SVN, and consistent with a military posture that the U.S. credibly would maintain indefinitely, thus making a Communist attempt to "wait us out" less attractive.

> I believe it is time to adopt the second approach for three reasons: (1) if MACV estimates of enemy strength are correct, we have not been able to attrite the enemy forces fast enough to break their morale and more U.S. forces are unlikely to do so in the foreseeable future; (2) we cannot deploy more than 470,000 personnel . . . without a high probability of generating a self-defeating runaway inflation in SVN, and (3) an endless escalation of U.S. deployments is not likely to be acceptable in the U.S. or to induce the enemy to believe that the U.S. is prepared to stay as long as it is required to produce a secure non-communist SVN. . . .[24]

[24] Ibid., pp. 108–110.

45

Thus, the secretary of defense finally seemed to have adopted an overall strategic concept for the conduct of the war in Vietnam. But it was not the concept advocated by or even acceptable to the military leaders, from the field commanders to the Joint Chiefs of Staff. The civilian decision makers in the Department of Defense were beginning to question the concept developed by the military leaders, which had led to programs that were increasingly expensive and depressingly barren of tangible results. The illusion of quick military victory had largely dissipated, but even at this point there was no questioning or reevaluation of overall American objectives in South Vietnam.

The initial strategic concept emerged from a basic assumption that the military and political situation in South Vietnam in the spring and early summer of 1965 was irretrievably lost unless the United States committed substantial combat forces and unless Hanoi could be persuaded to cease its support of the Viet Cong. American military leaders saw no alternative to Americanizing the war and defeating the enemy on the ground. The way to accomplish this, traditionally, was to bring the maximum power to bear on the enemy and on his war-making capability. But American political leaders, although not questioning this strategy or explicitly advocating a different one, sought to limit U.S. involvement.

So the military was denied the resources for a rapid and maximum application of power against the enemy in North and South Vietnam and their contiguous areas, laying the groundwork for future charges that "gradualism" and "political restraints" had prevented victory. But even the gradual application of American power, a policy that frustrated the desire of the military for quick and decisive results, soon began to prove too costly to an administration determined to keep the economy on a peacetime footing and determined not to mobilize reserve forces. Further, this strategy could not, in the face of a matching North Vietnamese buildup, produce tangible results for a president interested in "coonskins on the wall."

46

Thus, during this period other alternatives were sought that would relieve the pressure on U.S. resources, especially manpower, yet would contribute to the military effort. Among these were a barrier plan proposed by McNamara, attempts to obtain the commitment of additional Free World forces to supplement American troops, and heightened diplomatic activity aimed at engaging the North Vietnamese in negotiations.[25]

The turn of the year saw the policy debate over basic U.S. tactics in South Vietnam continue as it became increasingly clear that the nature of our objectives, the political bases of our resolution, the desirable magnitude of our presence, and the ground and air strategy to be pursued were still not crystallized or carefully delineated within the administration. The civilians in the Defense Department continued to stress the theme of establishing security and stabilizing troop and bombing levels for the long haul. The military authorities continued to insist on their strategic concept designed "to defeat externally directed and supported communist subversion and aggression." They attacked the premise that the restoration of economic stability in SVN was of overriding importance, and regarded the ceiling of 470,000 men as inadequate and restrictive.

Thus, the secretary of defense, the Joint Chiefs of Staff, and the field commander were still not agreed on their understanding of the country's strategy and objectives in South Vietnam. This tended not only to aggravate a communications problem that had always hindered political-military planning, but placed the military on the defensive. The divergence between Washington policy and the military direction of the war was to assume great importance before the gap was closed. For the time being, however, ambiguity and uncertainty continued. The president apparently believed

[25] Johnson, *The Vantage Point*, pp. 250–256; Taylor, *Swords and Plowshares*, pp. 375–376; Cooper, *The Lost Crusade*, pp. 320–368; Kraslow and Loory, *The Secret Search for Peace in Vietnam*; Westmoreland, *A Soldier Reports*, p. 200.

that the best way to preserve harmony and encourage continued support from his military leaders was to keep the strategic concept ambiguous or undefined.

The underlying nature of this disagreement over strategic concept was being picked up both in the press and on Capitol Hill, as public disenchantment with the conduct of the war began to grow. This public disenchantment, involving both hawks and doves, reflected the debate within the administration. On the hawk side, many political figures traditionally friendly to the military were enlisted to speak out against bombing restraints and restricted force levels. Senator Stennis, chairman of the Armed Services Committee, declared that General Westmoreland's troop requests must be met "even if it should require mobilization or partial mobilization." Stennis later charged that "American commanders in Vietnam are not getting all the troops they want and the bombing of the North is overly restricted." And Chairman Mendel Rivers of the House Armed Services Committee called upon the United States "to flatten Hanoi if necessary and let world opinion go fly a kite."

On the other side of the issue, the "credibility gap" between administration statements and actions on the ground in Vietnam widened. A series of dispatches from Hanoi by Harrison Salisbury of the *New York Times*, which described civilian casualties caused by U.S. bombing, touched off a round of controversy as to the morality and effectiveness of the air campaign against North Vietnam. Moderate student leaders, in a letter to the president, noted a disparity between American statements about Vietnam and American actions there, indicated confusion about basic U.S. purposes, and warned of a drift "from confusion toward disaffection."[26]

[26] Salisbury's dispatches are compiled in Harrison E. Salisbury, *Behind the Lines: Hanoi, December 23, 1966–January 7, 1967*; see also Terence Smith, "Student Leaders Warn President of Doubts on War"; James Haskins, *The War and the Protest: Vietnam*. For reaction to the Salisbury book, see James Aronson, *The Press and the Cold War*, pp. 181–245. These pages also appeared under the title "The Sell-Out of the Pulitzer Prize," in *The Washingtonian Monthly*.

The public and the press were becoming increasingly wary of statistics and statements coming out of Washington. In January 1967 a Harris opinion poll showed that the public was just as likely to blame the United States for truce violations as the enemy. In early February the Pentagon acknowledged that it had lost 1,800 aircraft in Vietnam as opposed to the 622 "combat aircraft" it had announced earlier. Even the *Chicago Tribune*, in early March, surmised that either figures coming out of Vietnam were wrong or those coming out of the Pentagon were misleading. The paper cited a recent joint press conference held by Secretaries McNamara and Rusk in which they announced that Communist military forces in Vietnam had suffered tremendous casualties in the past few months, thus reducing their effectiveness significantly, but announcing in the next sentence that serious Communist activity in South Vietnam had "increased substantially." And even Bob Hope admitted that some performers had refused to participate in his annual Christmas tour of the war zone to entertain the troops because of their disapproval of American policy.[27]

The costs of the war were also being brought to the attention of the American people with increased emphasis. In mid-March, the House Appropriations Committee approved a $12 billion supplemental Defense appropriations bill, and a week later the Senate overwhelmingly approved a $20.8 billion military procurement appropriation. American casualties announced on March 10, 1967 were the highest for any week of the war: 232 killed in action, 1,381 wounded in action, and 4 missing in action, a total of 1,617 American casualties in one week. The realization grew that the war was likely to be long and costly.

The underlying controversy within the Pentagon over the ground strategy to pursue in Vietnam was soon brought into the open again. On March 18, 1967 General Westmoreland submitted to CINCPAC an analysis of his additional force

[27] Tom Buckley, "Hope Says Some Performers Refused Vietnam Trip."

requirements projected through June of 1968. Westmoreland indicated that although he had not strongly objected to the 470,000-man ceiling established earlier, reassessment of the situation had made it clear that that force, although enabling the United States to gain the initiative, did not permit "sustained operations of the scope and intensity required to avoid an unreasonably protracted war." Thus, General Westmoreland indicated, the minimum essential force needed to exploit success and to retain effective control of areas being cleared of enemy influence, was an additional two and one-third divisions with a total of twenty-one maneuver battalions. He considered the optimum force to be four and two-thirds divisions which, with supporting forces, would total some 200,000 men in addition to the 1967 ceiling of 470,000.[28]

After developing more detailed justification for these figures, the Joint Chiefs of Staff formally reported to the secretary of defense on April 20, 1967 that additional forces were needed to achieve the objectives *they* considered the United States to be pursuing in Vietnam. The JCS request reaffirmed the basic objectives and strategy that had been contained in each troop request since 1965, but which had now become a point of issue within the administration. The military leaders repeated their view that the U.S. national objective in South Vietnam remained the attainment of a stable and independent noncommunist government.

They indicated that the military missions necessary to achieve that goal were:

(a) Making it as difficult and costly as possible for the NVA to continue effective support of the VC and to cause North Vietnam to cease direction of the VC insurgency.

(b) To defeat the VC/NVA and force the withdrawal of NVA forces.

(c) Extend government dominion, direction and control.

[28] *U.S.–Vietnam Relations,* IVC(6)(b), pp. 61–67.

(d) To deter Chinese Communists from direct intervention in SEA.[29]

They then listed the three general areas of military effort that they felt were necessary in pursuit of those missions:

(1) Operations against the Viet Cong/North Vietnamese Army (VC/NVA) forces in SVN while concurrently assisting the South Vietnamese Government in their nation-building efforts.
(2) Operations to obstruct and reduce the flow of men and materials from North Vietnam (NVN) to SVN.
(3) Operations to obstruct and reduce imports of war-sustaining materials into NVN.[30]

The military leaders believed effort was inadequate in each of these areas. In South Vietnam, insufficient forces prevented the establishment of a secure environment for the people. In North Vietnam, an expanded bombing campaign was required to reduce infiltration of men and supplies to the South, and in the third area, relatively little effort had been permitted.

Therefore, in addition to the deployment of additional ground forces to South Vietnam, the Joint Chiefs strongly recommended increased effort against the enemy's strategic supply lines into North Vietnam. Again, the Joint Chiefs reiterated their belief that a reserve call-up and extension of terms of service were "the only feasible means of meeting the additional FY 1968 requirements in the stipulated time frame." And in another plea for an approved strategy for the conduct of the war, something they had been seeking since the first troop deployments in 1965, the military leaders recommended that their "military strategy for the conduct of the war in Southeast Asia . . . be approved in principle."[31]

Thus, the issues were squarely posed for the president and, indeed, he seems to have been brought in on the planning much earlier in this case than in previous force-planning

[29] Ibid., pp. 73–74.   [30] Ibid., p. 74.   [31] Ibid., p. 76.

sequences. On April 25, 1967, General Westmoreland returned to the United States, ostensibly to address the Associated Press annual convention in New York. He and General Wheeler met with the president on April 27. Westmoreland indicated to the president that if the troops he requested were not provided, the war would not necessarily be lost but progress would certainly be slowed. He admitted that it was likely that the enemy would also add more troops, although he felt we had reached the crossover point where "attritions will be greater than additions to the [enemy] force." General Westmoreland concluded by estimating that with 565,000 men, the war could well go on for three years, but with a total of 665,000 as he had requested, it could be over in two years. General Wheeler repeated to the president his concern about the possibility of military threats in other parts of the world.[32]

In the Defense Department, meanwhile, the search for alternatives to Westmoreland's troop request was intensive. The strategic concept upon which the request was based was attacked directly by the Defense civilians, who preferred the strategy stated by McNamara in November 1966. They argued that a limit to the number of U.S. forces had to be imposed, thereby "stabilizing" the ground conflict. The Joint Chiefs, of course, fought back, declaring that this position would not permit early termination of the war on terms acceptable to the United States, provided little capacity for initiating new actions or "maintaining momentum," and presented "an alarming pattern" of realignment of U.S. objectives and intentions in Southeast Asia.[33]

The arguments about strategy went on throughout the summer. But once again what should have been a fundamental argument as to American purposes in South Vietnam was reduced to the single issue of what force buildup could be supported without mobilizing the reserves. This issue surfaced publicly on June 23, 1967, on the eve of an-

[32] Ibid., pp. 82–85.
[33] Ibid., pp. 77–88, 105–136, 146–165, 178–214.

other trip to Saigon by Secretary McNamara. In the *Washington News*, Jim Lucas observed that the manpower squeeze was on in Vietnam and that General Westmoreland's latest request for troops could not be met without some sort of mobilization. Lucas added that it was obvious that the White House did not want any sort of mobilization before the next year's elections if it could possibly be avoided. The article pointed up personnel deficiencies that existed within Army and Marine ground units in Vietnam, and added that many of these units were operating below acceptable manpower levels. A similar article by Neil Sheehan in the *New York Times* on July 3, 1967, accurately reported General Westmoreland's optimum and minimum troop requests, indicated that the administration could not grant the manpower requested by the field commander without a partial mobilization of reserves and a significant increase in war costs, and pointed out the serious manpower shortages that were being created in Army forces around the world in order to meet current Vietnam requirements.[34]

The search for alternatives continued. In mid-July the president sent Maxwell Taylor and Clark Clifford to the Far East, ostensibly to visit allies and to explain American policy. Their real purpose of trying to induce nations that had contributed token ground forces to the effort in Vietnam to commit more troops was no secret. Their efforts, characterized in the press as the arm twisting of reluctant allies, met with little or no success; indeed, President Marcos of the Philippines refused to meet with the president's representatives.[35] This reluctance by Korea, Thailand, Australia, New Zealand, and the Philippines to feel a great deal of concern

[34] Jim Lucas, "Partial Mobilization?"; Neil Sheehan, "Joint Chiefs Back Troop Rise Requested by Westmoreland."

[35] Taylor, *Swords and Plowshares*, pp. 375–376. For accounts of Allied participation in the war, see Lieutenant General Stanley R. Larsen and Brigadier General James L. Collins, Jr., *Vietnam Studies: Allied Participation in Vietnam*; W. Scott Thompson, *Unequal Partners: Philippine and Thai Relations with the United States, 1966–75*, pp. 73–112.

about the situation in Vietnam had a profound effect upon Clifford. He was later to indicate that this trip and the reaction of these nations caused him to begin to question American policy in Vietnam.

In the meantime, analysts in the Defense Department had concluded that a total of 51,249 troops in maneuver battalions could be deployed to Vietnam without changing the policy of a one-year tour in Vietnam, without calling up reserves, and without deploying NATO-reinforcing units in the United States. In his budget message to Congress on August 3, 1967, President Johnson disclosed plans to dispatch "at least 45,000" additional troops to South Vietnam in that fiscal year, bringing the total authorized troop strength in the war zone to 525,000 American forces.[36] This was Program 5, officially published by the Defense Department on August 14.

This announcement was greeted by the press and the public with a certain resignation bordering on apathy. On August 7, 1967, in a long article from Saigon, John Apple of the *New York Times* cited the constant need for reinforcement as a measure of the U.S. failure to train an effective South Vietnamese army. He characterized the war as a "stalemate" and indicated that there could be no victory unless "the central fact of the allied war effort—the critical lack of commitment of South Vietnamese society to work for its own survival—is changed."[37] On the same day, General Harold K. Johnson, Chief of Staff of the Army, was reported to have stated in Saigon that there was "a smell of success" in every major area of the war.[38] The credibility gap grew, and the American public seemed generally to accept the more pessimistic view.

The policy differences within the administration were revealed in acrimonious detail in hearings on the air war in North Vietnam before Senator Stennis' Preparedness

---

[36] *Public Papers of Lyndon Johnson, 1967*, II, p. 736.
[37] R. W. Apple, Jr., "Vietnam: Signs of Stalemate."
[38] "U.S. Army Staff Chief Finds 'Smell of Success.' "

Investigating Subcommittee of the Senate Armed Services Committee in August 1967. Members of the subcommittee, known for their sympathies for the military, were concerned that restraints on bombing in the North were unnecessary, were contrary to military advice, and were prolonging the war. The civilian officials, primarily Secretary McNamara, who were imposing these restraints against sound military advice were undoubtedly the targets of the investigation. Senator Stennis explained the reasons for the inquiry. "The real question is whether we are doing what we can and should do *in the opinion of our military experts* [emphasis added] to hit the enemy when and where and in a manner that will end the war soonest and thus save American lives."[39]

The subcommittee heard first from the military leaders involved in the air war. They all maintained that the bombing had been much less effective than it might have been—and could still be—if civilian leaders had heeded military advice and lifted the overly restrictive controls. When Secretary McNamara appeared before the subcommittee on August 25, he took direct issue with these views. He defended the bombing campaign as having been carefully tailored to limited U.S. purposes in Southeast Asia. The secretary argued that those who criticized the limited nature of the bombing sought unrealistic objectives, those of breaking the will of the North Vietnamese and cutting off the infiltration of war supplies to the South. The air war, the secretary contended, was not a substitute for the arduous ground war being waged in the South.[40]

On August 31, 1967, the subcommittee issued its predictable report which accepted almost all of the military's criticisms and told the administration that "logic and prudence requires that the decision be with the unanimous weight of professional military judgment."

[39] U.S., Congress, Senate, Committee on Armed Services, *Air War Against North Vietnam*, part 1, p. 3 (hereafter cited as *Air War Against North Vietnam*).

[40] Ibid., part 4.

The Stennis report starkly exposed the policy rift within the administration. In an attempt to dampen the public effects of this rift, the president, in a news conference on September 1, 1967, which was largely devoted to the issue of bombing, praised the advice he had been receiving from his military leaders.[41] Subsequent bombing decisions, however, must have been even more stinging to McNamara than this seeming repudiation. On September 10, 1967, for example, North Vietnam's third port at Cam Pha, a target McNamara had counseled against bombing and had specifically discussed in his testimony, was struck for the first time.[42] The secretary of defense and the Joint Chiefs, it appeared, were on a collision course, with the president apparently leaning toward his military advisors.

As indicated, however, the great debate within the administration in 1967 was over the conduct of the ground war, and that debate revolved around one crucial factor— mobilization. When the president began to search for the elusive point at which the costs of Vietnam would become unacceptable to the American people, he always settled upon mobilization, the point at which reserves would have to be called up to support a war that was becoming increasingly distasteful to the American public. This constraint, with all its political and social repercussions, not any argument about strategic concepts or the "philosophy" of the war, dictated American war policy. The Joint Chiefs of Staff again failed to get agreement on a strategic concept for fighting the war. Indeed, a change in concept or in objectives was not even mentioned in the decision to allocate additional limited ground forces to the war. But the forces allocated, in numbers far below that deemed necessary by the military to pursue their tactical concept, would necessarily force a change in the way the war was pursued on the battlefield.

On this occasion, Secretary McNamara apparently felt

---

[41] *Public Papers of Lyndon Johnson, 1967*, II, pp. 816–825.
[42] *Air War Against North Vietnam*, part 4, pp. 279–282; *U.S.–Vietnam Relations*, IVC(7)(b), p. 101.

more strongly than he had in the past that the course to be pursued in Vietnam be reviewed and approved at the highest level. The secretary of defense forwarded a personal memorandum to the president on November 1, 1967 that spelled out his feeling that the continuation of the present course of action in Vietnam "would be dangerous, costly, and unsatisfactory to our people." In his memorandum, McNamara suggested alternative moves toward "stabilization of our military operations in the South . . . and of our air operations in the North, along with a demonstration that our air attacks on the North are not blocking negotiations leading to a peaceful settlement." McNamara concluded his unusual memorandum with three recommendations, strikingly similar to the ones he had made in August of 1966. First, he suggested that the United States announce that it would not expand air operations in the North or the size of combat forces in the South beyond those already planned. Second, McNamara proposed a bombing halt before the end of 1967. Finally, he favored a new study of military operations in the South aimed at reducing U.S. casualties and giving the South Vietnamese greater responsibilities for their own security.[43]

President Johnson gave McNamara's memorandum long and careful consideration. He had already addressed the alternative strategy advocated by the Joint Chiefs of Staff. At a White House luncheon on September 12, the president had asked his military advisors to recommend additional actions, within existing policy limitations, that would increase pressure on North Vietnam and accelerate the achievement of U.S. objectives in South Vietnam. Here, again, however, the military chiefs showed neither flexibility nor creativeness. In their reply, on October 17, 1967, the Joint Chiefs indicated, in rather a resigned tone, that they considered the rate of progress to have been and to continue to be slow largely because U.S. military power had been constrained

[43] Johnson, *The Vantage Point*, p. 372. For an account of the evolution in McNamara's thinking, see Trewhitt, *McNamara*, pp. 227–245.

in a manner that had significantly reduced its impact and effectiveness. Military operations had been hampered in four ways, they argued:

a. The attacks on enemy military targets have been on such a prolonged, graduated basis that the enemy has adjusted psychologically, economically, and militarily, e.g., inured themselves to the difficulties and hardships accompanying the war, dispersed their logistic support system, and developed alternative transport routes and a significant air defense system.
b. Areas of sanctuary, containing important military targets, have been afforded the enemy.
c. Covert operations in Cambodia and Laos have been restricted.
d. Major importation of supplies into NVN by sea has been permitted.

Pessimistically, the Joint Chiefs indicated that progress would continue to be slow as long as these limitations on military operations continued. The military leaders then listed a series of steps they believed should be taken. Their recommendations included removing restrictions on the air campaign against all militarily significant targets in NVN; mining NVN deep water ports and NVN inland waterways and estuaries north of 20 degrees, N; extending naval surface operations north of 20 degrees, N; increasing air interdiction in Laos and along NVN borders; eliminating operational restrictions on B-52s in Laos; expanding ground operations in Laos and Cambodia; and expanding and reorienting NVN covert programs. The president reviewed the JCS recommendations but pointed out that some of them had already been rejected previously and would not now be approved.[44]

It finally appeared that the military chiefs had accepted the political restrictions imposed upon them by the commander in chief. On November 27, 1967, in response to another presidential request to recommend military action in

[44] *U.S.–Vietnam Relations,* IVC(6)(b), pp. 222–223.

Southeast Asia over the next four months, the military chiefs reiterated their pessimistic analysis, "There are no new programs which can be undertaken under current policy guidelines which would result in a rapid or significantly more visible increase in the rate of progress in the near term."[45] Thus, the president was aware of how widely the secretary of defense's proposals varied from the recommendations of his military leaders.

Surprisingly enough, however, it does not appear that the military leaders threatened or even contemplated resigning to dramatize their differences with and opposition to the limitations on the conduct of the war insisted upon by the president and his civilian advisors.[46] President Johnson was aware of the possible political effects of such a military defection, and he had temporized in order not to push his loyal military leaders to such a point. Although he never approved the strategy that the Joint Chiefs continued to recommend, he never completely ruled it out either. He allowed the military chiefs a gradual increase in their combat forces and held out the possibility of greater combat authority in the future. He was successful in pointing out the political limitations that prevented his meeting all of their requests, while never finally rejecting those requests.

But now the alternatives seemed clear. President Johnson pondered McNamara's proposals over the next few weeks, consulting administration officials, close personal friends, and members of Congress. In light of later developments, it might be interesting here to note the reaction of certain of the president's advisors. Dean Rusk agreed with McNamara's proposal on stabilizing our effort and giving the South Vietnamese greater responsibility for their own security, but he was skeptical of an extended halt in the bombing. He did

[45] Ibid., pp. 225–226.

[46] One commentator has indicated that there were "vague hints" that some members of the Joint Chiefs had threatened to resign during the air-power hearings in August. See Hoopes, *The Limits of Intervention,* p. 90. For General Wheeler's reaction to this report, see Trewhitt, *McNamara,* p. 245.

think, however, that we should "take the drama out of our bombing" by cutting back on operations in the Hanoi-Haiphong area. Clark Clifford, on the other hand, felt that McNamara's plan would "retard the possibility of concluding the conflict rather than accelerating it." He felt that the Mc-Namara suggestions would appear to Hanoi as "a resigned and discouraged effort to find a way out of a conflict for which we had lost our will and dedication." Walt Rostow, now the president's national security advisor, favored holding forces to approved levels but opposed an unconditional bombing halt as signifying weakness both to Hanoi and to the American people.[47]

In an almost unprecedented step, President Johnson, on December 18, 1967, wrote a personal memorandum for the permanent files giving his view of McNamara's proposals. The president had concluded that a unilateral bombing halt would "be read both in Hanoi and the United States as a sign of weakening will," although he agreed with Rusk that we should "strive to remove the drama and public attention" from the bombing of North Vietnam. The president went a long way toward approving McNamara's concept of ground strategy. Although he considered that the announcement of a so-called policy of stabilization would have undesirable political effects, he also indicated that he could see no basis at the moment for increasing U.S. forces above the current approved level. Finally, the president accepted McNamara's suggestion that we review our military operations in South Vietnam with a view to reducing U.S. casualties and accelerating the turnover of responsibility to the GVN.[48] Shortly before, Johnson had announced that McNamara would soon leave his post as secretary of defense and would be appointed president of the World Bank. The decision to replace McNamara, however, had apparently been made long before. According to Major General Robert N. Ginsburgh: "McNamara's memorandum was not responsible for his being replaced. The president had made the decision that Mc-

[47] Johnson, *The Vantage Point*, pp. 373–377.
[48] Ibid., pp. 377–378, 600–601.

Namara had to go in August when McNamara testified before the Stennis Committee. At that time, McNamara and the Joint Chiefs had had a head-to-head confrontation over our bombing of North Vietnam. The president was angry. He decided to back the Joint Chiefs and ease McNamara out."[49]

But now, in December, the president did not back the Joint Chiefs. Although they may have been placated by the removal of McNamara, and were hopeful that their strategy would be approved by his successor, the president in large part had agreed with McNamara's proposed ground strategy.

The president had discussed the McNamara proposals with, among others, General Westmoreland, the ground commander in Vietnam. Westmoreland, summoned home along with Ambassador Bunker in mid-November to appear on television and before Congress in order to stress the progress being made in Vietnam, had himself become concerned with the likelihood of a long, drawn out war. To Westmoreland, the denial of the major portion of his last troop request seemed to indicate that the president had opted for such a course, and he had begun to think through a concept for conducting such a war that would be acceptable to the American people and that would promise some results in the long run. As Westmoreland saw it: "If we were not going to call up the reserves, there was a definite limit as to how many troops we could support in Vietnam. I had come up with the general formula of about 500,000, plus or minus 10 percent. I had talked with McNamara about this, and I had consulted General Johnson, Chief of Staff of the Army, trying to get a fix on what was considered the maximum number that could be supported if there were to be no change in policy."[50] Westmoreland broached his strategy to the president upon his re-

---

[49] Personal interview with Major General Robert N. Ginsburgh, August 25, 1975. See also Kearns, *Lyndon Johnson and the American Dream*, pp. 320–321; Charles W. Corddry, "McNamara Will Take World Bank Job When Defense Budget Is Set"; Max Frankel, "McNamara Takes World Bank Post: War Shift Denied"; Richard Harwood, "Will Leave Pentagon in Early '68"; Clayton Fritchey, "A Cabinet Lesson Seen in McNamara's Case"; "Exit McNamara."

[50] Personal interview with General William C. Westmoreland, September 16, 1973.

turn to the United States in November and, at the behest of the president, explained his concept to the committees on Armed Services in the Senate and the House.[51]

In a major address to the National Press Club on November 21, 1967, Westmoreland first explained his strategy in public. Placing the American effort in Vietnam in perspective, the field commander indicated that "the end begins to come into view." The final phase of the war "will see the conclusion of our plan to weaken the enemy and strengthen our friends until we become superfluous." In answer to a question, Westmoreland indicated further: "It is conceivable to me that within two years or less, it will be possible for us to phase down our level of commitment and turn more of the burden of the war over to the Vietnamese Armed Forces who are improving and who, I believe, will be prepared to assume this greater burden."[52]

As Westmoreland recalled: "It was the only strategy that I could come up with that was viable if there were no change in policy, if we were not going to widen the war, and if we were not going to call up our reserves. One of the things that worried me was my conclusion that this strategy bought a long war and that casualties on the battlefield were going to be heavy. It was my strategy, and I portrayed it as such. The administration was totally noncommital on it. They kind of nodded their heads and did not disagree. They just listened and did nothing about it."[53]

Thus, with the president's apparent agreement to study turning over more of the war to the Vietnamese while sending

[51] Johnson, *The Vantage Point*, p. 376; personal interview with General William C. Westmoreland, September 16, 1973.

[52] Address by General William C. Westmoreland, to the National Press Club, pp. 7, 11. For press comment, see Charles W. Corddry, "End to War in Sight for Commander"; David Holmberg, "Westy Had Headline Words"; "Saigon Slated for Larger DMZ Role"; Chalmers M. Roberts, "General's Timetable Calls for Victory After '68 Elections"; George C. Wilson, "General on Master Plan: South Vietnam Troops to Join DMZ Fighting."

[53] Personal interview with General William C. Westmoreland, September 16, 1973; see also Westmoreland, *A Soldier Reports*, p. 235.

no more American ground forces to Vietnam, and with General Westmoreland's specific and public enunciation of this policy of "Vietnamization" of the war, the debate about strategic concepts within the administration seemed to have ended. U.S. forces in Vietnam would be stabilized at 525,000, and the Vietnamese would carry a larger share of the load. This strategy promised a limit on the American commitment to Vietnam while putting emphasis on the essential role of the Vietnamese in defending their nation.

General Westmoreland's prediction proved remarkably accurate. Although the circumstances were vastly different from what he had foreseen, the first American troop withdrawals from Vietnam began some twenty months after his address.

THREE

✿✿✿

The Eve of Tet

THE United States entered 1968 in a mood of cautious optimism concerning the course of the war in Vietnam. Although the press and the Congress were becoming increasingly skeptical about the extent and the success of the American effort, the president and his principal advisors remained optimistic. Only Secretary McNamara, among the president's closest advisors, had expressed doubts about the course of the American effort, and his doubts found little sympathy in the highest levels of the administration.[1]

The opening stages of the Communist winter/spring offensive were being defeated with great loss to the enemy in a series of bloody battles along South Vietnam's borders during October and November of 1967.[2] President Johnson was further reassured by a group of distinguished private citizens whom he consulted on foreign policy matters from time to time. This group, later referred to as the Wise Men, assembled in Washington on November 2, 1967, and received a series of briefings on South Vietnam from government officials. The group, which was not exposed to McNamara's doubts, expressed general satisfaction with the conduct and the success of the military aspects of the war. Concern was expressed, however, about the public opinion problem that faced the administration, and a program to give the public

[1] Johnson, *The Vantage Point*, pp. 372–378, 600–601; *Air War Against North Vietnam*, part 4, pp. 274–373; see also Goulding, *Confirm or Deny*, pp. 168–213; Trewhitt, *McNamara*, pp. 237–244.

[2] Westmoreland, *Report on the War in Vietnam*, pp. 138–139. The overall enemy strategy that underlay these bloody and seemingly inconclusive battles was not realized until much later. See note 30, chapter 4.

Transmit optimism

a better appreciation of the issues and the successes of the American effort in Vietnam was recommended.[3]

To transmit his optimism to the country, Johnson had summoned General Westmoreland and Ambassador Bunker home to the United States later in November. In appearances before congressional committees and on the *Meet the Press* television show, both stressed the progress that was being made in Vietnam.[4] These appearances, as well as Westmoreland's speech to the National Press Club and the optimism expressed by other members of the administration, seemed to offer some hope that there would be, at last, an end to the war.

The president was also convinced of the growing confidence of the Vietnamese and of their motivation and ability to achieve a stable administration in Saigon.[5] How shallow

[3] The group at this meeting included Dean Acheson, George Ball, McGeorge Bundy, Clark Clifford, Douglas Dillon, Arthur Dean, Henry Cabot Lodge, Robert Murphy, Abe Fortas, and Generals Omar Bradley and Maxwell D. Taylor. See Taylor, *Swords and Plowshares*, pp. 377–378. Also personal interview with General Maxwell D. Taylor, December 28, 1972.

[4] National Broadcasting Company, *Meet the Press, Sunday, November 19, 1967*. For other comment, see *Public Papers of Lyndon Johnson, 1967*, II, pp. 1,045–1,055; Roy Reed, "Bunker Sees the President: Predicts Saigon Gain in '68"; "Westmoreland Here, Cites Vietnam Gains"; Carroll Kilpatrick, "Westmoreland Sees U.S. Phaseout in '69"; Charles W. Corddry, "Viet 'Phase-Down' Defined as Long-Term, Gradual Step"; Jerry Greene, "Westy Briefing Gives Johnson a Jaunty Airing"; Peter Grose, "War of Attrition Called Effective by Westmoreland"; Philip Dodd, "Lyndon Calls Parley on Viet Nam Policy"; James Reston, "Washington: Why Westmoreland and Bunker Are Optimistic"; Jack Bell, "Dissenters Unmoved by General"; Ward Just, "LBJ Musters Aides to Show Gains in War"; Joseph Kraft, "LBJ a Happening President Whether by News Break or Invention"; Louis Harris, "Johnson Regains Popularity"; Johnson, *The Vantage Point*, pp. 261, 376. For an account of the mood of the American command in Saigon see David Halberstam, "Return to Vietnam."

[5] Rostow, *Diffusion of Power*, pp. 452, 457. See also United States, Military Assistance Command, Vietnam, *1967 Wrap-Up: A Year of Progress*; Orr Kelly, "War Just About Over—In a Military Sense"; Howard Handleman, "The Coin Has Flipped Over to Our Side." For opposite or less optimistic views, see Bernard B. Fall, *Last Reflections*

and tenuous these gains might be, however, was disclosed in General Westmoreland's year-end assessment of the military situation. This assessment, which was furnished on January 26, 1968, and was little noticed in the excitement that followed, gave an optimistic view of the military situation, but was much less sanguine about political progress. "The GVN is not yet a ready and effective partner with its own people," General Westmoreland reported. "The Viet Cong infrastructure remains basically intact; and corruption is both corrosive and extensive."[6]

But, as had been true in the past, American progress depended almost totally on what Hanoi would do, what resources North Vietnam would devote to the war, and what strategy it would pursue. And Hanoi had long since begun to implement a new strategy that would, within a month after the new year began, dash American optimism and put the Johnson administration and the American public through a profound political catharsis. The massive Tet attack on the cities and towns of South Vietnam would engender the most soul-searching debate within the administration of the entire war.

By July of 1967 the North Vietnamese had decided upon a major revision in strategy from that of protracted war to what came to be known as "general offensive, general uprising." From Hanoi's standpoint, the war in the South was not going well. Their forces had not won a significant battle in two years. United States firepower had destroyed much of their reserves of men and supplies. Hanoi needed a decisive

---

on a War, pp. 163–171; Richard Critchfield, The Long Charade: Political Subversion in the Vietnam War; Robert Shaplen, Time Out of Hand: Revolution and Reaction in Southeast Asia, pp. 384–391; William R. Corson, The Betrayal, pp. 71–82; William A. Nighswonger, Rural Pacification in Vietnam; Dennis Bloodworth, An Eye for the Dragon: Southeast Asia Observed 1954–1970, p. 227; William Tuohy, "Newsmen's View of Viet War Fails to Match U.S. Optimism"; Ward Just, "The Heart-Mind Gap in the Vietnam War."

[6] COMUSMACV 61742, 260755Z January 1968, Subject: Annual Assessment CY 1967, quoted in U.S.–Vietnam Relations, IVC(6)(c), p. 2. See also Neil Sheehan, " '68 Gain Was Seen by Westmoreland."

victory in order to create the military, political, and psycho- *(Goals of Tet)* logical conditions that would destroy both the political foundations of the Saigon regime and political support for the war in the United States. Large-scale attacks across South Vietnam would precipitate a general uprising, destroying the Saigon government and making it psychologically and politically impossible for the United States to pursue the war.[7]

Operationally, Hanoi's plan was to distract and overextend United States forces through massive attacks on the frontiers, far from the populated areas. Having thus diverted attention by these large, costly, but deceptive battles, the major attacks would be directed against the government administrative structure in the towns and cities. With the collapse of the government and the expected general uprising of the population, the United States would be faced with a *fait accompli* —a crumbling government and army in South Vietnam. The United States would have no recourse but to enter into negotiations for peace leading to a coalition government and the withdrawal of American forces.[8]

As early as October, the Communist plan was put into effect with a series of bloody battles in remote areas along the

[7] Lieutenant Colonel Pham Van Son, *The Viet Cong Tet Offensive 1968*, pp. 44–46. Also Robert J. O'Neill, *The Strategy of General Giap Since 1964*, pp. 15–16; Oberdorfer, *Tet*, pp. 42–54; Shaplen, *Time Out of Hand*, pp. 391–392; Rostow, *Diffusion of Power*, p. 460; Lieutenant Colonel Dave R. Palmer, "The Summons of the Trumpet: A Soldier's View of Vietnam," unpublished manuscript, pp. 241–244; Denis Warner, "Gains and Losses in Saigon," p. 22; Joseph Alsop, "Captured Documents Indicate a Major Red Strategy Shift"; Charles Mohr, "War-Ending Victory Seen as Aim of Enemy Drive"; Sir Robert Thompson, "Viet Reds' Drive Was a Giap Masterstroke"; Douglas Pike, "The Tet Offensive: A Setback for Giap, But Just How Big?" pp. 57–61; Douglas Pike, *War, Peace, and the Viet Cong*, pp. 124–126; General Vo Nguyen Giap, *Big Victory, Great Task*.

[8] Hanson W. Baldwin, "Public Opinion in U.S. and South Vietnam is Viewed as Main Target of New Offensive by Vietcong"; Stanley Karnow, "What Are the Vietcong Trying to Prove?"; Stanley Karnow, "VC Aim Seen to Boost Its Role in Settlement"; Richard Wilson, "Hanoi Sure It Can Force a Political Solution"; Pike, *War, Peace, and the Viet Cong*, p. 127.

borders of South Vietnam. Determined North Vietnamese forces attacked the Marine base at Con Thien near the DMZ. Then Communist forces struck Loc Ninh and Song Be, farther south along the Cambodian border. Beginning November 3 and continuing for twenty-two days, the North Vietnamese fiercely attacked Dak To in the Central Highlands. December saw the fighting spread to the Delta.[9]

In January the enemy moved in strength against the Marine outpost at Khe Sanh near the DMZ. Two North Vietnamese Divisions were soon identified in the vicinity, the 325th Division and the 304th Division, an elite unit which had participated in the triumph at Dien Bien Phu.[10] Faced with this massive enemy buildup, General Westmoreland decided to hold Khe Sanh rather than withdraw. He felt that this base guarded the approaches to Quang Tri city and the two northern provinces of Quang Tri and Thua Thien. In addition, the apparent determination of the enemy to take the base argued for holding it in order to tie down large NVA forces that otherwise could move against the populated areas.[11] This border fight fit General Westmoreland's predilection for fighting on the frontiers and away from the populated areas, in any case. He believed that in these areas fires were more effective because they were not restricted by political constraints or by the presence of civilians. He defended this strategy in a cable to the chairman of the Joint Chiefs of Staff: "When we engage the enemy near the borders we often preempt his plans and force him to fight before he is fully organized and before he can do his damage. Although

[9] Westmoreland, *Report on the War in Vietnam*, pp. 138–139, 155–156. See also Oberdorfer, *Tet*, pp. 107–108; Palmer, "Soldier's View of Vietnam," pp. 232–233. The Westmoreland account is taken largely from: United States, Military Assistance Command, Vietnam, *Command History, 1968*. When these accounts coincide, the *Command History, 1968* will be cited.

[10] Captain Moyers S. Shore, *The Battle for Khe Sanh*, p. 29; Westmoreland, *Report on the War in Vietnam*, p. 182.

[11] Westmoreland, *Report on the War in Vietnam*, p. 163; Shore, *The Battle for Khe Sanh*, p. vi; Westmoreland, *A Soldier Reports*, pp. 335–337.

such fighting gets high visibility in the press, it has low visibility to the people of South Vietnam since it is not being fought in their front yard."[12]

The similarities between Khe Sanh and Dien Bien Phu, in terms of both terrain and enemy action, quickly attracted the attention of the American press and public. The president followed the action closely and had a terrain model of the battle area constructed in the White House Situation Room.[13] Having decided to defend Khe Sanh, General Westmoreland simply could not permit the position to be taken. "The question was," Westmoreland stated, "whether we could afford the troops to reinforce, keep them supplied by air, and defeat an enemy far superior in numbers as we waited for the weather to clear, built forward bases, and made other preparations for an overland relief expedition. I believed we could do all of those things."[14] The Korean Marine brigade was shifted from the South to the Danang area to relieve United States Marines so that they could shift northward if necessary. Operation NIAGARA, a reconnaissance and firepower program in support of the outpost, was begun, with Westmoreland personally directing B-52 strikes in support of the beleaguered outpost.[15]

As the Viet Cong began extensive infiltration of South Vietnam's cities prior to attacking them, indications of the Viet Cong plan began to reach United States officials. An intelligence summary prepared in Saigon on December 8 accurately predicted a "general counteroffensive and general uprising" designed to lure allied units to the border areas, al-

[12] MACV 11956, 101011Z December 1967; Westmoreland, *A Soldier Reports*, p. 146.

[13] Personal interview with Walt W. Rostow, December 4, 1972.

[14] Westmoreland, *Report on the War in Vietnam*, p. 163. For an analysis of the differences between Khe Sanh and Dien Bien Phu, and for press comment, see notes 37 and 38, chapter 4.

[15] Personal interview with General William C. Westmoreland, September 16, 1973. Westmoreland habitually directed all B-52 strikes in Vietnam, but the Khe Sanh battle was the first time these strikes were closely integrated with tactical air operations. Personal interview with Major General Robert N. Ginsburgh, August 25, 1975.

low the Communists to control the country's armed forces and local administration, and force the Americans "to withdraw from South Vietnam in a short period of time."[16] Indeed, the attack order for the Communist offensive had been captured by American forces on November 19, 1967. The order stressed that strong military attacks would be used "in coordination with the uprisings of the local population to take over towns and cities." In releasing this document to the press on January 5, however, the United States press release cautioned that the document could not be taken as conclusive evidence that such an order had been given and might represent merely an internal propaganda document "designed to inspire the fighting troops."[17] Washington intelligence analysts were inclined to think the coming campaign was to be merely a continuation of past Communist strategy.[18]

By the 20th of December, General Westmoreland reported to Washington that he believed "the enemy has already made a crucial decision regarding the conduct of the war. . . . His decision, therefore, was to undertake an intensified country-wide effort, perhaps a maximum effort, over a relatively short period."[19] Even so, some in higher headquarters were not convinced. On December 26, Admiral Sharp, Commander in Chief, Pacific, informed Washington that "most of the evidence we hold points toward the approach of an important but not final period in the enemy situation. He may be considering further changes concerning the future conduct of the war. The likelihood of a final effort in the winter-spring offensive sometime after Tet cannot be discounted but remains remote."[20]

Westmoreland remained convinced, however, that the

[16] Rostow, *Diffusion of Power*, pp. 462–463.
[17] U.S., Mission in Vietnam, *Captured Document Indicates Final Phase of Revolution at Hand.*
[18] Rostow, *Diffusion of Power*, p. 463.
[19] MAC 12397, General Westmoreland to General Wheeler, 200609Z December 1967.
[20] Admiral Sharp to General Wheeler, 261858Z December 1967.

enemy would make his major effort in the two northern provinces of I Corps. On January 15 he reported to Washington that "the odds are 60-40 that the enemy will launch his planned campaign prior to Tet." He indicated that he was moving two brigades of the 1st Cavalry Division and two battalions of ARVN Airborne Troops to I Corps, and that he was "accepting a calculated risk in the III Corps area."[21] On the 21st he reiterated his belief that "the enemy plans a coordinated offensive designed to seize and hold key objectives in the northern two provinces."[22] On the 22nd, he reported evidence that the enemy "will attempt a multi-battalion attack on Hue city, and he may sally out of the Hai Laing jungle base area to attack Quang Tri city. . . . I believe the enemy will attempt a countrywide show of strength just prior to Tet." He later indicated that "as expected, January 25 is shaping up as D-Day for widespread pre-Tet offensive action on the part of the VC/NVA forces."[23]

Although an attack was felt to be imminent, it was initially inconceivable to the American command and to the South Vietnamese that military action would come during the Tet holidays. Tet is the Vietnamese holiday celebrating the arrival of the Chinese lunar New Year. But it is much more than that. It has been described as "a combination All Souls' Day, a family celebration, a spring festival, a national holiday and an overall manifestation of a way of life." In North Vietnam as well as in South Vietnam, it is the nation's most important and most sacred holiday, universally cherished by every religious group and social class.[24] The unique and peaceful

[21] MAC 00686, General Westmoreland to Admiral Sharp and General Wheeler, 151214Z January 1968.

[22] MAC 00982, General Westmoreland to Admiral Sharp, January 21, 1968.

[23] MAC 01049, General Westmoreland to Admiral Sharp, January 21, 1968; MAC 01108, General Westmoreland to Admiral Sharp and General Wheeler, 231328Z January 1968; MAC 01218, 251421Z January 1968, General Westmoreland to Admiral Sharp.

[24] U.S., Military Assistance Command, Vietnam, *Command Information Topic 5–65, Vietnamese Tet*; Ann Caddell Crawford, *Customs and Culture of Vietnam*, pp. 189–190.

nature of the Tet holiday had been stressed throughout the course of the Vietnam war. Beginning in 1963, the Communists had proclaimed annual battlefield cease-fires for Christmas, New Year, Buddha's birthday, and Tet. The Saigon government and the United States followed suit beginning with Christmas 1965.[25] These recurrent holiday truces quickly became expected in Vietnam although the United States command complained of massive Communist violations and supply movements during the truce periods.[26] Very few Americans were aware that the greatest feat of arms in Vietnam's history was considered to be the epic surprise attack by Nguyen Hue (Quang Trung) on the Chinese garrison in Hanoi during Tet of 1789.[27]

By early January, General Westmoreland felt that, in view of the obvious enemy buildup, the Tet cease-fire should be cancelled. However, the Vietnamese demurred. The army, as well as the rest of the nation, looked forward to the traditional respite. It was agreed, however, that the cease-fire would be limited to a thirty-six-hour period [1800, January 29 to 0600, January 31] rather than the forty-eight hours previously scheduled.[28] By January 24 both Ambassador Bunker and General Westmoreland, in a joint message to the president, indicated that it was undesirable to have any truce in Quang Tri, the DMZ, and at least part of North Vietnam.[29] The president agreed that the cease-fire would not

[25] Westmoreland, *Report on the War in Vietnam*, p. 111.

[26] *Command History, 1968*, pp. 375–376.

[27] Duncanson, *Government and Revolution in Vietnam*, p. 53; Nguyen Van Thai and Nguyen Van Mung, *A Short History of Vietnam*, pp. 210–211; Joseph Buttinger, *The Smaller Dragon: A Political History of Vietnam*, p. 265; Helen B. Lamb, *Vietnam's Will to Live: Resistance to Foreign Aggression from Early Times Through the Nineteenth Century*, p. 58.

[28] MAC 00338, General Westmoreland to Admiral Sharp, 090331Z January 1968; MAC 00764, General Westmoreland to Admiral Sharp, 080840Z January 1968; CINCPAC 200323Z January 1968; MAC 00943, 200843Z January 1968; CINCPAC 100249Z January 1968, Subject: *Tet Standdown; Command History, 1968*, p. 376.

[29] Saigon 16851, Joint Embassy/MACV Message, 241222Z January 1968, Subject: *Tet Ceasefire*.

apply in the I Corps area, the DMZ, or North Vietnam south of Vinh.[30] President Thieu concurred, but indicated he would withhold public announcement of these exceptions until six hours before the cease-fire began.[31] But the Vietnamese announcement never came. Saigon was in a festive mood on the eve of Tet. For the city dwellers, the war seemed remote. At least half the ARVN had departed for their homes to celebrate Tet.[32] President Thieu was celebrating at his wife's hometown of My Tho in the Mekong delta.[33]

According to the lunar calendar, the Year of the Monkey was to begin on Tuesday, January 30. In a virtually unnoticed action, however, the North Vietnamese government announced that the celebration would begin one day earlier. Thus, the families of North Vietnam were able to celebrate the important first day of Tet together in peace, prior to the anticipated retaliatory American air raids.[34]

[30] State 104215, Secretary of State to American Embassy, Saigon, 250109Z January 1968; JCS 8282, JCS to CINCPAC, CINCSAC, 261714Z January 1968, Subject: *Tet Ceasefire.*

[31] JCS 8282, 261714Z January 1968.

[32] Pham Van Son, *The Viet Cong Tet Offensive*, pp. 25–26; Westmoreland, *Report on the War in Vietnam*, p. 159; *Command History, 1968*, p. 881.

[33] Oberdorfer, *Tet*, p. 133.

[34] Ibid., pp. 73–74.

FOUR

☆☆☆

The Tet Offensive and United States Reaction

IN THE early morning hours of January 31, 1968, the enemy launched a series of simultaneous and coordinated attacks against the major population centers in III and IV Corps Tactical Zones (CTZ). Attacks had been launched against the major cities of I and II CTZ the previous night.[1] During the period January 30-31, 39 of South Vietnam's 44 provincial capitals, 5 of its 6 autonomous cities, and at least 71 of 245 district towns were attacked by fire and ground action.[2] The offensive was aimed primarily at civilian centers of authority and military command installations. At 9:45 A.M. on Tuesday, January 30, the United States and Saigon governments cancelled the Tet truce, which by then had become meaningless.[3]

In Saigon the enemy attack began with a sapper assault on the American Embassy, rapidly followed by assaults on Tan San Nhut Air Base, the Presidential Palace, the RVNAF Joint General Staff (JGS) headquarters compound, and other government installations. Large enemy forces infiltrated into Hue and captured the Imperial Citadel and most of the

---

[1] MAC 01438, General Westmoreland to Admiral Sharp, 301255Z January 1968; *Command History, 1968*, pp. 376, 386, 390, 397, 884, 890, 894–895, 902.

[2] CIA Intelligence Memorandum, "Communist Units Participating in Attacks During the Tet Offensive, 30 January through 13 February 1968," dated February 21, 1968, pp. 3–4. Initially, there was some confusion as to the actual number of province and district towns attacked. The *Command History, 1968*, p. 129, lists 27 provincial capitals and 58 district towns. President Johnson, in *The Vantage Point*, p. 382, lists 36 provincial capitals "and about one-fourth of the 242 [*sic*] district capitals."

[3] COMUSMACV Msg 300325Z January 1968.

city. Hue was in enemy hands, despite heavy reinforcement by the United States and Vietnamese forces, until February 25.[4] The fighting continued throughout the country and gradually tapered off by February 13.

A textbook prepared and used at the United States Military Academy in the study of the Vietnam war states: "The first thing to understand about Giap's Tet offensive is that it was an allied intelligence failure ranking with Pearl Harbor in 1941 or the Ardennes offensive in 1944. The North Vietnamese gained complete surprise."[5] Although this may be an exaggeration, there is no doubt that the American command had not anticipated the true nature of the Viet Cong attacks. General Westmoreland acknowledged: "The extent of this offensive was not known to us, although we did feel it was going to be widespread. The timing was not known. I frankly did not think they would assume the psychological disadvantage of hitting at Tet itself, so I thought it would be before or after Tet. I did not anticipate that they would strike in the cities and make them their targets."[6]

President Johnson, in the midst of the Tet period, directed

[4] *Command History, 1968*, pp. 129–131. For other details of the fighting, see pp. 376–400, 883–904; the South Vietnamese version is contained in Son, *Viet Cong Tet Offensive*, pp. 71–437. For details of the battle of Hue, see Oberdorfer, *Tet*, pp. 198–235; also Douglas Pike, *The Viet-Cong Strategy of Terror*, pp. 41–64; Stephen T. Hosmer, *Viet Cong Repression and Its Implications for the Future*, pp. 45–51; Lieutenant General Willard Pearson, *Vietnam Studies: The War in the Northern Provinces, 1966–1968*, pp. 29–72. For details of the fighting in Saigon, Hue, and Dalat, see Palmer, "A Soldier's View of Vietnam," pp. 260–273; also Denis Warner, "The Defense of Saigon." Fighting in the Delta is covered in Harvey Meyerson, *Vinh Long*, pp. 128–149; Major General William B. Fulton, *Vietnam Studies: Riverine Operations 1966–1969*, pp. 148–155. For the North Vietnamese version, see *South Vietnam: A Month of Unprecedented Offensive and Uprising* and *Scenes of the General Offensive and Uprising*.

[5] Lieutenant Colonel Dave R. Palmer, *Readings in Current Military History*, p. 103. See also Warner, "Gains and Losses in Saigon," pp. 23–24.

[6] Personal interview with General William C. Westmoreland, October 23, 1972. See also Westmoreland, *Report on the War in Vietnam*, p. 157.

his Foreign Intelligence Advisory Board to investigate the charge that the North Vietnamese offensive had caught the American command by surprise. A working group of intelligence analysts (with representatives from the Central Intelligence Agency, Defense Intelligence Agency, State Department, National Security Agency, and Joint Staff) was established to assist the Foreign Intelligence Advisory Board in its investigation. This group spent March 16 to 23, 1968, in Saigon. They interviewed intelligence analysts and examined all intelligence reports that had been available to the American command. The conclusions of this working group were as follows:

> . . . the intensity, coordination, and timing of the enemy attack were not fully anticipated. Ambassador Bunker and General Westmoreland attest to this. The most important factor was timing. Few U.S. or G.V.N. officials believed the enemy would attack during Tet, nor did the Vietnamese public.
>
> A second major unexpected element was the number of simultaneous attacks mounted. U.S. intelligence had given the enemy a capability of attacking virtually all the points which he did in fact attack and of mounting coordinated attacks in a number of areas. He was not, however, granted a specific capability for coordinated attacks in all areas at once. More important, the nature of the targets was not anticipated.
>
> Underlying these specific problems was a more basic one: most commanders and intelligence officers at all levels did not visualize the enemy as capable of accomplishing his stated goals as they appeared in propaganda and in captured documents. Prevailing estimates of attrition, infiltration, and local recruitment, reports of low morale, and a long series of defeats had degraded our image of the enemy.[7]

[7] *Intelligence Warning of the Tet Offensive in South Vietnam, April 11, 1968,* pp. 3–5, declassified December 3, 1975, for the House

Charges have since been made that U.S. intelligence officials systematically and deliberately had downgraded estimates of the strength of Viet Cong forces because they feared public reaction if increases in enemy troop strength were published. This resulted, it has been further alleged, in underestimating enemy military capabilities. These charges have been denied, but in any case, as James R. Schlesinger, former director of the Central Intelligence Agency, has stated, "The intelligence at that time was deficient."[8]

The Communist leaders had made a radical departure from their strategy of prolonged war. They sought decisive objectives, which were considered sufficiently important to justify paying a very high price. Their purposes in thus changing their strategy were twofold. Their first goal was to destroy GVN military and political control, generate a spontaneous

---

Select Committee on Intelligence. See also Taylor, *Swords and Plowshares*, p. 383. For indications that the attack was not anticipated in IV Corps see Meyerson, *Vinh Long*, pp. 103–104 and Donald Kirk, "U.S. Colonel in Delta Denies Getting a Warning on Raids." The attack was anticipated in III Corps, and troops were disposed around Saigon to deal with it. Personal interview with General Fred C. Weyand, December 27, 1973. Also see *Command History, 1968*, pp. 894–895; Westmoreland, *Report on the War in Vietnam*, p. 157; Rostow, *Diffusion of Power*, p. 464.

[8] For General Abram's comments on possible adverse press reaction to an announcement of increased enemy strength, see MAC 7840, 200251Z August 1967. See also Westmoreland, *A Soldier Reports*, p. 416; Lou Cannon, "'67 Viet Data Said Concealed"; Samuel A. Adams, "Vietnam Cover-Up: Playing War With Numbers"; "Letters: The Cult of Misintelligence"; statement of Samuel A. Adams before the House Select Committee on Intelligence; George Lardner, Jr., "False Data Blamed in '68 Tet Surprise"; John M. Crewdson, "False Troop Data in Vietnam Cited"; David S. Broder, "Ford Urges Balanced Tet View"; Norman Kempster, "Former CIA Aide Disputes Charges on Tet Offensive"; Jack Anderson and Les Whitten, "Numbers Game on Tet Offensive"; Columbia Broadcasting System Television Network, *Face the Nation, September 21, 1975; Guest—James R. Schlesinger*, p. 13; statement of Lieutenant General Daniel O. Graham, USA, director, Defense Intelligence Agency, before the House Select Committee on Intelligence; statement of William E. Colby, director, Central Intelligence Agency, before the House Select Committee on Intelligence; Don Oberdorfer, "Intelligence in Tet Fight Held Success."

uprising or create the impression of spontaneous uprisings against the GVN, and cause the disaffection of the ARVN.[9] To these ends, the initial assaults were conducted by Viet Cong forces, while NVA forces were retained for follow-up attacks and exploitation. In these objectives, however, the enemy failed. Throughout the country there was no instance in which the Viet Cong were welcomed by the population, and there were no defections from political or military ranks. Indeed, the ARVN fought valiantly in almost every case, although it was caught in a "pre-Tet" posture, with half its personnel on leave and with security relaxed.[10]

The second purpose of the Communist attack was psychological. The attacks apparently were designed "to discourage the United States, to shake the faith of the people of South Vietnam in the ability of the United States and their own Government to protect them, and to impress all concerned with the strength and popular support of the Viet Cong." This would leave Hanoi in a position of strength from which it could negotiate a cease-fire and the eventual withdrawal of American forces. Ambassador Bunker indicated that, based on the above analysis, he considered the "primary purpose of the operation to be psychological, rather than military."[11] In this objective, the Communists were more successful.

[9] MAC 01592, General Westmoreland to General Wheeler, 031512Z February 1968. See also CIA Intelligence Memorandum, February 21, 1968, pp. 3–4; *Command History, 1968*, pp. 70–72.

[10] Saigon 17920, American Embassy, Saigon to Secretary of State, 041100Z February 1968, Subject: *Thirty-Seventh Weekly Message*. For a North Vietnamese appraisal, see Oriana Fallaci, "North Vietnam Commander Admits 500,000 Men Lost, Vows to Win." See also *Command History, 1968*, p. 881; Pike, *War, Peace, and the Viet Cong*, p. 127.

[11] Saigon 17908, American Embassy, Saigon to Secretary of State, 040905Z February 1968, Subject: *Motives Behind Current VC/NVA Offensive*. In this message, Ambassador Bunker quotes from Liberation Radio (FBIS B020659) and from the dispatches of Joseph Cabanes, Agence France-Presse correspondent in Hanoi. See also Saigon 21321, Ambassador Bunker to the President, March 6, 1968, Subject: *Forty-Second Weekly Message*; Pike, *War, Peace, and the Viet Cong*, pp. 129–130; O'Neill, *The Strategy of General Giap*, p. 17.

General Westmoreland reported the unfavorable psychological effects on the Vietnamese people to include "added fear and respect of Communist capabilities, more fence-straddling by the uncommitted, and greater war weariness. . . . From a realistic point of view, we must accept the fact that the enemy has dealt the GVN a severe blow. He has brought the war to the cities and the towns and has inflicted damage and casualties on the population." On the other hand, Westmoreland pointed out some of the favorable psychological factors. "There is anger at the Communist violence and atrocities," he reported.[12]

Thus, although it soon became apparent to the American command in Saigon that the enemy had suffered a severe military defeat and had paid a high price for the change in strategy, losing large numbers of high-quality troops, the question remained whether he had secured in spite of his losses a decisive psychological victory, both in Saigon and in the United States. The public, the media, and the government in the United States were shocked by the unexpected attacks. President Johnson had received the intelligence reports of an anticipated Viet Cong winter attack from his field commanders and White House staff, and he took these reports seriously. As Major General Robert N. Ginsburgh, Walt Rostow's military assistant, recalled: "In late November, Rostow became impatient with the large number of captured documents which he felt were not being properly exploited. He arranged to have translations sent directly to the White House as well as the Defense Intelligence Agency. Beginning in early December, one week ahead of the intelligence community, Rostow became convinced of a coming attack and

---

[12] MAC 01614, 040959Z February 1968, General Westmoreland to General Wheeler; see also Tom Buckley, "Offensive is Said to Pinpoint Enemy's Strengths"; Murray Marder, "U.S. Experts Concede Gain by VC"; Newbold Noyes, "Offensive Poses Challenge to the People of America and South Vietnam"; Stanley Karnow, "Tremendous Blow Struck at Allies, Vietcong Claims"; "After the Tet Offensive"; "Hanoi Attacks and Scores a Major Psychological Blow"; Everett G. Martin, "The Devastating Effect on the People."

talked to the president of a coming winter-spring offensive. Whereas the Washington community was shocked by Tet, the president and Rostow were not. In retrospect they underestimated the reaction of the public. But they knew that what the enemy was saying would indeed happen."[13]

In Canberra, Australia, to attend memorial services for Prime Minister Harold Holt, President Johnson, on December 21, told the Australian cabinet, and repeated to the Pope on December 23, that he foresaw "kamikaze" tactics by the North Vietnamese in the weeks ahead. But little effort was made to alert the American public to the probability of such attacks, and the public consequently was ill-prepared for the trauma of Tet. In what he later admitted to be a mistake, Johnson had excised a long section dealing with Vietnam from his State of the Union message. In that speech, the president merely emphasized again the progress that had been made in Vietnam during the past year and indicated the attempts currently being pursued to establish peace talks with North Vietnam.[14]

Thus, the scope, intensity, and strength of the Viet Cong attacks caused extreme surprise and shock throughout the United States. Extensive television coverage of the offensive brought the blood, agony, and destruction of the battle directly into American homes and was a key factor in forming the popular conception of what had happened on the battlefield during the Communist offensive. The attack on the American embassy and the public killing of a Viet Cong terrorist by General Loan, chief of South Vietnam's National Police, were particularly disturbing.[15] Daily press reports filed from all

[13] Personal interview with Major General Robert N. Ginsburgh, August 25, 1975. See also Harry Kelly, "Reveal 8-Day Lag in Army's Viet Spy File."

[14] *Public Papers of Lyndon Johnson, 1968–69*, I, p. 25; Johnson, *The Vantage Point*, pp. 378–381; Albert H. Cantril, *The American People, Viet-Nam and the Presidency*, p. 5.

[15] Oberdorfer, *Tet*, pp. 159–161, 163–171; Taylor, *Swords and Plowshares*, pp. 384–385.

parts of Vietnam also contributed to the sense of disaster, as they concentrated on reporting the destruction caused by the initial Communist attacks throughout Vietnam. One single quotation in a press report had a tremendous impact. "It became necessary to destroy the town to save it," an American major was reported to have said to newsmen in explaining how it had been necessary to rout the Viet Cong who had occupied the delta village of Ben Tre.[16] This widely repeated sentence seemed to sum up the irony and the contradictions in the use of American power in Vietnam and caused many to question the purpose of our being there. If we had to destroy our friends in order to save them, was the effort really worthwhile, either for us or for our friends?

The official cables from Saigon quickly showed the true nature of the military reaction to the enemy's attacks. The Viet Cong was suffering severe casualties. The South Vietnamese army was reacting well, and the civil populace was not rising up to greet and support the Viet Cong in the cities. But this situation was not being reflected in news reports or on television in the United States. Those reports continued to emphasize the shock, surprise, extent, and power of the unexpected enemy offensive. Even some government officials, in spite of having access to these Saigon reports, reflected the mood of the country. Harry McPherson, a presidential speech writer and special counsel, recalled his reaction:

> I felt we were being put to it as hard as we ever had, and I was extremely disturbed. I would go in two or three mornings a week and study the cable book and talk to Rostow and ask him what had happened the day before, and would get from him what almost seemed hallucinatory from the point of view of what I had seen on network television the night before. . . . Well, I must say that I mistrusted what he said, although I don't say with any

16 "U.S. Bombed Viet Town to 'Save' It"; Bernard Weinraub, "Survivors Hunt Dead of Bentre, Turned to Rubble in Allied Raids"; Oberdorfer, *Tet*, pp. 184–185.

confidence that I was right to mistrust him, because, like millions of other people who had been looking at television the night before, I had the feeling that the country had just about had it, that they would simply not take any more. . . . I suppose, from a social scientist point of view, it is particularly interesting that people like me—people who had some responsibility for expressing the presidential point of view—could be so affected by the media as everyone else was, while downstairs, within fifty yards of my desk, was that enormous panoply of intelligence-gathering devices—tickers, radios, messages coming in from the field. I assume the reason this is so, the reason I put aside my own interior access to confidential information and was more persuaded by what I saw on the tube and in the newspapers, was that like everyone else who had been deeply involved in explaining the policies of the war and trying to understand them and render some judgment, I was fed up with the "light at the end of the tunnel" stuff. I was fed up with the optimism that seemed to flow without stopping from Saigon.[17]

William Bundy was also pessimistic:

I quickly came to the view that the attacks had been damaging to the North, but they had also been shattering to the South, especially in the area of pacification. The net balance, therefore, depended on whether the country could pull itself together. My view of the situation was formed by reports from people in the field out in Vietnam. I remember in particular one view that impressed me. Leroy Wehrle, who was with the AID office in Washington, was a staunch fellow with wide experience in Vietnam. He wrote a memo on February 5 which said that the South Vietnamese were through, that they had too many

[17] Personal interview with Harry C. McPherson, Jr., December 21, 1972. See also Tom Wicker, "Vietcong's Attacks Shock Washington"; Hugh Sidey, "Shaken Assumptions About the War"; Murray Marder and Chalmers M. Roberts, "Reds' Offensive Leaves U.S. With Maze of Uncertainties."

defects in their society to survive this blow. It was a poignant memo which said in effect, "They've had it." That memo reflected my view for a period.[18]

The president's first reaction was to counter this adverse press and television coverage and reassure the American public. On the 31st of January, at the height of the Tet fighting, General Westmoreland received the following instructions from the chairman of the Joint Chiefs of Staff: "The President desires that you make a brief personal comment to the press at least once each day during the current period of mounting VC/NVA activity. The purpose of such statements should be to convey to the American public your confidence in our capability to blunt these enemy moves, and to reassure the public here that you have the situation under control."[19]

In case there was any doubt, these instructions were repeated to both General Westmoreland and Ambassador Bunker later that same day by George Christian, press secretary to the president: "We are facing, in these next few days, a critical phase in the American public's understanding and confidence toward our effort in Vietnam. . . . To be specific, nothing can more dramatically counter scenes of VC destructiveness than the confident professionalism of the Commanding General. Similarly, the dire prognostications of the commentators can best be put into perspective by the shared experience and wisdom of our Ambassador. . . . Appearances by you, in the immediate situation, will make a greater impact here at home than much of what we can say."[20]

Subsequently, Rostow repeated to Ambassador Bunker and General Westmoreland the president's "hopes" that Westmoreland would give "an authoritative military appreciation" at least once a day and that Bunker would "make

[18] Personal interview with William Bundy, October 11, 1972.
[19] JCS 8691, 311401Z January 1968, Chairman, JCS to COMUSMACV.
[20] CAP 80383, 312152 January 1968, George Christian to Ambassador Bunker and General Westmoreland.

authoritative comments on the non-military aspects of events at appropriate times." Without this authoritative guidance, Rostow indicated, "the correspondents take over rather wildly, without poise and perspective and authority that only you two command."[21]

Ambassador Bunker, in view of the scarcity of solid information, limited himself to a background briefing in which he could not be quoted directly. His briefing received little attention. General Westmoreland dutifully met with the press on February 1. His report was hardly reassuring, however, as he emphasized the next phase in the enemy campaign, which was yet to come and which would be the largest phase, involving attacks in the Quang Tri/Thua Thien area.[22]

Westmoreland and Bunker agreed that it would be both unnecessary and unwise for them to hold a press conference daily, as this might give the press the impression that they were panicking. It was decided that a different senior officer would brief each day on some particular aspect of the situation.

President Johnson held his first press conference following the Tet attack on February 2. He indicated that "the stated purposes of the general uprising have failed."[23] He enlisted his cabinet to put forward the administration view and to calm and reassure the American people. In subsequent weeks, Secretary of State Rusk and Secretary of Defense McNamara appeared on a special hour-long edition of NBC's *Meet the Press*; Undersecretary of State Nicholas Katzenbach appeared on CBS's *Face the Nation*; and Presidential Assistant Walt W. Rostow was on ABC's *Issues and Answers*.[24] But despite

[21] Rostow to Ambassador Bunker and General Westmoreland, February 3, 1968.

[22] Press Conference, General William C. Westmoreland, Joint United States Public Affairs Office (JUSPAO), Saigon, February 1, 1968.

[23] *Public Papers of Lyndon Johnson, 1968–69*, I, pp. 155–163.

[24] U.S., Congress, Senate, Committee on Foreign Relations, *Background Information Relating to Southeast Asia and Vietnam*, p. 59. See also Lawrence Stern, "McNamara, Rusk: A Mood Contrast."

these efforts of the administration to emphasize the positive military side of the Tet offensive, to the American people and to the press it remained a disaster.

A feeling of frustration and gloom had settled over official Washington. The government had been shaken, not only by the Tet offensive, but by Communist initiatives in other parts of the world. In Korea, an assassination plot by North Korea against South Korea's President Park had been broken up at the last minute. Then the intelligence ship, the USS *Pueblo*, and its crew had been seized by North Korea. Intelligence reports indicated that a crisis might develop around Berlin. The administration could not be certain that these events did not represent a concerted Communist offensive designed to embarrass and defeat the United States not only in Vietnam but elsewhere in the world.[25]

Even the usually imperturbable Rusk began to show the pressure and strain. At a "backgrounder" press conference at the State Department on February 9, Rusk blew up at persistent questions concerning the failure of the United States intelligence in Vietnam. "There gets to be a point when the question is whose side are you on?" the secretary upbraided the startled newsmen. "I don't know why . . . people have to be probing for the things that one can bitch about."[26]

Against this backdrop, General Westmoreland was predicting a third round of Communist military action against the beleaguered forces at Khe Sanh. As early as January 31, while most of the major cities had been under attack, Westmoreland had reported that these attacks were "diversionary efforts while the enemy prepares for his major attack in northern I CTZ."[27] He emphasized in his press conference on

[25] Johnson, *The Vantage Point*, p. 385.

[26] Chalmers M. Roberts, *First Rough Draft: A Journalist's Journal of Our Times*, pp. 261–262; Oberdorfer, *Tet*, pp. 170, 366–367; Bernard Gwertzman, "War Again Strains U.S.-Press Ties"; Murray Marder, "Strain of Tension is Showing at Top"; Ted Lewis, "Mr. Anonymous Loses His Cool in Viet Briefing."

[27] MAC 01448, 310918Z January 1968, General Westmoreland to General Wheeler.

February 1 that the coming attack "will involve the commitment of the largest number of troops ever committed by the enemy to date" and indicated to Washington that it was likely that "the uncommitted NVA forces elsewhere in the country would conduct complementing offensive operations."[28]

Westmoreland felt that the ultimate enemy objective was the occupation of Vietnam's two northern provinces. Khe Sanh, he felt, was not particularly important in and of itself, but only as a gateway to Quang Tri and the lowlands. Westmoreland thought the enemy would attempt to bypass the strong point in order to attain his ultimate objectives farther to the east. "I put the minimum number of troops into Khe Sanh to hold the area, and the maximum number that I could supply by air if that became necessary. The soundness of this rationale is borne out by the success the enemy had in 1972. He moved into Khe Sanh without opposition and took over all of Quang Tri province. But at this time, I didn't think he would be foolish enough to expend resources on Khe Sanh. I thought he would bypass it."[29] Whether the enemy really planned to attack and occupy the two northern provinces of South Vietnam, as Westmoreland felt, or whether the massing of enemy forces near Khe Sanh was merely a diversion to draw American forces away from the cities has not been established with certainty. According to the MACV *Command History, 1968*, the enemy moved against Khe Sanh "in order to divert a major portion of our resources to a remote area while he attacked the major cities of RVN."[30] A full-scale enemy assault never occurred

[28] MAC 0152, 031512Z February 1968, General Westmoreland to General Wheeler.

[29] Personal interview with General William C. Westmoreland, September 16, 1973.

[30] *Command History, 1968*, p. 883; Shore, *The Battle for Khe Sanh*, p. 54; Hoopes, *The Limits of Intervention*, p. 144; also Lee Lescaze, "Khe Sanh: A U.S. Obsession?"; Orr Kelly, "Loc Ninh Fight Significant"; Joseph Kraft, "Khesanh Situation Shows Viet Foe Makes Strategy Work"; Tom Buckley, "Generals Ponder Foe's DacTo

at Khe Sanh, but again, it is not known conclusively whether this was by plan or whether the massive American air effort in support of Khe Sanh broke up the preparations for such an assault.[31]

Westmoreland may have felt that he need not "put any great emphasis on Khe Sanh *per se*," but the view was quite different in Washington. The parallels between Khe Sanh and Dien Bien Phu had been apparent to the White House since Khe Sanh had been invested in early January. The thought of an American Dien Bien Phu following on the heels of the Tet offensive was enough to shake the administration to its roots. As General Ginsburgh recalled: "The president was worried about Khe Sanh. Beginning in late December, Walt Rostow indicated to him that captured documents indicated that the North Vietnamese intended to reenact Dien Bien Phu. The president raised the question as to whether Khe Sanh should be held. He said he wanted to know what Westmoreland thought and what General Wheeler thought of his opinion. Westmoreland indicated he proposed to defend Khe Sanh, and the Joint Chiefs of Staff endorsed his view."[32]

At a meeting at the White House on January 29, General Wheeler, the chairman of the Joint Chiefs of Staff, presented to the president, at his request, a written statement indicating that the Joint Chiefs supported General Westmoreland's confidence that Khe Sanh could be held.[33] But the president's

---

Aims." In his article, Buckley quotes Lieutenant General William B. Rosson as follows, "They succeeded damn well in making us draw strength from the coast, if that's what they wanted to do." See also Giap, *Big Victor, Great Task*, pp. 60–71.

[31] Bernard C. Nalty, *Air Power and the Fight for Khe Sanh*, p. 105; Oberdorfer, *Tet*, pp. 110–111; Shore, *The Battle for Khe Sanh*, p. 71; O'Neill, *The Strategy of General Giap*, pp. 15–16.

[32] Personal interview with Major General Robert N. Ginsburgh, August 25, 1975.

[33] Personal interview with General Maxwell D. Taylor, December 28, 1972. See also JCS 01316, 041642Z February 1968, General Wheeler to General Westmoreland; "Joint Chiefs Endorse Defense of Khesanh."

concern was not alleviated by this unprecedented written statement from his military advisors. Indeed, it was reinforced by another military advisor, General Maxwell D. Taylor. Since his resignation as ambassador to South Vietnam, Taylor had served in the White House as a special consultant.[34] He had visited CIA headquarters on January 31 to examine closely the situation map of the enemy buildup around Khe Sanh and had become concerned about the exposed position of the American forces. He expressed his misgivings to the president and to Rostow:

> I was deeply concerned that the enemy would take advantage of bad weather. I was concerned about the difficulties of supplying our forces and bringing in reinforcements and supplies by helicopter under the artillery fire which one could anticipate from the heavy guns which the enemy had emplaced. It seemed to me unlikely that our 175mm. guns to the east could be very effective in supporting the garrison at Khe Sanh, and I was afraid that the organic artillery of the Marines could not be supplied continuously with the necessary ammunition to realize their full potential.[35]

Rostow and the president shared Taylor's unease, and this was transmitted to General Westmoreland on February 1. "Assuming that bad weather descends on the Khe Sanh/DMZ area and the enemy initiates his expected attack in strength against Khe Sanh," a cable from General Wheeler asked, "how will you be able to reinforce the garrison at Khe Sanh?"[36]

Westmoreland had directed his staff, on January 27, to make a thorough military analysis of the Dien Bien Phu battle and a comparison of it to the Khe Sanh situation so

[34] Taylor, *Swords and Plowshares*, pp. 359–360.
[35] Personal interview with General Maxwell D. Taylor, December 28, 1972.
[36] JCS 01147, 010351Z February 1968, General Wheeler to General Westmoreland, Subject: *Khe Sanh.*

that all possible counteractions could be taken.[37] Confident of his ability to defeat the enemy, he now tried to reassure the president. First, Westmoreland pointed out, he had air power, both tactical and B-52s, "by orders of magnitude over that at Dien Bien Phu." In addition, he had reinforcing artillery and vastly improved techniques of aerial delivery, by helicopter if necessary. "This capability of reinforcement by fire alone could have changed the course of battle at Dien Bien Phu," Westmoreland stated.[38]

But the president was not reassured. General Wheeler reported to Westmoreland the president's concern that the situation could become so serious "that he could be confronted with a decision to use tactical nuclear weapons to redress the balance—a decision which he does not want to be forced to make."[39] Westmoreland's reply in this case was not so reassuring. "The use of tactical nuclear weapons should

[37] *Command History, 1968*, pp. 785–786. The final report was promulgated on March 10, 1968 and was given wide distribution. A portion of the report appears in Rostow, *Diffusion of Power*, pp. 694–696. See also Westmoreland, *A Soldier Reports*, pp. 337–338 and Shore, *The Battle for Khe Sanh*, pp. 145–146. For authoritative accounts of the battle of Dien Bien Phu, see Jules Roy, *La Bataille de Dien Bien Phu*; Bernard B. Fall, *Hell in a Very Small Place: The Siege of Dien Bien Phu*; Paul Grauwin, *Doctor at Dienbienphu*. For the North Vietnamese version, see General Vo Nguyen Giap, *People's War, People's Army*.

[38] MAC 01586, 031225Z February 1968, General Westmoreland to General Wheeler, Subject: *Khe Sanh*. For press reaction to the Khe Sanh situation, see Roland Evans and Robert Novak, "Policy Makers and Generals Worry Over Massive Buildup at Khe Sanh"; Ward Just, "Khe Sanh: Holding the End of the Line"; Orr Kelly, "4 Divisions Threatening Marine Post"; Joseph C. Goulden, "Foe's Hit and Run Raids are Hard to Counter"; William McGaffin, "Khe Sanh Battle Near—No Dien Bien Phu in Sight: Pentagon"; Bernard Weinraub, "56 Marines Die in Battles in Tense Northern Sector"; Hedrick Smith, "U.S. Girding at Khesanh to Avoid a 'Dienbienphu': Washington Mood Tense"; Edward Mortimer, "Vets of Dienbienphu Appraise Khesanh"; Peter Braestrup, "Khesanh Waits and Probes Strategy"; Orr Kelly, "What Can U.S. Win at Khesanh?"; Neil Sheehan, "Khesanh: Why U.S. is Making a Stand"; Beverly Deepe, "Khe Sanh: Legacy of Westmoreland."

[39] JCS 01272, 030332Z February 1968, General Wheeler to General Westmoreland, Subject: *Khe Sanh*.

not be required in the present situation," he replied, since he had received permission to use a special artillery ammunition with greatly improved antipersonnel capabilities. However, should the situation in the DMZ change dramatically: "We should be prepared to introduce weapons of greater effectiveness against massed forces. Under such circumstances, I visualize that either tactical nuclear weapons or chemical agents would be active candidates for employment."[40]

"Because the enemy had uncommitted divisions in North Vietnam," General Westmoreland later recalled, "I was sensitive to the possibility of a massive attack across the DMZ. This would have been the worst possible case."[41]

Khe Sanh was the topic of conversation during a long White House luncheon on February 3. There was continuing concern that U.S. forces might be forced to withdraw from the outpost, thereby providing the enemy with a great psychological victory, both in the United States and in South Vietnam. Alternative courses of action that might relieve the pressure on Khe Sanh were discussed. One suggestion was a

[40] MAC 01586. There was much press speculation during this period about the possible use of nuclear weapons to keep Khe Sanh from being overrun. See Marquis W. Childs, "A-Bombs Reported Stockpiled in Vietnam"; George C. Wilson, "No A-Arms Requested for Vietnam, U.S. Says"; Hedrick Smith, "Wilson Cautions on A-Arms in War"; "Possible Viet A-Bomb Use Studied, McCarthy Suspects"; Charles W. Corddry, "A-Bomb Use Never Urged, Officers Say"; John W. Finney, "Anonymous Call Set Off Rumors of Nuclear Arms for Vietnam"; John W. Finney, "Wheeler Doubts Khesanh Will Need Atom Weapons." President Johnson tried to put an end to this speculation, first by having his press secretary announce on February 9 that the president had received no requests to use nuclear weapons in Vietnam, and then by stating, in his press conference on February 16, "No recommendation has been made to me. Beyond that, I think we ought to put an end to that discussion." *Public Papers of Lyndon Johnson, 1968–69*, I, p. 234. Despite the president's statement, the speculation did not immediately stop. See Joshua Lederberg, "A-Weapons Must be Limited if Used in South Vietnam"; Jerome S. Cahill, "Scott Opposes A-Weapon Use in Vietnam War"; Murray Marder, "A-Arms in Vietnam Seen Barred by Pact."

[41] Personal interview with General William C. Westmoreland, September 16, 1973. See also Westmoreland, *A Soldier Reports*, p. 338.

diversionary amphibious operation north of the DMZ to cut the North Vietnamese supply lines.[42] Other suggestions included an attack in the eastern portion of the DMZ area across the DMZ to link up relief forces with the garrison at Khe Sanh. But the meeting concluded there was no feasible way of making a diversion that would affect the battle in the near future. The mood of this meeting has been summed up by Taylor:

> There was an air of gloom over the discussion as the participants contemplated the gravity of the situation and the uncertainty of our ability to hold Khe Sanh without heavy losses. While no one suggested that we should not be there, it was quite apparent that most of us wished that we were not. However, no one suggested withdrawal, as it was apparent that the die was cast, and we would have to fight it out on this line. I tried rather feebly to make the point that Khe Sanh was only an outpost, and no one should expect an outpost to be a Verdun. However, the others present recognized that we ourselves had done a great deal to build up the importance of Khe Sanh in the minds of the public, and it was going to be very difficult to explain to our own people or anyone else that Khe Sanh was a minor outpost and the outcome of the battle unimportant.[43]

[42] The concept of an amphibious feint north of the DMZ was suggested by General Westmoreland on January 24, 1968. The principal objective would have been to force the enemy to take defensive countermeasures, thereby reducing the threat to Khe Sanh and northern I CTZ. Planning was approved by the Joint Chiefs of Staff under strict limitations. The plan, designated PACIFIC GROVE, remained on the shelf for possible future implementation. *Command History, 1968*, pp. 781–782.

[43] Personal interview with General Maxwell D. Taylor, December 28, 1972. For a similar view, see Denis Warner, "Khe Sanh and Dien Bien Phu," p. 18; also Denis Warner, "Report from Khe Sanh"; Max Frankel, "U.S. Girding at Khesanh to Avoid a 'Dienbienphu': Johnson Holds Reins."

FIVE

☆☆

Emergency Augmentation

THE initial military reaction in Washington to the Tet offensive was directed toward the air war. On February 3, the Joint Chiefs of Staff renewed an earlier proposal for reducing the restricted zones around Hanoi and Haiphong.[1] The JCS request, however, did not seem to the president to offer General Westmoreland any immediate assistance. Although Secretary Rush and Clark Clifford advocated added pressure on the North, the president decided at a meeting at the White House on February 13 not to take additional action against North Vietnam.[2]

Focusing on Khe Sanh and the possibility of an American defeat there, the president was determined that General Westmoreland would have all the forces he required to prevent such a defeat. On February 3, Wheeler reported to Westmoreland that "the President asked me if there is any reinforcement or help that we can give you."[3] Westmoreland, confident of his ability to handle the situation at Khe Sanh, but concerned with improving his ability to support his forces in I CTZ, replied that his major requirement was an additional squadron of C-130 cargo aircraft and some heavy air-drop equipment. He also requested faster delivery of replacement helicopters.[4] In a later cable Westmoreland cited additional material requirements "in response to the President's offer of assistance."[5]

[1] JCSM 78–68, February 3, 1968, quoted in *U.S.–Vietnam Relations*, IVC(7)(b), pp. 144–145.
[2] Johnson, *The Vantage Point*, p. 387.
[3] JCS 01272.
[4] MAC 01586.
[5] MAC 01717, 070236Z February 1968, General Westmoreland to General Wheeler, Subject: *Khe Sanh*.

By February 8 Westmoreland's staff had embarked on an in-depth study to determine what additional resources would be required in the coming year. In his message to General Wheeler announcing this study, Westmoreland indicated that his number one priority would be to accelerate the modernization of the RVNAF so that they could assume a greater share of the burden. Westmoreland also foresaw the need for an additional American division as well as a Korean division later in 1968, "particularly if operations in Laos are authorized."[6]

Although this study provided the basis for the troop request that was to come from Saigon later in the month, Washington was not concerned with "long-range" requirements at this time. Khe Sanh and the possibility of a second round of enemy attacks were on the minds of Washington planners. The difference in mood between Washington and Saigon was illustrated by a rather testy reply that General Westmoreland received from General Wheeler concerning these long-range requirements. The chairman of the Joint Chiefs of Staff stated that long-range requirements should be held up until later in the year. Emphasizing that "we can handle only one major problem at a time," Wheeler cautioned Westmoreland that he feared "until we have fully sorted out and acted upon your immediate requirements stemming from the present situation in Vietnam, the fulfilling of those requirements could very well be jeopardized by adding your longer range requirements at this particular time."[7]

The immediate requirement, of course, was to prevent the loss of Khe Sanh. During the night of February 5 the Khe Sanh combat base came under heavy rocket, artillery, and mortar fire. An enemy ground assault was beaten off.[8] In

---

[6] MAC 01812, 081557Z February 1968, General Westmoreland to General Wheeler.

[7] JCS 01589, 090020Z February 1968, General Wheeler to General Westmoreland. Westmoreland's reply indicating that he understood is in MAC 01848, 091220Z February 1968, General Westmoreland to General Wheeler.

[8] Shore, *The Battle for Khe Sanh*, pp. 64–66.

the early morning hours of February 7 the North Vietnamese, employing tanks for the first time, overran the Lang Vei Special Forces camp, five miles southwest of Khe Sanh.[9] On the night of February 7 enemy forces also moved on Danang, while heavy fighting in Hue continued.[10] General Westmoreland had foreseen that additional American forces would be needed in I CTZ to meet the enemy threat. A MACV forward headquarters was established at Phu Bai (just south of Hue) on February 9, a brigade of the 101st Airborne Division was ordered from the Saigon area to northern I Corps, and logistical units were positioned to support additional forces as they came into the area.[11] Westmoreland was taking a calculated risk in thinning his forces throughout South Vietnam in order to meet what he saw was the main enemy threat in the two northern provinces, but he felt the risk was small. As Westmoreland recalled: "The most skillful maneuver, from a military standpoint, was the way we shifted forces to meet military contingencies. We shifted forces in a timely way to a number of areas without giving the enemy an advantage in other areas. When the enemy committed himself in one area and was defeated, we could redeploy forces to go on the counteroffensive and give greater security in that area. The timing was deliberate in order to get the maximum advantage from our military strength."[12]

But Washington was not so confident of Westmoreland's ability to handle the situation with the forces at hand. If the siege of Khe Sanh was designed to thin out American forces so that the Viet Cong could conduct a second wave of attacks on the cities, it was possible that ARVN would not survive, and a coalition government would become a strong possibility. General Wheeler voiced these fears to Westmoreland on February 8:

[9] John A. Cash, "Battle of Lang Vei."

[10] *Command History, 1968*, pp. 885–887.

[11] Ibid., p. 378. Also personal interview with General William C. Westmoreland, September 16, 1973.

[12] Personal interview with General William C. Westmoreland, September 16, 1973.

There is a theory, which could be logical, that overall enemy strategy is to attack and attrite the ARVN, thereby destroying them and ultimately gaining acceptance by the people of a coalition government which would request the withdrawal of United States forces from South Vietnam. In other words, massive Khe Sanh buildup is alternative threat to enforce a syphoning off of troops from the south, thereby reducing security of the population and affording opportunities to destroy ARVN units. Also such a strategy could afford an opportunity to attack in force along the DMZ if you do not respond by a buildup of your forces in northern I Corps.[13]

General Wheeler closed his cable with some blunt advice that showed the gravity with which Washington viewed the situation: "The United States Government is not prepared to accept a defeat in South Vietnam. In summary, if you need more troops, ask for them."[14]

Then began a military minuet that emphasized again the different views Saigon and Washington took of the situation

[13] JCS 01529, 080448Z February 1968, General Wheeler to General Westmoreland. A Viet Cong Central Office for South Vietnam (COSVN) order published on February 1 and later captured by the United States 9th Infantry Division indicated that the Viet Cong strategy closely approached General Wheeler's "theory." The document, analysing the first day's developments and directing continuation of the attacks, described a two-part strategy. First, the enemy would threaten several localities (Khe Sanh, Hue, Dacto, Saigon). If the United States overcommitted itself in one area, the enemy would strike in another. Or the enemy could strike in one area in an effort to make the United States overcommit itself and thus prepare the way for attacks in different places. The second part of the strategy called for exerting psychological pressure on RVNAF and on the people by having enemy troops near cities and towns and by attacking by fire and ground probes. Thus, the second wave of attacks was not set to any timetable, but depended on the development of the situation. This document is summarized in MAC 02701, 260731Z February 1968, General Westmoreland to Admiral Sharp. The text of the document appears in Saigon 20925, American Embassy, Saigon to Secretary of State, March 1, 1968, Subject: *Central Office for South Vietnam, February 1, Assessment of the Situation.*

[14] JCS 01529.

in South Vietnam. General Westmoreland, now more confident of his ability to meet any new Communist attacks even though his forces were stretched thin, worried mainly about his logistic ability to support the large American buildup in the northern part of the country. The president, on the other hand, was not so sanguine. A defeat in South Vietnam, whether at Khe Sanh or other South Vietnamese cities, would have global repercussions that were unacceptable to the president.[15] Johnson was determined to send his field commander whatever means were at his disposal to prevent the possibility of such a defeat.

In reply to General Wheeler's cable, Westmoreland indicated that, although he felt that he could hold Khe Sanh, it was conceivable that it would be lost and have to be recaptured. Such a recapture would be a difficult and costly operation. "It is only prudent to plan for the worst contingency, in which case I will definitely need reinforcements. . . .These units would be essential on the assumption that we receive a setback in Quang Tri and Thua Thien provinces. . . . In this area, a setback is not probable but conceivable."[16] Westmoreland then indicated he did not need these forces now, but that plans should be made to deploy them in the unlikely event that he suffered a defeat. In such a case, he proposed that the 82nd Airborne Division and one-half of a Marine division, the units offered him by General Wheeler, be put ashore in an amphibious landing when surf conditions permitted, which would be sometime in April.[17]

But the president was not interested in sending troops in April to recapture Khe Sanh. In his subsequent cable, General Wheeler pointed out the president's difficulty: "From a political and psychological viewpoint, it would be very difficult for all concerned if he [the VC] were to consolidate control long enough to surface even a few of his so-called

---

[15] Rostow, *Diffusion of Power*, p. 495.
[16] MAC 01810, 081440Z February 1968, General Westmoreland to General Wheeler.
[17] Ibid.

Committees for the Alliance of National and Peace Forces [*sic*]. Considering the possibility that a few ARVN units may falter here and there, this would seem to pose additional requirements for the employment of United States forces."[18] Thus, Wheeler hinted, additional redeployments might be desirable earlier than April. "Please understand that I am not trying to sell you on the deployment of additional forces which in any event I cannot guarantee. However, my sensing is that the critical phase of the war is upon us, and I do not believe that you should refrain from asking for what you believe is required under the circumstances."[19]

By this time, Westmoreland was beginning to appreciate Washington's reasoning. He recalled: "It seemed to me that for political reasons or otherwise, the president and the Joint Chiefs of Staff were anxious to send me reinforcements. We did a little sparring back and forth. My first thought was not to ask for any, but the signals from Washington got stronger."[20]

Thus, Westmoreland's reply on February 9 was more specific: "Needless to say, I would welcome reinforcements at any time they can be made available." Westmoreland foresaw that these troops would allow him to go on the offensive as soon as the enemy attack was defeated. "It is conceivable," he reported, "that a six-month loan of these units would turn the tide to the point where the enemy might see the light or be so weakened that we could return them. . . . In summary, I prefer a bird in the hand than two in the bush."[21]

[18] This had already happened in Hue, where the Viet Cong occupation lasted for some twenty-six days. The Alliance of National, Democratic, and Peace Forces had broadcast an appeal over Liberation Radio on February 2, 1968, for the people of Hue to rise up against the "Americans and puppets who are at the end of their trail." Pike, *War, Peace, and the Viet Cong*, p. 22. See also R. H. Shackford, "Hanoi Launches Big Political Push."

[19] JCS 01590, 090021Z February 1968, General Wheeler to General Westmoreland.

[20] Personal interview with General William C. Westmoreland, September 16, 1973.

[21] MAC 01858, 091633Z February 1968, General Westmoreland to General Wheeler.

By February 10 Westmoreland was reporting to Washington that additional troops could be used in the area that worried the administration the most, Khe Sanh and the two northernmost provinces. Westmoreland indicated to General Wheeler that "additional forces from CONUS would be most helpful in permitting us to rapidly stabilize the current situation. . . . The enemy build-up in the north constitutes the greatest threat to South Vietnam. To contend with this threat requires a corresponding and significant increase in our strength in the northern two provinces. We are deploying forces to this area now. . . . However, in view of the widespread ongoing enemy offensive against provincial capitals, population centers, and key installations in the remainder of the country, further deployment of friendly forces out of these areas involves a risk that I am not prepared to accept at this time."[22]

General Westmoreland's messages were discussed at length at the White House on the afternoon of February 11.[23] As reported by General Wheeler, Westmoreland's message was interpreted as expressing the following: "You could use additional United States troop units, but you are not expressing a firm demand for them; in sum, you do not fear defeat if you are not reinforced. . . . Additional forces would give you increased capability to regain the initiative and go on the offensive at an appropriate time."[24]

Westmoreland's reply on February 12, so carefully prompted by General Wheeler, was firm and direct: "I am expressing a firm request for troops, not because I fear defeat if I am not reinforced, but because I do not feel that I can fully grasp the initiative from the recently reinforced enemy without

[22] MAC 01924, 110308Z February 1968, General Westmoreland to General Wheeler.

[23] Those in attendance were Secretaries Rusk and McNamara, Richard Helms, Generals Taylor and Wheeler, Clark Clifford, and Walt Rostow. Johnson, *The Vantage Point*, pp. 386–387.

[24] JCS 01695, 120108Z February 1968, General Wheeler to General Westmoreland.

them. On the other hand, a setback is fully possible if I am not reinforced and it is likely that we will lose ground in other areas if I am required to make substantial reinforcement in I Corps."[25]

That same day, February 12, the Joint Chiefs of Staff forwarded their plan for reinforcement to the secretary of defense. They emphasized that the deployment of the 82nd Airborne Division and two-thirds of a Marine division/wing team without a simultaneous call-up of some 120,000 Army and Marine Corps reserves would seriously drain our available combat forces. But General Wheeler was thinking of more than just Vietnam. He saw the opportunity to restore the capacity of the American military to meet contingencies other than Vietnam. Failing to mention General Westmoreland's evaluation, which General Wheeler had so carefully coaxed out of him, the Joint Chiefs provided the secretary of defense with their own evaluation of the situation: "It is not clear at this time whether the enemy will be able to mount and sustain a second series of major attacks throughout the country. It is equally unclear as to how well the Vietnamese Armed Forces would be able to stand up against such a series of attacks if they were to occur. In the face of these uncertainties, a more precise assessment of USMACV's additional force requirements, if any, must await further developments. The Joint Chiefs of Staff do not exclude the possibility that additional developments could make further deployments necessary."

Based on this assessment of the situation, the Joint Chiefs recommended that:

a. A decision to deploy reinforcements to Vietnam be deferred at this time.

b. Measures be taken now to prepare the 82nd Airborne Division and 6/9 Marine division/wing team for possible deployment to Vietnam.

[25] MAC 02018, 121823Z February 1968, General Westmoreland to General Wheeler.

c. As a matter of prudence, call certain additional Reserve units to active duty now. Deployment of emergency reinforcements to Vietnam should not be made without concomitant callup of Reserves sufficient at least to replace those deployed and provide for the increased sustaining base requirements of all Services. In addition, bring selected Reserve force units to full strength and an increased state of combat readiness.[26]

Thus, for perhaps the first time in the history of American involvement in Vietnam, the Joint Chiefs of Staff failed to recommend the immediate deployment of the troops requested by the field commander, a request that they had carefully coaxed from him. For years, Vietnam deployments had been based not on the military demands of the situation but on the forces available to the United States without the politically explosive necessity of a reserve call-up. This had caused a tremendous impact not only on the strategic reserve within the United States but on American forces deployed elsewhere in the world, particularly in Korea and in Europe. These units had been stripped of leaders and men with critical skills in order to support the American commitment in South Vietnam.[27]

The president was anxious to send whatever additional forces were needed by his field commander in Vietnam to prevent a politically damaging defeat. Faced with this fact and with Communist threats in Korea, Berlin, and possibly elsewhere in the world, the Joint Chiefs of Staff had decided, at long last, that resources were being drawn too thin. If the president wanted to send these forces, if he felt that

[26] JCSM 91–68, February 12, 1968, Subject: *Emergency Reinforcement of COMUSMACV*, quoted in *U.S.–Vietnam Relations*, IVC(6) (c), pp. 2–6.

[27] Lieutenant Colonel John D. Bruen, "Repercussions from the Vietnam Mobilization Decision"; Hanson W. Baldwin, "The Case for Mobilization"; Juan Cameron, "The Armed Forces' Reluctant Retrenchment," pp.173–174; Hanson W. Baldwin, *Strategy for Tomorrow*, pp. 11, 41; Hanson W. Baldwin, "U.S. Manpower Needs for War."

his field commander needed them, then this might be an opportune time to force him to bite the bullet on a reserve call-up. General Wheeler and the Joint Chiefs saw Tet as an opportunity to force the president's hand and to achieve their long-sought goal of a mobilization of reserve forces. They had laboriously solicited an "emergency" request for reinforcements from a supposedly beleaguered field commander, and now it was up to the president to provide the forces to meet this battlefield emergency, as well as possible emergencies elsewhere in the world.

But again the president was not prepared to make that decision and held the Joint Chiefs of Staff at bay. At a meeting at the White House on February 12, the decision was made "unanimously" to send one brigade of the 82nd Airborne Division and a Marine regimental landing team to General Westmoreland immediately. The subject of a reserve call-up was discussed. General Wheeler, of course, was in favor, while McNamara was opposed. The president directed them to study the problem further and to agree on a recommendation.[28]

The approved deployments were directed almost immediately by the Joint Chiefs and publicly announced. Airlift of the brigade from the 82nd Airborne Division, at a strength of approximately 4,000, was to begin on February 14, and the brigade was to close in Vietnam not later than February 26, 1968. The Marine Corps regiment was to close in SVN not later than February 26 also. The regiment (reinforced) less one battalion, was to be deployed by air from California at a strength of about 3,600. One battalion (reinforced), which was then embarked, was to be deployed by surface at a strength of about 1,600. Logistic support elements for both forces put the total deployment strength at 10,500.[29]

[28] Johnson, *The Vantage Point*, p. 386.
[29] JCS 01724, 122047Z February 1968, General Wheeler to Admiral Sharp; JCS 9911, 121820Z February 1968, Subject: *Deployment of Army and Marine Corps Forces to SVN*.

The Joint Chiefs of Staff reacted almost immediately to the president's decision to deploy these forces without a concomitant reserve call-up. On February 13, 1968, they forwarded to the secretary of defense their recommendation that approximately 46,000 reservists be called to active duty immediately and that some 140,000 be brought to a high state of readiness for immediate call-up "that could be responsive to further COMUSMACV force requirements. . . . COMUSMACV has already indicated the potential need for these units at an early date."[30] In addition, the Joint Chiefs pointed out the desirability of legislation that would extend the terms of service for specialists with critical skills, that would extend enlistments involuntarily for all enlisted personnel, and that would enable the armed forces to call up selected individual reservists.

A reserve call-up was again discussed at the White House on February 13. The president, remembering the complaints about the call-up of reserves during the Berlin crisis of the Kennedy administration and, much more recently, complaints about the failure to use effectively those who had been called up during the *Pueblo* crisis in January, was not convinced. He asked: "Why is it necessary to call up reserve units at this time? If we decided on a callup, how large should it be? Could we reduce the numbers by drawing on forces stationed in Europe or South Korea? Could we avoid by drawing on forces stationed in Europe or South Korea? Could we avoid or at least postpone individual reserve callups? If reserves were called, where would they be assigned? How long would they serve? What would be the budgetary implications? Would congressional action be necessary?" The president said he would take no action until he received satisfactory answers to these and several other questions.[31] Thus, the issue of a reserve call-up was deferred

---

[30] JCSM 96–68, February 13, 1968, Subject: *Emergence Reinforcement of COMUSMACV*, quoted in *U.S.–Vietnam Relations*, IVC(6)(c), pp. 6-12.

[31] Johnson, *The Vantage Point*, p. 387.

again. The Joint Chiefs of Staff believed the deferral seriously impaired their ability to conduct the war in Vietnam and made it difficult, if not impossible, for them to provide against military contingencies in other areas of the world. It was an issue that would be brought up again.

With the decision to provide this "emergency" augmentation to General Westmoreland, the policy-making process in Washington slowed appreciably for the following ten days. The president decided to visit the troops he had ordered to Vietnam to say farewell to them personally. He first went to Fort Bragg, North Carolina, to visit the paratroopers of the 82nd Airborne Division on February 17. From there he flew to El Toro, California to see the Marines who were leaving for Vietnam, and then spent the night on the carrier *Constellation*, which was returning for another tour of duty off the Vietnam coast. He also visited General Eisenhower in California.

The visit to Fort Bragg proved for the president to be one of the most moving and troubling of the entire Vietnam war. He addressed the troops and shook hands personally with as many as he could. The paratroopers, many of whom had just recently returned from a combat tour in Vietnam, were grim. The film clips of the president shaking hands with the solemn but determined paratroopers on the ramps of their aircraft revealed a deeply troubled leader. He was confronting the men he was asking to make the sacrifice, and they displayed no enthusiasm.[32] "These visits with brave men were among

[32] Allegations have been made that the men President Johnson met at Fort Bragg were substitutes for the men who actually were going to Vietnam, but who were not available on short notice because they were attending a farewell beer party. Thus, it has been alleged, the president was "conned" into bidding farewell to these substitutes, who were not scheduled to go to Vietnam; many of them were nonplussed by the ceremony. See Benjamin F. Schemmer, "The Day the President Got Conned." Of this story, Brigadier General Donald D. Blackburn has stated: "There was no intent to deceive the president. We substituted and filled in with men in order to put our best foot forward. We, in effect, filled in the blanks of a battalion. It was a representative, symbolic group. All of the men involved, as a matter of fact, rotated to

the most personally painful meetings of my Presidency,"
Johnson later confessed:

> The men with whom I talked and shook hands were
> strong and serious. I told them I regretted more than they
> would ever know the necessity of ordering them to Viet-
> nam. I spoke personally with as many as I could. I remem-
> ber vividly my conversation with one soldier. I asked him
> if he had been in Vietnam before. He said: "Yes, sir, three
> times." I asked if he was married. He said: "Yes, sir." Did
> he have any children? "Yes, sir, one." Boy or girl? "A boy,
> sir." How old is he? "He was born yesterday morning, sir,"
> he said quietly. That was the last question I asked him. It
> tore my heart out to send back to combat a man whose
> first son had just been born.[33]

It may well be that the dramatic decisions of the succeeding
month and a half had their genesis in those troubled conversations.

Vietnam in a relatively short time. There was no indication of any
lack of responsiveness on the part of the troops. The spirit was all
there." Personal interview with Brigadier General Donald D. Blackburn, March 9, 1976. See also Fred S. Hoffman, "LBJ Was Not Hoodwinked at Ft. Bragg"; Don Hirst, "Was LBJ Bilked at Bragg?"; Phil
Stevens, "Troop Switch? Baloney!"; George Beveridge, "The Army's-
Conning-of-LBJ Story." In any case, the effect upon the president was
the same. The original allegations were subsequently modified and
substantially withdrawn. See Colonel John G. Jameson, Jr., "A Letter
to the Editor: AFJ's Bum Dope on LBJ's Farewell."

[33] Johnson, *The Vantage Point*, pp. 387–388. Also *Public Papers of
Lyndon Johnson, 1968–69*, I, pp. 316–317. For the reaction of the men
on the carrier *Constellation*, see McPherson, *A Political Education*,
pp. 426–427. For the president's remarks at Fort Bragg, El Toro, and
on the *Constellation*, see *Public Papers of Lyndon Johnson, 1968–
1969*, I, pp. 238–243. For remarks made by Rostow at a press conference in California, see U.S., Congress, *Congressional Record*, Vol.
114, Part 3, pp. 3,700–3,701 (hereafter cited as *Congressional Record*). For press reaction, see Max Frankel, "Johnson Confers with
Eisenhower; Briefs Him on War"; Frank Cormier, "Johnson Sees
Eisenhower, Troops in Tour"; Carroll Kilpatrick, "President Plans
Short Notice For Trips."

SIX

☆ ☆

The Troop Request

ON February 12, 1968, General Wheeler told Westmoreland that he was considering a trip to Vietnam within a few days "to obtain at firsthand your thoughts as to the situation and corrective measures needed."[1] Now, as the augmentation forces had been dispatched and as the pace of decision making in Washington slowed, a semblance of normality returned to the American command organization. The president agreed with General Wheeler that he should go to Vietnam to find out "what Westmoreland felt he had to have to meet present needs" and what he thought he would need in the coming year in the way of troops, equipment, and other support.[2] In his message to General Westmoreland announcing his visit, General Wheeler gave broad scope to his purpose: "As you would surmise, the Administration must face up to some hard decisions in the near future regarding the possibility of providing you additional troops, recouping our strategic reserves in CONUS, and obtaining the necessary legislative support in terms of money and authorities. The President and Secretary McNamara have decided to defer until my return consideration of the foregoing important matters."[3]

General Westmoreland attached great significance to this portion of the cable. To him, it was an indication that the administration was ready to abandon the strategy of gradualism it had been pursuing and perhaps allow him the troops

[1] JCS 01695, 120108Z February 1968.
[2] Johnson, *The Vantage Point*, p. 388; also Columbia Broadcasting System, "LBJ: The Decision to Halt the Bombing," p. 15.
[3] JCS 01974, 172017Z 1968, General Wheeler to General Westmoreland.

and authority he had long wanted in order to end the war "in a reasonable timeframe." Westmoreland felt that he had already seen some evidence "that the president and his advisors were receptive to proposals concerning a new strategy. There were signals from both Washington and the United States Pacific Command (CINCPAC) in Hawaii indicating that a reappraisal of national policy might result in lifting the previously imposed troop ceiling."[4] General Wheeler had indicated on February 4 that the White House was considering diversionary attacks, either north of the DMZ or in eastern Laos, to relieve the pressure on Khe Sanh.[5] On February 5 Admiral Sharp had informed General Westmoreland that there might be some inclination in Washington "to relax the military ceiling. During Secretary McNamara's interview on *Meet the Press* yesterday," Admiral Sharp reported, "he did not foreclose the possibility of additional forces for South Vietnam, but stated that military commanders had not expressed such a need. . . . It may be timely now to estimate any additional needs."[6]

This sense that a change in strategy was necessary fit in with Westmoreland's own thinking: "I envisaged a new approach to the war that would take timely advantage of the enemy's apparent weakness; for whereas our setback on the battlefield was temporary, the situation for him as it developed during February indicated that the enemy's setbacks were, for him, traumatic."[7]

In his initial assessment of future requirements, on February 8, Westmoreland had stated that his first priority would be to accelerate the modernization of RVNAF so they could assume a greater share of the war. He listed an

[4] Personal interview with General William C. Westmoreland, October 23, 1972.

[5] JCS 01316, 041642Z February 1968.

[6] CINCPAC 052353Z February 1968, Admiral Sharp to General Westmoreland.

[7] Personal interview with General William C. Westmoreland, October 23, 1972.

additional American division and an additional Korean division as third priority. At that time, as already indicated, his long-range requirements were rebuffed by an administration that was shaken by the Tet offensive and the siege of Khe Sanh. By February 12 Westmoreland had raised his sights and elaborated his views about the need for a new strategy:

> This has been a limited war with limited objectives, fought with limited means and programmed for the utilization of limited resources. This was a feasible proposition on the assumption that the enemy was to fight a protracted war. We are now in a new ball game where we face a determined, highly disciplined enemy, fully mobilized to achieve a quick victory. He is in the process of throwing in all his "military chips to go for broke." I must stress equally that we face a situation of great opportunity as well as heightened risk. However, time is of the essence here, too. I do not see how the enemy can long sustain the heavy losses which his new strategy is enabling us to inflict on him. Therefore adequate reinforcement should allow me to . . . capitalize on his losses by seizing the initiative in other areas. Exploiting this opportunity could materially shorten the war.[8]

General Wheeler and his party, which included Deputy Assistant Secretary of State Philip Habib and Major General William E. DuPuy, special assistant to the chairman for counterinsurgency and special activities (SACSA), arrived in Saigon at 10:00 A.M. on Friday, February 23. They immediately plunged into a series of briefings by General Westmoreland's staff. These briefings covered both the current military situation in South Vietnam and troop and material requirements for the future.

General Wheeler was not as optimistic about the battlefield situation as was General Westmoreland. The day he

[8] MAC 01975, 120612Z February 1968.

arrived in Saigon, the chairman received the following pessimistic "appreciation of the situation" from Rostow:

> The enemy is prepared to strike in the western highlands [Pleiku, Kontum, Dacto]. He is apparently bringing major units in toward Saigon. He is, of course, positioned to attack at both Khe Sanh and Quang Tri. He has forces around Hue and Danang. . . . In the Delta, especially, but elsewhere as well, he is moving rapidly to exploit the relative vacuum in the countryside. . . . There is the suggestion in intelligence that additional North Vietnamese regulars are being brought south—perhaps two additional divisions. It may well be that the enemy is about to make a virtually total effort with the capital he has in hand.[9]

General Wheeler's peace of mind was not helped by a rocket attack on Saigon during his first night there. One round landed near his quarters, and, fearing that his billet had been targeted by Viet Cong gunners, General Wheeler moved into a room next to that of General Westmoreland in the Combat Operations Center.

Neither was Wheeler as optimistic about the possibility of Washington having a change of heart over geographic restrictions on the war. Since the very beginning of large-scale ground involvement in Vietnam, the Joint Chiefs of Staff had repeatedly requested authority to extend the ground war into Laos in order to cut the Ho Chi Minh trail and to cross the Cambodian border to eliminate Communist base areas. These requests had been repeatedly rejected by the president and the secretary of defense. There was little indication that they would be more favorably considered at this time, unless an American defeat were imminent. Indeed, in a discussion at the White House on February 12, some sentiment was voiced for pulling back to a strategy that would "give away no territory of value but avoid combat with the enemy in ter-

[9] OSD 02175, 232225Z February 1968, Rostow to Wheeler, TDY, Saigon.

rain and weather favoring him," perhaps concentrating our defenses further to the east.[10]

General Wheeler's major worry at this time, other than preventing a defeat in Vietnam, was the state of United States forces worldwide. Because there had been no reserve call-up, resources were being stretched too thin, and, in Wheeler's view, a new decision concerning national manpower resources was required. The Marine Corps was already unable to sustain its Vietnam deployments. The Army had skeletonized units throughout the world in order to provide the leadership and critical skills to meet the Vietnam buildup. The 82nd Airborne Division represented the only combat-ready deployable division in the United States, and two of its brigades had been stripped to fill a third brigade for deployment to Vietnam.[11]

In the face of this American military inadequacy, the North Koreans were behaving in a warlike manner. There were indications of trouble in Berlin and the Middle East. General Wheeler felt, quite correctly, that if a serious emergency arose that required the commitment of United States military force to an area other than Vietnam, the United States might not be able to act.

Thus, given General Westmoreland's optimism and the apparent diminution of the Communist capability to inflict a decisive defeat upon the South Vietnamese and American forces, it was difficult to base a request for additional forces on the current situation in Vietnam. Given the reluctance of the administration to approve an expanded ground war in Indochina, it appeared unappealing to base a request on such a new and forceful strategy.

The troop request that Westmoreland and Wheeler came up with was designed to meet both global and local interests. It addressed a series of contingencies that would pro-

[10] JCS 01695, 120108Z February 1968, General Wheeler to General Westmoreland.
[11] JCSM 96–68, February 13, 1968.

vide both commanders with reserve forces depending on the situation. "We reviewed in depth the various contingencies which would influence our future troop requirements in South Vietnam," Westmoreland recalled, "and we prepared an outline plan for the deployment of additional forces." He added:

> Furthermore, we were conscious of our responsibility for addressing a vast spectrum of contingencies from the worst to the best—even if we anticipated that later policy decisions might preclude us from being able to exercise certain options or alternative strategies. The worst case involved a collapse of the GVN, the capability of North Vietnam to commit major additional forces in the South, and the withdrawal of the ROK Forces. . . .
> At the other end of the spectrum, the best case involved a stable dynamic GVN that could move immediately toward manpower mobilization and initiate an aggressive recovery effort. If this case materialized and additional forces were authorized, these forces would enable us to support a new strategy to "reinforce success" and apply greatly increased pressure on the enemy.[12]

Generals Wheeler and Westmoreland and their staff assistants came up with three "force package requirements." The immediate increment, to be deployed by May 1, 1968, consisted of approximately 108,000 men. Two additional increments, to be ready for deployment on September 1, 1968, and December 31, 1968, respectively, came to approximately 42,000 and 55,000 men each, for a grand total of about 205,000 men.[13] These figures were later refined by the Joint Staff on the basis of detailed troop lists furnished by MACV. There was a "clear understanding" between the two com-

[12] Personal interview with General William C. Westmoreland, October 23, 1972.
[13] Report of the Chairman, JCS, Subject: *Situation in Vietnam and MACV Force Requirements*, February 27, 1968, quoted in *U.S.-Vietnam Relations*, IVC(6)(c), pp. 12–15.

manders that only the first increment was earmarked for Vietnam. The two additional increments would be deployed if the North Vietnamese were successful or if new and expanded strategic guidance were approved. Otherwise, the two increments would reconstitute the strategic reserve in CONUS.[14] "There was the question of getting the reserves in the bank," General Westmoreland indicated. "The availability was the first thing, and then deployment would be in accordance with what the requirements were and what the strategy would permit. . . . In other words, the requirements would materialize only if the reappraisal of national policy being conducted in Washington resulted in the approval of new strategic objectives."[15]

General Wheeler and his party left Saigon on February 25. He and General DuPuy wrote and edited their report en route to Honolulu. A stop was made there to advise Admiral Sharp, the commander in chief, Pacific, of the decisions made. Admiral Sharp's headquarters was theoretically in the chain of command between Saigon and Washington, but he had been bypassed frequently in the past month by direct communications between Wheeler and Westmoreland. From Honolulu, General Wheeler's report was cabled to Washington at the president's request.

In his report to Washington, General Wheeler emphasized the gravity of the situation in South Vietnam and said nothing about a new strategy, about contingencies that would determine the level of forces required there, or about reconstituting the strategic reserve for possible use independent of Vietnam. Indeed, his report contained a very somber and pessimistic picture of the South Vietnamese government and army:[16]

[14] Personal interview with General Earle G. Wheeler, November 8, 1972.
[15] Personal interview with General William C. Westmoreland, October 23, 1972. See also Lloyd Norman, "The '206,000 Plan'—The Inside Story."
[16] Report of the Chairman, JCS, February 27, 1968, pp. 12–15.

—The enemy is operating with relative freedom in the countryside, probably recruiting heavily and no doubt infiltrating NVA units and personnel. His recovery is likely to be rapid; his supplies are adequate; and he is trying to maintain the momentum of his winter-spring offensive.

—The RVNAF held up against the initial assault with gratifying and, in a way, surprising strength and fortitude. However, ARVN is now in a defensive posture around towns and cities and there is concern about how well they will bear up under sustained pressure.

—The initial attack nearly succeeded in a dozen places, and defeat in those places was only averted by the timely reaction of United States forces. In short, it was a very near thing.

—There is no doubt that the RD Program has suffered a severe setback.

—RVNAF was not badly hurt physically—they should recover strength and equipment rather quickly (equipment in 2–3 months—strength in 3–6 months). Their problems are more psychological than physical. . . . The defensive posture of ARVN is permitting the VC to make rapid inroads in the formerly pacified countryside. ARVN, in its own words, is in a dilemma as it cannot afford another enemy thrust into the cities and towns and yet if it remains in a defensive posture against this contingency, the countryside goes by default. MACV is forced to devote much of its troop strength to this problem.

Insofar as United States troop strength was concerned, General Wheeler reported that, although United States forces had lost none of their pre-Tet capability, MACV had been forced to deploy 50 percent of all United States maneuver battalions into I Corps. With the enemy preparing an attack against Khe Sanh/Hue/Quang Tri, and at the same time planning an attack in the Central Highlands and around Saigon while keeping the pressure on throughout the remainder of the country, "MACV will be hard pressed to meet adequately all threats. Under these circumstances, we must be prepared to accept some reverses."

But General Wheeler well knew that the president was not "prepared to accept some reverses." Thus, he continued, the central thrust of United States strategy must be to defeat the enemy offensive. If this were done, the situation would be greatly improved over the pre-Tet situation. Future military objectives were described as follows:

> First, to counter the enemy offensive and to destroy or eject the NVA invasion force in the north.
> Second, to restore security in the cities and towns.
> Third, to restore security in the heavily populated areas of the countryside.
> Fourth, to regain the initiative through offensive operations.

But the accomplishment of each of these tasks would take large numbers of American troops:

1. *Security of Cities and Government.* MACV recognizes that United States forces will be required to reinforce and support RVNAF in the security of cities, towns and government structure. At this time, 10 United States battalions are operating in the environs of Saigon. It is clear that this task will absorb a substantial portion of United States forces.

2. *Security in the Countryside.* To a large extent the Viet Cong now control the countryside. Most of the 54 battalions formerly providing security for pacification are now defending district or province towns. MACV estimates that United States forces will be required in a number of places to assist and encourage the Vietnamese Army to leave the cities and towns and re-enter the country. This is especially true in the Delta.

3. *Defense of the Borders, the DMZ and the Northern Provinces.* MACV considers that it must meet the enemy threat in I Corps Tactical Zone and has already

deployed there slightly over 50% of all United States maneuver battalions. United States forces have been thinned out in the highlands, notwithstanding an expected enemy offensive in the early future.

4. *Offensive Operations.* Coupling the increased requirement for the defense of the cities and subsequent re-entry into the rural areas and the heavy requirement for defense of the I Corps Zone, MACV does not have adequate forces at this time to resume the offensive in the remainder of the country, nor does it have adequate reserves against the contingency of simultaneous large-scale enemy offensive action throughout the country.

The conclusion was obvious and inevitable: "Forces currently assigned to MACV, plus the residual Program Five forces yet to be delivered, are inadequate in numbers and balance to carry out the strategy and to accomplish the tasks described above in the proper priority."

General Wheeler then described the forces he and General Westmoreland considered necessary to contend with and defeat the enemy threat he had described:

1. *Immediate Increment, Priority One*: To be deployed by 1 May 1968. Major elements include one brigade of the 5th Mechanized Division with a mix of one infantry, one armored and one mechanized battalion; the Fifth Marine Division (less RLT-26); one armored cavalry regiment; eight tactical fighter squadrons; and a groupment of Navy units to augment on going programs. (Total: 107,938)

2. *Immediate Increment. Priority Two*: To be deployed as soon as possible but prior to 1 September 1968. Major elements include the remainder of the 5th Mechanized Division, and four tactical fighter squadrons. It is desirable that the ROK Light Division be deployed within this time frame. (Total: 41,796)

3. *Follow-On Increment*: To be deployed by the end of

CY 1968. Major elements include one infantry division, three tactical fighter squadrons, and units to further augment Navy programs.

The troop list developed in Vietnam by the two military leaders had been designed to serve many purposes. Under the best possible circumstances, it would provide some additional troops to the Vietnam commander, but most importantly, it would allow reconstitution of the strategic reserve. These forces would, of course, be available to the United States commander in Vietnam if a political decision were made to adopt a new strategy of expanding the war. In the worst possible case, the collapse of the GVN, the troop list would provide for further Americanization of the war.

But in his report to the president, General Wheeler did not mention the best contingency, a stabilization of the situation in Vietnam with few additional forces required. Neither did he mention reconstitution of the strategic reserve, the possibility of an expanded strategy, or the fact that all three troop increments would be needed in Vietnam only with an expanded strategy. Wheeler put the worst possible case forward as though it represented the current situation in South Vietnam.

As Wheeler recalled the substance and thrust of his report: "I emphasized how Westy's forces were badly stretched, that he had no capability to redress threats except by moving troops around. I emphasized the threat in I Corps. More attacks on the cities were, I said, a possibility. I argued that Westy needed flexibility and capability. I talked about going on the offensive and taking offensive operations, but I didn't necessarily spell out the strategic options."[17]

Thus, the chairman of the Joint Chiefs of Staff, in stressing the negative aspects of the situation in Vietnam, again saw Tet and the reaction to it as an opportunity, perhaps the last opportunity, to convince the administration to call up the

[17] Interview with General Earle G. Wheeler, quoted in Henry, "February, 1968," p. 24.

reserve forces and to reconstitute a military capability within the United States that would allow some military flexibility to meet other contingencies. Vietnam was the excuse but was not necessarily to be the major beneficiary of a call-up of reserve forces.

There has been speculation as to what would have happened if General Wheeler had gone to Vietnam earlier, or if McNamara had been sent instead of Wheeler. According to General Ginsburgh: "The reason General Wheeler's trip was postponed was that Secretary McNamara had been called to testify before Congress on the Tonkin Gulf incidents of 1964. The president wanted Wheeler to go to Vietnam, but he delayed until after the hearings. In early February the president was very warlike and seriously considered going all out to help Westmoreland. If Wheeler had gotten out and back earlier with his report, the president might have acted more quickly, and history would have been different."[18]

And Townsend Hoopes, then undersecretary of the Air Force, has speculated that if McNamara had gone instead of Wheeler, he might have prevailed upon the military commander, as he had in the past, to scale down his request for troops.[19]

McNamara, who had only three days left to serve as secretary of defense, remained businesslike to the very end. With the president in Texas, McNamara convened a luncheon meeting at the Pentagon on February 26 to discuss the Wheeler report and to determine how to proceed. Present were the service secretaries and their military chiefs of staff.

The magnitude of the request stunned many of those gathered around the table. Paul Ignatius, secretary of the Navy, and Townsend Hoopes, representing the secretary of the Air Force, voiced their doubts about the necessity for this large increase in troops for Vietnam. McNamara ex-

[18] Personal interview with Major General Robert N. Ginsburgh, August 25, 1975. See also U.S., Senate, Committee on Foreign Relations, *The Gulf of Tonkin, the 1964 Incidents.*
[19] Hoopes, *The Limits of Intervention*, pp. 163–164.

pressed his view that meeting the Wheeler request would require some 400,000 more men on active duty and would cost $10 billion in the first year. Although he had long ago come to the conclusion that force levels in Vietnam should be stabilized for the long haul, McNamara asked each service to analyze the request according to three alternatives: (1) full compliance; (2) partial compliance; (3) an examination of alternative political and military strategies in Vietnam. But in order to move ahead rapidly, he asked the services to concentrate their studies on the first alternative, that the troop request be met in full.[20]

The president's principal advisors met on February 27 to discuss the Wheeler report. McNamara presented the three options that he had formulated the day before and indicated the cost in men and dollars. He spelled out his third option, however, in terms of the strategy he had recommended before. Under this option we would maintain the status quo on troop commitments, protect only "essential" areas, and reduce offensive operations in unpopulated regions. McNamara's own feeling was that either doing a great deal more or doing very little more both had the advantage of clarity, but he did not understand the strategy of putting in 206,000 more men. That, he indicated, was neither enough to do the job nor an indication that our role in Vietnam must change.[21] But McNamara believed the decision should not be made in haste. Secretary of the Treasury Fowler suggested that providing the forces Wheeler requested could break the stalemate in Congress concerning the president's request for a surtax. As he put it, the whole enterprise—Vietnam forces, global reserves, taxes—must be put to the American people as an "act of national will" in terms that transcended Vietnam and Southeast Asia.[22]

The initial reaction of Rostow, the president's special

[20] Ibid., pp. 159–163.
[21] Johnson, *The Vantage Point*, p. 390.
[22] Personal interview with Henry H. Fowler, December 28, 1972. See also Rostow, *Diffusion of Power*, p. 704.

assistant for national security affairs, was to support the request. He felt there was a hawkish balance in the country and a desire on the part of the public to do something about the situation. He also felt that our military forces were over-extended in general, and that this should be corrected.[23]

However, Rostow agreed there were many implications that had to be considered before making a decision. In reporting the meeting to the president, he did not state his own reaction but indicated that the "only firm agreement" among the advisors was that "the troop issue raised many questions to which you ought to have clear answers before making a final decision." Among the questions that needed answering, Rostow indicated to the president, were the fol-lowing: "What constituted the military strategy and tactics underlying the troop proposals? What budgetary and balance-of-payments problems would these proposals raise? How could such an increase be justified to the American people? How would Europe and the Communist capitals react? What peace proposals should be included in any Presidential state-ment? What was the South Vietnamese capacity to carry the load in the days ahead?"[24] Rostow recommended that after hearing General Wheeler's report the president should estab-lish "an intensive working group," to be chaired by Clark Clifford, which would "go to work full time to staff out the al-ternatives and their implications."[25]

At 6:00 A.M. on February 28, General Wheeler flew into Andrews Air Force Base, Maryland and went directly to the White House. He joined the president and his senior advisors at breakfast and presented a summary of his report.[26]

[23] Personal interview with Walt W. Rostow, December 4, 1972. Rostow wrote a memorandum to clarify his thoughts on the subject, but did not forward it to the president. Rostow, *Diffusion of Power*, pp. 703–704.

[24] Johnson, *The Vantage Point*, p. 390.

[25] Ibid.

[26] At the breakfast table in the Executive Mansion that morning, in addition to Wheeler, were Vice President Humphrey, Secretaries Rusk and McNamara, Secretary of Defense-designate Clifford, General Taylor, Deputy Secretary of Defense Paul Nitze, CIA Director Helms, Walt Rostow, George Christian, and Tom Johnson. Ibid.

He stated: "This offensive has by no means run its course. The scope and the severity of his [the enemy's] attacks and the extent of his reinforcements are presenting us with serious and immediate problems." He indicated that General Westmoreland needed a reserve force of "about two divisions." Wheeler said that in his judgment if we did not send troops in the numbers suggested, we might have to give up territory, probably the two northernmost provinces of South Vietnam.

McNamara, in his valedictory meeting as a member of the cabinet, voiced his disagreement. He felt that adding some 200,000 men would merely be more of the same and would not make a major difference. The North Vietnamese, as they had in the past, would simply add men to match our increases. The secretary of defense said he would recommend nothing beyond the emergency augmentation forces already on their way to Vietnam. He believed that the key was the South Vietnamese army. He recommended giving it increased resources and responsibilities. Such a course might entail the loss of some territory or a few hamlets to the enemy, but it would limit United States losses in dollars and men and would help to ease the growing dissension in the country.[27]

Wheeler indicated that even though it would be impossible to meet his proposal for deploying some 100,000 men by May 1, the package he had outlined could be accepted as a long-range plan.[28]

"Wheeler's report had really ominous overtones to it," Clifford recalled: "It seemed to me he was saying that the whole situation was a precarious one, and we had to have additional troops. I thought (and everyone else did) that he was saying he needed 206,000 additional troops in Vietnam. Whatever the reason, he made a case for 206,000 more men. He came back with a story that was frightening. We didn't know if we would get hit again, many South Vietnamese units had disappeared, the place might fall apart politically."[29]

[27] Ibid., pp. 391–392.
[28] Ibid., p. 392.
[29] Personal interview with Clark Clifford, November 16, 1972.

The choices the chairman of the Joint Chiefs of Staff had presented the president were not attractive. To accept and meet General Wheeler's request for troops would mean a total United States military commitment to South Vietnam, a further Americanization of the war, a large call-up of reserve forces, and a need to put the economy on a semiwar footing to meet vastly increased expenditures—all in an election year and at a time of growing domestic dissent, dissatisfaction, and disillusionment about the purposes, conduct, and cost of the war. On the other hand, to deny the request for troops, or to attempt again to cut it to a size that could be sustained by the thinly stretched active forces, would surely signal that an upper limit to the United States military commitment in South Vietnam had been reached and that a satisfactory end to the war had been pushed far into the future.

The president was understandably reluctant to make such a judgment without a full study of all the implications. He asked Clifford, his long-time friend and advisor and his incoming secretary of defense, to head a group to study the problems involved. "He had not been living with Vietnam day in and day out as the others had," the president has written, "and I thought that a new pair of eyes and a fresh outlook should guide this study." The last thing the president said to Clifford at this grim meeting on February 28 was: "Give me the lesser of evils. Give me your recommendations."[30] This was to be a difficult task which, in the end, would engender the most soul-searching debate within the administration during the whole history of the war as to what course of action to take. It would become one of the most controversial episodes in recent American history.

[30] Johnson, *The Vantage Point*, pp. 392–393.

SEVEN

☆☆☆

The Clifford Task Force: A-to-Z Reassessment

CLARK CLIFFORD was no stranger either to government service or to policy debates concerning Vietnam. He had come to the White House under President Truman and served there from May 1945 until February 1950 as a young special counsel. Leaving government, he established a private law practice in Washington. His political shrewdness, eloquence, and contacts within the government quickly made this practice extremely successful, and he was soon reputed to be the highest paid professional man in the country. In 1960, Clifford was chosen by President-elect Kennedy to act as his transition planner and liaison with the Eisenhower administration in the interval between election and inauguration. Kennedy subsequently appointed him a member of and then chairman of the Foreign Intelligence Advisory Board.[1]

Although he chose not to remain in public service, Clifford's wide contacts with American business leaders, as well as his political acumen, was valued by Kennedy, and he relied on Clifford's advice. Lyndon Johnson, after the assassination, also came to rely on him. Both presidents often used Clifford to sound out business leaders concerning administration policies. Since he was not a member of the administration, Clifford could look dispassionately upon these policies and temper his advice with the knowledge of how an important element of the business and financial elite of the nation would view them.[2]

---

[1] Joseph C. Goulden, *The Superlawyers: The Small and Powerful World of the Great Washington Law Firms*, pp. 76–93; Clifford, "A Viet Nam Reappraisal," p. 604.

[2] Goulden, *The Superlawyers*, pp. 99–100, 102–104; personal interview with Harry C. McPherson, Jr., December 21, 1972.

Johnson, in particular, came to value Clifford's advice on a whole range of issues. He became an "old and trusted friend whose advice was always cogent, clear and effective."[3] In 1966 he accompanied Johnson to the Manila Conference. The president offered him a cabinet position, but Clifford preferred to maintain his independence and his law practice. He dealt with Johnson as an equal, which was perhaps unique in the Johnson administration. "The president and I had a frank relationship throughout," Clifford recalled. "He had nothing I wanted. I was older than he. Our relationship was on an entirely different basis than some of his other advisors."[4] After leaving office, Johnson indicated that Clifford (along with Abe Fortas) had been consulted on every major decision of his presidency. Indeed, the president was quite proud that Clifford had agreed, in early 1968, to accept the position of secretary of defense. He looked upon him as a stalwart upon whom he could lean for policy support after his disappointment with McNamara.[5] Clifford explained his decision to serve as follows:

I had been offered previous positions in the administration by President Johnson, one of which had been a cabinet position. I had taken the posture that these positions were really not in a field in which I was mostly interested and for which I was best prepared. I felt it unwise to go into them. One position was that of attorney general. I didn't want that position. I indicated that I felt I should be used in the fields in which I was interested and for which I was best prepared. Those fields were international relations and national preparedness. I had used this argument in avoiding other governmental positions. I felt that I should make my contribution in the fields of foreign policy and national security. I adhered to that position. It was a strong position on my part. At this time, however, the president called

[3] Johnson, *The Vantage Point*, pp. 235–237.
[4] Personal interview with Clark Clifford, November 16, 1972.
[5] Personal interview with Harry C. McPherson, Jr., December 21, 1972.

me in, sat me down, and told me he wanted me in Defense. He had me, in effect, hoisted on my own petard. I had told him that this was the field in which I wanted to work. He said that this was in my field and that it was an opportunity to render a valuable service to the country. I was not in a position to challenge his point.

In addition, I did have some background in Defense. One of the first assignments I undertook for President Truman way back in 1945 was on the question of the unification of the services. I worked on that for four or five years. I was involved in writing the Unification Act of 1947 and further legislation in 1949. Those were very real accomplishments. In 1960 President Kennedy appointed a group to plan for futher unification of the Armed Forces. I was a member of that group. So the subject of national defense had been of continuing interest to me for a number of years. The first evening President Johnson spoke to me about this, I agreed. We reached agreement on my serving that very evening.[6]

Clifford's acceptance of the position of secretary of defense pleased the president, but it was viewed without enthusiasm by the high-level civilians in the Pentagon. They were McNamara people, and no one except possibly Cyrus Vance would have been really welcome as McNamara's successor. Clifford was looked upon by these officials as a crony of the president, picked for his political connections rather than his knowledge of defense matters, a man who had never run anything except a small law firm. The McNamara men in the Pentagon did not want a political dilettante, a Mr. Smooth, a man reportedly interested mostly in money and creature comforts. In particular, they did not want a hard liner, a man who had the reputation of advocating the bombing of North Vietnam as a solution to the war. Moreover, they feared he had been appointed as a caretaker, in the waning months of the first Johnson administration, to

---

[6] Personal interview with Clark Clifford, November 28, 1972.

conciliate Congress and the public until after the presidential election.[7]

Serving under Secretary McNamara, the principal civilian assistants at the Defense Department had come to share with him, and, indeed, had helped him to shape, a view of the United States involvement in Vietnam that varied from that of both the military and the State Department. This view had been embodied in McNamara's memorandum to the president of November 1, 1967.

Upon the appointment of Clifford, many of these senior officials contemplated leaving government; they did not relish the idea, nor could they honestly serve a cabinet official whose views were completely different from their own, a secretary who put his faith in what they felt was the repudiated policy of bombing North Vietnam as a solution to the war. The issue for these subcabinet officers, many of whom had already served for a number of years and had helped fashion our Vietnam policy, became whether they could work with this secretary of defense—whether they could make his views consistent with their own.

Paul Warnke, assistant secretary of defense for international security affairs, was the Defense official who would be closest to and have the most influence on the new secretary of defense. He would see Clifford most often. Others with important voices and with frequent access to Clifford included Paul Nitze, deputy secretary of defense, and Phil G. Goulding, assistant secretary of defense for public affairs. Clifford's daily meetings with these officials were probably much more important than the formal Task Force meetings in clarifying the new secretary's view of United States policy in Vietnam during the early days of his tenure.[8]

Nitze was both an experienced and an independent-minded public servant. He felt strongly that our effort in Vietnam had

---

[7] Goulding, *Confirm or Deny*, pp. 309–311; John Maffre, "Clifford Denies He's Only a Caretaker."

[8] Goulding, *Confirm or Deny*, pp. 312–314.

distorted United States policy in other important areas of the world. He saw the situation in this way: "It seemed to me to be clear that we were running into enormous difficulties outside of Vietnam with respect to our policies as a whole with respect to our NATO allies, for the Program One forces, and, most importantly, for the domestic support in the United States for an outward-looking foreign policy. . . . One shouldn't take as absolute the objective of denying the subversion of South Vietnam by force. Clearly that was an important objective, but it ought to be looked at in relation to our other objectives and policies as a whole."[9]

Nitze felt that we had not defined the relationship of our objectives in Vietnam to other national objectives. Clearly there were limits to the magnitude of forces we could send and the length of time we could keep them there, but these limits had not been made explicit. Our stated objectives in Vietnam, he felt, had led to an open-ended commitment, and the history of our involvement in South Vietnam had been the recurring issue of reinforcing weakness as opposed to "the humiliation of settling for less than our objectives." But the time had now come, he felt, for a review of our Vietnamese policy in the context of our total global political and military strategy.[10]

While serving as secretary of the navy, Nitze had become convinced that bombing the North would neither force Hanoi to the conference table nor cut off the small amount of supplies and forces needed to sustain the war in the South. Further, the bombing raids on the North posed the threat of further escalation. He recalled:

> When I was secretary of the navy and Harold Brown was secretary of the air force, Mr. McNamara asked Harold and me to take a look at the effectiveness of the air at-

[9] Personal interview with Paul Nitze, October 6, 1972.
[10] Ibid.; also Deputy Secretary of Defense, "Memorandum on Strategic Guidance," March 3, 1968, pp. 4–5.

tack on North Vietnam, interdicting supplies into South
Vietnam, and what, if anything, could be done in order to
improve its effectiveness in that regard. I used the Navy
staff and he used the Air staff. . . . Off the results of our investigation, there was really an impossibility, no matter
what you did, of improving the effectiveness to such a level
that the North Vietnamese would not have enough supplies for their efforts in South Vietnam, quite apart from
the general pressure of air attacks on North Vietnam. . . .
I saw nothing after I became deputy secretary of defense
which changed my view on that.[11]

Therefore, Nitze believed we should call off the bombing
of North Vietnam entirely and thus reduce the risk of escalation. In doing this, he felt, we could get a commitment from
North Vietnam not to violate the 17th parallel either with
artillery fire or by the movement of forces.[12] This was a view
that Clifford was later to find very attractive.

Coupled with limiting the resources we committed to South
Vietnam and halting the bombing of the North, Nitze felt
that new strategic guidance should be issued to our ground
commander in South Vietnam. In summary, this guidance
would direct him to concentrate on helping the GVN and
RVNAF to recover their pre-Tet effectiveness while providing maximum security to the populated areas of South Vietnam. This would necessarily require a reduction in the emphasis on and resources allocated for frontier defenses and
search-and-destroy operations in remote areas.[13]

Nitze felt that the crucial question in Vietnam in the near
term was "who would pick themselves out of the dust first,"
and therefore the things that could be done fast were of the
greatest importance. This led him to believe Westmoreland
should be sent some 50,000 additional troops no later than
June "to supply the necessary stiffening to the GVN's ef-

[11] Personal interview with Paul Nitze, October 6, 1972.
[12] Ibid.
[13] Ibid.; also Memorandum from Deputy Secretary of Defense,
pp. 1–3.

forts." He also felt that the strategic reserve should be reconstituted by a reserve call-up. "I thought that it was wholly improvident to further tap the strategic reserve of the United States, where you would have no flexibility to reinforce at all."[14]

Paul Warnke, assistant secretary of defense for international security affairs, had views far different from Nitze, but in many essential aspects they coincided. Warnke believed the United States had made a mistake by going into Vietnam in the first place. He felt that statements of progress coming from the field commanders were illusory and that we had achieved only a stalemate. Concerning the military situation at the end of 1967, he recalled: "My own view was that basically it was irrelevant, because we were not making any sort of political progress. I figured that we were just focusing on the wrong thing. I figured we were winning, we could continue to win, we could win every year; it still wouldn't make any difference unless you could make political progress. My guess was that at the end of a year we would still be in the same place except another 10,000 Americans would have been killed."[15]

Warnke had helped convince McNamara that a new strategy was necessary in Vietnam. "Basically, the strategy that I felt should be followed was that set forth in the memorandum that Secretary McNamara sent to President Johnson in November. At that stage we felt that you ought to diminish the American participation, that you ought to cut back the bombing, that you ought to try and get into negotiations and, if that failed, you ought to be in a position in which you should remain at a lower level of combat for a longer period of time."[16]

The task, then, that Warnke felt he faced at the beginning of March was to convert Clifford, a hawk who had long had a reputation for supporting massive bombing in the North,

[14] Personal interview with Paul Nitze, October 6, 1972.
[15] Personal interview with Paul Warnke, November 17, 1972.
[16] Ibid.

to his point of view. He knew that if the new secretary approved the Wheeler-Westmoreland proposals, most of the careful restrictions and limitations he and McNamara had for so long fought to impose on military operations in Indochina would soon go overboard. As Warnke saw the situation: "As far as I was concerned, the issue was whether or not I could work with this particular secretary of defense, whether his policy or his approach was consistent with mine. In the case of McNamara, it was clear to me that it was. In the case of Clark, I was hopeful that it would be. If not, I certainly would not have fought him; I would have quit."[17]

Clifford did not have a well-developed or comprehensive strategic concept concerning the role of the United States in Southeast Asia. His view of America's strategic interest in this part of the world had been awakened during the transition between the Eisenhower and Kennedy administrations. At the final meeting between the outgoing and incoming presidents, at which Clifford was present, Eisenhower emphasized to the new president the importance of Laos in the defense of Southeast Asia. Clifford accepted that judgment, and supported Kennedy in his evolving belief of the importance of Vietnam to the defense of all Southeast Asia.[18] He was consulted by President Johnson about the increase in American troop commitment to South Vietnam in 1965. He was not enthusiastic about this action, but once American troops were committed, Clifford staunchly opposed the bombing pause over the Christmas 1965–New Year 1966 holiday season.[19] As late as November of 1967, in commenting to the president on McNamara's suggestion for a bombing halt, Clifford stated his objections: "Would the unconditional suspension of the bombing, without any effort to extract a *quid pro quo* persuade Hanoi that we were firm and unyielding in our con-

[17] Ibid.
[18] Clifford, "A Viet Nam Reappraisal," pp. 603–604. See also Dwight D. Eisenhower, *The White House Years: Waging Peace 1956–1961*, pp. 607–612.
[19] Johnson, *The Vantage Point*, pp. 148–149, 236–237. Also Clifford, "A Viet Nam Reappraisal," p. 606.

viction to force them to desist from their aggressive designs? The answer is a loud and resounding 'no.' It would be interpreted by Hanoi as (a) evidence of our discouragement and frustration, and (b) an admission of the wrongness and immorality of our bombing of the North, and (c) the first step in our ultimate total disengagement from the conflict."[20]

Clifford later gave this rationale for his position:

> I supported President Johnson on Vietnam. I believed in our policy. I accepted the original domino theory—that is a simple way to describe it—and felt we had to oppose it. I had been through the reality of Soviet aggressive expansionism in my days in the Truman Administration. I compared that with this situation in Southeast Asia. . . . Our policy seemed to be bringing us out where we wanted to come out. As long as I thought we were making progress, that we were coming out where we wanted, I supported the policy. A perfect illustration occurred during a meeting of the so-called Wise Men, who met with the president in November of 1967. That group was unanimous, there was not a dissenting voice, except perhaps George Ball, regarding the president's policy. We told him he was on the right track, and the president was comforted by that. We felt that way because we were making progress toward our goals that had been set. We had a winning game and shouldn't change. It seemed we were going to prevail, so the pressure should be kept on.[21]

But doubts had begun to arise in Clifford's mind. In the late summer of 1967 he and General Maxwell Taylor had gone to Asia at the president's request to discuss with the various governments concerned the possibility of their making or increasing troop commitments to Vietnam. It quickly had become apparent that these countries did not share the

[20] Johnson, *The Vantage Point*, p. 375.

[21] Personal interview with Clark Clifford, November 16, 1972; see also Christian, *The President Steps Down*, p. 77. For an account of the Wise Men meeting see Taylor, *Swords and Plowshares*, pp. 377–378.

same degree of concern about the war in Vietnam as did the United States. As Clifford recalled: "I came back with doubts. It bothered me that, as I discussed the domino theory, I found a unanimous attitude on the part of the leaders in the countries we visited that they just didn't accept it. This created doubts, but these doubts were not sufficient to change my mind. It didn't change my basic attitude. I supported the president's policy."[22]

An indication of Clifford's feeling was manifested during his confirmation hearings before the Senate. On September 29, 1967, in a speech at San Antonio, President Johnson had offered a new basis for stopping the bombing of North Vietnam, one with fewer and less stringent conditions than any proposal that had been previously offered to Hanoi: "As we have told Hanoi time and time and time again, the heart of the matter is this: The United States is willing to stop all aerial and naval bombardment of North Vietnam when this will lead promptly to productive discussions. We, of course, assume that while discussions proceed, North Vietnam would not take advantage of this bombing cessation or limitation."[23] This offer came to be known as the "San Antonio formula," and was subjected to varying interpretations within the United States government. Dean Rusk has indicated that the formula was left "deliberately vague as an attempt to elicit any kind of response from Hanoi."[24]

Clifford, in his briefings at the State Department prior to his confirmation hearings, had learned to his dismay that the San Antonio formula was being interpreted by the State Department to mean that, in return for a bombing halt in the North, the North Vietnamese must stop sending men and

---

[22] Personal interview with Clark Clifford, November 16, 1972; also Clifford, "A Viet Nam Reappraisal," pp. 606–607. For a more optimistic view see Taylor, *Swords and Plowshares*, pp. 375–376.

[23] *Public Papers of Lyndon Johnson, 1967*, II, p. 879; also Johnson, *The Vantage Point*, pp. 267–269; *U.S.–Vietnam Relations*, IVC(7)(b), pp. 101–103.

[24] Personal interview with Dean Rusk, January 22, 1973.

material into South Vietnam. Clifford felt that this interpretation rendered the San Antonio formula virtually meaningless as a path to negotiations, as it was totally unrealistic to expect North Vietnam to abandon its men in the South by failing to provide them with clothing, food, munitions, and other supplies.[25]

Thus, in his testimony before the Senate Armed Services Committee, Clifford gave his own liberalized interpretation of the San Antonio formula, an interpretation that he felt was more realistic and would offer a suitable condition for negotiations. The essential portion of his testimony was as follows:

SENATOR THURMOND:

When you spoke of negotiating, in which case you would be willing to have a cessation of bombing, I presume you would contemplate that they would stop their military activities, too, in return for a cessation of bombing.

MR. CLIFFORD:

No, that is not what I said.

I do not expect them to stop their military activities. I would expect to follow the language of the President when he said that if they would agree to start negotiations promptly and not take advantage of the pause in the bombing.

SENATOR THURMOND:

What do you mean by taking advantage if they continue their military activities?

MR. CLIFFORD:

Their military activity will continue in South Vietnam, I assume, until there is a cease fire agreed upon. I assume that they will continue to transport the normal amount of goods, munitions, and men, to South Vietnam. I assume that we will continue to maintain our forces and support our forces during that period. So what I am suggesting in

[25] Clifford, "A Viet Nam Reappraisal," p. 608.

the language of the President is, that he would insist that they not take advantage of the suspension of the bombing.[26]

Several days later, the Clifford testimony, despite concern as to its utility, was confirmed by the State Department as the position of the United States government. While this amounted to a considerable softening, it was still short of the unconditional bombing halt the North Vietnamese were demanding.

This incident provided a clue to the frame of mind that Clifford brought to his task as secretary of defense: "As it so happened, the State Department made a concession to my point of view, feeling that rather than make an issue of it, they would go along. But there was something working inside me that indicated I was searching for a negotiated settlement."[27]

Clifford was to learn quickly how different the perspective and knowledge of the outside advisor was from that of the responsible administrator and policy maker. As a private citizen, he had not delved deeply into the justifications for our Vietnam policies. As the secretary of defense, he was completely and immediately immersed in the painfully difficult and complex decisions required by General Wheeler's report.

Even before he took office, Clifford had, in his conversations with McNamara, learned of McNamara's disillusionment with the bombing campaign.[28] Nitze had also pressed his views upon the new secretary, and Townsend Hoopes,

[26] U.S., Congress, Senate, Committee on Armed Services, *Nomination of Clark M. Clifford to be Secretary of Defense*, pp. 20–21. Also Chalmers M. Roberts, "Clifford Formula on Lull Defined."

[27] Personal interview with Clark Clifford, November 28, 1972. According to Major General Ginsburgh, however, the president was not pleased with Clifford's interpretation: "The president realized he had been had. He could not repudiate his secretary of defense-designate, but the president's disillusionment with Clark Clifford began here." Personal interview with Major General Robert N. Ginsburgh, August 25, 1975.

[28] Goulding, *Confirm or Deny*, pp. 306–312.

undersecretary of the Air Force, had written Clifford a personal letter recommending a bombing pause as well as a less aggressive ground strategy with fewer casualties.[29] Clifford listened and read but gave no sign of agreement. His education into the intricacies of the strategic and political implications of the Vietnam war was beginning. —

This education proceeded quickly. On the afternoon of February 28, Clifford chaired the first meeting of the group that was to help him examine the Wheeler recommendations. Among those present, in addition to Clifford, were Secretaries Rusk, McNamara, and Fowler, Undersecretary of Defense Nitze, Richard Helms of the CIA, Walt Rostow, and General Maxwell Taylor. General Wheeler was not there as the president had asked him to report to the cabinet on his trip to Saigon.[30]

At this initial meeting, Clifford gave the group, which came to be known as the "Clifford Task Force," his understanding of the task assigned them by the president. There is some variation among the participants concerning the scope of the instructions given Clifford by the president. President Johnson has indicated that, on February 28, based upon his instructions, Rostow prepared a directive to the Task Force to guide its work. This directive, labeled a "draft" at McNamara's suggestion so that it could be changed as the study progressed, was sent to the principals to guide their work. When the Task Force had finished, the final version of the directive was signed and sent to Clifford and Rusk for their permanent records. The president's directive, as he recalled it, called for a broad analysis of alternatives. It stated:

> As I indicated at breakfast this morning, I wish you to develop by Monday morning, March 4, recommendations in response to the situation presented to us by General Wheeler and his preliminary proposals. I wish alternatives

[29] Hoopes, *The Limits of Intervention*, pp. 151–155.
[30] Johnson, *The Vantage Point*, p. 394.

examined and, if possible, agreed recommendations to emerge which reconcile the military, diplomatic, economic, congressional, and public opinion problems involved. In particular, I wish you to consider, among other things, the following specific issues:

What military and other objectives in Vietnam are additional United States forces in Vietnam designed to advance?

What specific dangers is their dispatch designed to avoid?

What specific goals would the increment of forces if recommended aim to achieve in the next six months or over the next year?

What probable Communist reactions do you anticipate in connection with each of the alternatives you examine?

What negotiating postures should we strike in general?

What modifications, if any, would you recommend with respect to the San Antonio formula?

What major congressional problems can be anticipated and how should they be met?

What problems can we anticipate in United States public opinion and how should they be dealt with?

You should feel free in making this report to call on the best minds in this Government to work on specific aspects of the problem, but you should assure the highest degree of security up to the moment when the President's decision on these matters is announced.[31]

Clifford, however, has written that he has no knowledge of and never received any such directive. His understanding of his objective was "to determine how this new requirement could be met. We were not instructed to assess the need for substantial increases in men and material; we were to devise the means by which they could be provided."[32]

[31] CBS interview with Lyndon Johnson, pp. 17–19. For the text of the draft directive, see Johnson, *The Vantage Point*, p. 397.
[32] Clifford, "A Viet Nam Reappraisal," p. 609.

"At the beginning of the work of the Task Force, I guarantee there was no directive. I didn't see a directive at all," Clifford recalled. "It is quite clear in my mind that we had no written directive. None was received by the time we finished our deliberations and turned in our report. When you file a report, you refer to the directive under which you have been working. It establishes the frame of reference of the report. In my report to the president, there is no reference to any directive."[33]

The climate at the White House in the days following the Tet offensive further led Clifford to the view that his task was to determine how to furnish Westmoreland the troops he desired. As Clifford recalled it:

Since the beginning of the Tet offensive, there had been a series of meetings with the military. The president repeatedly asked them if they were sure they had everything they needed to avert defeat. The president often during this period referred to Lincoln and McClellan, where McClellan had charged he had not been given the resources to accomplish his military tasks. President Johnson let us know without any doubt that he would give to Westmoreland what he needed. . . . There was no doubt in my mind that the president's attitude was that we should see that General Westmoreland had everything he needed, that we were to find out how we could send what was needed and what the impact would be on the rest of the government and the country. But the overall attitude was: What must we do to send to General Westmoreland what he needed?[34]

Indeed, this attitude was later reflected by the president: "At the beginning of March 1968, I was concerned that we might have to contribute considerably more to Vietnam— more men, more equipment, more money. . . . If Westmoreland had insisted that only a large number of reinforcements

[33] Personal interview with Clark Clifford, November 16, 1972. See also Townsend Hoopes, "LBJ's Account of March, 1968."
[34] Personal interview with Clark Clifford, November 16, 1972.

135

stood between his men and disaster, I would have managed to find them somewhere."[35]

Apparently there was actually a directive from the president, which went to the State and Defense departments. However, it also seems clear that this directive did not direct a thorough reassessment of alternative strategies in Vietnam nor did it affect the direction taken by the Clifford Task Force.

William Bundy referred to a presidential directive in a memorandum he wrote outlining the specific papers to be written by the Clifford Task Force. This memo stated: "Secretary of Defense and Secretary of State will meanwhile consider the draft directive received from the White House. Directive will be redrafted before Saturday meeting to fit the approach being followed by the Task Force."[36] But Bundy now has no recollection of the directive. He recalled: "I don't think anybody in that room said, 'What's our directive?' Our directive was to look hard at this recommendation. The clear flavor of the discussion was that we would look first and foremost at the proposed 206,000 increase in men and forces, and give that a very hard look; I won't say receive it sympathetically, but at least receive it initially as the motion before the court. That something would be done in that direction was the feeling of the first day or so of the discussion."[37]

The facts, according to Morton Halperin, deputy assistant secretary of defense and one of Warnke's chief assistants, were as follows:

> I think that it is pretty clear that there was a directive, but that it did not influence the Task Force. It was never referred to in any of the meetings of the Task Force. It was not appended to the document, which is standard

[35] Johnson, *The Vantage Point*, pp. 415, 423.

[36] "Outline of Subjects and Division of Labor on Viet Nam Staff Study," Memorandum from William Bundy to Clark Clifford Task Force, February 29, 1968, quoted in *U.S.–Vietnam Relations*, IVC (6)(c), pp. 16–17.

[37] Personal interview with William Bundy, March 5, 1973.

procedure if you are working from a presidential directive. I think that, fundamentally, what Clifford assumed he was doing was analyzing Westmoreland's request to see whether or not he should get all or some of it. If you look at the directive, I feel that this is consistent with the notion that the alternatives to be examined were alternative numbers to send to Westmoreland. There is nothing in what the president said in his memoirs or in the directive that suggests that he was looking for a fundamental reassessment of our policy. So I think in a sense Clifford is right when he says our job was to see how to implement it, if you add whether it was to be all of it or some of it. The president is right when he says he didn't tell Clifford just to implement it; he told him to examine the alternatives.[38]

Thus, to the Defense civilians, veterans of many bureaucratic battles over the level of troops to be assigned to Vietnam, the president's request to study alternatives called for a study similar to those that had followed previous troop requests. The request would be assessed in terms of what could be made available without a call-up of reserve forces. This figure would be taken to the field commander by the chairman of the Joint Chiefs of Staff. The field commander's request would then be modified to fit what could be provided, allowing the president to claim truthfully that he had met every request for troops from the field commander. This had been the procedure followed in the past, both with Program 4 forces in 1966 and with the request for Program 5 forces in 1967. It was the procedure that the military expected would be followed in this instance.

Warnke also saw Wheeler's request as a routine troop request that would be handled in the same manner as past requests. He recalled:

The guidance that we got from Clark was that we were to consider Westy's request and to determine the manner in which it should be filled. I thought of it as being the

[38] Personal interview with Morton H. Halperin, December 27, 1972.

same sort of exercise that McNamara always went through with Westmoreland. Westy would come in with a request and then that request would be sort of massaged, and Bob and Westy would agree on a figure, always something less than Westy had asked for, but always the request was granted. What he had put in for now was the exact number that had been cut out of his previous request. This was a complete catch-up request. I did not regard it as an emergency situation, and I don't think that any of the civilian leadership in the Pentagon regarded it as an emergency situation. Most of us who had been in the Pentagon prior to that time regarded it as being nothing but a catch-up request, the same thing that Westy and Bus Wheeler had been urging all along.[39]

There were, however, certain differences between this troop request and others that had been considered previously at the Pentagon. All previous requests for troops had always revolved around the vital single issue of what force buildup could be supported without a mobilization of reserve forces. But it was precisely this domestic restraint that the chairman of the Joint Chiefs of Staff was challenging at this point. He was using the shock of the Tet offensive to attempt once more to break through the mobilization barrier so that the military chiefs could both reconstitute their strategic reserve and finally pursue the war in the way they thought best.

The second difference this time was the new secretary of defense. Unfamiliar with the system established by Secretary McNamara and the military, and unfamiliar with the fact that the mobilization level, not any argument about strategic concepts, had dictated American war policy, Clifford felt his task was not to question the troop request, but to devise the means for meeting it.

In this initial meeting, which was the only meeting of the Task Force attended by Dean Rusk, both Walt Rostow and Secretary of the Treasury Henry Fowler advocated approval

[39] Personal interview with Paul Warnke, November 17, 1972.

of some portion of the Wheeler request. Rostow emphasized that a sharp distinction had to be made between the number of troops that could be immediately made available to Westmoreland and those that could not be made available until a later time. The former should be provided, Rostow argued, while provision of the latter should be investigated with great care in order to understand all the implications. As Rostow recalled: "The one thing I contributed of substance was to indicate the importance of separating the consideration of forces into two parts, what we could send to Westmoreland by, say, June 1, to fight the present battle, and then to consider those that would arrive only later in the year and be needed in the long run."[40]

Secretary Fowler was quite clear as to the serious economic costs that would be associated with meeting Wheeler's request for additional forces, and his frank assessment of these costs must have been sobering to his colleagues. The required increases in military expenditures in fiscal years 1968 and 1969 associated with meeting Wheeler's troop request, the secretary of the treasury pointed out, would have to be met by dollar-for-dollar tax or budgetary action to avoid serious effects on the domestic economy and to preserve the stability of the dollar.

In order to get the president's tax bill passed, Fowler indicated, Congress would insist that at least 25 to 30 percent of the additional military costs be met by cuts in domestic programs, other defense expenditures, and perhaps foreign aid. The secretary doubted that, even under these conditions, it would be possible to increase taxes enough to cover the increased expenditures. Thus, there would be significant adverse effects on the economy and on the dollar in any event. Furthermore, Fowler did not believe Congress would stop with the 25 to 30 percent cuts that the administration might be willing to accept. He foresaw the following additional congressional actions: domestic programs most central

[40] Personal interview with Walt Rostow, December 4, 1972; also Rostow, *Diffusion of Power*, pp. 520, 702–704.

to the Great Society and the problems of poverty and the cities would be further cut; the defense budget would be cut, although probably less; foreign aid would be virtually gutted by a cut of 50 percent or more. Fowler indicated that only an "act of national will"—in an election year—could avert these results. He concluded that the case, no matter how well it was presented, was unlikely to generate such an act.[41]

This initial Task Force meeting, therefore, raised fundamental questions at the very beginning. Could enough troops to make a difference be sent to Vietnam in a reasonable time? Could the economy stand the shock of a major mobilization? Where would the manpower come from? What were our essential political objectives in Vietnam? How could additional forces help to achieve those objectives? What objectives could be achieved by these forces in the next six months; over the next year? What would be the reaction of the public to a large increase in forces in Vietnam, coupled with mobilization and economic controls? Was there a finite limit to the national commitment to Vietnam?

The education of Clifford was continuing. As he later recalled: "Until the day-long sessions in March, I had never had the opportunity of intensive analysis and fact-finding. Now I was thrust into a ruthlessly frank assessment of the situation by the men who knew the most about it. Try though we would to stay with the assignment of devising means to meet the military's requests, fundamental questions began to recur over and over."[42]

Clifford's reaction was one of shock. Prompted by the Defense Department officials on his staff, he began to ask these fundamental questions, which had not been asked in years, questions to which there were no easy answers. As he recalled, the entire focus of the inquiry began to change: "When we began to talk of the impact of sending 206,000 men, of calling up the necessary reserves, of the fragility of

[41] Handwritten notes by William Bundy, February 29, 1968; also Rostow, *Diffusion of Power*, p. 704.
[42] Clifford, "A Viet Nam Reappraisal," pp. 609–610.

the dollar, we faced the fact that the impact on the country would be enormous. The financial considerations alone were appalling. When we entered into discussions and saw the problems involved, the question quickly changed from, 'How could we send the troops to Westmoreland?,' to 'What is the most intelligent thing to do for the country?' "[43]

Thus, by the time the Task Force met again on February 29, the focus had changed. Clifford now indicated to the group that he felt the real problem to be addressed was not how to send 206,000 troops to Vietnam. Rather, the real questions had become: Should we follow the present course in Vietnam? Could it ever prove successful even if vastly more than 206,000 troops were sent? The answers to these questions and the formulation of alternative courses open to the United States were now to be the initial focus of the review. Clifford indicated that certain military options also were to be examined. These ranged from adding 206,000 troops and removing current restrictions on ground and air operations to making no change in total authorized force levels.[44]

Clifford also asked General Wheeler to get from General Westmoreland the answers to a series of questions that had not been answered adequately during the discussion of the previous day. These questions, which were cabled to Westmoreland that day, included the following:

1. What military and other objectives are additional forces designed to advance?
2. What specific dangers are their dispatch to SVN designed to avoid, and what specific goals would the increment of force, if recommended by [the committee] aim to achieve in the next six months? over the next year?

[43] Personal interview with Clark Clifford, November 16, 1972.
[44] Handwritten notes by Morton Halperin from conversation with Paul Warnke, February 29, 1968, quoted in *U.S.–Vietnam Relations,* IVC(6)(c), pp. 16–17.

3. Should there be any variance in our political objectives in South Vietnam?
4. Habib stated that Thieu believes that the ARVN can be expanded this year by an additional 30,000 over the 65,000 now in your program. Is this possible?
5. Are you having any success in getting the GVN to thin out the ARVN from urban areas in order to undertake offensive action against the enemy in the hinterland?
6. Have Freddy Weyand and General Khang been able to get started on a coordinated plan of action against enemy elements deployed around Saigon?
7. What alternative military strategies could you adopt with Program 5 forces, plus the six additional battalions recently deployed, which would defend adequately the essential areas and population of South Vietnam?
8. Would the evacuation of Khe Sanh and the establishment of a defense line located further to the east improve or degrade your military situation in I CTZ north exclusive of political considerations?
9. Is it feasible to leave the cleaning and defense of the Delta entirely to the Vietnamese?[45]

Several papers, to be completed and discussed by the Task Force on Saturday, March 2, were assigned at this meeting. The general division of labor and outline of subjects to be considered was made a matter of record by William Bundy as follows:

1. What alternative courses of action are available to the United States?
   Assignment: Defense—General Taylor—State (Secretary)
2. What alternative courses are open to the enemy?
   Assignment—Defense and CIA
3. Analysis of implications of Westmoreland's request for additional troops.

[45] JCS 02430, 292339Z February 1968, General Wheeler to General Westmoreland.

Series of papers on the following:

Military implications—JCS

Political implications—State

    (Political implications in their broadest domestic and
    international sense to include internal Vietnamese
    problem.)

Budgetary results—Defense

Economic implications—Treasury

Congressional implications—Defense

Implications for public opinion—domestic and international—State

4. Negotiation Alternatives

Assignment—State[46]

The main work in preparing a paper for Secretary Clifford to present to the president, then, was to be done within the Defense Department. Of the papers done outside the Pentagon, only those on negotiations and South Vietnamese domestic policies prepared by Bundy and Habib at State and General Taylor's on alternative strategies went to the White House. The other materials contributed by CIA, State, Treasury, and the Joint Staff were fed into the deliberative process at the Pentagon but were not included as specific papers in the final product. Thus, the dominant voice in the consideration of alternatives as the reassessment progressed was to be that of the Defense civilians.

Clifford received from his assistant secretaries a pessimistic and disenchanted view of the situation and prospects in Vietnam that differed sharply from his perception before he became secretary of defense. Although these papers did not appear outside the Pentagon and many of them were not presented to senior members of the Task Force other than Clifford, the dark picture of United States failure in Vietnam they provided was to have a profound effect upon his subsequent thinking and, through him, upon the policy goals of the United States. The main thrust of the papers prepared in

[46] Memorandum from William Bundy to Clifford Task Force.

the Defense Department was that more of the same in South Vietnam would simply not achieve decisive results and, indeed, would be far too costly to the United States to remain a viable policy.

The assistant secretary of defense for systems analysis, Alain Enthoven, in examining United States objectives in South Vietnam, painted for the secretary of defense a bleak picture of failure:

Since the original commitment of large United States forces in 1965, our stated objectives have been to:

1. Make it as difficult and costly as possible for NVN to continue effective support of the VC and cause NVN to cease its direction of the VC insurgency.

   While we have raised the price to NVN of aggression and support of the VC, it shows no lack of capability or will to match each new US escalation. Our strategy of "attrition" has not worked. Adding 206,000 more US men to a force of 525,000, gaining only 27 additional maneuver battalions and 270 tactical fighters at an added cost to the US of $10 billion per year raises the question of who is making it costly for whom.

2. Extend GVN dominion, direction and control over SVN.

   This objective can only be achieved by the GVN through its political and economic processes and with the indispensable support of an effective RVNAF. The Tet offensive demonstrated not only that the US had not provided an effective shield, it also demonstrated that the GVN and RVNAF had not made real progress in pacification—the essential first step along the road of extending GVN dominion, direction and control.

3. Defeat the VC and NVA forces in SVN and force their withdrawal.

   The Tet offensive proves we were further from this goal than we thought. How much further remains to be seen.

144

4. Deter the Chinese Communists from direct intervention in SEA.

   This we have done successfully so far; however, greatly increased US forces may become counterproductive.

We know that despite a massive influx of 500,000 US troops, 1.2 million tons of bombs a year, 400,000 attack sorties per year, 200,000 enemy KIA in three years, 20,000 US KIA, etc., our control of the countryside and the defense of the urban areas is now essentially at pre-August 1965 levels. We have achieved stalemate at a high commitment. A new strategy must be sought.[47]

In examining several strategies in order to determine which, if any, would most likely bring success in the future, Enthoven and his staff found only one that held out any promise:

1. *No change but increase the resources.*
   This strategy alternative is implicit in the recommendations of MACV and CJCS. . . . In brief, the MACV and CJCS recommendations are for additional forces to regain this ground lost since January 1968. Nothing is said as to whether still more US forces will be required to finish the job. Another payment on an open-ended commitment is requested.

2. *Widen the War.*
   Adoption of this alternative would require more forces than are now being considered and it runs further risks of involving China and the USSR. The course of events already set in motion could lead to adoption of this alternative; increasing US forces in SVN would undoubtedly increase the possibilities of it.

3. *Opt Out of the War.*
   The price of quitting now would include the undermining of our other commitments worldwide, bitter dis-

[47] OASD/SA, Draft Memorandum, Subject: *Alternative Strategies,* dated February 29, 1968, quoted in *U.S.–Vietnam Relations,* IVC (6)(c), pp. 27–28.

sension at home, and a probable resurgence of active Chinese-USSR territorial aggrandizements.

Before Tet we could have done this with less risk than now.

4. *Resuscitate GVN and RVNAF*

This option is to return to the concept of a GVN war with US assistance instead of the present situation of a US war with dubious GVN assistance.

Adoption of this alternative requires:

a. A solid commitment to a US force ceiling. This commitment must be communicated to the highest levels of GVN/RVNAF and our own military leaders.

b. A skillful conditioning of US and world opinion to the limited US commitment to the South Vietnamese war and to our right of withdrawal if GVN/RVNAF determination or performance wavers.

c. A statement that the US objective in SVN is to develop the GVN capability to defeat the VC and NVA forces in SVN and force their withdrawal.[48]

Thus, these analysts concluded that the highest priority must be given to "getting RVNAF moving," most especially in providing them with modern equipment; "RVNAF modernization should take precedence over equipping all US forces except those deploying to the combat zone."[49]

Other systems analysis papers concluded that "the enemy's current offensive appears to have killed the (pacification) program once and for all," and cited statistics to show that in the past the North Vietnamese had been able to match the United States buildup in South Vietnam with their own buildup. Statistics were also used to project the cost to the United States in casualties resulting from various deployment options and various strategies on the ground. These projec-

[48] Ibid., pp. 28–29.
[49] OASD/SA, Draft Memorandum, Subject: *The Status of RVNAF*, undated, quoted in *U.S.–Vietnam Relations*, IVC(6)(c), pp. 28–29.

tions showed that a shift to a population control strategy that was unchallenged by the enemy would stabilize United States casualty rates.[50]

Phil G. Goulding, the assistant secretary of defense for public affairs, emphasized to Clifford that there seemed to be no action that would unify the country. He felt that in terms of public reaction the question to answer was what available option would have the most success in bringing together those who supported the president's actions in Vietnam and isolating the opposition. In analyzing the various options, Goulding divided the public into hawks, doves, and middle-of-the-roaders. He felt that the program proposed by General Wheeler, or a variation of it, of increased deployments to Vietnam accompanied by reserve call-ups, extra expenditures, and increased taxes would receive an extremely negative reaction from all elements. These measures, he stated:

> . . . will make the doves unhappy because we become more and more enmeshed in the war. They will make the hawks unhappy because we still will be withholding our military strength, particularly in the North. And the middle-of-the-roaders who basically support the President out of conviction or patriotism will be unhappy because they will see the ante going up in so many ways and still will not be given a victory date, a progress report they can believe or an argument they can accept that all of this *is* in the national interest. (Further, they will read in the dissent columns and editorials that 18 months from now, when the North Vietnamese have added 30,000 more troops, we will be right back where we started.)[51]

[50] OASD/SA, Draft Memorandum, Subject: *Pacification Slow-down,* undated, quoted in *U.S.–Vietnam Relations,* IVC(6)(c), p. 26; OASD/SA, Draft Memorandum, Subject: *Data for Analysis of Strategies,* undated, quoted in *U.S.–Vietnam Relations,* IVC(6)(c), p. 29.

[51] Phil G. Goulding, Draft Memorandum, Subject: *Possible Public Reactions to Various Alternatives,* undated, quoted in *U.S.–Vietnam Relations,* IVC(6)(c), pp. 30–32.

Thus, according to Goulding, the decision to deploy additional troops of any significant number had to be accompanied by some "new" move. Two new moves were contemplated, either deployment plus expanded bombing of the North or deployment plus a visible peace campaign based on a pause in the bombing of the North. The second course, Goulding indicated, might help unite the country. A "peace campaign" option, he felt, "would be more favorably received by the nation than the deploy/escalate North, since it would, in the public mind, offer more hope of an eventual solution to the war."

A fourth option, denial of the Westmoreland request and continuing the war "as is," would please no one, according to Goulding: "The hawks (and the military) would protest vehemently. They would be less satisfied, and the doves would be more satisfied by this failure to take new initiatives toward peace."[52]

The advantages of the fifth option—denial of General Westmoreland's requests and a change in strategy in South Vietnam—were overwhelming from the standpoint of public affairs, the paper concluded:

> The pain of additional deployments, Reserve callups, increased draft calls, increased casualties, extended tours would be eliminated. The hazards of bombing escalation would be eliminated. The dangers of a bombing pause would be eliminated. The frustration of more-and-more-and-more into the endless pit would be eliminated. What the people want most of all is some sign that we *are* making progress, that there is, somewhere, an end. While this does not necessarily show progress, it does show change. It does show the search for new approaches. . . . It would prevent the middle-of-the-roaders from joining the doves. While the doves want a pause, I would think they would prefer this to deployment-mobilization plus pause. While the hawks want to escalate in the North, most of them (not

52 Ibid.

all) also want an end to increased ground strength in the South. I believe that we would be successful in getting members of Congress to make speeches in support of this.[53]

In summary, Goulding's paper concluded that the fifth option, no further deployment of troops and some unspecified change in strategy (although not a bombing escalation or bombing pause), would be most acceptable to the American public and would tend to unify the country. Also acceptable, but not as desirable in his opinion, would be an increase in troop deployment coupled with a peace initiative, probably a pause in the bombing of the North.

Although both Enthoven and Goulding advocated some change in strategy in Vietnam, it was in Warnke's office of international security affairs that such a strategy had received the most thought and the most detailed formulation. Warnke did not share the pessimism of other Defense officials that Clifford would be an unreconstructed hawk. One of Warnke's deputy assistant secretaries, Richard Steadman, had accompanied Clifford and General Taylor on their trip to the Far East in the summer of 1967 and had reported Clifford's doubts as a result of that trip. Warnke also had interpreted Clifford's remarks concerning the San Antonio formula during his confirmation hearings as leaving his options open with regard to the bombing campaign in the North. He recalled: "I recognized that he was an intelligent man and that he had some questions about our Vietnam policy. It was pretty obvious to me after the opening sessions that we had in Clark what I regarded as a real ally. It wasn't a question of capturing his ear; it was a question of arming him with the ammunition to do what we all thought ought to be done."[54]

Warnke had gathered together a group of young officials with wide and varied experience in Vietnam. Most of them were junior in rank but had a keen understanding of the

[53] Ibid.
[54] Personal interview with Paul Warnke, November 17, 1972.

149

political and military situation in Vietnam based upon long service there. They had long been frustrated by the military emphasis in United States programs. This military overemphasis, they felt, was at the expense of, and indeed might preclude, progress in what they viewed as the equally important nonmilitary political areas in Vietnam. Working under two of Warnke's deputy assistant secretaries, Morton Halperin and Richard Steadman, this group of experts prepared a draft memorandum for the president, which undertook to examine alternative strategies in Vietnam that would promise greater success in the future.[55] Halperin and his associates thus saw in this task an opportunity that they had long sought. As they viewed the situation, there was now to be little or no constraint placed on a new examination of the total Vietnam policy of the United States. Halperin later recalled:

> We had worked for McNamara, and we believed in what McNamara was doing, and we had to decide if we could really work with Clifford. We had to really—not educate him—but turn him around. And this was quite deliberate. Clifford, in effect threw us a ball by saying, "Prepare a draft report." I don't think there was any doubt in our minds that we were going to write what we thought even if that meant we all got fired. I think that most of us felt that if Clifford was not going to let us continue to fight for what we were fighting for, then there was no point in staying. Our report was the first memo that got general circulation in the government which really attacked the fundamental motives in the Vietnam war—and the military had no answer to it.[56]

[55] Working directly under Leslie Gelb, acting director of the Policy Planning Staff, this group included, at one time or another, Frank Scotton, Richard Holbrooke, Richard Moorestein, Colonel Volney Warner, Colonel Paul Gorman, Lieutenant Colonel Herbert Schandler, and Major Charles M. Cooke. Personal interview with Leslie Gelb, January 5, 1973.

[56] Personal interview with Morton Halperin, December 27, 1972.

The paper prepared by these young men, and approved by Warnke, took a pessimistic view of the situation in South Vietnam and gave a bleak assessment of what would happen if our current strategy were continued. Our current strategy would not put the United States in a position to drive the enemy from South Vietnam or to destroy him, even with increased American forces. The likely enemy response would be a matching increase in forces. Therefore, the paper concluded: "The current strategy thus can promise no early end to the conflict, nor any success in attriting the enemy or eroding Hanoi's will to fight. Moreover, it would entail substantial costs in South Viet Nam, in the United States, and in the rest of the world."

These substantial costs would indeed preclude the attainment of United States objectives. In South Vietnam "the presence of more than 700,000 US military can mean nothing but the total Americanization of the war. There is no sign that ARVN effectiveness will increase, and there will be no pressure from the US or the GVN for ARVN to shape up if the US appears willing to increase its force levels as necessary to maintain a stalemate in the country."

In the United States, the effects would be equally unfortunate:

> We will have to mobilize reserves, increase our budget by billions, and see US casualties climb to 1,300-1,400 per month. Our balance of payments will be worsened considerably, and we will need a larger tax increase—justified as a war tax, or wage and price controls. . . .

> It will be difficult to convince critics that we are not simply destroying South Vietnam in order to "save" it and that we genuinely want peace talks. This growing disaffection accompanied, as it certainly will be, by increased defiance of the draft and growing unrest in the cities because of the belief that we are neglecting domestic problems, runs great risks of provoking a domestic crisis of unprecedented proportions.

Thus, if our current strategy, even with increased troops, could not promise an early end to the conflict, what alternatives were available? No American ground strategy and no level of United States forces alone could by themselves accomplish our objective in South Vietnam, the draft memorandum stated:

> We can obtain our objective only if the GVN begins to take the steps necessary to gain the confidence of the people and to provide effective leadership for the diverse groups in the population. ARVN must also be turned into an effective fighting force. If we fail in these objectives, a military victory over the NVN/VC main forces, followed by a US withdrawal, would only pave the way for an NLF takeover.
>
> Our military presence in South Vietnam should be designed to buy the time during which ARVN and the GVN can develop effective capability. In order to do this, we must deny the enemy access to the populated areas of the country and prevent him from achieving his objectives of controlling the population and destroying the GVN.

The memorandum concluded that MACV should be told that his mission was to provide security to populated areas and to deny the enemy access to the population; that he should not attempt to destroy the enemy or to drive him out of the country. MACV should be asked to recommend an appropriate strategy and to determine his force requirements to carry out this objective with the minimum possible casualties.[57]

However, in the next section of the memorandum, the authors relieved MACV of this responsibility by sketching one possible strategy (obviously the preferred one) that it

[57] Draft Memorandum for the President, Subject: *Alternative Strategies in SVN*, 3rd Draft, March 1, 1968, Annex II, Alternative Courses of Military Action, quoted in *U.S.–Vietnam Relations*, IVC (6)(c), pp. 36–37.

should be possible to pursue "without substantially increasing our level of forces in South Vietnam, thus avoiding the adverse domestic and foreign consequences sketched above."

The strategy outlined in the memorandum was designed to attain the initiative along the "demographic frontier." It consisted of the following:

These forces currently in or near the heavily populated areas along the coast should remain in place. Those forces currently bordering on the demographic frontier* should continue to operate from those positions, not on long search-and-destroy missions, but in support of the frontier. Eight to 10 battalions from the DMZ areas would be redeployed and become strategic reserve in I Corps; six battalions from the interior of II Corps would be redeployed to Binh Dinh province as a strategic reserve for defense of provincial capitals in the highlands. As security is restored in the previously neglected populated areas of coastal Vietnam, additional US battalions would move forward to the demographic frontier. . . .

Based just beyond the populated areas, the forces on the demographic frontiers would conduct spoiling raids, long-range reconnaissance patrols and, when appropriate targets are located, search-and-destroy operations into the enemy's zone of movement in the unpopulated areas between the demographic and the political frontiers. They would be available as a quick reaction force to support RVNAF when it was attacked within the populated areas. Where RVNAF patrolling in the populated areas is inadequate, US forces would be in a position to assist.

* This frontier runs along the eastern foothills of the Annamite chain, from Quang Tri Province to Phan Thiet in Binh Thuan, cuts across SVN along the northern edge of the Delta from Phuc Tuy to the Cambodian Border in Tay Ninh. Garrisons would be established as at Bong Son and An Khe.

The advantages of the demographic strategy of population security were seen to be numerous:

1. It would become possible to keep the VC/NVA off balance in their present zone of movement. This area is now largely available to them for maneuver and massing, no more than a day's march from any of the major cities north of Saigon.

2. It would lengthen enemy LOC's from their sanctuaries in Laos and Cambodia. Base areas and LOC's within SVN would be the subject of attack and disruption, without extending the war to neighboring countries.

3. RVNAF, knowing the availability of support from US reaction forces, would perform more aggressively.

4. This would permit the patrolling and securing of populated areas to be accomplished primarily by Vietnamese forces.

5. US forces would keep active in what is now the enemy's zone of movement, no longer presenting static positions against which the enemy can mass and attack. This, plus his increased logistical problems, would reduce US casualties while increasing his. In effect, we would force him to come to us, fight on terrain of our choosing.

6. The increased patrolling of the populated areas by RVNAF combined with US actions in the zone of movement would make it harder for the enemy to mass against and attack targets within the populated areas. This would reduce civilian casualties and refugee generation.

7. Garrisoning US forces closer to RVNAF would facilitate joint operations at the maneuver level (battalion, company), again increasing RVNAF aggressiveness.

8. With RVNAF thus supported by US forces, it can be expected to remain in uniform and engage in operations as long as it is paid and fed.[58]

[58] Draft Memorandum for the President, March 1, 1968, Annex III, Population Security, quoted in *U.S.–Vietnam Relations*, IVC (6)(c), pp. 38–39.

No disadvantages of this strategy were noted in the memorandum. The detailed troop deployments required to implement the strategy were listed by corps area.[59]

Based upon this self-styled analysis of the deficiencies of
our current strategy and the desirability of a strategy of
protecting the demographic frontier, the paper recommended
the following presidential actions:

1. State that our political objective is a peace which will
leave the people of South Vietnam free to fashion their
own political institutions . . . and that the primary role of
US military forces is to provide security in the populated
areas of South Vietnam rather than to destroy the VC/
NVA or drive them out of the country. We should plan on
maintaining the posture necessary to accomplish this
objective for a considerable period.

2. Approve the immediate dispatch of an additional
10,500 military personnel to South Vietnam.

3. Approve an accelerated and expanded program of
increased fire power and mobility for ARVN and other
elements of the GVN Armed Forces.

4. Send General Taylor to Saigon to explain the
strategy to MACV and the GVN, and to request General
Westmoreland to develop a strategy and force requirements to implement the military objectives stated.

5. Dispatch one or two high-level civilians to Saigon
with General Taylor to warn the GVN that it must broaden
their [sic] base of political support, end its internal bicker-
ing, purge corrupt officers and officials, and move to
develop efficient administration and effective forces. They
should also begin a discussion of negotiations while informing the GVN of the increased support to be provided
for ARVN.

[59] Draft Memorandum for the President, March 1, 1968, Appendix,
Strategy by Corps Tactical Zone, quoted in U.S.–Vietnam Relations,
IVC(6)(c), pp. 39–41.

6. Deliver a Presidential address to the American public, explaining our new strategy in light of the enemy's new tactics.[60]

In short, then, according to the reassessment of our strategy in South Vietnam, no ground strategy and no level of additional United States forces alone could achieve an early end to the war. That could be done only if the Vietnamese government took the steps necessary to provide effective military and political leadership to its people. In order to speed up this process, the memorandum proposed a sweeping change in American ground strategy based on a decision not to increase United States forces substantially as General Westmoreland and the Joint Chiefs desired. The United States would limit its objectives in South Vietnam and adopt a strategy of population security along a demographic frontier, foregoing costly search-and-destroy operations in remote areas. This would give the government of Vietnam time to organize and develop democratic institutions and would give RVNAF time to grow in effectiveness while United States forces provided a protective screen for the populated areas at minimum cost in resources and casualties.

This paper had a tremendous impact on Secretary Clifford. It raised additional questions in his mind that had not been addressed by the nation's military leaders. The questions that had previously been asked by McNamara had been concerned with how many troops could be sent to South Vietnam without disturbing the economy and without necessitating a reserve call-up. But now these more fundamental questions had been raised, and the entire strategy had been brought into question by the Defense civilians. What effect would additional forces have on the war in South Vietnam? Would these forces hasten victory? How long would it take to achieve decisive results? How many troops would ultimately be needed?

[60] Draft Memorandum for the President, March 1, 1968, Appendix, Effects of Strategy on Interior Provinces, quoted in *U.S.–Vietnam Relations*, IVC(6)(c), pp. 41–42.

The issues raised in Warnke's paper were discussed at Secretary Clifford's 8:30 meeting in his office on March 1. It was at these daily meetings, rather than in the more confused Task Force meetings, that Clifford reviewed with his staff the most important questions facing him each day.[61] Generally present at these meetings were Nitze, Warnke, Goulding, George Elsey, a special assistant to Clifford, and Colonel Robert Pursley, military aide to Clifford. On March 1 General Wheeler was also present. The chairman of the Joint Chiefs of Staff was appalled at the apparent repudiation of American military policy in South Vietnam contained in the memorandum. He detected two "fatal flaws" in the population security strategy:

1. The proposed strategy would mean increased fighting in or close to population centers and, hence, would result in increased civilian casualties.
2. By adopting a posture of static defense, we would allow the enemy an increased capability of massing near population centers, especially north of Saigon.[62]

General Wheeler was equally appalled at the statement that "MACV does not clearly specify how he would use the additional forces he requests, except to indicate that they would provide him with a theater reserve and an offensive capability." It was just this offensive capability that was necessary, he felt—and had so stated in his report to the president—to restore security in South Vietnam and to take advantage of the heavy enemy losses.

The debate continued in Clifford's office on the following day. Warnke gave his answer to General Wheeler's two fatal flaws of the population control strategy:

1. *Increasing Fighting in the Cities.* General Wheeler is concerned that the proposed strategy will mean increased fighting in or close to population centers and, hence, will

[61] Goulding, *Confirm or Deny*, pp. 319–321.
[62] *U.S.–Vietnam Relations*, IVC(6)(c), p. 42.

result in increased civilian casualties. . . . If the enemy continues to choose to fight in the cities, we will have no choice but to engage him in those areas at the cost of civilian casualties. The proposed strategy may actually reduce civilian casualties if we can succeed in attacking enemy concentrations before he can attack the cities. . . . By freeing forces now engaged along the DMZ and in lightly populated highlands for active offensive operations near population centers, we should make the enemy effort against cities less effective.

2. *Enemy Ability to Mass Near Population Centers.* General Wheeler's concern that under the proposed strategy the enemy will be more capable of massing near population centers north of Saigon is difficult to understand. In fact, prior to Tet, because we were operating primarily along the coast, along the DMZ, and in the highlands, we were permitting the enemy to mass along the demographic frontier as he did prior to the Tet offensive. In fact, one of the advantages of the new strategy is that we will be able to keep the enemy off-balance in this area. General Wheeler may believe we advocate a posture of static defense. This is not true. In the strategy sketched in the paper, one of the primary missions of US forces would be to operate in this area, remain highly mobile and carry out attacks against suspected enemy base camps.[63]

General Wheeler fought back with arguments contained in two documents. The first was a message from General Westmoreland which answered specific questions asked of him on February 29 about the planned use of additional forces. The first question concerned the military "and other" objectives additional forces were designed to advance. General Westmoreland was ambitious, indeed, and stated that these objectives were to:

[63] OASD/ISA, Memorandum for the Secretary of Defense, Subject: *General Wheeler's View of the Two Fatal Flaws in the Population Control Strategy*, dated March 2, 1968, quoted in *U.S.–Vietnam Relations*, IVC(6)(c), p. 43.

(1) Defeat and evict from SVN the new NVA units now present in western Quang Tri and central Thua Thien Provinces, to include the Ashau Valley and base areas 131 and 114.

(2) Maintain positive governmental and military control over Quang Tri and Thua Thien Provinces, particularly the populous areas of the coastal lowlands and the DMZ area. Be prepared to block or interdict the infiltration/invasion routes from NVN through Laos.

(3) Destroy VC/NVA main force units and base areas in the remainder of I Corps and in the northeastern coastal and northwestern Laos border areas of II Corps.

(4) Reduce the "calculated risk" currently entailed in our economy of force posture in II and III Corps by providing the added flexibility and "punch" of an armored cavalry regiment.

(5) Conduct aggressive and continuing offensive campaigns throughout the coastal areas of II Corps and into traditional enemy base areas and sanctuaries in III Corps along the Cambodian border; especially in war zones "C" and "D." Restore the offensive combat and pacification momentum lost in III Corps as a result of the enemy's Tet offensive and the requirement to transfer the 101st Airborne Division (-) to I Corps to stem the NVA incursion into Quang Tri.

(6) Be prepared for contingency operations if required.

The second question asked by General Wheeler had been: "What specific dangers are their dispatch to SVN designed to avoid, and what specific goals would the increment of force aim to achieve: In the next 6 months? Over the next year?" In his answer, General Westmoreland was loquacious and somewhat vague as to specific missions for these forces:

. . . additive forces would serve to forestall the danger of local defeats due to the tactical degeneration or temporary disorganization of some ARVN units in the event of another general enemy offensive coupled with a massive

159

invasion across the DMZ. The need to be prepared to support or reinforce ARVN units that are surprised by the nature and intensity of VC/NVA attacks became manifest during the enemy's Tet drive and must be recognized in US troop requirement and deployment plans for the foreseeable future. . . .

Provision of the immediately required additional forces also would make it possible to apply continuous pressure to some degree in all corps areas and thus reduce the danger of allowing the enemy the opportunity to solicit support from the population and to reorganize, refit, and recoup so that he could soon field rejuvenated units, despite heavy losses suffered during the Tet offensive. These forces will also make it possible to retain that degree of flexibility and rapid responsiveness necessary to cope with an apparent new enemy tactic of searching for thin spots in our force structure or deployment in order to launch his concentrated mass attacks. . . .

Over the next year the increment of force would make it possible to:

A. Move progressively from north to south with a continuing series of hard hitting offensive campaigns to invade base areas, interdict and disrupt infiltration routes, and eliminate or evict VC/NVA forces from SVN.

B. At the same time, the highly mobile exploitation force (two divisions) would be available to counter enemy aggression or to exploit opportunities for tactical success anywhere in SVN without reducing the minimal essential force necessary to guarantee maintenance of security in those areas where successful military campaigns have already been waged. . . .

C. With the total additive combat forces requested it will be possible to deal with the invader from the north, and to face with a greater degree of confidence the potential tank, rocket and tactical air threat as well as ever present possibility that he may reinforce with additional elements of his home army.[64]

The second document used by General Wheeler was an analysis by the Joint Staff of the military implications of the deployment of various levels of United States forces in South Vietnam. These options were those the secretary of defense had indicated should be addressed at the Task Force meeting of February 29. Again, however, the conclusions of the Joint Staff were vague and imprecise. By sending General Westmoreland some 206,000 additional men and relaxing restrictions on operations in Cambodia, Laos, and North Vietnam, the Joint Staff indicated the following would be accomplished:

a. Assuming no additional deployments, break enemy offensive and permit early and sustained operations against the enemy.

b. Permit simultaneous operations against enemy main force, base areas, and border sanctuaries.

c. Permit resumption of program to develop effectiveness of RVNAF.

d. Permit greater employment of air assets in conducting an expanded air campaign against NV, Laos, Cambodia.

Sending fewer troops than requested and not relaxing operational restrictions would slow the rate of progress. Adding only 50,000 troops would "probably secure the cities but would be insufficient to . . . restore security in the countryside." Adding no additional forces would mean that allied forces would remain in a defensive posture and "US objectives in South Vietnam cannot be achieved."[65]

[64] MAC 02951, 020947Z March 1968, General Westmoreland to General Wheeler, quoted in *U.S.–Vietnam Relations*, IVC(6)(c), pp. 44–46.

[65] Organization of the Joint Chiefs of Staff, Plans and Policy Directorate, Short Range Plans Branch, J–5, Subject: *Analysis of CO-MUSMACV Force Requirements and Alternatives*, dated March 1, 1968, quoted in *U.S.–Vietnam Relations*, IVC(6)(c), pp. 46–49.

Secretary Clifford was troubled by the vagueness and the lack of precision of the Westmoreland and Wheeler plans. As he recalled:

> I couldn't get hold of a plan to win the war, there was no plan for winning the war. It was like quicksilver to me. If you picked up one ball, there would be two or three others bouncing around. Our plan seemed to be that continual attrition hopefully would force the enemy at some unknown time in the future to come to terms. But when I attempted to find out how long it would take to achieve our goal, there was no answer. When I asked how many more men it would take, would 206,000 men do the job, no one could be certain. I couldn't find out how many more guns and planes, how much more time was needed. It was a dead end.[66]

The senior members of Clifford's Task Force met again on March 2 and 3. These meetings, General Taylor recalled, "were a rather disorderly crossfire of individual expressions of opinion."[67] As Nitze recalled these sessions: "Each of us put our views onto paper, and I think we had fifteen pieces of paper drafted by members of the Task Force or by the JCS. But those papers tried to set forth as clearly as the authors could their views and the argumentation of those views."[68]

Secretary Fowler continued to be adamant in pointing out the fiscal implications of a large increase in military expenditures. His memorandum pointed out that the defense measures responsive to the situation would entail an increase in budgetary outlays of $2.5 billion in fiscal 1968 and $10 billion in fiscal 1969, with an adverse impact on the balance of payments of $500 million. Thus, the adoption of a defense program of this nature would have to be accompanied by a judgment concerning the desirability of economic stabiliza-

---

[66] Personal interview with Clark Clifford, November 16, 1972. Also Clifford, "A Vietnam Reappraisal," pp. 610–612.

[67] Taylor, *Swords and Plowshares*, p. 388.

[68] Personal interview with Paul Nitze, October 6, 1972.

tion measures, to include standby credit controls and a temporary freeze of wages, salaries, and prices.[69]

In a memorandum that he sent directly to the White House as well as to the Task Force, General Taylor reiterated his view that 25,000 men be sent to General Westmoreland, that the strategic reserve be reconstituted, and that Westmoreland be given new strategic guidance "which would assist him in establishing the priorities for his efforts necessary to bring his mission within capabilities of those forces allotted him." This new guidance, General Taylor felt "should make it clear that Westmoreland's mission was primarily the suppression of attacks on the cities, the restoration of order in the areas attacked at Tet, and the creation of a mobile reserve ready to pass to a vigorous offensive with the resumption of favorable weather in the spring."[70]

Rostow later remarked that he was appalled at Warnke's paper and viewed it as excessively pessimistic. He felt the paper reflected to a great degree the tone and phrasing of an unclassified paper written and circulated within the government by Daniel Ellsberg, a former Defense official. "It was scandalous that they used the actual language from the Ellsberg memorandum," he recalled, "which Ellsberg admitted was based on no access to official information."[71]

[69] Personal interview with Henry H. Fowler, December 28, 1972.

[70] Undated Memorandum, Subject: *Vietnam Alternatives*, signed M.D.T., quoted in *U.S.–Vietnam Relations*, IVC(6)(c), pp. 22–24. Also Taylor, *Swords and Plowshares*, pp. 388–389.

[71] Personal interview with Walt W. Rostow, December 4, 1972. See also Rostow, *Diffusion of Power*, pp. 495, 519–520, 700, 702, and Daniel Ellsberg, Memorandum for the Record, Subject: *Impact of the Winter-Spring Offensive*, February 28, 1968. The ISA draft did use some of the wording of the Ellsberg memo in describing the current situation in Vietnam and read more into the Tet offensive than had been noted by other observers. The following paragraph in the ISA paper is taken almost verbatim from page 4 of Ellsberg's memorandum:

It is unlikely that the GVN will rise to the challenge. It will not move toward a Government of National Union. Current arrests of oppositionists further isolate and discredit it, and possibly foreshadow the emasculation of the Assembly and the undoing of all promising political developments of the past year. Furthermore, it is possible that the recent offensive was facilitated by a newly

As the Task Force deliberations proceeded, there was no audible opposition to sending Westmoreland some 25,000 men at once and little or no enthusiasm for sending him the 206,000 requested by General Wheeler. The real debate came over new strategic guidance for Westmoreland and the direction this guidance should take. No one at this time seriously considered extending military authority to operate in Laos, Cambodia, and North Vietnam. Although Rostow had consistently felt the war could only be materially shortened by putting substantial United States ground forces across the Ho Chi Minh Trail in Laos or into the southern part of North Vietnam, he did not press this view.[72]

Most of the members of the Task Force felt that any new strategic guidance would move in the direction of a popula-

---

friendly or apathetic urban environment, and a broad low-level cooperative organization that had not existed on the same scale before. If, in fact, the attacks reflect new VC opportunities and capability in the cities, then the impact of the attacks themselves, the overall military response, and the ineffective GVN political response may still further improve the VC cause in the cities, as well as in the countryside. Even if the political makeup of the GVN should change for the better, it may well be that VC penetration in the cities has now gone or will soon go too far for real non-Communist political mobilization to develop.

See *U.S.–Vietnam Relations*, IVC(6)(c), p. 34. However, Rostow errs in stating that the conclusions of the two papers were similar. The Ellsberg memo predicted a conclusion disastrous to United States objectives. It stated that "things are going to get much worse; and then they will not get better. . . . I think that the war is over." The ISA paper, on the other hand, stressed the nonmilitary aspects of our strategy and concluded that we were at a stalemate in Vietnam but that we could "obtain our objective . . . if the GVN begins to take the steps necessary to gain the confidence of the people and to provide effective leadership for the diverse groups in the population." See *U.S.–Vietnam Relations*, IVC(6)(c), p. 370. Also personal interview with Leslie Gelb, January 5, 1973. For other views of Ellsberg's pessimistic conclusions, see Roland Evans and Robert Novak, "A Tet Memo from Ellsberg"; and John P. Roche, "Recollections of Ellsberg."

[72] Rostow, *Diffusion of Power*, p. 704. Walt W. Rostow, "Aftermath: Losing Big: A Reply," p. 10; personal interview with Walt W. Rostow, December 4, 1972. Also see *U.S.–Vietnam Relations*, IVC (3), pp. 131–133.

tion control strategy, which would require few additional American forces, would upgrade the role of the South Vietnamese armed forces, and would settle in for the long haul. General Wheeler saw the writing on the wall and hinted of this strategy to General Westmoreland. On March 2 he cabled that the committee had had a lengthy discussion of the present status of the Vietnamese armed forces. He requested that Westmoreland furnish him as much meaningful information as was available "forthwith."[73]

Clifford had found Warnke's draft "quite persuasive," and felt strongly the need to give General Westmoreland new strategic guidance. He had come to realize that the strategy then being followed and the new strategy being advocated by the military could lead to an unending troop commitment and a further United States take-over of the war, and voiced his concern about this. But Clifford's doubts at this time were mildly stated. He felt that his report to the president should not be too dramatic, but should be subtly worded to indicate initial doubts and the possibility of a later change.[74] Taylor, although arguing for new strategic guidance, doubted that such guidance could be announced at that time without serious military and psychological damage to the country. Rostow believed that any change in strategic guidance required detailed review with Westmoreland and doubted whether population security really meant a change in strategy.[75]

The discussion continued with no consensus emerging about the best form for the strategic guidance, which most of the participants felt was necessary. Finally, at the end of the long session, William Bundy suggested that someone had to summarize the conclusions reached during the discussion into a report to the president. He and Warnke assumed this task.[76]

[73] JCS 02506Z March 1968, General Wheeler to General Westmoreland.

[74] Personal interview with Clark Clifford, November 28, 1972.

[75] William Bundy, handwritten notes, March 2-3, 1968.

[76] Personal interview with William Bundy, October 11, 1972.

Meanwhile, word of the tenor of the Task Force deliberations had reached the various military headquarters in the Pacific, and the senior military commanders made eleventh-hour bids to buttress their case for a more aggressive strategy. Admiral Sharp, commander in chief, Pacific, had always been an outspoken advocate of a more aggressive air campaign against North Vietnam, which was his particular responsibility. On March 1 he again made a plea for removing restrictions on this campaign, which had "hampered the effectiveness of our forces." He phrased his plea in terms of the overall reevaluation of strategy in Vietnam and stated: "To permit the enemy to fight the war in his way is to permit him to take the strategic offensive while US and Free World forces remain on the strategic defensive. . . . The Rolling Thunder campaign is the only means available to US forces for the conduct of a strategic offensive against what we must recognize as a determined enemy." The admiral "strongly recommended" that all restrictions on air operations over North Vietnam "other than those against foreign shipping, hospitals, schools, and population be lifted."[77]

On March 2 General Westmoreland urged anew that United States forces be authorized to drive into Laos to cut the Ho Chi Minh Trail as soon as the necessary forces were available. The next day he reported that Communist action in Laos was reaching the critical point and asked for serious consideration of a plan for United States forces to intervene through Thailand under the sponsorship of the Southeast Asia Treaty Organization.[78]

On March 4 Admiral Sharp again laid out the options as he saw them: "It seems to me we are at a crossroads. We have the choice of using our military power at full effectiveness with provision of the necessary forces, or we can continue a campaign of gradualism and accept a long drawn-out contest, or we can retreat in defeat from Southeast Asia and

---

[77] CINCPAC to JCS, 010823Z March 1968, Subject: *Rolling Thunder Air Campaign in North Vietnam, April through September 1968*; also Oberdorfer, *Tet*, p. 288.
[78] Oberdorfer, *Tet*, p. 288.

leave our Allies to face the Communists alone." To Admiral Sharp the choice seemed obvious. "I suggest that we need to think and act in an aggressive, determined, and offensive manner. . . . Now we need to get tough in word and deed, the only policy that the Communists understand." Sharp recommended that a combined amphibious and air campaign against North Vietnam be authorized and undertaken "as the weather and the current situation permits."[79]

But the military's demands for an aggressive and expanded strategy were swimming against the tide of opinion in Washington. All these plans required a political decision to widen the war and increase American forces at a time when most officials who had participated in the secret Pentagon meetings felt that the American commitment had already exceeded the bounds of our national interest.

The formal report of the Clifford Task Force was polished and refined at the Pentagon. The draft memorandum for the president prepared by Warnke and Bundy differed markedly in tone from the initial memorandum presented to the Clifford group earlier in the week. Gone was any discussion of grand strategy. The memorandum recapitulated the request for additional military personnel and indicated that General Wheeler believed that this request should be met and that action should be taken to increase and improve the strategic reserve within the United States. To achieve these goals, however, it would be necessary to increase the strength of the armed forces by some 511,000 men by June 30, 1969. This could be accomplished by calling up 262,000 reservists, by increasing draft calls, and by extending terms of service.[80]

The secretary of defense, in his memorandum to the president, recommended:

> 1. An immediate decision to deploy to Vietnam an estimated total of 22,000 additional personnel (approximately 60% of which would be combat). An immediate

[79] CINCPAC to Wheeler, 032253 March 1968; also Oberdorfer, *Tet*, p. 288.
[80] Draft Memorandum for the President, March 4, 1968, quoted in *U.S.–Vietnam Relations*, IVC(6)(c), pp. 52–53.

decision to deploy the three tactical fighter squadrons deferred from Program 5 (about 1,000 men). This would be over and above the four battalions (about 3,700 men) already planned for deployment in April which in themselves would bring us slightly above the 525,000 authorized level. . . .

2. Either through Ambassador Bunker or through an early visit by Secretary Clifford, a highly forceful approach to the GVN (Thieu and Ky) to get certain key commitments for improvement, tied to our own increased effort and to increased US support for the ARVN. . . .

3. Early approval of a Reserve call-up and an increased end strength adequate to meet the balance of the Westmoreland request and to restore a strategic reserve in the United States, adequate for possible contingencies worldwide . . . (about 245,000 men).

4. Reservation of the decision to meet the Westmoreland request in full. While we would be putting ourselves in a position to make these additional deployments, the future decision to do so would be contingent upon:

a. Reexamination on a week-by-week basis of the desirability of further deployments as the situation develops;

b. Improved political performance by the GVN and increased contribution in effective military action by the ARVN;

c. The results of a study in depth, to be initiated immediately, of possible new political and strategic guidance for the conduct of US operations in South Vietnam, and of our Vietnamese policy in the context of our world-wide politico-military strategy. . . .

5. No new peace initiative on Vietnam. Restatement of our terms for peace and certain limited diplomatic actions to dramatize Laos and to focus attention on the total threat to Southeast Asia. . . .

6. A general decision on bombing policy, not excluding future change, but adequate to form a basis for discussion with the Congress on this key aspect. Here your advisers are divided:

168

a. General Wheeler and others would advocate a substantial extension of targets and authority in and near Hanoi and Haiphong, mining of Haiphong, and naval gunfire up to a Chinese Buffer Zone;

b. Others would advocate a seasonal step-up through the spring, but without these added elements.[81]

Attached to the basic report were eight appendixes which elaborated on the reasoning that led to the recommendations. Tab A reviewed the justification for immediately sending some additional forces to Vietnam. There was an urgent need, it was stated, both practical and psychological, to send such forces as could be gotten to Vietnam in time to affect the situation within the coming four or five months.[82] Tab B elaborated on what should be done to increase the effectiveness of Vietnamese efforts in conjunction with the United States troop increase. Two possible GVN reactions to the deployment of additional United States forces were foreseen. The reaffirmation of the American commitment would be welcomed, would add to the feeling of confidence, and might stiffen the GVN's will at a time "when the tasks it faces are rather monumental." On the other hand, there was always the danger that the Vietnamese would be tempted to relax behind the refuge of American power, and the sense of anxiety and urgency that had resulted from the Tet offensive could suffer. The memorandum indicated, however, that the Vietnamese government had the capacity to take civil and military actions that would materially improve the political climate and sense of security within South Vietnam, as well as its image in the United States. The United States would have to be prepared to make specific demands upon the Vietnamese government in order to get it to take a wide range of decisions and actions. A list of specific and tough demands, ranging from mobilization to a "fundamental change in the attitude and dedication of the leadership" was

[81] Ibid.
[82] Draft Memorandum for the President, March 4, 1968, Tab A, The Justification for Immediate Additional Forces in South Vietnam, quoted in *U.S.–Vietnam Relations,* IVC(6)(c), pp. 53–54.

included. The appendix recommended that a high-level mission, probably headed by the secretary of defense, go to Saigon to emphasize to the Vietnamese that improved governmental performance was essential; that any further United States support must be matched by Vietnamese action; and that the United States would do what was necessary to improve the capability of RVNAF.[83]

Tab C consisted of a brief justification for increasing the strategic reserve. The basic argument was that we would then be prepared to provide the additional ground, sea, and air forces involved in General Westmoreland's request if the military situation required. In addition, the unsettled situation in many parts of the world made this buildup "a prudent action entirely apart from possible Vietnam contingencies."[84]

Relegated to Tab D was the Task Force's major effort—the arguments for an in-depth study of the need for a change in strategic guidance for General Westmoreland. This appendix reflected Warnke's view and quickly repudiated the military's recommendations for massive reinforcements and the extension of the war. That plan, according to the Task Force paper, did not provide any really satisfactory answer to the problem in Vietnam: "There can be no assurances that this very substantial additional deployment would leave us a year from today in any more favorable military position. All that can be said is that the additional troops would enable us to kill more of the enemy and would provide more security if the enemy does not offset them by lesser reinforcements of his own. There is no indication that they would

[83] Draft Memorandum for the President, March 4, 1968, Tab B, Increasing the Effectiveness of Vietnamese Efforts in Conjunction with a United States Troop Increase, quoted in *U.S.–Vietnam Relations*, IVC(6)(c), pp. 54–58. Portions deleted from the government edition can be found in *The Pentagon Papers, Gravel Edition*, IV, pp. 578–579.

[84] Draft Memorandum for the President, March 4, 1968, Tab C, Justification for Increasing the Strategic Reserve, quoted in *U.S.–Vietnam Relations*, IVC(6)(c), p. 58.

bring about a quick solution in Vietnam and, in the absence of better performance by the GVN and the ARVN, the increased destruction and increased Americanization of the war could, in fact, be counterproductive."[85]

There were many other reasons for conducting a study of our Vietnamese policy in the context of worldwide United States political and military strategy. No matter what the result in Vietnam itself, we will have failed in our purpose, the memorandum stated, if:

a. The war in Vietnam spreads to the point where it is a major conflict leading to direct military confrontation with the USSR and/or China;

b. The war in Vietnam spreads to the point where we are so committed in resources that our other worldwide commitments—especially NATO—are no longer credible;

c. The attitudes of the American people towards "more Vietnams" are such that our other commitments are brought into question as a matter of US will;

d. Other countries no longer wish the US commitment for fear of the consequences to themselves as a battlefield between the East and the West.[86]

Although the memorandum indicated that the "exact nature of the strategic guidance which should be adopted cannot now be predicted," it pointed toward a population-security strategy by stating that there could be no prospect of a quick military solution to the aggression in South Vietnam and that a study of the issue might show that General Westmoreland "should not be expected either to destroy the

[85] Draft Memorandum for the President, March 4, 1968, Tab D, Necessity for In-Depth Study of Vietnam Policy and Strategic Guidance, quoted in *U.S.–Vietnam Relations*, IVC(6)(c), pp. 58–60. Deleted portions appear in *The Pentagon Papers, Gravel Edition*, IV, p. 581.

[86] Draft Memorandum for the President, March 4, 1968, Tab D, Necessity for In-Depth Study of Vietnam Policy and Strategic Guidance, quoted in *U.S.–Vietnam Relations*, IVC(6)(c), pp. 58–60.

enemy forces or to rout them completely from South Vietnam." The kind of open-ended American commitment that might be required to achieve such military objectives could not even be estimated.[87] Thus, the current strategy of "destroying the enemy forces in South Vietnam" and a new strategy that would expand the geographic limits of the war were clearly repudiated as requiring resources beyond the capability or inclination of the United States to commit. For the first time, a lid had been put firmly upon the level of commitment of American forces to the struggle in Vietnam.

Tab E had been prepared by William Bundy and discussed negotiating options and possible diplomatic actions that could be taken in conjunction with a buildup of United States forces. It was a lengthy argument for doing nothing that had not already been done. The paper indicated that the San Antonio formula was "rock bottom" as a condition for stopping the bombing and entering into talks. This position represented the belief widely held at the time that negotiations, in spite of continuing contacts through third parties, were still out of the question. In the wake of the ferocious attacks in South Vietnam, new initiatives could only be construed by Hanoi as evidence of allied weakness and "would be extremely unwise at the present time." Hence, no new initiatives were recommended.[88]

Tab F contained the two opposing views concerning the bombing campaign against North Vietnam. As already noted, the Clifford group was split on bombing policy. The Joint Chiefs of Staff, as they had often done in the past, recommended "a coordinated and sustained air campaign" against North Vietnam to include closing the port of Haiphong. But the Joint Chiefs were careful to hedge about what results

[87] Ibid.
[88] Draft Memorandum for the President, March 4, 1968, Tab E, Negotiating Posture Options and Possible Diplomatic Actions, quoted in *U.S.–Vietnam Relations*, IVC(6)(c), pp. 60–62. See also *U.S.–Vietnam Relations*, IVC(7)(b), pp. 171–172.

might be expected, and pointed out that for the next several months, bad weather would partially offset the new measures. The second paper, drafted by Warnke, tersely and emphatically rejected all of the JCS recommendations for expanding the air war. An expanded campaign, Warnke argued, would be militarily ineffective and would involve unacceptable political risks. Instead, he argued for optimizing "the political value of the attacks" by destroying "clearly important military and economic targets without excessive population damage."[89]

In the light of subsequent developments, it is interesting to note that neither side considered a partial reduction, pause, or cessation of the bombing of the North. The San Antonio formula was regarded as eminently reasonable, and the North Vietnamese failure to respond to it was interpreted as evidence of their general lack of interest in negotiations at that time. Similarly, since the promise of a complete cessation of the bombing had been made if the San Antonio conditions were fulfilled, it was felt that something less than a complete cessation would be equally ineffective in getting Hanoi to the negotiating table.

The final two tabs of the Clifford memorandum, Tabs G and H, contained Goulding's analysis of what the public reaction would be to increased troop commitments and the calling up of reserve forces.[90]

Thus, the memorandum forwarded to the president by the secretary of defense, the result of a period of frantic consultation, writing, and reassessing, was in many ways similar to all the other studies that had been triggered by troop re-

[89] Draft Memorandum for the President, March 4, 1968, Tab F, Military Action Against North Vietnam, Tab F–1, The Campaign Against North Vietnam, quoted in *U.S.–Vietnam Relations,* IVC (6)(c), p. 62; also *U.S.–Vietnam Relations,* IVC(7)(b), pp. 168–170, 173–180.

[90] Draft Memorandum for the President, March 4, 1968, Tab G, Difficulties and Negative Factors in the Course of Action; Tab H, Problems We Can Anticipate in United States Public Opinion, quoted in *U.S.–Vietnam Relations,* IVC(6)(c), pp. 62–63.

quests from the field commander in Vietnam. The litany seemed familiar: We will furnish what we can presently furnish without disrupting the normal political and economic life of the nation, while we study the situation as it develops.

Other reasons for not meeting all of Westmoreland's requests were adduced. The situation in South Vietnam was not clear. The ability of the government and of the army to survive and to improve was in serious question. The ability of the United States to attain its objectives in South Vietnam by military force of whatever size was not apparent. The Task Force report, therefore, seemed to recommend that we continue rather haltingly down the same road, meanwhile consulting the map more frequently and in greater detail to make sure we were on the right road.

But this time there was a difference. Although no new strategy was recommended, for the first time it was recognized and made explicit that new strategic guidance was required, that a reassessment of our strategy in Vietnam was needed, that a limit to United States involvement in South Vietnam had to be determined, and that any number of American troops could not achieve our objectives without significant improvement in the ability of the Vietnamese government to win popular support and to fight aggressively for its own security.

Asked to assess alternative levels of reinforcement to be sent to Vietnam, the senior officials who prepared and approved the March 4 memorandum had arrived at a more fundamental question. This question was, indeed, what difference in the war, what progress toward victory, would the buildup requested by the military leaders actually make? The civilian leaders were prepared to go a long way toward meeting the military's request for reinforcements and for a partial mobilization in order to be prepared to meet additional contingencies. More importantly, however, these officials finally came to realize that no military strategy could be successful unless a South Vietnamese political and military entity was capable of winning the support of its people. Thus, for the first time, United States efforts were to be made contingent upon specific reforms undertaken by the South Vietnamese, and United States leverage was to be used to elicit these reforms. South Vietnam was to be put on notice that the limit of the United States' patience and commitment had been approached.

The Clifford report represented a compromise. In this case, it was a compromise brought about by differences between the Defense civilians and the chairman of the Joint Chiefs of Staff and his officers. Initially, Warnke's office had prepared a draft presidential memorandum that had indeed reassessed United States strategy in South Vietnam, found it faulty, and recommended a new strategy of protecting the demographic frontier using basically the United States forces already present. The chairman of the Joint Chiefs of Staff found fatal flaws in this strategy, could not accept the implied criticism of past strategy in the proposal, did not think that the Defense Department civilians should be involved in issuing specific guidance to the military field commander, and supported his field commander in his request for the forces required to allow him to "regain the initiative." The compromise reached, of course, was that although new strategic guidance seemed to be needed, a decision on this guidance should be deferred pending a complete political and military reassessment of United States strategy and objectives in Vietnam in the context of our worldwide commitments.

William Bundy saw the purpose of the report as follows: "We felt we should make modest recommendations with enough caveats and appendices so that the idea would come through that no decision should be made until this had been walked around a great deal. . . . Big questions remained. There were stop signs—caution signs—all over this draft. This was quite deliberate. We had fulfilled our mandate, but there were all sorts of questions remaining. . . . Anybody could see that this was perfectly clear, that no president would decide on the basis of these recommendations."[91]

"The actual recommendations were a small part of the report," recalled Warnke, "and the rest of it was an effort to get the attention of the president, to get him to focus on the wider questions."[92] Equally important, the seed of doubt concerning United States strategy and direction in Vietnam had been planted in Clifford's mind. This seed was to grow rapidly in the following weeks.

[91] Personal interview with William Bundy, October 11, 1972.
[92] Personal interview with Paul Warnke, November 17, 1972.

EIGHT

☆ ☆

The President Ponders

THE Clifford report was presented to the president at a meeting at the White House on the evening of March 4. A copy was distributed to everyone at the table.[1] Clifford pointed out that his report made a sharp distinction between present needs and the longer-run question of overall strategy and military posture. He felt that his short-range recommendations were urgently needed to meet the immediate situation in Vietnam, as well as other possible contingencies there and elsewhere. But in the longer run, he pointed out, there were many difficulties. He felt that the president should ponder hard before he took additional measures.[2]

Walt Rostow, still upset with the Defense civilians who had written most of the report, pointed out to the president the extremely pessimistic nature of some of it. The president acknowledged later that he had indeed detected a deep sense of pessimism not only in the report but from those around the table as well. "I have never seen some of our stalwarts in our operation in Washington dealing with the Southeast Asia theater that were as depressed as they were after Tet," he stated.[3] But he himself had been encouraged by the detailed information he was receiving daily from his representatives in Saigon. Indeed, on Sunday, February 24, the day after General Wheeler left Saigon, General Westmoreland, in an extensive interview with Wes Gallagher of the Associated

[1] Johnson, *The Vantage Point*, pp. 396–397.

[2] Personal interview with Clark Clifford, November 28, 1972; Johnson, *The Vantage Point*, pp. 397–398.

[3] Personal interview with Walt W. Rostow, December 4, 1972; Johnson, *The Vantage Point*, p. 398; CBS interview with Lyndon Johnson.

177

Press, likened the enemy offensive to the Battle of the Bulge in World War II and stated that the enemy "suffered a military defeat." This encouraging picture was repeated in other reports, culminating in a cable on March 3, in which the field commander reported that throughout Vietnam, United States forces were "moving to a general offensive."[4]

The discussion concerning ground strategy in South Vietnam continued at the Tuesday luncheon at the White House the next day.[5] The conversation centered on whether it would be better to take some firm and decisive action early in the crisis, as advocated by the military, or to deal with the situation by gradual steps. Rostow urged the president to go to the country and demand a maximum effort in response to the enemy attacks so as to force an early end to the war. Public opinion polls had shown an upward surge in public support of the war after the shock of the Tet attacks. Rostow felt that this "rally-round-the-flag" effect upon public opinion would continue. This concept holds that a large number of citizens are inclined to support the country's leadership no matter what it does. Thus, meaningful public opinion, Rostow felt, would not really form until the president had taken a position. Then the public would be influenced significantly by that position and tend to support it. As Rostow saw it: "You don't have any public opinion on an issue until the president states what he wants to do. If the president makes a good case, the public will go along. The president could have gotten support for a reserve call-up at the time, but the case diminished as time progressed."[6]

[4] Johnson, *The Vantage Point*, p. 396; personal interview with Walt W. Rostow, December 4, 1972; Wes Gallagher, "Foe Can't Stand Long War"; "Outlook Assessed by Westmoreland."

[5] Those present were Secretaries Rusk and Clifford, Generals Wheeler and Taylor, CIA Director Helms, Walt Rostow, George Christian, and Tom Johnson. Johnson, *The Vantage Point*, p. 399.

[6] Personal interview with Walt W. Rostow, December 4, 1972. See also Walt W. Rostow, *The United States in the World Arena*, pp. 511–515; Rostow, *The Diffusion of Power*, p. 520. The rally-round-the-flag phenomenon is also discussed (and confirmed) in John E. Mueller, "Presidential Popularity from Truman to Johnson," pp.

But the president was not prepared to take any drastic action at this time. In reviewing the long discussion of the previous day, Johnson indicated that he felt that he was "about to make a rather basic change in strategy." The president recognized that the United States was now making its further commitment to Vietnam dependent upon the Vietnamese themselves doing more. He apparently accepted this new direction and told Clifford "to take whatever steps are necessary" to increase the effectiveness of ARVN by providing more helicopters, additional M-16 rifles, and other equipment. "Let's give the South Vietnamese the best equipment we can," the President said. "It had become clear to all," Rostow recalled, ". . . that we couldn't send more Americans with M-16s over to Vietnam when the Vietnamese didn't have M-16s of their own. We had to produce enough M-16s to send to the Vietnamese rather than sending our own troops."[7]

[handwritten margin note: Change in tactics / equipment]

21–22; see also Kenneth N. Waltz, "Electoral Punishment and Foreign Policy Crisis," in James N. Rosenau, ed., *Domestic Sources of Foreign Policy*, p. 272; Tom Wicker, "In the Nation: Peace, It's Wonderful"; Richard E. Neustadt, *Presidential Power: The Politics of Leadership*, p. 100; Burns Roper, "The Public Looks at Presidents"; Nelson Polsby, *Congress and the Presidency*, p. 25; Richard J. Barnet, *The Roots of War*, p. 270. This phenomenon works in both directions. If the administration is using increasing force, the public will respond like hawks; if it is seeking peace, the public responds like doves. See John E. Mueller, "Trends in Popular Support for the Wars in Vietnam and Korea," pp. 368–369; also Seymour Lipset, "The President, the Polls, and Vietnam"; Sidney Verba et al., "Public Opinion and the War in Vietnam"; Milton J. Rosenberg et al., *Vietnam and the Silent Majority*, pp. 24–28. Thus, Rostow seems to misinterpret support for the president's deescalatory policies in March 1968 as being an increase in dove sentiment in the country. See Rostow, *The Diffusion of Power*, pp. 481–482; also Philip E. Converse and Howard Schuman, "Silent Majorities and the Vietnam War."

[7] Personal interview with Walt W. Rostow, December 4, 1972. Colt was the sole producer of M-16 rifles for the army and owned exclusive manufacturing and proprietary rights to this weapon. The company at first refused to license other manufacturers, and the army vacillated in securing these manufacturing rights and maintaining the security of the production base. The rights were not acquired by the army until June 30, 1967 when Colt was unable to produce enough

As the meeting drew to a close, the president told General Wheeler to inform General Westmoreland "to forget the 100,000 [*sic*]. Tell him 22,000 is all we can give at the moment."[8] There is strong evidence, however, that the president was not actually that definite on the troop issue. Apparently no message was sent to General Westmoreland informing him of this decision. And subsequent discussions among the president's advisors at the White House and in their soundings on Capitol Hill seemed to indicate that the question of sending large numbers of additional troops to Vietnam remained an open one.

Nevertheless, some doubt had been introduced into Johnson's mind concerning both the efficacy and the necessity for a large troop buildup in Vietnam. Johnson later told his advisors that they had moderated his judgment at the meeting on March 4. "At that time I had almost been ready to call up a large number of reserves not for Vietnam alone but to strengthen our overall military position; to ask Congress for the authority to call additional selected reservists; and to continue to push hard for the tax bill on that basis. My

---

rifles to meet urgent requirements in Vietnam. A competitive award to a second producer was scheduled for June 1968, with initial production scheduled for August 1969. Based upon the president's order of March 5, 1968, Deputy Secretary of Defense Nitze on March 6 directed the army to expand and accelerate production immediately. This led to awards to General Motors and Harrington and Richardson. In a prodigious feat of manufacturing, these two firms began delivering M-16 rifles to the army in November 1968, some twelve months ahead of schedule. Personal interview with J. F. Merritt, January 5, 1973. See also U.S., Congress, House of Representatives, Committee on Armed Services, *Report of the Special Subcommittee on the M-16 Rifle Program*; U.S., Congress, Senate, Committee on Armed Services, *Additional Procurement of M-16 Rifles*; U.S., Congress, House of Representatives, Committee on Armed Services. *Selected Aspects of M-16 Rifle Program Contracts*; U.S., Congress, House of Representatives, Committee on Armed Services. *Hearings Before the Special Subcommittee on the M-16 Rifle Program*; Charles W. Corddry, "Time, Not Price, Was Guide in Rifle Pacts, Army Says."

[8] Johnson, *The Vantage Point*, p. 399.

opinion had changed as a result of what I had heard from my advisors and what I saw happening on the ground in Vietnam."[9]

The totally negative approach of the Clifford report to any new negotiating initiative troubled the president. However, in discussing the subject with his advisors on March 4, he received little reassurance. Rusk described the possibility of peace talks as "bleak" at that moment. Philip Habib, the State Department representative who had accompanied General Wheeler to Saigon, had reported to the secretary that the universal opinion in Saigon seemed to be that the United States would be faced with a major crisis, given the environment in South Vietnam after the Tet offensive, if Hanoi were to accept the San Antonio formula and engage us in negotiations at that time.[10]

Since the first of the year, Nitze, Katzenbach, and Rostow had been working on a special committee at the undersecretary level devoted to developing, among other things, United States negotiating positions in case talks did begin. According to Nitze, this group had concluded that a peace initiative might be possible after the enemy's winter/spring offensive had been defeated, "no later than May or June."[11]

The United States, since the early spring of 1965, had indicated its willingness to engage in talks or negotiations with the enemy. But this readiness to negotiate had always been balanced by a need to negotiate from strength. Although some thought had been given to blocking out a negotiating strategy, little agreement on key negotiating issues had been reached, and almost no thought had been given to coordinating United States and South Vietnamese negotiating objectives. Thus, efforts to bring the United States and the North

9 Ibid., p. 406.
10 Johnson, *The Vantage Point*, p. 398; also Philip C. Habib, Memorandum to the Secretary of State, Subject: *Observations on the Situation in Vietnam*, February 28, 1968.
11 Personal interview with Major General Robert N. Ginsburgh, August 25, 1975.

Vietnamese to the negotiating table had always foundered on misunderstanding, obstinance, lack of coordination, mistrust, or military initiatives that indicated "lack of goodwill."[12]

Dean Rusk had been criticized for viewing Vietnam as essentially a military problem.[13] There was no doubt that the military aspects of the struggle in Vietnam received primary, if not exclusive, attention. This did not bother Rusk, however. He described his role as follows: "President Johnson used to say that Secretary McNamara was his right hand in terms of denying to the North Vietnamese the ability to conquer South Vietnam and that I was his left hand, trying to bring this matter to a conclusion by political processes."[14] Rusk saw himself as a personal advisor to the president rather than as a maker and advocate of a specific policy. He was more inclined to give the president the alternatives, let him make the decision, and then see that the decision was carried out.[15]

Rusk had attended only the initial meeting of the Clifford Task Force at the Pentagon, and had not returned to subse-

[12] Cooper, *The Lost Crusade*, Chapters 11–14; also Kraslow and Loory, *The Secret Search for Peace in Vietnam*. Personal interview with Major General Robert N. Ginsburgh, August 25, 1975.

[13] Roger Hilsman, *To Move a Nation: The Politics of Foreign Policy in the Administration of JFK*, p. 421; Cooper, *The Lost Crusade*, pp. 254–255; David Halberstam, *The Best and the Brightest*, p. 347; Stanley Hoffmann, *Gulliver's Troubles, Or the Setting of American Foreign Policy*, pp. 282–284; Henry Fairlie, *The Kennedy Promise: The Politics of Expectation*, pp. 322–324. As Hoffman points out, the problem of having a secretary of state forceful enough to keep political considerations from being displaced by purely military ones is not a new one. See Dean Acheson, *President at the Creation*, pp. 126, 158–159, 428, 430–431; Arthur M. Schlesinger, Jr., *A Thousand Days: John F. Kennedy in the White House*, pp. 199, 759–760, 868; Roland A. Paul, *American Military Commitments Abroad*.

[14] Personal interview with Dean Rusk, January 22, 1973. See also "Dean Rusk Looks Back on Vietnam"; John B. Henry II and William Espinosa, "The Tragedy of Dean Rusk," p. 186.

[15] Hilsman, *To Move a Nation*, pp. 35–36, 40–43; Joseph Kraft, "Washington Insight: The Enigma of Dean Rusk"; Henry and Espinosa, "The Tragedy of Dean Rusk," p. 180. Rusk did not come into office with this view. See Hilsman, *To Move a Nation*, pp. 15, 24–25.

quent meetings. He saved his advice for the only person that mattered, Lyndon Johnson. The secretary of state opposed the military's request for large additional forces. He felt that the military situation was in hand in Vietnam and that large increases in American forces would enable the South Vietnamese to avoid taking the measures necessary to revitalize their governmental and military machinery. As Rusk saw the situation: "I felt that we had enough force in Vietnam to do what was required. My own impression was that we had established a military position in South Vietnam by the end of 1967 which the North Vietnamese could not possibly have overrun by military action. I think they knew this in Hanoi; the Tet offensive in 1968 proved it."[16]

Rusk thought that President Johnson was wrong in asking General Westmoreland if any additional troops were needed: "It is in the very nature of the military to request more troops. General Marshall used to tell me: 'Give the generals one-half of the troops they ask for and then double their mission.' "[17] Rusk was also aware of the drain on the strategic reserve, but took a realistic view of this: "There was concern about the strategic reserve in this country, so I could understand those who wanted to rebuild it. But even there, I wasn't all that concerned with doing it right away. In one sense, the forces in Vietnam were a general reserve if they were needed in a place of higher priority. So I wasn't that concerned about the general reserve."[18]

Rusk also did not view General Wheeler's request for troops as an emergency measure designed to ward off disaster in Vietnam. "I had no real doubt about the capacity of our forces on the ground to deal with the situation," he stated. "South Vietnamese, US, and other allied main forces in South Vietnam were intact and had the capability of restoring the situation."[19] Rusk realized that the 206,000 men requested by the military was a contingency figure, partly related to the general reserve. "Under certain conditions, we might need

[16] Personal interview with Dean Rusk, January 22, 1973.
[17] Ibid.   [18] Ibid.   [19] Ibid.

forces up to that amount, but I thought those contingencies were remote."[20]

Rusk further believed that negotiations could not succeed until military operations by both the United States and South Vietnam had made it "pretty clear to North Vietnam that they would not be able to succeed militarily."[21] But he recognized that although the Tet offensive had been a military failure from the standpoint of the North Vietnamese, its impact would cause significant changes in the United States. "The political and psychological impact in the United States was very different. It could only lead to the conclusion that the Tet offensive was a brilliant success from the North Vietnamese point of view. Unhappily, differences on the home front in the United States almost certainly encouraged Hanoi to persist in the hope of obtaining politically what they could not get militarily."[22]

Thus Rusk felt that the only way to remove this problem from "the battlefield to the conference table" was to regain public confidence so that the United States could continue to exert military pressure on North Vietnam. He saw this military pressure as a necessary prelude to negotiations, and stated: "During one period they had little incentive to negotiate because they thought they were going to succeed militarily. During the remainder of the period they had little incentive to negotiate because they thought that divisions within the United States would make it unnecessary for them to do so."[23]

Thus, from Rusk's standpoint, negotiations with Hanoi would not be fruitful under the prevailing circumstances. North Vietnam had no incentive to negotiate following the psychological shock of Tet on the American people and, as has already been indicated, starting negotiations under the present circumstances could prove disastrous to the South

[20] Ibid.
[21] "Dean Rusk Looks Back on Vietnam."
[22] Personal interview with Dean Rusk, January 22, 1973.
[23] "Dean Rusk Looks Back on Vietnam."

Vietnamese government in its attempts to rally its people. But some initiative had to be taken to restore the administration's credibility and thereby make it domestically tolerable to continue the war until the enemy realized that he could not prevail militarily.

Rusk found his thinking mirrored in an article prepared by a group of British intellectuals, including Barbara Ward, which had been referred to him by the British ambassador to Washington, Sir Patrick Dean. The article attempted to describe an alternative to either United States withdrawal from South Vietnam or a massive invasion of the North, and indicated that the Communists had invented an alternative that the Americans should adopt: "It is called 'fighting and negotiating.' At some convenient point this spring, America should do two things simultaneously, stop the bombing of the North and mobilize more men for Vietnam. It should announce that it will talk at any time, appoint negotiators, appeal to world opinion, remind Hanoi of its offers to talk and conduct a major peace offensive. At the same time, it would reinforce its armies in the South and continue the talk of 'pacification.' "[24]

Rusk had forwarded this article to the president on March 4, prior to the report of the Clifford Task Force. This in itself was an unusual practice, so the president knew that Rusk took the article seriously. When, during the course of the discussion on March 4, Rusk suggested to the president that most of the bombing of North Vietnam could be stopped during the rainy season without great military risk, the president knew that Rusk had given this idea some thought. In the absence of any other negotiating recommendation, the president grasped at this possibility. "Really get on your horses on that," he told Rusk.[25]

The next day, at the White House luncheon meeting, Rusk proposed that the following paragraph be included in a speech the president would make on Vietnam in the near

[24] Johnson, *The Vantage Point*, p. 399.
[25] Ibid.; see also "Dean Rusk Looks Back on Vietnam."

future: "After consultation with our allies, I have directed that US bombing attacks on North Vietnam be limited to those areas which are integrally related to the battlefield. No reasonable person could expect us to fail to provide maximum support to our men in combat. Whether this step I have taken can be a step toward peace is for Hanoi to determine. We shall watch the situation carefully."[26]

Rusk then read a memorandum he had prepared which expanded upon and clarified this bombing-pause proposal. He viewed the partial cessation of bombing as an alternative to sending additional troops to Vietnam. He recommended that the action be announced without conditions. This would make the offer more attractive in two ways. First, if Hanoi rejected the gesture, then the United States, with increased public support, would have a free hand to continue the war as before. Second, if Hanoi made any positive response to the offer, which Rusk doubted would occur, then an unconditionally stated offer would have a better chance of leading to talks.

Rusk suggested, therefore, that his proposal should replace the San Antonio formula, with its complicated strictures of "not take advantage" and "prompt and productive" talks. The secretary of state urged that such "theological debates about words be avoided." Instead, the problem should be placed on the "de facto level of action." He added that it was important not to embroider the statement with all sorts of "conditions" or "assumptions." "Just take the action," he said, "and see whether anybody is able to make anything out of it."[27]

However, Rusk's memorandum made an implicit condition to the maintenance of any such bombing pause. A bombing pause would only be a "peace initiative" if the other side responded. The decision to resume the bombing would not be made until after Hanoi's intentions become evident. If the North Vietnamese failed to respond to the offer, either

---

[26] Johnson, *The Vantage Point*, p. 400.
[27] Ibid.; also *U.S.–Vietnam Relations*, IVC(7)(b), pp. 180–181.

by offering to enter into peace talks or by reciprocating militarily, the bombing could be resumed. Thus, the other side's reaction would not be prejudged. The United States would wait and see before deciding to resume bombing.[28]

Rusk's memorandum explicitly stated that the purpose of a limited bombing cutback was to offset growing public opposition to the war, but that it was also possible that there would be some favorable response from Hanoi. In any case, the memorandum argued, a partial stoppage of the bombing would not entail military risks at that time of the year. Weather conditions would cause a reduction in the bombing in any event. Rusk felt the northeastern monsoon season made it a good time to make this gesture. A partial cessation would not mean a major military sacrifice because most of the sorties were being flown in the southern part of North Vietnam during the rainy season. The redirection of the United States bombing effort to Laos during this period was taken for granted by the Joint Chiefs.[29]

In addition, the secretary of state included two conditions under which the United States bombing campaign would be resumed immediately: a major enemy attack on Khe Sanh or a second wave of attacks on the cities of South Vietnam. Rusk described his thoughts as follows: "I must confess that I thought bombing in the far north was expendable from a military point of view. I did not believe that the 5 percent of our sorties that were flown there were producing comparable effects on the battlefield compared to the cost."[30]

But Rusk, like the President, was opposed to a total halt in the bombing. "We had a sense of obligation to the fellow on the ground not to deprive him of support on the ground, in the DMZ, or on the Ho Chi Minh trail. In the absence of any serious indication that Hanoi would do business, a complete halt would make it rough on the fellows on the ground

---

[28] Personal interview with Dean Rusk, January 22, 1973.
[29] Personal interview with General Earle G. Wheeler, November 8, 1972; also Johnson, *The Vantage Point*, p. 400.
[30] Personal interview with Dean Rusk, January 22, 1973.

in South Vietnam. Thus, I was for a partial, not a complete, halt."[31]

Clifford apparently did not oppose Rusk's suggestion. However, he felt that the conditions for resuming the bombing should be made explicit and should be announced. But Rusk was adamant. "That won't work, this reciprocity won't work," he stated.[32]

The idea of a partial bombing pause as a means of inducing negotiations, of course, was not new in the administration. Previous holiday pauses in the bombings had been accompanied by offers to extend them if Hanoi indicated a willingness to negotiate. A pause in May 1965, and a thirty-seven day pause in December 1965 and January 1966, had been accompanied by a massive diplomatic effort to engage the North Vietnamese in talks.[33] Similar efforts, including a letter from President Johnson to Ho Chi Minh inviting him to indicate what reciprocity might be expected from a bombing halt, were made during the Tet truce of 1967.[34] All these bombing pauses had been greeted by North Vietnam with massive efforts to resupply its forces and a reiteration of its position that only unconditional cessation of the bombing could lead to talks.[35]

More recently, in May 1967, both Secretary of Defense McNamara and Walt Rostow had advocated to the president a bombing cessation north of the 20th parallel.[36] And in November 1967 McNamara had formally proposed to the president a cessation of the bombing of North Vietnam by

[31] Ibid.

[32] CBS interview with Lyndon Johnson.

[33] Johnson, *The Vantage Point*, pp. 136–137, 233–241; *U.S.–Vietnam Relations*, IVC(3), pp. 106–128; IVC(7)(a), pp. 20–50; Cooper, *The Lost Crusade*, pp. 291–296.

[34] Johnson, *The Vantage Point*, pp. 252–256; Cooper, *The Lost Crusade*, pp. 251–268; *U.S.–Vietnam Relations*, IVC(7)(b), pp. 3–8. For the text of the letters see Johnson, *The Vantage Point*, pp. 582–596.

[35] Melvin A. Gertov, "Hanoi on War and Peace," in John R. Boettiger, comp., *Vietnam and American Foreign Policy*, p. 62.

[36] Johnson, *The Vantage Point*, pp. 366–370; *U.S.–Vietnam Relations*, IVC(7)(b), pp. 43–53.

the end of the year. His reasons paralleled those to be presented by Rusk in March. McNamara wrote: "The bombing halt would have dual objectives. We would hope for a response from Hanoi, by some parallel reduction in its offensive activity, by a movement toward talks, or both. At a minimum, the lack of any response from Hanoi would demonstrate it is North Vietnam and not the United States that is blocking a peaceful settlement."[37]

Although Rusk had initially opposed the bombing pause of December 1965, he quickly came to the conclusion that such pauses were useful. In 1965 he had indicated that his first concern was to be able to demonstrate to the American people that we had done everything we could to find the way to a peaceful settlement. Second, he stated: "It is our deepest national purpose to achieve our goals by peace, not war. If there is one chance in ten, or twenty, that a step of this sort could lead to a settlement . . . I would take it." Finally, he thought bombing pauses would help place the responsibility for continuing the war where it rightly belonged, on Hanoi, "and on those who were saying that only our bombing of the North stood in the way of peace."[38]

Rusk continued to maintain this position in subsequent years. He believed his role was to seek a diplomatic solution to the war. His latest views on the bombing of North Vietnam had been set forth to the president in response to McNamara's November 1 memorandum. Rusk at that time had indicated his own dissatisfaction with the bombing as a way to peace. He suggested that the United States should carry out just enough bombing north of the 20th parallel to prevent North Vietnam's antiaircraft guns from being moved south and to keep large numbers of people occupied with repairing damages and maintaining communications so that they could not be sent south into combat. He felt, however, that we should "take the drama out of our bombing" by cut-

[37] Johnson, *The Vantage Point*, pp. 372–376.
[38] Johnson, *The Vantage Point*, p. 236; *U.S.–Vietnam Relations*, IVC(7)(a), pp. 23–26.

ting back on strikes in the Haiphong–Hanoi area. Rusk did not believe we should permit "a complete sanctuary in the northern part of North Vietnam and thereby eliminate this incentive for peace." He was therefore skeptical that an extended pause in the bombing as suggested by McNamara would lead to negotiations. His attitude toward such an extended pause was that "Hanoi would call any pause (i.e., not permanent) an ultimatum. We know of their 'fight and negotiate' strategy discussions. For those in the outside world pressing for a halt in the bombing, no pause would be long enough."[39]

For Johnson, a bombing pause was not an attractive peace proposal. The experience of the thirty-seven-day pause and the diplomatic initiatives that had accompanied it in December 1965–January 1966 influenced him for the remainder of his tenure. His two close confidants and unofficial advisors, Abe Fortas and Clifford, reportedly told him that the January bombing pause was his "worst mistake" in the Vietnam war. He was to refer to these fruitless diplomatic efforts of early 1966 again and again, both privately and publicly, whenever another pause or cessation of the bombing was suggested.[40] As the president explained it: "We had stopped the bombing, not once or twice, but eight different times from 1965 to the beginning of 1968. Five other times we had ruled out attacks on military targets in or around Hanoi and Haiphong for extended periods. The net result of all these bombing pauses was zero for us, because the enemy used every pause to strengthen its position, hastily pushing men and supplies and equipment down the roads of North Vietnam for massive infiltration into the South."[41]

Why, then, did Johnson give serious consideration to the Rusk proposal at this time? There seem to be two reasons. First, it was the only peace proposal available to him. The

[39] Johnson, *The Vantage Point*, pp. 376–377.
[40] Cooper, *The Lost Crusade*, pp. 295–296.
[41] Johnson, *The Vantage Point*, p. 241. For a list of the bombing pauses, see p. 578.

Clifford Task Force, to the president's obvious disappointment, offered no new peace initiatives. A total halt in the bombing did not seem to be a viable alternative in view of the military situation at Khe Sanh and in the northern portion of South Vietnam adjacent to the DMZ. Although a pause in the bombing did not appear to be an attractive offer to North Vietnam in view of Hanoi's continued insistence on a total cessation of the bombing as a condition for entering negotiations, it could possibly result in a peace offer if Hanoi had actually been as badly hurt militarily by its Tet offensive as Johnson's military commanders insisted. In any case, a bombing pause north of the 20th parallel would offer little military risk during the rainy season and might stop the deterioration in public support for the war.

Second, the proposal had been made by Rusk. Rusk was not in the habit of writing memoranda unless he had given considerable thought to the matter at hand. He stated his rationale as follows: "I didn't write a lot of memos for general circulation in the government. I did not circulate around the government a lot of hypothetical memoranda because I did not want to shape and in any way limit the freedom of discussion that ought to go on in government before decisions are made."[42] Thus, the president realized from the way Rusk had presented his suggestion and from the fact that he had prepared a written memorandum on it that Rusk was not just thinking aloud. As the president saw it: "He was a deliberate man, a judicious man, a careful man. And he didn't get on his horses as quick as I did on some things."[43]

Therefore, at the end of the meeting, Rusk gave a written copy of his proposal to Clifford so that it could be studied within the Defense Department. A cable was prepared for Ambassador Bunker the following day by William Bundy describing the proposal and asking for Bunker's judgment as to whether it could be sold to the South Vietnamese. But the president decided not to send this cable. He was concerned

[42] "Dean Rusk Looks Back on Vietnam."
[43] CBS interview with Lyndon B. Johnson.

that the proposal might become widely known and "destroyed before it had a fair trial."[44]

Other reasons were probably important to the president. Rejection by the South Vietnamese was a distinct possibility. In addition, Secretary Rusk had been called to testify before the Senate Foreign Relations Committee in open session on March 11. President Johnson has suggested that he wanted to protect his secretary of state from having to disclose the possibility of such an initiative under questioning by the less than sympathetic senators. This would have been difficult if a formal proposal had been sent to Saigon for consideration.[45]

Rusk's proposal was not greeted with enthusiasm in the Defense Department. Warnke, especially, was highly critical. Warnke, perhaps alone in government, felt that the San Antonio formula had been fulfilled by the North Vietnamese and that a bombing halt should be ordered on that basis. A partial cutback in the bombing, such as that proposed by Rusk, "was a pull-back from the San Antonio formula, and weakened it," Warnke felt. "As a consequence, I was against it."[46] Warnke felt that the Rusk proposal was merely a gesture designed to rally American and world opinion. He felt that such a gesture might well regain support for the president on the home front, but would not be enough to get North Vietnam to the negotiating table, and could spoil the opportunity for other peace initiatives for a long time in the future. He felt that a nonresponse from Hanoi would increase hawkish pressure on the president to resume the bombing, thus perpetuating an old policy he had long felt to be bankrupt.[47]

Clifford was going through an intensive period of education and of soul searching. He was beginning to be convinced that the military course being pursued by the United States in Vietnam was endless as well as hopeless, and would lead

[44] Johnson, *The Vantage Point*, p. 401.
[45] CBS interview with Lyndon B. Johnson.
[46] Personal interview with Paul Warnke, November 17, 1972.
[47] Ibid.

neither to victory or peace. He felt that the Rusk proposal was not conciliatory and would not lead to negotiations. It would merely mean the intensified use of force against North Vietnam when North Vietnam rejected the offer.[48] Yet only the day before, Clifford, through his Task Force, had recommended a "seasonal step up" in the bombing of the North. Where was the strategic concept that would break this vicious circle and put the nation on the road to peace? Clifford's search for such a concept continued.

[48] Personal interview with Clark Clifford, November 16, 1972.

NINE

✿✿✿

The Climate of Opinion

PUBLIC opinion studies and polls have shown how little public support for the war changed between the fall of 1967 and the spring of 1968 despite the momentous events that occurred during that period. Overall support for the war itself showed small swings closely tied to how well the war was going, but the majority of the public clung to a position of support.[1] Indeed, the crisis of Tet caused an initial upward surge in public support for the war (figure 1).[2] But the battles at Tet also reinforced the feeling of the American people that the war was bogged down, that a military solution would not be found in the near future. And this view of a military stalemate continued to be reflected in the media. The leaders

[1] Hazel Erskine, "The Polls: Is War a Mistake?" pp. 135, 143–150; Louis Harris, "Confidence Shaken But Majority Rejects Vietnam Pullout"; "Sizing Up the Public on the War"; Mueller, "Trends in Popular Support for the Wars in Korea and Vietnam," p. 365; Mueller, "Presidential Popularity from Truman to Johnson," pp. 28–30; Jerome H. Skolnick, *The Politics of Protest*, p. 44; Cantril, *The American People, Viet-Nam and the Presidency*, pp. 5–7. The definition of "support" for the war is, of course, vital. Some commentators noticed a large increase in the number of doves after March 1968, while others interpret this as public support for the president's bombing pause and peace initiative. See Converse and Schuman, "Silent Majorities and the Vietnam War," pp. 20–21; Harlan Hahn, "Correlates of Public Sentiment About War: Local Referenda on the Vietnam Issue," p. 1,189; Gallup Opinion Index, "New Wave of Pessimism on Vietnam Conflict Found Throughout Nation," p. 6; Gallup Opinion Index, "Sharp Increase Found in Number of Doves," p. 15; Rostow, *Diffusion of Power*, pp. 481–483; Rosenberg et al., *Vietnam and the Silent Majority*, pp. 38–39; John E. Mueller, *War, Presidents and Public Opinion*, p. 57.

[2] The chart is from Mueller, "Trends in Popular Support for the Wars in Korea and Vietnam," p. 364. Used by permission. See also Louis Harris, "War Support Spurts After Tet Attacks"; "Poll Finds Rise in War Support From 61% to 74% in 2 Months."

194

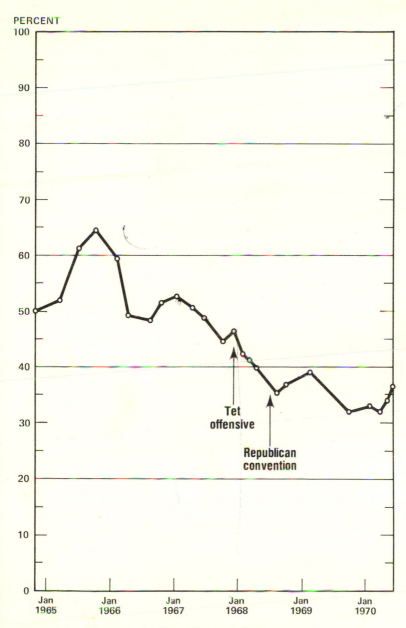

Figure 1. Support for the Vietnam War

of American opinion, the commentators, editorial writers, columnists, educators, and business leaders, many of whom had been uneasy and uncertain before, now became convinced that the war was being lost or, at the very best, could not be won without a vast expenditure of additional resources.[3]

Thus the shock and anger of the first days of Tet soon gave way to a sense of futility and despair among this vocal section of the population and colored the atmosphere in which decisions were made. The view propounded by these leaders of opinion was that the country was becoming increasingly divided over and disenchanted with the current Vietnam strategy and would no longer settle for more of the same, with no indication of an eventual end to the conflict. The feeling grew that the cost of the war was no longer worth the goals for which it was being fought.

There is some dispute as to the objectivity of both press and television coverage of the Tet battles, as well as to the influence that this coverage had on the opinion of the mass of the American public.[4] It has been alleged that the media re-

[3] Rostow, *Diffusion of Power*, pp. 484–496; Sidney Verba and Richard A. Brady, "Participation, Preferences, and the War in Vietnam"; Rosenberg et al., *Vietnam and the Silent Majority*, pp. 30–33; Joseph Kraft, "Short-Term Swings of Opinion Blind LBJ to Basic U.S. Mood"; Louis Harris, "U.S. Reacts With Sober Determination to Step-Up of War."

[4] Oberdorfer, *Tet*, pp. 239–241; Michael J. Arlen, *Living Room War*, pp. 168–173, 111–122; Ben H. Bagdikian, *The Information Machine*; Douglas Cater and Philip L. Geyelin, *American Media: Adequate or Not?*; Edith Efron, *The News Twisters*, p. 47; Rod Holmgren and William Norton, eds., *The Mass Media Book*; Warren K. Agee, ed., *Mass Media in a Free Society*; Arthur Krock, *The Consent of the Governed*; Robert MacNeil, *The People Machine*; James B. Reston, *The Artillery of the Press: Its Influence on American Foreign Policy*; William L. Rivers, *The Adversaries*; Donald F. Roberts and Wilbur Schramm, eds., *The Process and Effects of Mass Communication*; Robert Stein, *Media Power: Who Is Shaping Your Picture of the World?*; Alan Wells, ed., *Mass Media and Society*; Edmund Ions, "Dissent in America: The Constraints on Foreign Policy," pp. 8–12; George Will, "Does TV Bias Matter?"; "Blood on the Screen"; "Living Room War—Impact of TV"; Robin Day, "Troubled Reflections of a TV Journalist," pp. 78–88; Richard Harwood, "Power of the Press: Myth or Reality?"; Bernard C. Cohen, "For-

ported the initial destructive Viet Cong attacks in detail, but failed to follow up and emphasize the rather quick recovery of U.S. and South Vietnamese forces and the rather substantial military defeat suffered, in the end, by the Viet Cong forces.

In any case, the shock and carnage of the first Tet attacks were brought home vividly to the American public by television. The opinion of a large number of Americans as to what the results of the Tet offensive implied for United States policy in Vietnam was formed by this extensive and dramatic television coverage. Television news analyses, as opposed to strict reporting, also had a substantial influence. The analysis presented by Walter Cronkite of CBS News on the evening of February 27th was particularly dramatic:

> It seems now more certain than ever that the bloody experience of Vietnam is to end in a stalemate. This summer's almost certain standoff will either end in real give-and-take negotiations or terrible escalation; and for every means we have to escalate, the enemy can match us, and that applies to invasion of the North, the use of nuclear weapons, or the mere commitment of one hundred or two hundred or three hundred thousand more American troops to the battle. And with each escalation, the world comes close to the brink of cosmic disaster.
>
> To say that we are closer to victory today is to believe, in the face of the evidence, the optimists who have been wrong in the past. To suggest we are on the edge of defeat is to yield to unreasonable pessimism. To say that we are mired in stalemate seems the only realistic, yet unsatisfactory, conclusion.[5]

---

eign Policy Makers and the Press"; Benjamin D. Singer, "Violence, Protest, and War in Television News: The U.S. and Canada Compared"; Peter Braestrup, *Big Story: How the American Press and Television Reported and Interpreted the Crisis of Tet 1968 in Viet Nam and Washington.*

[5] For the analysis that led Cronkite to this decision, see Oberdorfer, *Tet*, pp. 246–251.

Presidential Press Secretary George Christian later stated that when Cronkite made this statement, "the shock waves rolled through the Government."[6] Rostow has claimed that "the massive uninhibited reporting of the complex war was generally undistinguished and often biased." He also admits, on the other hand, that military and civil authorities were not effective in presenting a "clear and persuasive" picture of the course of events in Vietnam.[7] The assertions of the president, his senior aides, and his military commanders had been rendered suspect by their previous optimism and by the obvious destruction being wrought upon the people and cities of South Vietnam. The objectives of United States policy began to be questioned and the cost began to appear too high in relation to the likely results.

Important segments of the American press reflected this outlook. James Reston of the *New York Times* asked, "What is the end that justifies this slaughter? How will we save Vietnam if we destroy it in the battle?"[8] The *Wall Street Journal* asked, "Are developments on the ground making hash of our original, commendable objectives? . . . If practically nothing is to be left of government or nation, what is there to be saved for what?" The editorial bluntly suggested: "We think the American people should be getting ready to accept, if they haven't already, the prospect that the whole Vietnam effort may be doomed; it may be falling apart beneath our feet. The actual military situation may be making academic the philosophical arguments for the intervention in the first place."[9] In a biting piece of satire, the humorist Art Buchwald likened the situation to the Little Big Horn, with General Custer issuing optimistic statements concerning high

---

[6] William T. Small, *To Kill a Messenger*, p. 123. Also Lawrence Laurent, "Walter Cronkite Speaks Out on Vietnam."

[7] Rostow, *Diffusion of Power*, p. 502.

[8] James Reston, "Washington: The Flies That Captured the Flypaper"; also Gay Talese, *The Kingdom and the Power*, p. 497.

[9] "The Logic of the Battlefield." See also Min S. Yee, "The U.S. Press and Its Agony of Appraisal"; John W. Fenton, "Switches by Press on War Reported."

enemy casualties and indicating that the battle "had just turned the corner and he could now see the light at the end of the tunnel."[10]

These themes continued to appear in the newspapers and spread to the leading news magazines. *Atlantic* and *Harper's* devoted entire issues to Vietnam.[11] On March 11, writing in *Newsweek*, Walter Lippmann stated that the possibility of a United States "defeat" in Vietnam was causing a shock throughout the country. This shock was all the greater, Lippmann concluded, because it was so unexpected:

> Three months after General Westmoreland came home last autumn the Army is on the defensive. Three months after our Ambassador in Saigon came home to reassure us, the whole political program in the villages and the cities is in ruins. . . . Lyndon Johnson thinks he is fighting a limited war because he does not escalate as fast as some of the generals would like him to. The fact is that his war aims are unlimited: they promise the pacification of all of Asia. For such unlimited ends it is not possible to win a war with limited means. Because our aims are limitless, we are sure to be "defeated."[12]

Time magazine, in its edition of March 15, wrote that "increasingly intelligent debate at home concerns formulas that would lead to some form of disengagement. . . . It indicates that for the US, 1968 has brought home the awareness that victory in Vietnam—or even a favorable settlement—may simply be beyond the grasp of the world's greatest power."[13]

Focus to this growing dissatisfaction with the American effort in Vietnam was provided by a startlingly accurate ac-

[10] Art Buchwald, " 'We Have Enemy on the Run' Says Gen. Custer at Big Horn."

[11] Henry Raymont, "Harpers and Atlantic Put Out 'Vietnam' Issues"; Dan Wakefield, "Supernation At Peace and War," pp. 39–105; Norman Mailer, "The Steps of the Pentagon," pp. 47–142.

[12] Walter Lippmann, "Walter Lippmann on Defeat," p. 25.

[13] "The War."

count, published in the *New York Times* on March 10, of the troop request from Vietnam and of the policy reassessment that was being conducted within the administration. The story also made clear the growing doubt of many administration officials about the course of United States policy in South Vietnam. Written by Neil Sheehan and Hedrick Smith, the story stated:

General William C. Westmoreland has asked for 206,-000 more American troops for Vietnam, but the request has touched off a divisive internal debate within high levels of the Johnson Administration.

A number of sub-Cabinet civilian officials in the Defense Department, supported by some senior officials in the State Department, have argued against General Westmoreland's plea for a 40 percent increase in his forces "to regain the initiative" from the enemy. . . .

The contention of these high ranking officials is that an American increase will bring a matching increase by North Vietnam, thereby raising the level of violence without giving the allies the upper hand. . . .

The President has not yet decided on the question of substantial increases in American forces in Vietnam. . . . Nonetheless, the scope and depth of the internal debate within the Government reflect the wrenching uncertainty and doubt in this capital about every facet of the war left by the enemy's dramatic wave of attacks at Tet, the Asian New Year holiday, six weeks ago. More than ever this has left a sense of weariness and irritation over the war. Officials themselves comment in private about widespread and deep changes in attitudes, a sense that a watershed has been reached and that its meaning is just now beginning to be understood. . . .

But at every level of Government there is a sense that the conflict, if expanded further, can no longer be called "a limited war." Officials acknowledge that any further American involvement carries serious implications for the civilian life of the nation—not only the call-up of military reserves and enactment of a tax increase, but problems with the budget, the economy and the balance of payments.[14]

Sheehan and Smith then went on to describe with amazing accuracy the position taken by the Defense civilians in the deliberations of the Clifford Task Force.

The effect of the story was electric. As Hedrick Smith recalled:

> The story broke in the *Times*' early editions on the Saturday night of the Gridiron Club dinner [March 9], where the Washington journalistic elite were all gathered. I was there as a guest of James Reston. At about 10:00 P.M., the news of the story hit the room. It moved like wind through a field of wheat. It really had an impact, and people reacted. George Christian [presidential press secretary] was surrounded by reporters. I could physically see the impact of this story. It was one of the greatest journalistic thrills I've ever had—actually to see a live audience respond to a major story that I had helped report and write.[15]

The story, having been brought to the attention of the Washington press corps in so dramatic a fashion, was promptly picked up by other newspapers and by the end of the next day had reached from one end of the country to the other. The article, which was precise, accurate, and difficult to refute, increased public skepticism concerning our policy in Vietnam. If things were really going so well and if the Tet battles had been such a great victory as the administration continued to proclaim, why, the public asked, was it necessary to send an additional 200,000 American troops to Vietnam?

This skepticism was reinforced as other influential media

[14] Neil Sheehan and Hedrick Smith, "Westmoreland Requests 206,-000 More Men, Stirring Debate in Administration."
[15] Personal interview with Hedrick Smith, October 13, 1975.

voices spoke out strongly against the proposed course in Vietnam. The same evening that the story appeared (March 10), NBC television concluded a special program on Vietnam with the following comment: "Today, if published reports are correct, the President has before him a request for another two hundred thousand men to help restore the situation to what it was. This has brought warnings the enemy will match any new force we put into the field. All that would be changed would be the capacity for destruction. . . . Laying aside all other arguments, the time is at hand when we must decide whether it is futile to destroy Vietnam in order to save it."[16]

The *New York Times* story, as Rostow recalled "churned up the whole eastern establishment and created a false issue. It caused an unnecessary crisis and distorted things. It overrode the hopeful news and had quite substantial effects on public opinion. It gave a false picture of the situation."[17]

President Johnson, of course, was furious at the news leak. He knew the effect this would have on public and congressional critics of the war. The president suspected that the story had been leaked by low-level Pentagon civilians in order to put pressure on him to see things their way. He also suspected some political motivation, since the article appeared two days before the New Hampshire primary.[18]

But the president was mistaken. The story had been pieced together, as most such stories are, from a variety of sources, and the very multiplicity and diversity of these sources indicated the great controversy at all levels of the executive branch as well as in Congress that had been engendered by the troop request. The initial indication of the struggle within

[16] *Frank McGee Sunday Report*, March 10, 1968, quoted in Oberdorfer, *Tet*, p. 273.

[17] Personal interview with Walt W. Rostow, December 4, 1972. See also Chalmers M. Roberts, "War is Undergoing Searching Scrutiny"; Frederick Taylor, "Request for More Vietnam Troops Studied by White House: Some Oppose Any Buildup."

[18] Johnson, *The Vantage Point*, p. 402.

the Pentagon had indeed come from a Pentagon official. As Edwin L. Dale, Jr., economics reporter in the Washington bureau of the *New York Times*, recalled: "I was having cocktails at the home of Congressman Bill Moorhead. We were classmates at Yale and close friends. I got into a conversation with Townsend Hoopes, who had been a class ahead of us at Yale. He disclosed to me in this conversation that there was a group forming in the Pentagon that was beginning to resist sending more troops to Vietnam. He told me nothing more, nothing classified."[19]

This conversation reached the ears of Sheehan and Smith at the *Times*' Washington bureau, and they went to work to develop the story. As Sheehan described their reaction: "On Monday morning Ed Dale told us about this conversation he had had with a senior administration official, subcabinet level, who had made very derogatory remarks about another troop request from the military and who had indicated that a big argument was going on in the administration over this request. It had been clear to Smith and me that something was up, that there was some internal dissent about Tet. This remark by Dale, given the climate of opinion, was enough to provoke us into making serious inquiries."[20]

Within minutes of starting these inquiries, confirmation of the troop request and the debate within the administration was obtained from quite different sources on Capitol Hill. Sheehan called a staff aide of a conservative senator, a hawk on the war and a good friend of the military. As he recalled:

> I used the reporter's technique of implying precise knowledge, and he told me instantly that General Westmoreland had come in with a request for "a couple of hundred thousand" troops. He gave an indication of the fight going on between the Joint Staff, who supported the request, and the Defense civilians, who didn't want to send the troops. Simultaneously, Smith called one of his sources on Capitol

[19] Personal interview with Edwin L. Dale, Jr., October 21, 1975.
[20] Personal interview with Neil Sheehan, October 20, 1975.

Hill and came up with a precise figure of 206,000 men, but we were uncertain whose figure this was, whether it had originated with Westmoreland or the Joint Chiefs of Staff. I then went to other sources and got a little piece of the argument from one and ran it by another. No one individual ever gave the full story, and some didn't realize how much they did tell me by denying or confirming my statements. It was not until Friday, however, that I could confirm that the 206,000-man request was Westmoreland's figure, that it had come from him. We were able to write definitely at that point that Westmoreland had asked for another 206,000 troops. That made a hard news lead on which to hang the larger story of the policy debate which the request had provoked.[21]

Although Smith had obtained a precise troop request figure immediately, he viewed the policy debate within the administration as the more interesting and important part of the story. He recalled: "I got the precise figure, and Neil confirmed that it had come from Westmoreland. There were two essential lines of information which hit us simultaneously from two different sets of sources, the tremendous size of the request and the debate within the administration. I was more impressed with the second element, thought it to be much more interesting, and kept working on it. If we hadn't quickly gotten confirmation of the debate, the story on the troop request alone would have been a one-column story in the middle of the week."[22]

[21] Ibid.

[22] Personal interview with Hedrick Smith, October 13, 1975. See also Braestrup, *Big Story*. For speculation that Daniel Ellsberg was the ultimate source of the news story, see Jack Anderson, "Daniel Ellsberg: The Other News Leak." Hedrick Smith had the following comment: "I'm skeptical, knowing where the information came from, that Daniel Ellsberg had anything to do with it. Although I don't know the ultimate source from whom my sources got the story, I know that Ellsberg was not a direct source." Both Smith and Sheehan, in personal interviews, denied that their story was politically motivated or had any connection with the New Hampshire primary. It appeared when it did, they state, only for pragmatic and competi-

How did these congressional (and other) sources learn of the troop request and the debate within the administration? As Sheehan later speculated:

> The story was all over Capitol Hill on both sides, hawk and dove. Indeed, Lyndon Johnson might have been partly responsible. He talked regularly on the phone to Senator Russell. My principal source was on the staff of a senator not unacquainted with Russell, and one who shared his views. My impression was that senior military people were trying their Capitol Hill contacts to gain support for the troop request. They were talking to Westmoreland's friends on the Hill to go to bat for him. On the other side, there was profound disillusionment and disagreement with our policy. Some of the junior military people to whom I talked were very disturbed that Westmoreland had asked for additional troops at that point. They thought it was the worst possible thing to do psychologically. So people were willing to talk. That's why we could put the story together in such detail.[23]

William G. Miller, assistant to Senator John Sherman Cooper, described the situation as follows: "There are fifty senators who have had more direct experience in foreign and military affairs than does the political leadership in any administration. As far as information on key issues in which the senators are vitally interested goes, if there was any illusion that what was going on could be kept from Congress, it was indeed an illusion. There is an interlocking network based on long-standing close relationships between Congress and key people in the bureaucracy at all levels which kept Congress fully informed."[24]

Disenchantment with the war had been growing in Con-

---

tive reasons: getting the facts as nearly complete as possible and getting the story out on Sunday to beat the competition of the weekly news magazines.

[23] Personal interview with Neil Sheehan, October 20, 1975.

[24] Personal interview with William G. Miller, September 30, 1975.

gress since the spring of 1967, reflecting the growing distaste for the war throughout the country.[25] A large number of legislators realized that the war was a stalemate with no early hope for victory. General Westmoreland's visit to Congress in November had been designed to reverse this trend, and had succeeded for a time in abating the surge against the war policy being pursued in Vietnam.

But the Tet offensive again raised the issue of United States policy in Vietnam and renewed the antiwar sentiment, especially in the Senate. The Tet attacks confirmed many senators' doubts about the direction and cost of the American effort in Vietnam and also brought similar doubts to many fence-sitters and supporters of the war. Miller described the situation as follows: "Tet was a dramatic episode in reaction against the continuing war that had been building for a long time. To some senators, reports from the president that things were going well in Vietnam were regarded as a studied rejection and an affront to them. It was not clear to the senators that Lyndon Johnson did not propose to continue the buildup in Vietnam as recommended by his military advisors, and to them this had become an intolerable policy."[26]

Of special concern to many legislators was the fact that the president had entered into a war and had deployed over half a million men into combat with what they felt was inadequate consultation with the Congress. They were determined to have a stronger voice in future decisions and were determined to be consulted before any decision was made to increase troop strength in Vietnam significantly.

A number of prominent senators had interrupted debate on civil rights on March 7 to make this clear to the president. The chief issue, said Senate Foreign Relations Commit-

---

[25] Don Oberdorfer, "The 'Wobble' in the War on Capitol Hill"; David S. Broder, "Young House Members Seek Over-All Viet Strategy Review"; "The List Grows."

[26] Personal interview with William G. Miller, September 30, 1975.

tee Chairman J. William Fulbright, "is the authority of the Administration to expand the war without the consent of Congress and without any debate or consideration by Congress."[27] This view was echoed by his colleagues. "I think we must insist upon that," stated Senator Clifford Case. "I think we cannot any longer evade a responsibility of a share in the decision. . . ."[28] "I think it would be a mistake," Senator Robert Kennedy declared, ". . . for the President to take a step toward escalation of the conflict . . . without having the support and understanding of the Senate, and of the American people."[29] Senate Majority Leader Mike Mansfield, no foe of the president, was also concerned. "We are in the wrong place and we are fighting the wrong kind of war," he stated, while crediting the president with having "tried hard and vigorously and consistently to find a way to the negotiating table."[30]

The *New York Times* article appeared the day before Secretary of State Rusk was scheduled to testify before the Senate Foreign Relations Committee. The members of the committee respected and understood Rusk. They felt that, although he was in error in continuing to support the war in view of its impact on the country, he had maintained his integrity and had never lied to them.[31] Thus, the chairman, in an unusual statement, noted at the outset of the hearings:

> I know that you understand, and that those in this room and the public at large will understand, that the discussion

[27] *Congressional Record*, p. 5,645. See also John W. Finney, "War Doubts in Senate"; Lyle Denniston, "Senators Demand Voice in Viet Troop Buildup"; John W. Finney, "Criticism of War Widens in Senate on Build-up Issue."

[28] *Congressional Record*, p. 5,656.

[29] Ibid., p. 5,647.   [30] Ibid., p. 5,659.

[31] Personal interview with William G. Miller, December 1, 1972. However, the committee had been critical of Rusk for previously refusing to testify on Vietnam in open session. See John W. Finney, "Senate Panel to Press Rusk for a Debate on War"; "Mansfield Acts to End Row on Rusk Refusal"; "Rusk's TV Appearance Provokes Senate Panel"; "Mansfield Backs Rusk on Secrecy."

between you and the committee about the foreign aid program in general and about Vietnam in particular is not inspired in any way by any personal animus toward you. Every member of this committee has a high regard for you personally. All of us—and I particularly—recognize that few officials in Washington today have performed their duty to their country with greater devotion and energy than you have. The fact that many of us disagree with your views in no way implies that we do not have a profound respect for your intelligence and integrity and that we do not admire your devotion and sense of duty.[32]

But the senators were also aware of the impact of the media and Rusk's testimony was televised live. During his two-day grilling, Rusk testified for a total of six and one-half hours on March 11 and for four and one-half hours on March 12. This was the most prolonged questioning of a cabinet officer ever broadcast to the American people.[33]

Rusk sidestepped all attempts to pin him down on a possible increase in troops or other elements of future Vietnam strategy. "I think it would not be right for me to speculate about numbers or possibilities," he stated, "until the President has had a chance to look at all the information and consult with his advisors."[34] Rusk stated that although "there is no specific recommendation in front of the President at the present time, . . . [the] entire situation is under consideration from A to Z. . . . The facts and problems and opportunities are being looked at, but I can't speculate about decisions that have not been made or conclusions that have not been reached. . . . We are looking at the situation, studying it from every angle but we have not come to conclusions

[32] U.S., Congress, Senate, Committee on Foreign Relations, *Hearings, Foreign Assistance Act of 1968, Part I–Vietnam*, p. 1 (hereafter cited as *Hearings, Foreign Assistance Act of 1968*).

[33] Johnson, *The Vantage Point*, p. 403. Also personal interview with William G. Miller, December 1, 1968.

[34] *Hearings, Foreign Assistance Act of 1968*, p. 41.

and the President does not have specific—and that means detailed factual—action recommendations in front of him at the present moment."[35]

Although he was not questioned on this point by the committee, Secretary Rusk chose to repeat his statement of February 14 concerning the probability of negotiations with North Vietnam. A flurry of intensive diplomatic explorations in January and early February had led to speculation about the possibility of negotiations. Soundings by government leaders in India, the Soviet Union, Italy, and France, and by Secretary General Thant of the United Nations with North Vietnamese representatives had encouraged what the administration viewed as false hopes for such talks. Rusk's statement in February had sought to dampen these rising expectations and seemed to signify that the administration had given up hope of entering talks in the near future: "At no time has Hanoi indicated publicly or privately that it will refrain from taking military advantage of any cessation of the bombing of North Vietnam. Nor has it shown any interest in preliminary discussions to arrange a general cease-fire."[36]

In his testimony before the committee, Rusk volunteered a similar statement, probably for the same reason—to discourage speculation that peace talks were imminent. To the committee, Rusk stated, "It is quite clear from our recent contacts with Hanoi that they would not accept a partial cessation of the bombing as a step toward peace in any way, shape or form." But the secretary left the door open for further administration attempts to enter into peace talks. He told the committee: "That does not mean that, as we

[35] Ibid., pp. 41, 99. This was reiterated and further explained for the committee on March 30, 1968, by General David M. Shoup. See U.S., Congress, Senate, Committee on Foreign Relations, *Present Situation in Vietnam*, p. 12.

[36] "Rusk's Statement of February 15, 1968 on Probability of Peace Talks"; Hedrick Smith, "Rusk Says Hanoi Spurns U.S. Terms for Negotiation"; Henry Tanner, "Thant Confers With Hanoi Representative"; Robert C. Doty, "Fanfani Saw 2 Hanoi Aides."

move into the future, we won't consider examining that and all other proposals that we can get our hands on or that we can think up ourselves."[37]

The televised Senate hearings, which were characterized by Senator Mundt as an "educational forum," served that purpose in that they brought home to the administration and to the American people the growing dissent within the committee and within the Congress concerning the direction of United States policy in Vietnam and the determination of the Senate to be consulted on any further troop deployment to Vietnam. *Time* magazine stated that the session had "laid out, occasionally with eloquence, the basic positions of the Administration and its less extreme critics." But the hearings also presented to the nation the theme that Rusk reiterated time and time again—the theme that this country must stand by its commitments.[38]

Meanwhile, the education of Clark Clifford, which had begun and had proceeded so rapidly in the Pentagon, was continuing on Capitol Hill. Subsequent to the report of the Clifford Task Force, the new secretary, often accompanied by General Wheeler, undertook an active schedule of meetings with congressional leaders, especially with members of the Senate and House Armed Services Committees, in order to gauge opinion on Capitol Hill.

This opinion quickly became evident. "They were loath to a reserve call-up," General Wheeler recalled.[39] Clifford was especially impressed with the views of Senator Russell, the influential chairman of the Senate Armed Services Commit-

[37] *Hearings, Foreign Assistance Act of 1968*, p. 25.

[38] "Standoff." See also David Lawrence, "Implications in Quizzing Rusk"; Chalmers M. Roberts, "Vietnam Doubts, Misgivings Persist"; "Impervious to Reality"; "Rusk Turns Bear"; "As Mr. Rusk Has Been Saying . . ."; "Contribution of the Hearings"; Clayton Fritchey, "Rusk Commitment Thesis Lambasted"; Crosby S. Noyes, "Views of Rusk, Fulbright Panel Irreconcilable"; Joseph Kraft, "The Dean Rusk Show."

[39] Personal interview with General Earle G. Wheeler, November 8, 1972.

tee, who thought we had made a mistake getting into Vietnam in the first place.[40] "The more I got into it, the more I began to reach the decision that Senator Russell was right, that we shouldn't have gone in in the first place," Clifford recalled.[41] Senator Henry Jackson later recalled his sessions with Clifford: "About four of us blocked an attempt, right after Tet, to get a quarter million more troops out there. I opposed it, because I said we must start to wind this thing down. . . . That's a bit of history that has never been discussed at any great length. They were not committee meetings. We had discussions on it and we opposed it—Senator Russell, Senator Stennis, Clark Clifford."[42]

Senator Jackson believed this congressional opposition was decisive in Clifford's thinking at this time. "We had a series of lunches," Jackson recalled:

> The chairman of the Joint Chiefs of Staff and Clark Clifford met with Senators Stennis, Russell, Young, Margaret Chase Smith, and myself. We just made it very clear that we just couldn't support a large increase in the number of troops in Vietnam. Clifford and Wheeler presented it jointly, in fairness, and said that it was only analysis at that time. Clifford was skeptical, he couldn't see any end to it. Our reaction was that he would have to depend on us and that we wouldn't support it. I would suspect that the reaction he got from us was decisive in his decision making. If we wouldn't support it, who would? Clifford was dismayed. Our reaction was definitely a part of his thinking, and must have been one of the decisive factors that influenced him.[43]

[40] For some of Senator Russell's views, see Theodore Draper, *Abuse of Power*, pp. 153–155 and Joseph C. Goulden, "Johnson Strategists Ponder Crisis Over War Escalation."

[41] Personal interview with Clark Clifford, November 28, 1972.

[42] "Interview with Senator Henry M. Jackson."

[43] Personal interview with Senator Henry M. Jackson, March 25, 1973. See also Brigadier General S.L.A. Marshall, "New Defense Secretary's Flexibility Lights Up the Senate."

Senator Margaret Chase Smith had a different reaction. She recalled these meetings as follows:

> I had the very definite impression that Secretary Clifford and President Johnson were trying to get key members of Congress to make the decision and take the responsibility politically (at least share it). My reaction was that, since only the President had all of the information and since Congress could not possibly know as much as the President on what was needed, this was not feasible. Key members of Congress could only give their individual reaction to what was told them. I was not sure that the whole story was told to them and subsequent events support my doubt on this score.
>
> My individual reaction was that, with the loss of so many men and the huge expenditures, we could not abruptly withdraw and pull out and that if a few more men would produce success I would support a small addition of troops being sent. . . . I was not loath to a Reserve call-up. On the contrary, I felt that the Reserve should be called up for that was its purpose and mission. . . . I reasoned that as the war continued at an indecisive pace resulting from a limited effort it would increasingly touch more American families with the loss of lives of their sons and husbands and consequently the war would grow increasingly unacceptable to them.[44]

Senator Mansfield also met with Clifford, although he does not recall seeing General Wheeler during this time. He recalled these meetings in the following manner: "I respected his concern for the way things were going and the need for finding some solution to the war in Indochina. He was, of course, aware of how I felt about our involvement from the very beginning and all I did was encourage him to do everything he possibly could to bring about an end to the war."[45]

[44] Personal correspondence from Senator Margaret Chase Smith, August 31, 1973.

[45] Personal correspondence from Senator Mike Mansfield, May 21, 1973.

Congress was also impressed by continued expressions of optimism from General Westmoreland's headquarters in Saigon. As a result of his meetings with members of Congress, Clifford had General Wheeler, on March 8, cable General Westmoreland to the effect that optimistic statements such as ones made by a "senior military spokesman" and published by the *New York Times* on March 7, had an unfortunate impact in Congress "in connection with your request for additional forces." The chairman stated, "That request would be hard, perhaps impossible, to sell if we do not adopt a sober and conservative attitude as to the political, economic and psychological situation in South Vietnam."[46]

General Westmoreland responded the same day with a somewhat testy cable indicating that he was "the senior military spokesman referred to," but stating he would conform to the secretary's guidance "consistent with intellectual honesty as to my appraisal of the situation."[47] This exchange of cables was further evidence of the difference in Saigon and Washington's views of the Tet offensive. General Westmoreland, concerning this guidance from Washington, stated: "I was a little nonplussed. It seemed to be rather inconsistent. Here I was being accused of asking for reinforcements on an emergency basis, and yet I was being told not to be optimistic when I was trying to make an objective appraisal of the situation."[48]

In the meantime, Clifford had been asked to testify before the Fulbright Committee immediately following the testimony of the secretary of state. But Clifford, still uncertain as to the depth of his commitment to the administration's Vietnam policy, begged off with the excuse that he was too new in office and too preoccupied with Vietnam to be able to offer

[46] CJCS 02721, 080048Z March 1968, General Wheeler to General Westmoreland and Admiral Sharp; also Gene Roberts, "U.S. Command Sees Hue, Not Khe Sanh, as Foe's Main Goal."

[47] MAC 03280, 081357Z March 1968, General Westmoreland to General Wheeler.

[48] Personal interview with General William C. Westmoreland, October 23, 1972.

mature judgments on the military assistance program, which was the ostensible purpose of the hearings. The president, aware of Clifford's growing doubt, was also not anxious to have him testify in the hostile Senate arena and over nation-wide television. Johnson and Clifford, with the concurrence of the Senate committee, agreed that Nitze, the deputy secretary of defense, should testify.

Nitze, fully aware that the testimony would involve a defense of the administration's policies, refused to testify on the grounds that he was not in a position to defend these policies. He handed Clifford a letter he had prepared for the president, stating his position that further troop deployments to Vietnam would threaten United States commitments elsewhere in the world. The letter concluded with a short paragraph saying that in view of his stated position, he could well understand that the president might want his resignation. Nitze recalled his position as follows:

> I'm perfectly prepared to accept an administration decision which, from a narrow ground, I might have disapproved of but on which I could see that higher authority with a broader grasp could have considerations in mind that I didn't have in mind, and then defend that. But I felt that I understood the problem as well as the next man, and nobody was prepared to explain to me what these broader considerations were. In fact, I felt the situation was reversed, that I was paying more attention to the broader considerations than higher authority was. Now under those circumstances, I was not the man to send up to testify. . . . It wasn't a great break with the administration. It was just that you operate in a certain way, and that's the way you are going to operate. I couldn't do it any other way.[49]

Clifford was shaken by Nitze's letter, both by its content and by the reception he knew it would receive from Johnson, who was acutely sensitive on the matter of loyalty. He agreed

[49] Personal interview with Paul Nitze, October 13, 1972.

to forward the letter to the president if Nitze would delete the reference to his readiness to "not continue" in office. This was done, and the rest of the letter went to the White House. From that day, Nitze was never again invited to the Tuesday luncheons at the White House.[50]

Clifford and the president then decided that Warnke should testify for the Defense Department. Warnke agreed, despite his profound misgivings about Vietnam policy. Fulbright, however, insisted that the committee would accept only Clifford or Nitze, and that the committee would wait until notified that one or the other was prepared to testify. So the ball was back in Clifford's court.

There is reason to believe that this was the point where Clifford's growing but unresolved doubts crystallized into a firm conviction that our strategy had to turn to that of seeking a peaceful solution. Moved by the sincerity and eloquence of his assistants, Nitze, Warnke, and Goulding, concerned by the obvious disaffection among his friends in Congress, unconvinced by the generals of the Joint Chiefs of Staff, Clifford's own thoughts coalesced. Certainly, the idea of having to defend this dubious and unsuccessful policy before informed and hostile congresssional critics focused his doubts. "When Clark Clifford had to face up to the possibility that he might have to defend the administration's policy before the Fulbright committee, his views changed," recalled Nitze.[51]

As Clifford explained his dilemma, he searched for answers, but could find none:

> I could not find out when the war was going to end; I could not find out the manner in which it was going to end;

[50] This incident is described in detail in Kalb and Abel, *Roots of Involvement*, pp. 231–232, and Hoopes, *The Limits of Intervention*, pp. 198–200, and was confirmed in a personal interview with Paul Nitze on October 13, 1972. Nitze, in any case, only attended the Tuesday luncheons as a stand-in for MacNamara when the secretary of defense was unable to attend. Personal interview with Major General Robert N. Ginsburgh, August 25, 1975.

[51] Personal interview with Paul Nitze, October 13, 1972. William Bundy expressed the same opinion in a personal interview on October 11, 1972. Also Hoopes, *The Limits of Intervention*, pp. 200–201.

I could not find out whether the new requests for men and equipment were going to be enough, or whether it would take more and, if more, when and how much; I could not find out how soon the South Vietnamese forces would be ready to take over. All I had was the statement, given with too little self-assurance to be comforting, that if we persisted for an indeterminate length of time, the enemy would choose not to go on. . . . I was convinced that the military course we were pursuing was not only endless, but hopeless. A further substantial increase in American forces could only increase the devastation and the Americanization of the war, and thus leave us even further from our goal of a peace that would permit the people of South Vietnam to fashion their own political and economic institutions. Henceforth, I was also convinced, our primary goal should be to level off our involvement, and to work toward gradual disengagement.[52]

Clifford saw Fulbright privately and, in a frank talk, informed the chairman of his growing doubts about the administration's Vietnam policy. As Fulbright recalled the meeting: "Clifford indicated to me that he was going through a review of United States policy in Vietnam. He made the case that he didn't want to make a public statement until that review had been completed. I didn't feel that it was appropriate for him to come before the committee until this review had been completed."[53]

The two men agreed that if Clifford were to testify while the matter was still being debated within the administration, it might damage the prospects for changing the administration's policy. Fulbright, heartened by what he heard, wrote the secretary of defense that he could testify in the future at his own convenience. As the chairman stated it: "It is the view of the Committee on Foreign Relations that the subject

[52] Clifford, "A Vietnam Reappraisal," pp. 611–613.
[53] Personal interview with Senator J. William Fulbright, November 2, 1973. See also Kalb and Abel, *Roots of Involvement*, p. 233; Hoopes, *The Limits of Intervention*, pp. 200–201.

of military assistance is of such significance that the Secretary of Defense should be heard in public session as in the past. The Committee is, of course, aware of the need for you to familiarize yourself with the subject and will hold itself available for your appearance at your convenience."[54]

Thus, Clifford moved closer to making up his mind on the road the United States should follow in bringing the war in Vietnam to a conclusion. But as he was to discover, "to reach a conclusion and to implement it are not the same, especially when one does not have the ultimate power of decision."[55]

[54] Letter from J. W. Fulbright, Chairman, to the Honorable Clark Clifford, Secretary of Defense, dated March 21, 1968.

[55] Clifford, "A Vietnam Reappraisal," p. 613.

TEN

☆☆

Politics and Economics

PRESIDENT JOHNSON had been remarkably successful in keeping the Vietnam war "above politics." He assiduously cultivated bipartisan support for the war and used every means available to demonstrate that his decisions concerning Vietnam were simply an extension of the policies and actions of his predecessors in the White House.[1] Consensus was for him a technique of governing and of leading. He had taken great pains to insure that the Tonkin Resolution in 1964 received bipartisan congressional support.[2] He was especially successful at generating public expressions of approval from the most popular Republican of them all, General Dwight D. Eisenhower.[3]

Vocal opposition to the war in Vietnam up to 1968 had come either from nonpolitical groups largely unassociated with either political party or from a small number of Democratic legislators. On the other side, occasional complaints from the political right that the president had adopted a "no win policy" in Vietnam were continually being undercut

---

[1] Brandon, *Anatomy of Error*, p. 31; Sam Houston Johnson, *My Brother, Lyndon,* pp. 198, 204–205; Tom Wicker, *JFK and LBJ: The Influence of Personality on Politics,* pp. 198–206; Johnson, *The Vantage Point,* pp. 448–468; Hugh Sidey, *A Very Personal Presidency: LBJ in the White House,* pp. 70–83.

[2] Eric F. Goldman, *The Tragedy of Lyndon Johnson,* pp. 177–183. Also Anthony Austin, *The President's War,* pp. 37–120; Windchy, *Tonkin Gulf,* p. 317; Goulden, *Truth is the First Casualty,* pp. 37, 48–79; U.S., Congress, Senate Committee on Foreign Relations, *The Gulf of Tonkin, the 1964 Incidents.* See also J. William Fulbright, *The Crippled Giant: American Foreign Policy and Its Domestic Consequences,* pp. 181–191.

[3] Johnson, *The Vantage Point,* p. 131.

by public statements from General Westmoreland—a man highly respected by the right—who always insisted he was receiving all the troops and support he had asked of the president and was getting them as fast as he needed or could absorb them. Johnson recognized the importance of full support from his field commander. At the Honolulu conference in February 1966, he told Westmoreland, "General, I have a lot riding on you. . . . I hope you don't pull a MacArthur on me."[4]

A growing discontent with the war had begun to jell within the student movement. This discontent, however, was not well organized, was leaderless, and seemed in no position to challenge the nomination of an incumbent president with Johnson's political skill and power. One man, however, slowly came to the conclusion that, however hopeless the odds, the incumbent president and his war policies must be challenged. On November 30, 1967, Senator Eugene McCarthy announced his candidacy for the Democratic nomination for president, thus becoming the leader of an insurgency that was to rip apart the Democratic party.[5]

McCarthy made his decision to challenge the president's position because of a "recent announcement from the Administration of plans for continued escalation and intensification of the war in Vietnam and . . . the absence of any positive indications . . . for a compromise or negotiated political settlement."[6] But the McCarthy campaign, in its early days, seemed disorganized and passionless and seemed merely to suggest how little support there was for the dove position on Vietnam. McCarthy had reluctantly been persuaded to enter the New Hampshire primary in order to rally

[4] Westmoreland, *A Soldier Reports*, p. 159; Sidey, *A Very Personal Presidency*, p. 82.

[5] Eugene J. McCarthy, *The Year of the People*, pp. 1, 265–267; also Theodore H. White, *The Making of the President, 1968*, pp. 71–80; Richard C. Stout, *People*, pp. 67–77.

[6] McCarthy, *The Year of the People*, p. 265.

this support insofar as it existed, but the threat to Johnson seemed remote.[7]

Robert Kennedy had seemed to the dissident Democrats to be the natural candidate to carry their banner. He had a broad base of power, he had the Kennedy name, and he had already broken with the administration on Vietnam. Kennedy had been under pressure for some time to challenge the president for the nomination, but the political professionals whose judgment he trusted told him he could not succeed and that he would shatter the party if he tried.[8] So Kennedy, at a breakfast meeting at the National Press Club on the morning of January 30, 1968, the very eve of Tet, declared himself out of the presidential race "under any foreseeable circumstances."[9]

The Tet offensive, however, legitimitized the Vietnam war as a political issue. First, it seemed to provide dramatic evidence that the government, the Johnson administration, had deceived the people and, consequently, could not be trusted. Second, Tet liberated politicians, journalists, and commentators from their previous commitments to the war. The situation had now changed dramatically and new solutions, new approaches seemed to be called for. Third, the psychological blow suffered in Vietnam made legitimate, indeed necessary, the search for alternative policies. It was a time for reassessment of American purposes and policies in Vietnam not only within the administration but within the whole political process of the nation. All of America seemed to yearn for the magic solution, the way to peace with honor. The public opinion polls, which showed continued public support for the war, held no comfort for Johnson: the polls

[7] Lewis Chester, Godfrey Hodgson, and Bruce Page, *An American Melodrama: The Presidential Campaign of 1968*, pp. 82–83; Arthur Herzog, *McCarthy for President*, pp. 79–88; McCarthy, *The Year of the People*, pp. 65–66; David Halberstam, "McCarthy and the Divided Left," pp. 42–44.

[8] David Halberstam, *The Unfinished Odyssey of Robert Kennedy*, pp. 8–9, 12, 38–39, 48–49; Theodore H. White, *The Making of the President, 1968*, pp. 158–160.

[9] Jules Witcover, *85 Days: The Last Campaign of Robert F. Kennedy*, pp. 15–17.

also showed that confidence in the president's conduct of the war lagged far behind public support for the war itself and was declining (figure 2).[10]

Shortly after Tet, then, the challengers to the president in both parties began to speak up. The Vietnam war and especially the Johnson administration's conduct of it had become the major political issue of the still embryonic presidential campaign. This issue dominated all other public concerns.

Johnson stood aloof from the political battle. As an incumbent president facing a series of international and domestic crises and carrying the burden of a reevaluation of national policies in Vietnam, he declined to enter primary contests other than those in which, as a candidate, he was legally obligated to have his name on the ballot.[11] He knew of the mood of the nation, but he did not feel that either McCarthy or Kennedy would be a threat. His political advisors had no doubt that he would be the Democratic nominee for president.[12]

Thus, the results of the New Hampshire primary, the nation's first, held on March 12, the day Rusk completed his testimony before the Fulbright committee, came as a shock.[13] McCarthy, the peace candidate, had made a surprisingly strong showing in a primary he had entered reluctantly, partly because of the supposed hawkish predilection of the New Hampshire electorate. In fact, when the write-in vote had been tallied later in the week, McCarthy had come within several hundred votes of defeating the president in the popular vote.[14] Although Johnson's name had not been

[10] Gallup Opinion Index, "Johnson's Popularity," p. 2. Used by permission. See also George Gallup, "Johnson Rating in Poll Hits Low"; "Johnson's Rating on Vietnam Drops"; George E. Reedy, *The Twilight of the Presidency*, p. 68.

[11] John Herbers, "Johnson Rejects Primary Contests"; "Johnson Bars Bid in Massachusetts."

[12] Sam Houston Johnson, *My Brother, Lyndon*, pp. 237–238; Johnson, *The Vantage Point*, p. 538.

[13] Sam Houston Johnson, *My Brother, Lyndon*, p. 238.

[14] Chester et al., *An American Melodrama*, pp. 79–81; Theodore H. White, *The Making of the President, 1968*, pp. 83–89. First-hand accounts of the New Hampshire campaign are found in McCarthy,

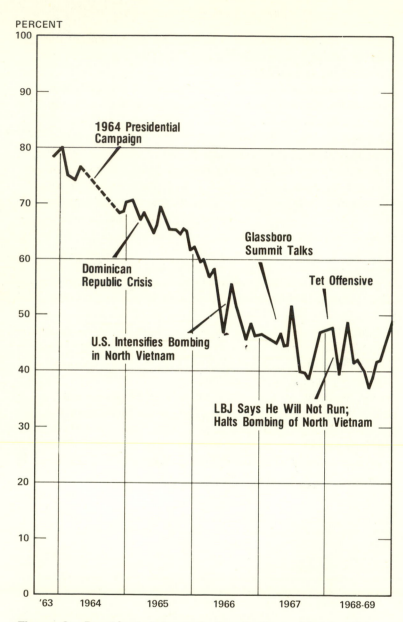

PERCENT

Figure 2. President Johnson's Popularity as Measured by the Gallup Poll

on the ballot, the Democratic organization had made it clear that they expected a massive write-in campaign to display the voters' enthusiasm for the president.

The reaction across the country to the New Hampshire vote was profound. Although the election had little importance in terms of ultimate voting power, it had vast psychological implications. It was clear that Johnson, the master politician, had been successfully challenged, not by an attractive and appealing vote getter, but by a less strong, less attractive candidate who had been able to mobilize and focus the growing discontent and disillusionment caused by the war.

The election was widely heralded as a repudiation by the voters of the administration and its Vietnam policies, and it buoyed the hopes of the president's critics in both parties. Later analysis has shed more light on the motives of the voters in New Hampshire and has called into question the assumption that the vote for McCarthy was a peace vote. Doubtless, those who voted for McCarthy in the primary were much more dissatisfied with Johnson's policies on Vietnam than were those who voted for Johnson. But among the McCarthy voters, those who were dissatisfied with Johnson for not pursuing a *harder* line in Vietnam outnumbered those who wanted a withdrawal by a margin of nearly three to two. Indeed, studies have shown that of those who favored McCarthy before the Democratic convention but who had switched to some other candidate by November, a plurality switched to Wallace.[15]

Nevertheless, the New Hampshire results posed an acute dilemma for Robert Kennedy. With the president's vulnerability on Vietnam demonstrated, should Kennedy, his premier

---

The Year of the People, pp. 67–87; Stout, *People*, pp. 146–182; Jeremy Larner, *Nobody Knows: Reflections on the McCarthy Campaign of 1968*, pp. 34–41; Herzog, *McCarthy for President*, pp. 85–99.

[15] See Philip E. Converse, Warren E. Miller, Jerold G. Rusk, and Arthur C. Wolfe, "Continuity and Change in American Politics: Parties and Issues in the 1968 Election," pp. 1,083–1,105.

political opponent on this and other issues, now throw his hat in the ring? Kennedy huddled with his advisors during the four days following the primary in New Hampshire. He still felt that if he could turn Vietnam policy about, that if he could force the administration to make an active search for peace, but he would have no need to run against Johnson. Kennedy relayed to the president, through Clifford, his suggestion that a commission of nationally eminent Americans be appointed to study and reassess Vietnam policy with a view toward seeking a road to peace. The plain but unspoken pledge was that if the president would change his policy on the war, Kennedy would agree not to run for president. But the president rejected this proposal, and, on March 16, Kennedy, after informing the president and Senator McCarthy, announced he would be a candidate for the Democratic presidential nomination.[16]

For President Johnson, the threat was now real. McCarthy, even in the flush of a New Hampshire victory, could not reasonably expect to unseat the incumbent president. But Kennedy was another matter. His candidacy gave the peace movement instant respectability. The president now faced the prospect of a long and divisive battle for nomination within his own party against a very strong contender, with the albatross of an unpopular war hanging around his neck.

Criticism of the president continued to mount. Spurred by the New Hampshire voters' indication of massive public disaffection with the president's conduct of the war, 139 members of the House of Representatives joined in sponsoring, on March 18, a resolution calling for an immediate congressional review of United States policy in Southeast Asia.[17]

At the regular weekly luncheon on March 19 of the people

[16] Theodore H. White, *The Making of the President, 1968*, pp. 161–166; Witcover, *85 Days*, pp. 47–69; Henry A. Zeiger, *Robert F. Kennedy; A Biography*, pp. 136–137; "Kennedy's Secret Ultimatum."
[17] John W. Finney, "139 in House Support Drive for a Review of Policy in Vietnam."

working on the president's campaign, the distinct possibility that Johnson might lose the upcoming Wisconsin primary was discussed. James L. Rowe, Jr., leader of this group, indicated that he "thought somebody ought to be blunt to the president."[18] In a memorandum to the president that same day, Rowe indicated he was "writing with the frankness that, I think, has existed between us." Assessing the aftermath of Tet from a purely political standpoint, Rowe wrote: "*The President* must do something dramatic (not gimmicky) *before* the Wisconsin primary. . . . Somehow or other, somewhere or other the picture of the President as the man who would go anywhere, do anything in his desperate search for Peace has been lost. McCarthy and Kennedy are the candidates of peace and the President is the war candidate. He must do something exciting and dramatic to recapture the peace issue."[19] Johnson had become a wartime president, and the country now hungered, indeed seemed to demand, a move toward peace in Vietnam.

During these busy days of March, another great crisis, this one of an economic nature, also demanded the president's attention. This monetary crisis stemmed from a basic decision taken in 1965, when the buildup in Vietnam first began, that the nation could afford to wage a two-front war, the war in Vietnam and the domestic war against poverty, without economic controls and without raising taxes. The theme was clearly stated in the president's budget message of 1966: "We are a rich Nation and can afford to make progress at home while meeting obligations abroad—in fact, we can afford no other course if we are to remain strong. For this

---

[18] Personal interview with James L. Rowe, Jr., December 29, 1975. Others present included Robert Burkhardt, William Connell, Richard Maguire, Cliff Carter, Lawrence O'Brien, and Martin Friedman. Marvin Watson represented the White House. See also Steven V. Roberts, "McCarthy Appeal Wide in Wisconsin."

[19] Memorandum for The President, "Peace with Honor in Vietnam," March 19, 1968, signed James Rowe. Also personal interview with James L. Rowe, Jr., December 29, 1975.

reason, I have not halted progress in the great and vital Great Society programs in order to finance the cost of our efforts in Southeast Asia."[20]

But things did not work out as well as anticipated, primarily because the expenditures required for the war were vastly underestimated. Thus, 1966 witnessed the most rapid price inflation in the United States since the Korean war.[21] To meet this situation, the president, in his 1967 State of the Union message, requested that Congress enact a 6 percent (later raised to 10 percent) surcharge on personal and corporate taxes, to be effective July 1, 1967, and "to last for two years or for so long as the unusual expenditures associated with our efforts in Vietnam continue."[22]

The president's proposal was received coolly in Congress. Wilbur Mills, powerful chairman of the House Ways and Means Committee, felt that approval of the tax increase would indicate support of the president's policy of carrying out his Great Society programs and carrying on the Vietnam war at the same time. Mills felt that any tax increase should be accompanied by a cut in expenditures. But Johnson was unwilling to propose any cuts in his Great Society programs.

This stalemate, which Mills eventually won, resulted in congressional inaction on the tax bill until its eventual passage and signature into law on June 28, 1968.[23] Mean-

[20] U.S., Bureau of the Budget, *Budget of the United States Government for the Fiscal Year Ending June 30, 1967*, p. 7; also U.S., Congress, Joint Economic Committee, *Economic Effect of Vietnam Spending, Hearings*, p. 205. Portions of these hearings were published by the Center for Strategic Studies, *Economic Impact of the Vietnam War*.

[21] U.S., President, *Economic Report of the President Transmitted to the Congress, January 1967*, p. 5; Arthur M. Okun, *The Political Economy of Prosperity*, pp. 70–77; Phillip Cagan et al., eds., *Economic Policy and Inflation in the Sixties*, pp. 49–55; U.S., Congress, Joint Economic Committee, *Economic Effect of Vietnam Spending*, pp. 206–207; *Public Papers of Lyndon Johnson, 1967*, I, p. 8.

[22] Okun, *The Political Economy of Prosperity*, pp. 83–85; U.S., President, *Economic Report of the President, January 1967*, pp. 9–12.

[23] Lawrence C. Pierce, *The Politics of Fiscal Policy Formation*, pp. 148–172; U.S., Congress, House of Representatives, Committee on Ways and Means, *President's 1967 Surtax Proposal, Hearings*, Part I; U.S., Congress, House of Representatives, Committee on Ways and

while defense and domestic spending continued at a high level, so inflation continued. The United States surplus in its international balance of payments dwindled rapidly in the final months of 1967, resulting in a fourth-quarter deficit of $7 billion.[24] This deficit, together with the devaluation of the British pound in November 1967, generated serious uncertainties in the international monetary markets and made the dollar particularly vulnerable to attack. As a result, internal conditions in the United States were subjected to intense scrutiny throughout the world. The Tet offensive and its aftermath, with the prospect, announced in the press, of a vast increase in American forces in Vietnam and consequently a vast increase in American expenditures, accompanied by the continued stalemate on taxes, was enough to touch off another serious outbreak of speculative fever. In the first week of March, the gold pool had to sell some $300 million in gold. In the second week, speculation went almost out of control. The world's central banks had to supply some $1 billion in gold to meet the demand. The United States had lost $327 million to the speculators by March 14, and the president had to move.[25]

The London gold market was closed on March 16 to check the massive drain. Over the weekend, Treasury secretaries and heads of central banks from seven nations hastily assembled and met secretly in Washington. They established a new "two-tier" international gold exchange wherein gold could no longer be bought in the free market.[26]

Means, *President's 1967 Surtax Proposal: Continuation of Hearings to Receive Further Administration Proposal Concerning Expenditure Cuts*; Okun, *The Political Economy of Prosperity*, pp. 86–91.

[24] G. L. Bach, *Making Monetary and Fiscal Policy*, pp. 134–135; Johnson, *The Vantage Point*, p. 317; U.S., President, *Economic Report of the President Transmitted to the Congress, February 1968*, pp. 13–16.

[25] Johnson, *The Vantage Point*, p. 318.

[26] Personal interview with Henry H. Fowler, December 28, 1972. Also U.S., Board of Governors of the Federal Reserve System, *Fifty-fifth Annual Report of the Board of Governors of the Federal Reserve System, 1968*, pp. 331–332; Johnson, *The Vantage Point*, pp. 318–319; Bach, *Making Monetary and Fiscal Policy*, p. 137.

The crisis had been averted, but the underlying problem that gave rise to it had not been solved. The central bankers of the world remained understandably nervous about the stability of the dollar and the ability and willingness of the United States to put its financial house in order. Any great increase in defense outlays by the United States in Vietnam without cuts in expenditures for the Great Society or without increases in taxes could quickly lead to renewed speculation, the downfall of the dollar, and a vast international financial crisis. The world and national economies were very much on Johnson's mind as he pondered his course in Vietnam.[27]

[27] Johnson, *The Vantage Point*, pp. 406–407; "Guns and Butter—Failure of a Policy," pp. 27–29.

ELEVEN

✩ ✩

End of a Strategy

By mid-March, it was apparent that President Johnson was not going to approve the deployment of 206,000 additional troops or anything approaching it. The diminishing ground action in Vietnam had made it clear that another massive attack was unlikely. Public and congressional reaction showed that such an increase would be politically explosive and hard to justify. Financial considerations meant that any large increase could be made only at the expense of important domestic programs.

From that point, work on troop levels in Vietnam proceeded in two directions. First, an effort was made to refine United States troop estimates so that any increase of forces in Vietnam, as well as any reserve call-up to support that increase, would be held to the absolute minimum. Second, actions to strengthen the Vietnamese armed forces were emphasized. "This had by then become absolutely central to our thinking," William Bundy recalled.[1]

By March 8, the Joint Chiefs of Staff had indicated that some 30,000 troops, as opposed to the 22,000 previously recommended, could be quickly raised and deployed. In his cable to Westmoreland on March 8 informing him of this, however, General Wheeler reflected the changing situation in Washington: "I do not wish to shunt my troubles on to you; however, I must tell you frankly that there is strong resistance from all quarters to putting more ground force units in South Vietnam. . . . You should not count on an affirmative decision for such additional forces."[2]

[1] Personal interview with William Bundy, October 11, 1972.
[2] JCS 2767, 090130Z March 1968, General Wheeler to General Westmoreland.

General Westmoreland replied on March 11 with a request that the 30,000 increment be composed of seven maneuver battalions and a military police battalion.[3] Ambassador Bunker also indicated that although a force of this size would pose no problems, any larger increases could tend to Americanize the war further and give the Vietnamese an escape route from their responsibilities. "We need to maintain a careful balance between modernization of RVNAF and the buildup of our own forces," the ambassador added.[4]

The *New York Times'* article and congressional reaction to it had indicated the depth of opposition to a substantial force increase. General Wheeler's cable to Westmoreland informing him of the March 11 meeting at the White House and of the growing opposition in Congress to any further deployment of forces to South Vietnam ended with the following admonition: "I was directed to keep you informed of the status of our forces in the US so that you will not in the future be placed in the position of asking for something that does not exist or is not available."[5]

Such advice must have come as a shock to Westmoreland. He had already been perplexed and puzzled by the article in the *New York Times* alleging that he had asked for 206,000 more troops. He recalled:

When I read that in the *New York Times*, at first I didn't even recognize it. I didn't recognize what they were talking about, and then suddenly I realized that this was the plan that was put in the context of General Wheeler's request. I was busy with other things, and I had not realized that this had created such a big exercise. In any case, I never considered the plan developed by General Wheeler and me to be a demand per se for the deployment

[3] MAC 3385, 111500Z March 1968, General Westmoreland to General Wheeler, quoted in *U.S.–Vietnam Relations,* IVC(6)(c), pp. 71–72.

[4] Saigon 21733, 111142Z March 1968, American Embassy, Saigon to Secretary of State, quoted in Johnson, *The Vantage Point,* 405–406.

[5] JCS 02848, 122014Z March 1968, General Wheeler to General Westmoreland.

of additional forces or an "emergency" request for battle-field reinforcements. Rather, I considered it a prudent planning exercise designed to generate the military capability to support future tactical and strategic options consistent with policy determination. I used the phrase "force requirements" in the sense defined by the JCS, meaning forces that would be required to accomplish approved military objectives. In other words, the requirement would materialize only if the reappraisal of national policy being conducted in Washington resulted in the approval of new strategic objectives.[6]

Having responded to the chairman's request to determine plans and forces for the "worst possible contingency," the field commander was now being mildly chastised for requesting troops that "did not exist or were not available."

The president apparently finally decided, at a meeting at the White House on March 13, to deploy the 30,000 additional troops to South Vietnam. The decision was formalized by the deputy secretary of defense in a memorandum to the chairman of the Joint Chiefs of Staff on March 14.[7] But these deployments were not to be made. On March 14, the secretary of the army pointed out that 30,000 troops would not be sufficient. An additional 13,500 would have to be added to that figure in order to support and sustain the 10,500 emergency augmentation that had been sent to General Westmoreland in February.[8] The 30,000 deployment was held in abeyance while the services sought to determine if these 13,500 additional troops could be made available.

The president continued to confer with congressional leaders and with his secretary of the treasury. On March 19,

[6] Personal interviews with General William C. Westmoreland, October 23, 1972 and September 16, 1972. Also Westmoreland, *A Soldier Reports*, p. 358.

[7] Deputy Secretary of Defense, Memorandum for Chairman, Joint Chiefs of Staff, Subject: *Southeast Asia Deployments*, dated March 14, 1968, quoted in *U.S.–Vietnam Relations*, IVC(6)(c), pp. 71–72.

[8] Secretary of the Army, Memorandum for the Secretary of Defense, March 14, 1968, quoted in *U.S.–Vietnam Relations*, IVC(6)(c), p. 72.

he had received a message from Westmoreland describing his plan for a major offensive in I Corps to open Route 9 and relieve the forces at Khe Sanh. The ground war appeared to be going well. "I thought that if Westmoreland had enough confidence to launch an offensive with the forces he had in Vietnam, it would be wise to limit additional commitments," the president stated.[9]

By March 22, the president had decided to limit additional troop deployments to be sent to Vietnam to the 13,500 support forces necessary to sustain the emergency reinforcements sent in February. This would necessitate a reserve call-up of only 62,000.[10] Thus, the increase in United States forces was to be only a token. None of the 206,000-man increment proposed by Generals Wheeler and Westmoreland late in February was to be deployed. For the first time, a line had been drawn on the American ground force commitment to South Vietnam.

The decision to send only 13,500 men was not announced by the president. Indeed, the Pentagon continued to plan for the deployment of 30,000 men in addition to this small support element, and the 30,000 figure was mentioned in the press.[11] The president wanted to prepare his ground carefully and get the support of his military leaders for this drastic cutback of their stated requirements.

Improved Vietnamese performance was absolutely critical

[9] Johnson, *The Vantage Point*, pp. 407, 409–410. Details of Westmoreland's offensive are described in Westmoreland, *Report on the War in Vietnam*, p. 104; Shore, *The Battle for Khe Sanh*, pp. 132–144; Lieutenant General John J. Tolson, "Pegasus," pp. 9–19; John R. Galvin, "The Relief of Khe Sanh," pp. 88–94.

[10] Johnson, *The Vantage Point*, p. 415; *U.S.–Vietnam Relations*, IVC(6)(c), pp. 76–77.

[11] Assistant Secretary of Defense (Systems Analysis), Memorandum for Secretary of Defense, Subject: *Program #6 Summary Table (Tentative)*, dated March 23, 1968, quoted in *U.S.–Vietnam Relations*, IVC(6)(c), p. 76. The decision was not announced to the Pentagon until March 28, after the president had conferred with General Abrams. See *U.S.–Vietnam Relations*, IVC(6)(c), pp. 76–77. Also William Beecher, "565,000 Total Is In View: Strategy Change Weighed."

to limiting United States deployments to South Vietnam, and, initially, the South Vietnam government responded well. Washington and the American mission in Saigon did everything they could to encourage the South Vietnamese. The Vietnamese government had passed a mobilization decree in October 1967. This decree provided for sharply curtailed deferments and for lowering the draft age from 20 to 18. The decree was to become effective on January 1, 1968, but it had not been implemented before the Tet offensive. Even while recalling reservists during the Tet offensive, however, the Vietnamese government thought of postponing the drafting of 18- and 19-year olds until all other eligibles had been called up. Ambassador Bunker pointed out to President Thieu that this would engender further criticism in the United States to the effect that the Vietnamese were not carrying their share of the burden.

Responding to the American pressure, Thieu ordered an increase in the size of RVNAF of some 60,000 men over a six-month period. This would require the drafting of some 100,000 to 125,000 men. Thus, drafting of 19-year olds began on March 1, with 18-year olds to begin serving on May 1.[12] In addition, Ambassador Bunker reported that in the month following the Tet offensive, the number of volunteers for the Vietnam armed services was five times the level of the previous year and that approximately two and one-half times as many men reported for the draft in February 1968, as had in February 1967. This indicated, Bunker added, "a greater determination on the part of the GVN to increase the forces at its disposal."[13]

The president was encouraged by these accomplishments. He directed Ambassador Bunker to press President Thieu for an early speech that would describe to the American pub-

[12] COMUSMACV 07327, 150106Z March 1968, COMUSMACV to JCS, Subject: *RVNAF Force Levels*; also Saigon 20392, 250740Z February 1968, American Embassy, Saigon to Secretary of State, Subject: *Mobilization Pushed Up*.

[13] Saigon 22267, 161040Z March 1968, American Embassy, Saigon to Secretary of State, Subject: *GVN Mobilization Policy*.

lic these Vietnamese efforts in their own behalf.[14] In a speech of considerable substance delivered on the evening of March 20, Thieu reported on the efforts of his government to mobilize its manpower resources and to bear its share of the load. He announced a projected increase in the armed forces of 98,000 and indicated his government "must make greater efforts and accept more sacrifices" so as to demonstrate to its allies "that we deserve their support."[15]

With the decision to limit additional United States force deployments to a token number and with the indication that the South Vietnamese were prepared to take over a larger share of the ground war, the president, at a press conference on March 22, announced personnel changes that seemed to signal a new ground strategy in Vietnam. General Wheeler's tenure as chairman of the Joint Chiefs of Staff was extended for one year. General Westmoreland would leave his Vietnam post in mid-summer and would become Army Chief of Staff.[16] Although a successor to Westmoreland was not named, it was widely assumed that it would be his deputy, General Creighton Abrams. Since he had arrived in Vietnam, Abrams had been assigned by General Westmoreland to devote his major attention to improving the RVNAF. As their role was to be expanded, it seemed natural that Abrams would assume command.

Westmoreland had served the president well, and Johnson

[14] Personal interview with William Bundy, October 11, 1972. Also State 131330Z March 1968, Secretary of State to American Embassy, Saigon.

[15] Bernard Weinraub, "U.S. Aides Pleased by Thieu's Speech"; also Johnson, *The Vantage Point*, pp. 413–414.

[16] *Public Papers of Lyndon Johnson, 1968–69*, I, p. 340; for press commentary as to whether this signalled a change in strategy, see Joseph Alsop, "Westmoreland's Replacement Hints Wavering LBJ Support"; Charles Mohr, "Westmoreland Departure Could Spur War Changes"; Orr Kelly, "Westmoreland to Head Army—Regrets Leaving Vietnam Before Battle Is Over"; "Westmoreland's Nomination as Army Chief Could Portend Shift in U.S. Viet Policy"; "Westmoreland's Transfer"; Richard Dudman, "Moving Westmoreland May Not Alter Strategy"; Neil Sheehan, "Conflicts Over Asia: Within the Administration, a 'Kind of Malaise' Over Vietnam"; "Change of Command"; David Lawrence, "Viet War Under 'Intensive Review' "; "A New Policy for Vietnam."

was grateful. Although political public relations on the home front is not among the normal assignments of a field commander, the president employed Westmoreland in this role three times in 1967 alone.[17] Each time the general voiced his encouragement with the way things were going in Vietnam but carefully refrained, except in his November speech at the National Press Club, from predicting the future.

After the Tet offensive, General Westmoreland began to bear the brunt of congressional and press criticism for the Vietnam stalemate, primarily because of his optimistic public statements. He was identified in the public mind as the general who had predicted victory, had then been surprised by the enemy, and had requested 206,000 additional reinforcements.[18] President Johnson resented such criticism. "Westy did everything he was expected to do, and more," Johnson said. "I will not have him made a scapegoat."[19] The president expressed his confidence in Westmoreland publicly and in private throughout this period and indicated, in his press conference of February 16, that, as far as he was concerned,

---

[17] Westmoreland, *A Soldier Reports*, pp. 224–239; Ernest B. Furgurson, *Westmoreland, The Inevitable General*, pp. 326–327, 335; Oberdorfer, *Tet*, pp. 103–106.

[18] Drew Pearson, "Westy Likely to Keep Viet Post"; Peter Arnett, "Viet Red Drive Challenges U.S. Military Assumptions"; Beverly Deepe, "South Vietnam Shaken: Hardly a Hamlet Feels Safe"; Clayton Fritchey, "Westmoreland's Vietnam Strategy"; Drew Pearson, "Gen. Westmoreland Ouster Is Urged"; D. Gareth Porter, "People as the Enemy"; "Westmoreland's Strategy: Will It Pass the Acid Test?"; "Man on the Spot"; Keyes Beech, "Westmoreland's Image Tarnished by Red Drive." For an appraisal of General Westmoreland's strategy and performance in Vietnam, see Sir Robert G. K. Thompson, *No Exit from Vietnam, pp.* 122–144; Sir Robert Thompson, "Squaring the Error," pp. 442–453; Blair Clark, "Westmoreland Appraised: Questions and Answers"; Mark M. Boatner III, "The Unheeded History of Counterinsurgency"; Halberstam, *The Best and the Brightest*, p. 549; Lieutenant General Richard Stilwell, "Evolution in Tactics—The Vietnam Experience"; Frances FitzGerald, *Fire in the Lake: The Vietnamese and the Americans in Vietnam*, pp. 342–345; Jeffrey Race, *War Comes to Long An*, pp. 226–227; Meyerson, *Vinh Long*, pp. 150–154; Charles M. Fair, *From the Jaws of Victory*, pp. 369–416; Beverly Deepe, "Khe Sanh: Legacy of Westmoreland"; Ward Just, "Vietnam Notebook"; Adam Yarmolinsky, "Picking Up the Pieces: The Impact of Vietnam on the Military Establishment."

[19] Christian, *The President Steps Down*, p. 120.

"if there is any way General Westmoreland could go, it would be up."[20]

On March 23 President Johnson sent General Wheeler in secret to Clark Air Force Base in the Philippines to meet Westmoreland, to inform him of the situation facing the president at home, and to obtain his agreement on the small number of additional troops that would be furnished him. The two commanders met on March 24. As Westmoreland recalled this meeting: "He told me that a significant change in our military strategy for the Vietnam war was extremely remote, and that the administration had decided against a large call-up of reserves. Consequently, since we could not execute the strategic options that General Wheeler and I had discussed in February, the question of deploying major additional forces to South Vietnam became a mute issue."[21]

Westmoreland told the chairman he could hold his own and pursue his current strategy with the forces already provided him plus the 13,500 additional support forces the president had approved for deployment. "It was just a question of dragging out the war," Westmoreland stated. "In effect, it forced the Vietnamization strategy that I had proposed earlier as the only tactical option."[22]

Wheeler returned to Washington with Westmoreland's "request" for 13,500 additional troops. The commander in chief had made it obvious to the two military men, as it had become obvious to him, that "the moment had come to throw more weight behind the Vietnamese with their new spirit of confidence."[23] These troop deployments, as it turned out, were to be the final ones, the last increment of American military manpower committed to the Vietnam war.

[20] *Public Papers of Lyndon Johnson, 1968–69*, I, pp. 232–234; Charles W. Corddry, "Johnson to Recall Westmoreland From Vietnam Command in July to be New Army Chief of Staff—Westmoreland Attains No. 1 Goal."
[21] Personal interview with General William C. Westmoreland, October 23, 1972.
[22] Ibid. Also Westmoreland, *A Soldier Reports*, pp. 358–359.
[23] Johnson, *The Vantage Point*, p. 415.

TWELVE

☆☆

The Bombing Pause

DEAN RUSK had felt, early in March, that a bombing pause would be in the best interests of the nation and the president. It would involve little or no military risk during the monsoon season and would be an initiative that would help regain public support for the war. The president had told him to "get on his horse and get a plan." But the proposal had been greeted coldly by the civilians at the Defense Department, who felt it was a watering down of the San Antonio formula. The military, of course, including both the Joint Chiefs of Staff and CINCPAC, had advocated a vast step up in the bombing. Even Ambassador Bunker, in cables on March 1 and March 14, had pressed hard for additional bombing of North Vietnam, noting that the South Vietnamese had been shaken by our failure to respond in this fashion to the Tet offensive.[1] The chances for agreement within the administration for a bombing pause seemed bleak.

Now, in mid-March, with public opposition to troop increases growing and the ground situation in Vietnam improving, the question of a bombing pause, or halt, came up again and from a new quarter. On the evening of March 15, Arthur Goldberg, the ambassador to the United Nations, sent Rusk a detailed memorandum on Vietnam. Goldberg, who had resigned from a cherished Supreme Court seat to accept the United Nations post at the president's behest, had expressed himself before in a series of memoranda to the president. His view had always been that Vietnam was not susceptible to a military solution and that the United

---

[1] Personal interview with William Bundy, October 11, 1972. Also Saigon 22096, American Embassy, Saigon to Secretary of State.

States should move toward negotiations.[2] After the Tet offensive, it became apparent to Goldberg, as it had to Clifford, that the nation simply could not continue on its present course, and that a fresh move toward a political solution was necessary to prevent further erosion in public support for the war. He stated these views to the president: "In a democracy, you have to have the consent of the governed. While a president cannot operate with a fever chart, if he loses the consent of the governed, in a democracy, then you had better take drastic action to put you and the governed into compatibility."[3]

Goldberg at the time knew nothing of Rusk's bombing-pause proposal and felt, like many others in the nation, that the president was seriously considering a large increase in American troop strength in Vietnam. His proposal to the president, which was designed to move the nation toward negotiations and to regain public support, was as follows: "In specific terms, then, my suggestion, based on the San Antonio formula, means that—without announcing any conditions or time limit—we would 'stop' the aerial and naval bombardment of North Vietnam for the limited time necessary to determine whether Hanoi will negotiate in good faith; in my view this can best be determined by what actually happens

[2] Personal interview with Arthur Goldberg, January 24, 1973. President Johnson's version of Goldberg's appointment to the United Nations post is in *The Vantage Point*, pp. 543–544. Of this version, Goldberg says: "The president was not telling the truth. I never approached him, he called me. I never dreamed of approaching him. I was very happy on the Court, and he knew that to be the case. So, he just wasn't telling the truth. I accepted the post because I correctly felt that our country was in very great trouble over the Vietnam issue, and that I could not put my personal predilection which was, of course, to stay on the Court—my highest ambition—before the country's interest." See also Alfred Steinberg, *Sam Johnson's Boy: A Close-up of the President from Texas*, p. 779. For an assessment of Goldberg at the United Nations, see Arnold Beichman, *The "Other" State Department: The United States Mission to the United Nations—Its Role in the Making of Foreign Policy*, pp. 164–172.

[3] Personal interview with Arthur Goldberg, January 24, 1973.

during the talks rather than by any advance verbal commitments of the kind we have been seeking."[4]

Some reports indicate that in discussing the Goldberg proposal with his advisors in the White House on March 16, the president exploded in a rage, waved the memo in the air, and denounced it in colorful language.[5] Rostow, who was present, discounts these stories. He recalled the incident in this fashion: "The President was not outraged and shouting on a matter of obvious substance, but he expressed himself vividly, and he looked at the proposal negatively. He was very worried about the area near the DMZ. He felt, in those circumstances, that a total bombing halt would be militarily irresponsible."[6]

Rusk also remained opposed to a total bombing halt. He still favored a de facto halt in the bombing north of the 20th parallel to see "if we get a de facto response from Hanoi." But he thought the Goldberg proposal could be used as a stalking horse to get both the Americans and the Vietnamese in Saigon to agree on the partial bombing pause as an acceptable compromise. Rusk convinced the president that both his plan and the Goldberg proposal should receive a fair hearing from his advisors in Vietnam.

Consequently, that evening, March 16, a cable was dispatched to Ambassador Bunker outlining the two plans as "staff proposals" without indicating their authors or proponents. The first proposal, the Goldberg proposal, in effect, was contained in a single paragraph which stated that the plan would be to accept recent Hanoi statements as indicating that the North Vietnamese understood and had complied with the San Antonio formula; hence we would stop

---

[4] Johnson, *The Vantage Point*, p. 408. On March 18 Chester Bowles, the ambassador to India, presented a proposal for a bombing halt which was similar to Goldberg's, although he wanted other governments to take the responsibility for pressing the North Vietnamese to enter into meaningful negotiations. Ibid., pp. 408–409.

[5] Kalb and Abel, *Roots of Involvement*, p. 230; Oberdorfer, *Tet*, p. 296.

[6] Personal interview with Walt W. Rostow, December 4, 1972. Also Johnson, *The Vantage Point*, p. 408.

bombing North Vietnam. In outlining his own plan, which he stated was "more modest," Rusk included the entire memorandum that he had provided the president on March 5, explaining in detail why a bombing pause would not be harmful during the monsoon season. The secretary asked Ambassador Bunker if this proposal could be sold to Thieu in conjunction with a limited United States force increase and proposals for improving ARVN equipment. Rusk emphasized that it was his best judgment that the North Vietnamese would not respond with any real step toward peace, but that they might "hold their hand at Khe Sanh and against the cities for some time."[7]

It was patently obvious from the tone and content of the cable that the second alternative was the preferred one, and, as Rusk has indicated, "the response was predictable."[8] Ambassador Bunker, in his reply, confirmed that a total halt in the bombing would be very disturbing in its effect on the GVN. Even a reduction of the bombing to a point south of Vinh, Bunker reported, would have unsettling effects, but he felt it would be easier to obtain South Vietnamese agreement on such a limited bombing pause, especially if it was accompanied by increased military support for the Saigon government.[9] The assessment by the ambassador was limited to the political effects of a peace initiative in Vietnam. The military commander, General Westmoreland, was not consulted by Bunker nor were his views included in Bunker's reply.[10]

Thus, Rusk had his proof from the field that the South Vietnamese government would not readily accept a total bombing halt. "By the middle of March," Rusk recalled, "I had no doubt in my mind that the president was going to announce a partial bombing halt as I had suggested."[11]

[7] Personal interview with William Bundy, October 11, 1972. Also State 131772, Secretary of State to American Embassy, Saigon.

[8] Personal interview with Dean Rusk, January 22, 1973.

[9] Saigon 22548, American Embassy, Saigon to Secretary of State, March 20, 1968.

[10] Personal interview with General William C. Westmoreland, October 23, 1972.

[11] Personal interview with Dean Rusk, January 22, 1973.

THIRTEEN

Search for a Strategy

CLARK CLIFFORD was troubled. He had come to the conclusion that the American effort in Vietnam had in reality been directed toward achieving a military victory, a goal he was now convinced was impossible to attain. He was sure the war could not be won. He felt something had to be done to get negotiations started, but he did not have an alternative strategy in mind. As he saw it: "The big issue, really, was whether we would continue on to achieve what was really understood to be a military victory or whether some other means could be found for ending the war. I concluded that a military victory was unattainable within the restrictions that obtained at the time, these being public attitude, expense, our moral concepts, and the political realities of the period."[1]

But what policy should he recommend to change the direction of the war, what could be the first step? The men in the Pentagon on whose advice Clifford mainly depended, Nitze and Warnke, were adamantly opposed to Rusk's partial bombing-halt proposal. They looked upon it as a watering down of the San Antonio formula.[2] These advisors indicated to Clifford that the North Vietnamese would not respond to such a proposal and that it would simply play into the hands of those who wanted "a gesture that would fail." All this proposal would do, Clifford was convinced, would be to set the stage for an eventual reescalation of the war.[3] As Clifford recalled his view of Rusk's bombing-pause proposal:

I was never conscious during this period that Secretary Rusk deviated from policy. His idea concerning a bombing

[1] Personal interview with Clark Clifford, February 15, 1973.
[2] Personal interview with Paul Warnke, November 17, 1972.
[3] Personal interview with Morton Halperin, December 27, 1972.

pause was based upon the fact that bad weather would allow us to cut back the bombing as a gesture, that such a gesture wouldn't cost much. Then when the other side did nothing, we could bear down on them. His bombing-pause proposal seemed to me to be designed to provide the basis for greater pressure in the future. As far as I could tell, it really did not constitute a good faith effort to get negotiations started. This is my personal view. I interpreted it as a device to be presented that would cost nothing militarily because of the weather. But it was anticipated that it would be rejected, and this would be the basis for launching a more effective and far-reaching attack against North Vietnam. I did not get the impression at the time that there was a similarity in approach between Rusk and me.[4]

Clifford was interested in a more fundamental reassessment of American policy in Vietnam: "What I was arguing for was a real effort to start negotiations. I was urging a change in policy. Instead of our previous policy of the application of increasing force, I wanted to do what was necessary to get negotiations started."[5]

Clifford's advisors, alone in the government, were agreed that North Vietnam had indicated its acceptance of the San Antonio formula and had indicated a great deal of flexibility in stating its conception of a negotiated settlement.[6] But the president had made it abundantly clear, in discussing the Goldberg proposal and in other meetings, that a total cessation of the bombing was not an option he would accept at a time when American forces in the northern provinces of South Vietnam were seriously threatened by large numbers of North Vietnamese regular troops. "So we didn't really know what to propose, other than to not send any more troops," recalled Halperin.[7]

[4] Personal interviews with Clark Clifford, November 16, 1972 and February 15, 1973.
[5] Ibid.
[6] *U.S.–Vietnam Relations*, IVC(7)(b), pp. 186–189. Also personal interview with Paul Warnke, November 17, 1972.
[7] Personal interview with Morton Halperin, December 27, 1972.

Nevertheless, Clifford pressed on the president his views that a military victory in Vietnam was impossible, that a change in direction of American policy was necessary, and that a sincere negotiating proposal must be made. He was willing to risk his friendship with Johnson in the interest of having his views prevail. As Clifford recalled:

> I presented my views to the president, saying, in essence, "Instead of our continuing down the route we've been going, instead of sending an additional 200,000 men to Vietnam, let's give some kind of signal to Hanoi that we would like to find a basis for negotiations." I put it in the following terms several times, "The baby has to crawl before the baby can walk." If we can give them some signal, the baby will be crawling. If we get some signal from Hanoi in response, maybe we can pick the baby up, and it can walk a few steps. Then maybe we can give a signal, and the baby can walk a few more steps. By proceeding in these stages, we can end up where we want to end up, with a negotiated settlement.[8]

But Clifford was advocating a change in policy without a clear view of how to accomplish that change, of what that first step should be. As Rostow recalled these views:

> Clifford was very vague. He lectured all of us on the impossibility of military victory, but he did not advocate anything operational. He talked about things that had no operational substance. He offered no other solution. What shocked President Johnson was that he didn't know what Clifford wanted. The president wasn't going to enlarge the war, but he was going to hang in there. On the operational side, however, he had trouble getting Clifford to focus on a specific peace proposal. Clifford was at cross purposes with the president, not in specific acts of policy but in not stating lucid operational alternatives.[9]

[8] Personal interview with Clark Clifford, February 15, 1973. See also Clifford, "A Viet Nam Reappraisal," p. 613; Christian, *The President Steps Down*, pp. 78, 115.
[9] Personal interview with Walt W. Rostow, December 4, 1972.

And Harry McPherson, who was present at many of these meetings, remembered "that Clifford spoke in a way that didn't seem to set us on a clear course, but at the same time doubted the course we were on."[10]

Clifford agreed, to an extent, with this analysis. As he recalled: "It would be nice to be able to delineate with particularity a precise plan which sprang forth fully armed from my brow, but as in most things, it wasn't that clear. I felt we should take some small step, and then they would respond, and so on. I was urging a change in policy. Instead of our previous policy of the application of increasing force, I wanted to do what was necessary to get negotiations started."[11]

Clifford had been an effective, loyal, and able advisor to the president for years. Johnson respected him and valued his judgment and counsel; he had brought Clifford into the administration in 1968 with great pride. Clifford's contacts on Capitol Hill were outstanding; he was persuasive; he learned quickly; he would be the Gibraltar of the administration's policy in the Pentagon. As McPherson recalled: "The president said to me one day that Clifford was probably the only man in America who had made a million dollars in law fees in one year, and that he had been able to persuade that man to come into the administration during a bitter period. It wouldn't have been hard to think of bringing him in in 1965, when all was hope and triumph and there were new successes every day. But to come in at the end of an administration during a period of such turmoil was really something."[12]

But Clifford himself quickly came to question seriously whether our objectives in Vietnam could be achieved by the path we were following, and he continually pressed his views

[10] Personal interview with Harry C. McPherson, Jr., December 21, 1972.

[11] Personal interview with Clark Clifford, February 15, 1973.

[12] Personal interview with Harry C. McPherson, Jr., December 21, 1972.

on the president. Clifford's change of attitude was disturbing to Johnson, and as was his fashion, the president often gave the impression of tuning Clifford out and of being overly polite to him. Clifford recalled their relationship during this period as follows:

> As I was in the process of changing my mind, it had an impact on the president, and it was disturbing to him. He felt that when I came in, I was going to be a good, strong stalwart, a supporter of the status quo. As I changed, it was disturbing to him. He was irritated with me. It's difficult for a president to have his two senior advisors disagree. The fact that Secretary Rusk and I began to take different positions was disturbing and upsetting to him. The president made a great deal out of our differences. He was upset with me. The bloom was off our relationship. I was changing, but Rusk wasn't. He was more constant. Two or three times in the course of our meetings the President would refer to my plan as the "Clifford approach." In the early days of March, the president was harassed and dismayed and used such a designation as a term of opprobrium. He discounted its value and the results to be achieved by it.[13]

No president, indeed no man, likes to be told that his basic policy has been wrong, that he has lost control of a situation and cannot succeed, that his closest and most trusted advisors are misguided and are leading him even deeper into disaster, even if it is a close friend that is saying all this. So on occasion Clifford was rebuffed by the president and sometimes was not invited to meetings. But he continued forcefully to present his views, and the president continued to respect his opinions and to listen to him.[14] McPherson described

[13] Personal interviews with Clark Clifford, November 28, 1972 and February 15, 1973.

[14] Christian, *The President Steps Down*, p. 115.

Clifford's relationship with the president during this period in the following manner:

> Let me try to describe it for a moment as a novelist instead of as an historian in order to weave into it Lyndon Johnson's innermost thoughts, which we can't know. . . . Here is a man who has been an extremely able, loyal, and effective advisor to you for years and years. You value his counsel. But he begins seriously to question what we're doing in light of what can be achieved, and it begins to seem terrifically unbalanced to him. And he tells the president that the course we are on is a self-destructive one, that we can't win it this way.
>
> The president has been working with Rusk and Rostow. They had been disturbed by McNamara's behavior and views over the last year. There is kind of a beleaguered threesome, the president, secretary of state, and national security advisor. And now the man that the president brought in to replace McNamara is beginning to show signs of not having his head on straight on this issue. So from time to time, because he is this man you respect so much and are so proud of and who you need so much, you call him in and you listen to him, or you get on the phone for an hour with him.
>
> You patiently explain that he doesn't understand because he wasn't in the government, that we have had bombing pauses and diplomatic initiatives which proved that the North Vietnamese are not going to make peace. And he comes right back and in that corporate lawyer voice says, "Mr. President, it's just not going to do, and I really believe for your sake and for America's sake we have to get out."
>
> Well, if you're up there at the top and if you have the responsibility and if you've taken your country into this war and you have already lost 25,000 or 30,000 of your men and have undercut the financing for your whole Great Society programs and everything you hoped to do here

246

at home, you're not going to say, "All right, I made a mistake on that." So that means that for the next meeting, you don't invite Clifford. But two or three days later, you do listen to him again. That's how, as a novelist, I would look at it. I knew President Johnson pretty well, and I could just sense that was what went on.[15]

In his search for allies outside the Defense Department, Clifford had earlier called McPherson at the White House. McPherson recalled their conversation:

> He asked me how I stood on the war, and I told him I was getting awfully nervous about it and was beginning to have very serious fundamental doubts about it. He suggested that he was too, and that we should work very closely. I was to be his eyes in the White House. Having worked in the White House, he no doubt knew the value of having someone there to keep his eyes and ears open, and he was, I am sure, already aware that in turning this around he would face entrenched opposition from Rostow and the NSC staff. In the last ten days of March we talked almost daily, and I began to get more and more the feeling that he was really determined to turn it around. The way he put it was to the effect that "we're going to have to get our friend out of this situation."[16]

In his search for a strategy, Clifford and his advisors at Defense finally decided that the first step, as a signal to Hanoi, would have to be a cutback in the bombing of North Vietnam. But this was not expected to result in negotiations. A reciprocal step from Hanoi would indicate their intentions, and then additional steps would be taken as further signals. Clifford's staff gave as examples of the kind of step Hanoi might make in response to a bombing cutback, assurances that it would not attack from across the DMZ, or would not

[15] Personal interview with Harry C. McPherson, Jr., December 21, 1972.
[16] Ibid. Also McPherson, *A Political Education*, p. 431.

attack the cities in South Vietnam.[17] Clifford saw this developing in the following manner: "The step obviously that could give the first signal was a cutback in the bombing. The bombing was very controversial. My proposal was to cut it back and keep it cut back to see what we would get, what signal. Then we could go to the next deescalatory step. We would take the first faltering step, hoping that we might get some response from them to guide us to the next step."[18] Clifford's desire to receive some "assurance" from Hanoi as the bombing was cut back was seen by Rusk as attaching conditions to the cessation of the bombing, conditions that would be denounced by the North Vietnamese and would stand in the way of getting negotiations started.

President Johnson's reaction to the pressures building on him was to reaffirm publicly his Vietnam policies. On March 17 and March 18, in two blunt speeches to the National Alliance for Businessmen and the National Farmer's Union Convention, the president declared: "We must meet our commitments in the world and in Vietnam. We shall and we are going to win! . . . Hard choices are going to have to be made in the next few days. Some desirable programs of lesser priority are going to have to be deferred."[19] The president attacked directly the critics of his Vietnam policies. "We ought not let them win something in Washington that they can't win in Hue, in the I Corps, or in Khe Sanh. And we are not going to."

The president portrayed himself as following a prudent middle course between those who "think that we ought to get it over with, with a much wider war" and those who think "that you can have peace by talking for it, by wishing for it, by saying you want it, and all you need to do is pull back to the cities." He further declared that "we don't plan to let people influence us, pressure us, and force us to divide our Nation in a time of peril."[20]

[17] *U.S.–Vietnam Relations*, IVC(7)(b), pp. 187–190.
[18] Personal interview with Clark Clifford, February 15, 1973.
[19] *Public Papers of Lyndon Johnson, 1968–69*, I, pp. 402–413.
[20] Ibid., p. 412.

The political effect of these speeches was indicated to the president by his political advisor, James L. Rowe, Jr., in his March 19 memorandum:

> The President must change his tactics on the hard line. I am shocked by the number of calls I received today in protest against your Minneapolis speech. Our people on the firing line in Wisconsin said it hurt us badly. A number of "doves" called me to say they were against the President because of his Vietnam policy but were not resentful and bitter until the Minneapolis speech called them traitors. They said he should accept the fact and realize the country is divided over Vietnam and impugning their patriotism, as they say the speech did, merely infuriates them. Some people who support your Vietnam policy telephoned to say they thought the speech "hurt our side" a great deal.
>
> The Minneapolis speech said "win the war." . . . (The fact is hardly anyone today is interested in winning the war. Everyone wants to get out and the only question is how.)[21]

Rowe had also spoken to Clifford, asking him to "crank into the computer of decision" his views of the domestic political situation. He indicated to Clifford that "the word 'escalation' had obviously become the dirtiest of dirty words. . . . Any kind of escalation . . . is going to hurt us badly."[22]

Clifford, on hearing these speeches, felt that the president had committed his prestige to a continuation of a hard policy in Vietnam and that much ground had been lost in his attempts to change American policy: "I hadn't seen the speeches prior to their delivery. They were tough and hard-nosed. The president indicated that we would proceed down the same road, that we would not weaken."[23]

[21] Memorandum for The President, "Peace with Honor in Vietnam," March 19, 1968, signed James Rowe.

[22] Ibid.; also personal interview with James H. Rowe, Jr., December 29, 1975.

[23] Personal interview with Clark Clifford, November 16, 1972.

The president had decided after Tet that he would have to make a speech to the American people to explain his actions and decisions concerning the nation's effort in Vietnam. McPherson, his speech writer, had been working on this speech for weeks, but the confusion in the early days of February as to what to do had prevented him from finishing.[24] Johnson had given a good deal of thought to this speech. He planned to discuss the situation in Vietnam, clarify what the Vietnamese were doing for themselves, explain his plans for a modest increase in American forces in Vietnam, and, last, make a serious peace proposal.[25]

Background material for the speech arrived from the State Department on March 20; it contained the proposal Rusk had made two weeks earlier for a pause in the bombing north of the 20th parallel. The president met with his advisors on March 20 and March 22 to discuss this speech. Present at the March 20 meeting were the vice president, Arthur Goldberg, and McGeorge Bundy, as well as the president's usual advisors.[26] As the discussion passed around the room, it became clear that none of the president's advisors felt that the Rusk proposal would actually lead to negotiations with the North Vietnamese. Rusk reiterated his proposal and stated that "unless we are prepared to do something on bombing, there is no proposal for us to make."[27]

Clifford was convinced that the Rusk proposal did not go far enough and would not lead to negotiations. As he saw it: "Rusk believed that any conciliatory gesture would be misinterpreted by the other side. He felt we should keep the pressure on them. He really didn't have in mind a bombing cutback. He thought we could use the period of bad weather

---

[24] McPherson, *A Political Education*, p. 423.

[25] Johnson, *The Vantage Point*, p. 410.

[26] Ibid., pp. 411–413. Although the president in his book only discusses the meeting on March 20, most of his principal advisors whom I interviewed remember much more clearly the luncheon meeting on Friday, March 22. It was at this Friday meeting, apparently, that the major portion of the substantive discussion of a bombing pause took place.

[27] Ibid., p. 412.

in North Vietnam to make a lot over a bombing pause. It wouldn't cost much, and, assuming the other side rejected it, we could accelerate the use of force against them. His bombing-pause proposal seemed to me to be designed to provide the basis for greater pressure in the future."[28]

William Bundy confirms Clifford's view. As he recalled the discussions, the rationale for a bombing pause lay, not in its value in getting negotiations started, but in its utility in temporarily placating American public opinion: "In all of the discussions in which I participated, the general consensus was that the utility of the partial bombing pause lay in persuading the American people that we were seriously concerned about peace. The proposal, it was thought, would help to bring dissent down to a manageable level. If it was rejected—as we anticipated—we could then carry on and still hope to achieve our objectives."[29]

Clifford at this time repeated his suggestion for a cutback in the bombing as a first step, leading perhaps to the enemy's stopping firing rockets and artillery from the DMZ or perhaps agreeing to withdraw forces from the DMZ:

> I felt we should definitely make a move to start negotiations. I thought we should suggest some minor change in our formula to Hanoi to see if we could get talks started. One thing I suggested was to make an offer on the bombing, to cut back the bombing to some extent to see if they might take some step. Perhaps they would stop shelling our cities in the South. Then we should stay right with it, and make a series of moves of a conciliatory or deescalatory nature to see if this would lead to talks. These were responses they could make, not conditions for stopping.[30]

But Rusk saw this as imposing conditions on Hanoi, which they would not accept. "I felt that you should just stop the

[28] Personal interviews with Clark Clifford, November 16 and November 28, 1972.
[29] Personal interview with William Bundy, March 5, 1973.
[30] Personal interviews with Clark Clifford, November 16 and November 28, 1972.

bombing without imposing conditions," he stated, "and therefore keep your options open."[31] Clifford recalled that because of his frustration, the debate between himself and Rusk became rather sharp: "In a gentlemanly way, the sharpness was beginning to become apparent. Our ideas were completely different, and we wanted a bombing pause for entirely different reasons. What I was then arguing for was a real effort to start negotiations. I was urging a change in policy. Instead of our previous policy of the application of increasing force, I wanted to do what was necessary to get negotiations started."[32]

The discussion moved around the table from one man to another. William Bundy contributed the judgment that the Rusk proposal would probably not produce results. "It was too thick to drink and too thin to plow," he stated. The consensus of the group, Bundy concluded, appeared to be that "a bombing reduction was unlikely to produce a response, although it could have significant advantages in showing the U.S. determination to move toward peace and thus add to domestic support."[33]

As McPherson remembered that meeting "the consensus was that a halt at the 20th parallel would not bring about talks, and we could not halt altogether without jeopardizing our troops in I Corps. And the president said, 'Well, that looks like the way it is.' At that time it seemed to me that the signal that was being given to all of us was that we are not going to do it. I never had any instructions to put a bombing pause in the speech, or to seriously consider it."[34]

The president listened attentively to the discussion, and a conception of what he had to do apparently began to

[31] Personal interview with Dean Rusk, January 22, 1973.

[32] Personal interview with Clark Clifford, November 16, 1972. None of the other participants in this meeting with whom I have talked recalled this sharpness. See Christian, *The President Steps Down*, p. 115.

[33] Personal interview with William Bundy, October 11, 1972.

[34] Personal interview with Harry C. McPherson, Jr., December 21, 1972.

form in his mind. He later indicated that he felt certain by this time that the peace proposal he was determined to make would take the form of a cutback of the bombing to the 20th parallel as first suggested by Rusk.[35] But, as was his fashion, Johnson wanted to explore every possibility and gain the consensus of all his advisors before he announced any such decision. Also, stung by leaks to the press, the president was determined that premature disclosure would not be permitted to weaken or possibly destroy the chances for success of what he saw as a major peace initiative. "The president didn't want to flag what was in his mind and lose his freedom of action," Rusk stated. "He didn't like having these things put on paper and then later reading about them in the newspapers."[36]

Thus, at the conclusion of the meeting, Johnson, in apparent agreement with his advisors that a bombing pause was unlikely to get negotiations started with the North Vietnamese, directed that this peace initiative be removed from the speech and studied separately. Subsequent drafts of the speech contained neither this nor any other peace proposal.

Both Clifford and McPherson were discouraged by the results of the meeting. McPherson the next day sent the president a short memorandum of his own which recommended a sequence of negotiating steps similar to Clifford's. In his plan, the United States would announce that it had stopped the bombing north of the 20th parallel, and that it had sent representatives to Geneva and Rangoon to await the North Vietnamese. McPherson's scenario then closely followed Clifford's, although it ended the way Rusk foresaw: "They would say that wasn't enough; we'd have to stop it altogether. We would say that we could not do that so long as men and supplies were pouring down the trail. But we'd say, we will stop it altogether, if you will not mount attacks on the cities in I Corps, or upon Saigon; and if you will

[35] Johnson, *The Vantage Point*, p. 413.
[36] Personal interview with Dean Rusk, January 22, 1973; also Johnson, *The Vantage Point*, p. 413.

stop the shelling of South Vietnam from the DMZ. They'd say there could be no conditions; we must stop all the bombing. We'd express our regret that they had responded in the same intransigent way."[37]

Although this would not result in negotiations, McPherson indicated, "I thought it would show the American people, and people in other nations, that we were truly seeking them." The president sent McPherson's proposal to Rusk for his reaction. This reaction, which came two days later, was predictable. The plan to stop the bombing at the 20th parallel, of course, was what Rusk had been advocating for almost a month. But the secretary of state did not care for the idea of sending representatives to other capitals to wait for the North Vietnamese to appear. He would prefer, he indicated, to ask the two cochairmen of the Geneva Conference (the United Kingdom and the Soviet Union) and perhaps the members of the International Control Commission to be "available to talk to any interested parties about the possibilites of a peaceful settlement." But Rusk maintained his position that no conditions be attached to the bombing pause.[38]

Clifford and his colleagues in the Defense Department were discouraged to the point of desperation. As a good trial lawyer, Clifford had come to the conclusion that the president's case could not be won by the means being pursued. He had performed the hardest task a lawyer faces, that of telling his client that he is wrong, that he cannot win, and that he should make the best deal possible and settle. But Clifford saw no change forthcoming in a war policy that he felt would lead Johnson to disaster. He had talked to many of his friends in the business community and sensed the doubts that had also developed in their attitude toward the war. He concluded: "I didn't think the public was willing to support the policy we had been following. At that time, I had the feeling that we were at a crucial stage in the decision-making process. I thought it was going to take something very sub-

<hr>

[37] McPherson, *A Political Education*, pp. 432–433.
[38] Johnson, *The Vantage Point*, p. 419.

stantial to shift the president's attitude. I needed some stiff medicine to bring home to the president what was happening in the country."[39]

To provide this stiff medicine, Clifford proposed to the president that, before making a final decision, he consult with the Wise Men, the distinguished group that had supported and encouraged him in November. Clifford had received indications that the outlook of many of these individuals might have changed after the tumultuous days of January and February, and he wanted the president exposed to this change. Johnson welcomed Clifford's suggestion and told Rostow to set up a meeting.[40]

[39] Personal interview with Clark Clifford, November 28, 1972.
[40] Ibid. Also Johnson, *The Vantage Point*, p. 409.

FOURTEEN

☆☆

The Wise Men

SCHOLARS of the role of the presidency in the American scheme of government long have pointed out the isolation from the public that inevitably accompanies modern presidential power.[1] In the case of Lyndon Johnson, it has been charged that he reinforced this sense of isolation from reality by surrounding himself with a staff of acquiescent and like-minded sycophants who told him only the favorable things he wanted to hear. Thus, Johnson has been seen as being isolated from events taking place in the nation during the early days of 1968 and receiving only those reports and that advice that was passed to him by an inner circle of protective advisors.[2] Many of these advisors have indicated otherwise, however. As McPherson recalled this period: "The president wasn't a bit isolated from the press reaction to Tet. He was beginning to hear at this time complaints about the war from people who he really respected, members of Congress, leaders of industry, and leaders of other institutions in the country."[3]

[1] Reedy, *The Twilight of the Presidency*, pp. 10–16, 20, 30; George E. Reedy, *The Presidency in Flux*, pp. 11–14, 95–98; Philippa Strum, *Presidential Power and American Democracy*, pp. 51–75; Woodrow Wilson, *Constitutional Government in the United States*, p. 68.

[2] "Debate in a Vacuum," pp. 13–14; Charles W. Roberts, *LBJ's Inner Circle*, pp. 168–169; Sidey, *A Very Personal Presidency*, p. 269; Louis Heren, *No Hail, No Farewell*, pp. 180–185; Ralph L. Stavins, Richard J. Barnet, and Marcus G. Raskin, *Washington Plans an Aggressive War*, p. 199; Halberstam, *The Best and the Brightest*, pp. 627–628, 636–639; Hoopes, *The Limits of Intervention*, pp. 59–61; Theodore H. White, *The Making of the President, 1968*, p. 126; Strum, *Presidential Power and American Democracy*, pp. 47–49; John Emmet Hughes, *The Living Presidency: The Resources and Dilemmas of the American Presidential Office*, pp. 118–121.

[3] Personal interview with Harry C. McPherson, Jr., December 21, 1972.

And Rostow has written that "any man who tried to distort the flow of information to President Johnson would not have lasted two weeks in his job. . . . A president is extremely sensitive to the biases of his subordinates and to conscious or unconscious efforts to impose them. . . . My objective was not to determine the President's view but to make sure he had available the widest flow of information possible—a kind of intelligence ticker, if you like."[4]

The President made a point of seeking advice from people outside of government, as well as from his immediate staff, sometimes to the distraction of his appointed officials who had the responsibility for recommending and implementing policy based upon their knowledge and experience. The roles of Fortas and Clifford, prior to Clifford's appointment as secretary of defense, have already been mentioned. In addition, the president had summoned General Matthew Ridgeway to the White House on the day following the Tet offensive and received his advice on the necessity for re-constituting the strategic reserve.[5] Johnson had stopped to seek the advice of President Eisenhower in mid-February when he had flown out to bid farewell to the Marines being sent to reinforce General Westmoreland, and he continued to get advice throughout the month from friends and acquaintances outside of government.[6]

The changing public attitude toward his policy in Vietnam was soon to reach Johnson in forceful terms from people outside the government whom he admired and trusted, people who wielded great influence in the American political, business, and intellectual communities, and upon whom he had depended for advice and support in previous days. Late in February, the president had asked elder statesman Dean Acheson, a wise and trusted advisor, for his opinion about

[4] Walt W. Rostow, "Losing Big: A Reply," p. 10. See also Roche, "The Jigsaw Puzzle of History," p. 14.

[5] Johnson, *The Vantage Point*, p. 389.

[6] Rostow, *Diffusion of Power*, p. 466; W. Averell Harriman, *America and Russia in a Changing World: A Half Century of Personal Observation*, p. 125; Johnson, *The Vantage Point*, p. 414–415.

the course of American policy in Vietnam. Acheson declined to give his view as he did not have all the facts. The president had therefore given him authority, at Acheson's request, to interview officials of his own choosing in the State Department, CIA, and the Defense Department and gave instructions that these government officials should speak frankly. Acheson lost no time in conducting this inquiry among second- and third-level officials in these agencies. He consulted with William Bundy of the State Department, George Carver of the CIA, and several of the Defense Department officials whose views had been accepted by Clifford.

On March 15, three days after the New Hampshire primary and during the height of the gold crisis, Acheson reported his findings to the president. He told the president that, in his opinion, the time and resources necessary to accomplish our military objectives in South Vietnam were no longer available. The American public would support neither an increased effort nor even the present level of effort over an extended period. Acheson concluded that the ground war had to be changed, the bombing stopped or greatly reduced, and the war brought to a halt as soon as possible in keeping with the American commitment to South Vietnam. The president listened and was impressed with Acheson's frank view.[7]

On March 20 the President met privately with Arthur Goldberg to discuss his bombing-halt proposal. Although Johnson had reportedly denounced the proposal in no uncertain terms when it had been discussed with his closest advisors at the White House on March 16, Goldberg found this meeting "very pleasant." As Goldberg recalled the meeting: "The president indicated that he had read my memorandum thoughtfully, and that many aspects of it made sense. He indicated that there would soon be a meeting of a

---

[7] Oberdorfer, *Tet*, pp. 294–295; Kalb and Abel, *Roots of Involvement*, pp. 236–237; personal interview with William Bundy, October 11, 1972.

group of advisors that he had called upon from time to time. He said that he would very much appreciate it if I would attend that meeting and present the point of view which I had taken in my memorandum."[8]

The Wise Men, the group of presidential advisors summoned at Clifford's suggestion, assembled at the State Department on March 25. Those present were Dean Acheson, secretary of state under President Truman; George Ball, undersecretary of state in the Kennedy-Johnson period; McGeorge Bundy, special assistant to Presidents Kennedy and Johnson; Douglas Dillon, ambassador to France under President Eisenhower and secretary of the treasury under President Kennedy; Cyrus Vance, deputy secretary of defense under McNamara and a diplomatic troubleshooter for President Johnson; Arthur Dean, chief Korean war negotiator; John J. McCloy, High Commissioner to West Germany under President Truman and assistant secretary of war during World War II; General Omar Bradley, World War II commander and the first JCS chairman; General Matthew Ridgeway, Korean war commander and later NATO commander; General Maxwell Taylor, JCS chairman under President Kennedy and later ambassador to Saigon; Robert Murphy, a senior career ambassador of the Truman-Eisenhower period; Henry Cabot Lodge, former senator and twice ambassador to Saigon; Abe Fortas, a sitting associate justice of the Supreme Court and a personal advisor to President Johnson; and Arthur Goldberg, ambassador to the United Nations and a former secretary of labor and Supreme Court Justice.

The group met over dinner with Rusk, Clifford, W. Averell Harriman, Rostow, Richard Helms, General Wheeler, Nitze, Nicholas Katzenbach, and William Bundy. The outside advisors questioned the government officials extensively on the war, the pacification program, and the current condition of the South Vietnamese government.

[8] Personal interview with Arthur Goldberg, January 24, 1973.

After dinner, the senior government officials left, and the group received three briefings. Philip C. Habib, a deputy to William Bundy, delivered a frank briefing on the conditions in Vietnam after the Tet offensive. He covered such matters as corruption in South Vietnam and the growing refugee problem. Habib told the group that the Tet offensive had made it clear that the Saigon government was generally weaker than had been realized. He spoke with greater frankness than the group had previously heard. In addition to Habib, Major General William E. DePuy, special assistant to the Joint Chiefs for counterinsurgency and special activities, briefed the group on the military situation, and George Carver, a CIA analyst, gave his agency's estimates of conditions in the war zone.[9]

The briefings, according to General Taylor, were temperate and thoughtful presentations.[10] Goldberg, however, felt that the briefings were designed to show that Tet was a great victory, which he felt was not the case. He recalled the briefings as follows:

It just did not hold up in my mind. The briefing indicated that the enemy had lost 80,000 men killed in the Tet offensive. I asked the general what the normal ratio of killed to wounded would be. He said, as I recall, ten to one. And I said that that was a big figure and that, assuming that the Vietnamese were not as solicitous about their wounded as we were, and would not treat their slightly wounded or would put them back into combat when we would not, could we consider three to one to be a conservative figure for those rendered ineffective by wounds? And he said yes. And then I asked the question, "How many effectives do you think they have operating in the field?" And he said something like 230,000. And I said, "Well, General, I am not a great mathematician but with 80,000 killed and with a wounded ratio of three to

[9] Stuart H. Loory, "Hawk's Shift Precipitated Bombing Halt."
[10] Taylor, *Swords and Plowshares*, p. 390.

one, or 240,000 wounded, for a total of 320,000, who the hell are we fighting?" It didn't make any sense to me, and I didn't think that was a very good briefing. I like facts laid out. I thought there was a great obligation to tell the president the facts.[11]

General Ginsburgh saw another irony of the decision-making process in these briefings. He stated:

There is no question that if Wheeler and Rostow had briefed rather than DePuy and Carver, there would have been a different flavor to the briefings. They would have put a different emphasis on the situation. Without disparagement, DePuy and Carver didn't have the kinds of answers that Wheeler and Rostow could have given. Wheeler had originally been scheduled to give the briefing, but he had just come back from his trip to meet Westmoreland in the Philippines and hadn't had time to prepare. DePuy had been working on this briefing, and it was decided that he should give it. It was then decided that the other portions of the briefing should be given by someone comparable in rank to DePuy, and Carver and Habib were chosen.[12]

Rusk later indicated that he felt that, in going out of their way to explain the real problems that the nation faced in Vietnam, the briefers may have presented an unbalanced picture of the total situation.[13] In any case, the discussion continued on into the evening, and it was soon apparent that for many of these senior advisors, the nearly unanimous support for the president's Vietnam policy of the previous November had been replaced by a troubled skepticism.

The next day, the advisors assembled for lunch at the White House, and, subsequently, met with the president to

[11] Personal interview with Arthur Goldberg, January 24, 1973.
[12] Personal interview with Major General Robert N. Ginsburgh, August 25, 1975.
[13] Personal interview with Dean Rusk, January 22, 1973.

give him their views. General Abrams, Westmoreland's deputy in Vietnam, had returned from Clark Field with General Wheeler. The two generals had been closeted with the president that morning giving him a report on the tactical situation in Vietnam.[14] The president brought them to the meeting to give his advisors a firsthand description of the military situation in Vietnam.

General Wheeler disclosed to the group his recent trip and talk with General Westmoreland. He gave an optimistic picture of the military situation and mood in Saigon in contrast to the situation during his earlier visit in February. Abrams discussed the performance of ARVN units during the Tet offensive, concluded that they had in general fought well, and indicated that they could take on a larger part of the fighting in the future.[15] But as Rostow recalled, the Wise Men "were not focusing on Vietnam, but on the political situation in the United States."[16]

After lunch, the group reported to the president. Each individual expressed his view with the utmost frankness. McGeorge Bundy, acting as spokesman, reported a shift in views since the previous November. He said that the group in general no longer felt so hopeful about the possibility of slow and steady progress in Vietnam. Acheson reiterated his former advice that the objectives in Vietnam were too high considering the time and resources it would take to achieve them. Dean, Dillon, and Ball expressed similar sentiments. General Ridgeway read aloud before the group a paper he had written the night before expressing his views. He was opposed to further United States troop increases except to man a training establishment for the Vietnamese. The South Vietnamese, with American advice and equipment, should be given two years to develop a defense establishment

---

[14] Johnson, *The Vantage Point*, p. 416; also Murray Marder, "General Abrams, LBJ Confer on Vietnam"; Neil Sheehan, "General Abrams in Capitol, Sees President and Aides."

[15] Johnson, *The Vantage Point*, pp. 416–417.

[16] Personal interview with Walt W. Rostow, December 4, 1972.

capable of maintaining their political independence. At the end of the two years, American forces would begin to phase down. Lodge, General Bradley, and Vance agreed that the Vietnamese should be called upon to do more and that the United States objectives in South Vietnam should be lowered. Lodge felt that the basic thrust of the United States effort in the future should be directed toward territorial, constabulary, and counter-terrorist activities and away from military objectives. This reorientation of strategy and objectives, he felt, would make possible a drastic reduction in the number of American troops in South Vietnam. Ball and Goldberg reiterated their view that a bombing halt was necessary in order to get negotiations started. Goldberg also restated his view that Tet was a serious defeat as far as public opinion was concerned and that the president could not press on with the war in the absence of public support.

Some of the advisors disagreed strongly with these views. Murphy, Fortas, and General Taylor were dismayed by the pessimism of the others. But, of deep significance, the president stated that it seemed to him that "all the advisors expressed deep concern about the divisions in our country. Some of them felt that those divisions were growing rapidly and might soon force our withdrawal from Vietnam."[17]

Thus, the consensus of the group, except for the small minority who stood firm in support of the current policy, was that some action had to be taken to begin to reduce the American involvement in Vietnam and to find a way out. There was no sense of proposing a specific peace proposal, nor even agreement on whether a peace initiative would be

---

[17] Johnson, *The Vantage Point*, p. 418. See also Oberdorfer, *Tet*, pp. 309–315; Kalb and Abel, *Roots of Involvement*, pp. 245-249; Hoopes, *The Limits of Intervention*, pp. 214–218; Taylor, *Swords and Plowshares*, pp. 390–391; General Matthew B. Ridgeway, "Indochina: Disengaging," p. 588; Henry Cabot Lodge, *The Storm Has Many Eyes: A Personal Narrative*, p. 219; personal interview with Dean Rusk, January 22, 1973; personal interview with William Bundy, October 11, 1972; personal interview with Arthur Goldberg, January 24, 1972.

useful in the current situation. But all seemed to be convinced that an increase in American forces would be unthinkable and that the South Vietnamese should shoulder a greater share of the fighting.

The president was visibly impressed by the change in view of these eminent and trusted advisors. He put great faith in their opinions, and the considered views of Acheson particularly impressed him.[18] As Clifford recalled:

> The president could hardly believe his ears. I knew by his attitude. He dismissed Rusk, Rostow, and myself after their first reaction, so that they wouldn't be affected or inhibited by our judgment or that of other members of the administration. By the time he had finished, he said that "somebody had poisoned the well." He tried to find out who had done so. He called back George Carver and General DePuy. He was so shocked by the change in attitude of the Wise Men that he wanted to hear the briefings they had received. The meeting with the Wise Men served the purpose that I hoped it would. It really shook the president.[19]

And Goldberg recalled that "the president seemed very disturbed at the reaction of the group, namely, that we felt that Tet was not the great victory he had been told it was."[20]

The president sent for the briefers to have them repeat for his benefit what they had previously told his advisors. Carter and DePuy returned and repeated their briefings. Habib was informed of the president's wish for a repeat briefing just as he was leaving Washington. He chose to get on the airplane rather than return to the White House.[21]

Repeating the briefings could not alter the fact that a majority of the president's most trusted advisors had expressed the view that a new strategy had to be found for Viet-

[18] Personal interview with Dean Rusk, January 22, 1973.
[19] Personal interview with Clark Clifford, November 16, 1972.
[20] Personal interview with Arthur Goldberg, January 24, 1973.
[21] Personal interview with William Bundy, October 11, 1972.

nam. It was what these reactions meant as a reflection of broader opinion that most troubled the president. He later wrote of his reaction: "They were intelligent, experienced men. I had always regarded the majority of them as very steady and balanced. If they had been so deeply influenced by the reports of the Tet offensive, what must the average citizen of the country be thinking?"[22]

Thus, the meeting with the Wise Men seemed to have served the purpose that Clifford had anticipated it would. These trusted advisors had now brought home to the president what the newspapers and polls had been telling him for a month. The Tet offensive had increased the opposition within the country to the war. Further escalation would not be acceptable to a large and influential segment of the American public. It was necessary to call a halt, to change our policy, to restore some balance.

[22] Johnson, *The Vantage Point*, p. 418.

FIFTEEN

☆☆☆

The President Makes a Decision

LYNDON JOHNSON was troubled. His advisors had assured
him, and he had assured the country, that the Tet offensive,
overall, represented "the most disastrous Communist defeat
of the war in Vietnam."[1] But the people were not convinced.
Growing dissatisfaction with the war was evident in both the
Congress and the electorate. In addition, inflation and a growing gold outflow threatened the major achievements of the
Great Society.

The steadily improving military situation in South Vietnam and the unexpectedly decisive actions of the South Vietnamese government had already led the president to decide
to make only a small deployment of American forces and to
increase support for the South Vietnamese so that they could
share a greater part of the fighting.

Johnson was determined to continue to pursue United
States objectives in Vietnam, but he was also determined to
propose a serious peace initiative that would be meaningful
to the North Vietnamese, would temper public opposition
to the war, and would possibly lead to negotiations to deescalate or end the conflict. But what should be the nature
of such a peace proposal? How could a proposal be made that
could accomplish all these objectives without threatening the
security of American forces in Vietnam?

During the past months, several peace feelers had been
received from diplomatic sources around the world. Initiatives had been received from the Soviet Union, Italy,
Sweden, India, Denmark, the Papal delegate, the secretary
general of the United Nations, and others. All of them had

---

[1] Johnson, *The Vantage Point*, p. 383.

been vigorously pursued, and all of them had come to naught.[2] The president's advisors all agreed that a peace initiative would be desirable and, indeed, necessary to temper public opinion, but they were also agreed that Hanoi would not accept any such proposal until it was convinced that it could not achieve its objectives on the battlefield or on the American home front.

Now, within his own administration, there was doubt being manifested about the course of the American effort in Vietnam. Clifford, whom the president respected and depended upon so much, had raised questions about the effectiveness of the total American effort and had suggested that some way must be found to turn the war around, to find a step that would lead to the end of the war. These views had caused the president and Clifford to grow apart, although Johnson continued to listen to him.

But Johnson's faith in Rusk never wavered. He sought advice from all quarters, and he might blend these views into a decision, but in the end it was mainly Rusk's judgment he wanted and Rusk's judgment he followed.[3] Rusk had proposed a peace initiative, a bombing pause without conditions north of the 20th parallel. But even Rusk, although convinced that such a proposal would do much to halt eroding public support for the war in the United States, doubted that it would be successful in bringing Hanoi to the negotiating table. And although Rusk was his constant and trusted advisor, the president was impressed with the arguments of Clifford and the Wise Men that unity must be restored to the country in order to allow the continuation of efforts in South Vietnam.

Thus, the president faced a dilemma. How could Rusk's peace proposal be transformed from one that would merely influence American public opinion and have desirable political consequences into a proposal that would do these things

[2] Ibid., pp. 395–396, 401.
[3] Christian, *The President Steps Down*, p. 115; Chalmers M. Roberts, *First Rough Draft*, pp. 252–253.

267

but would also be acceptable to Hanoi as a sincere American effort to achieve negotiations? Some other dramatic action was needed.

The president began to weigh one course of action of which his advisors, except for Rusk, were not aware. As President Johnson has stated: "I was judging the possible impact of a peace move linked with an announcement of my decision to withdraw from politics at the end of my term. That consideration put things in another perspective. I knew some of my advisors were thinking of a peace move in terms of public opinion and political consequences. I was wondering whether a new offer might really lead to a settlement. That made a considerable difference."[4]

The president had been thinking for a long time about the possibility of not seeking a second term; the idea was not solely related to the situation in Vietnam. Johnson was influenced by many considerations: "I frankly did not believe ... that I could survive another four years of the long hours and unremitting tensions I had just gone through. . . . I also knew that the likelihood of obtaining the necessary Republican votes to propel a tax bill through Congress . . . would be close to zero if I were a candidate for reelection."[5] The possibility of renewed domestic turmoil in the cities in 1968 was also a factor. Johnson felt it possible that he might be faced with the decision whether or not to use federal troops. He stated, "I did not want the slightest suspicion to arise . . . that I had responded with too little or too much, too soon or too late, with one eye on the safety of our citizens and the other on Election Day."[6]

Johnson also felt that he had expended much of his capital with Congress and had accomplished most of what he was capable of accomplishing in the field of domestic social legislation. Thus, whatever else he could possibly accomplish

[4] Johnson, *The Vantage Point*, p. 413.
[5] Ibid., p. 425–426. Also Max Frankel, "Johnson Pullout Conceived in '65."
[6] Johnson, *The Vantage Point*, p. 426.

would have to be done in a short time, and would probably be done better as a noncandidate. "He recalled coming in as a Congressman and seeing FDR immobilized domestically over the Supreme Court issue," Walt Rostow stated. "He felt that he could beat Nixon, but wouldn't be able to accomplish anything in his second term. He had too many 'tin cans' tied to him. He had used up his capital on civil rights and on the war."[7]

As the president saw the situation: "A man who uses power effectively must also be a realist. He must understand that by spending power he dissipates it. Because I had not hesitated to spend the Presidential power in the pursuit of my beliefs or in the interest of my country, I was under no illusion that I had as much power in 1968 as I had had in 1964."[8]

And there was the problem of Vietnam, which had created such divisions and hostilities in American public life. Johnson had become the focus of these divisions. He was being challenged within his own party for the presidential nomination directly on the issue of his conduct of the war, a challenge almost without precedent for an incumbent president. Thus, if the president were to withdraw from the race, the war issue might be removed from political debate. For a time, some semblance of unity would be restored to the country, and political connotations might be removed from any peace initiative.

The president had discussed the possibility of not being a candidate with his family and with many of his closest advisors over a period of time.[9] He was seeking the proper

[7] Personal interview with Walt W. Rostow, December 4, 1972.

[8] Johnson, *The Vantage Point*, p. 433.

[9] Ibid., pp. 427–433. Also Lady Bird Johnson, *A White House Diary*, pp. 248, 260, 261; Westmoreland, *A Soldier Reports*, p. 233. The secret was well kept from Johnson's campaign workers, however. James Rowe had arranged for Theodore H. White to meet with and interview the president on March 26, 1968, immediately subsequent to the meeting with the Wise Men. As Rowe recalled the meeting: "He kept us waiting two hours, which was out of character. I was struck

forum so that any such announcement would have the maximum impact. His speech at the end of March seemed an excellent time to make this dramatic announcement for many reasons. It would follow Harry Truman's precedent and would provide enough time so that the remaining Democratic candidates could organize their campaigns.[10] Also he wanted his bombing-pause proposal to be made free of other political considerations. He later explained:

> I wanted that decision to be understood by the enemy and by everyone everywhere as a serious and sincere effort to find a road to peace. The most persuasive way to get this across, I believed, would be to couple my announcement of a bombing halt with the statement that I would not be a candidate for reelection.

> I had also hoped that the combined announcement would accomplish something else. The issue of Vietnam had created divisions and hostilities among Americans, as I had feared. I wanted to heal some of those wounds and restore unity to the nation. This speech might help to do that. I deeply hoped so.[11]

It is not clear exactly when President Johnson decided to make a bombing pause north of the 20th parallel the initiative for peace that would be coupled with his decision to withdraw as a candidate for reelection. He had been inclined toward

---

by how tired the president was. He cut off White's questions on politics and talked about what he had accomplished during his administration. He said that he had done more than FDR. When we left, I remarked to White that it sounded like a valedictory. But I also indicated that I had heard this several times and that he would be badly fooled if he thought the president was serious about not being a candidate. In fact, I was in the White House all day working on the campaign on the day the president quit." Personal interview with James H. Rowe, Jr., December 29, 1975. See also Theodore H. White, *The Making of the President, 1968*, pp. 114–116.

[10] Johnson, *The Vantage Point*, pp. 430–431.

[11] Ibid., p. 427. Also Kearns, *Lyndon Johnson and the American Dream*, pp. 340–348.

THE PRESIDENT MAKES A DECISION

Rusk's proposal throughout March, although it did not seem to promise the beginning of negotiations. Rusk has indicated that he felt the president was seriously considering this proposal on March 16, when it was communicated to Saigon. McPherson believed this initiative had been dismissed as late as the meeting with the president on March 22.

The president has indicated that on the evening of March 27, he had a long talk with Senate Majority Leader Mansfield at the White House and discussed, among other things, his planned statement. The president read to Mansfield portions of the latest draft of his speech and indicated that he "told him I intended to end all bombing north of the 20th parallel."[12]

But as Mansfield recalled that conversation, the president was not nearly so definite about his decision to announce a bombing halt:

> I met with the President from 6:00 p.m. that evening to 9:30 p.m. that evening, alone. At that time he read to me portions of an address he contemplated making the following Sunday and told me that he had five people working on it. When he finished reading the speech, I told him that I thought it would be a mistake to make the speech because it offered no hope to the people and it only indicated a further involvement. He did mention the possibility of ending the bombing north of the 20th parallel. Whether or not that decision was "hard" at that time I do not know. I urged him as strongly as I knew how to bring this tragic war to an end because it was an area in which we should not have become involved in the first place and it was an area which was not and never had been vital to our security.[13]

Thus, it seems that as late as the evening of March 27, Johnson had not firmly decided to include a partial bombing

---

[12] Johnson, *The Vantage Point*, p. 419.
[13] Personal correspondence from Senator Mike Mansfield, May 21, 1973.

halt in his speech. Although he was being propelled in this direction by the dictates of politics, the necessity to make some peace offer, and by the advice of his most valued advisors, he was still determined to keep all of his options open. He was still trying to get support for a firm policy. As Mansfield recalled:

> The President did raise the question of the proposal to increase U.S. forces in Vietnam by 206,000 which I said was madness. I referred to the report I had made to him in 1965 in which I had indicated at that time that if we continued along the path we were following then, we could eventually have an expeditionary force of upwards of 750,000 men in Vietnam. He did not mention that he was not going to seek reelection but he did say, as he was going to the Oval Office and I was leaving, that he wished that his leaders had stood with him more. I said nothing, but he then thanked me for always stating my honest opinions to him and said that he appreciated my candor.[14]

Work on the president's speech continued. On Thursday, March 28, Rusk, Clifford, Rostow, William Bundy, and McPherson met in Rusk's office to go over the latest draft; the speech was to be delivered in three days. Clifford was one of those who did not know or think that he knew what was in the president's mind. Although encouraged by the

---

[14] Ibid.; for Senator Mansfield's 1965 report, see U.S., Congress, Senate, *Two Reports on Vietnam and Southeast Asia to the President of the United States by Senator Mike Mansfield*. In recalling his conversation with the president, Senator Mansfield mistakenly stated on the floor of the Senate in a later debate, "As a matter of fact, the entire speech was read to me that evening, and I recall that in the speech a reference was made to a cessation of the bombing below [sic] the 20th parallel." *Congressional Record*, p. 8,659. But as McPherson points out (and as Senator Mansfield later recalled in the cited personal correspondence), there was no mention of a bombing pause in any of the draft speeches up to that time. Personal interview with Harry C. McPherson, Jr., December 21, 1972. For a view of the early conflict between Johnson and Mansfield on Vietnam, see Steinberg, *Sam Johnson's Boy*, pp. 775–777; 779–780. Also Clayton Fritchey, "Mansfield's Warnings on Asia Date Far Back."

reaction of the Wise Men and their impact on the president, he still felt a little shut out these last days of March. "I had not been fully conversant with the speech as the drafts had progressed," he recalled. "I can't recall whether I had seen the draft or not before I got to the State Department."[15]

The specific reason for meeting in Rusk's office that morning was to go over the draft and smooth it out. "This shouldn't have taken long, and I expected to be back by lunch," Clifford remembered.[16] There was no peace initiative or bombing halt in the speech, and Clifford, like Senator Mansfield the night before, felt the whole tone of the draft was inconsistent with the mood of the country. As he saw it:

> The draft was presented in such a manner that I thought delivery of it would be a tragic error. When I read that speech, I made about a twenty-minute speech of my own. I said this was the wrong speech, that it was a speech about war. What the president needed was a speech about peace. For example, the first sentence read, "I want to talk to you about the war in Vietnam." I wanted that changed to "I want to talk to you about peace in Vietnam." What I wanted to do, and did, was to turn it around. The draft was a hard-nosed, stern call for a continuation of the policy of the application of force and a call for public support for a continuation of a policy that would ultimately bring us out all right. I thought that was a completely incorrect approach.[17]

Clifford reiterated his plea that the speech should announce the first step toward winding down the war and reducing the level of violence by a bombing halt north of the 20th parallel. He repeated his plan that such an initial step should be followed by some small step from Hanoi, to be followed by other deescalatory steps.

[15] Personal interviews with Clark M. Clifford, November 28, 1972 and February 15, 1973.
[16] Ibid.
[17] Ibid.; also McPherson, *A Political Education*, p. 435.

Rusk, in William Bundy's words, was "remarkably amenable."[18] "I didn't attach that much importance to the meeting on the 28th," recalled Rusk. "By that time, I had no doubt that the president was going to include the partial bombing-halt proposal in the speech, and I knew it also probable that he was not going to stand for reelection. The tone of the speech, given these two major points, had to be adapted to those conclusions. The bombing-pause initiative had not been put in before because the president did not like having these things put on paper and then later reading about them in the newspapers. The president wasn't going to tip his hand."[19] Rostow agreed: "My view was that you didn't have a speech until the peace proposal was put in. We knew that this would be the big thing. It sat around waiting the proper time to put it in. Once the peace proposal was put in, the heart of it being right up front in the speech, the speech was written around it. Redrafting the speech around the peace proposal was no big deal."[20]

So at this point, Rusk agreed with Clifford that the time had come to insert the bombing-halt proposal in the speech. He called in a secretary and dictated a statement embodying his original proposal, a de facto bombing pause north of the 20th parallel. "Clifford thought he had to fight the hawks, Rusk and Rostow," Rostow stated. "But we didn't have to be persuaded. We had been thinking about a postoffensive peace proposal since autumn. We had to bring Clifford on board."[21]

But Clifford, not knowing of the president's apparent decision to announce the bombing halt, saw the situation much differently. As he recalled the meeting: "This was no charade. When I left that meeting my own feeling was that I had made the most substantial contribution to the resolution of that

[18] Personal interview with William Bundy, October 11, 1972.
[19] Personal interview with Dean Rusk, January 22, 1973.
[20] Personal interview with Walt W. Rostow, December 4, 1972.
[21] Ibid.

274

difficulty than any other I made during my days with President Johnson. Out of that session came another draft, a whole new tone for the speech. By the time we ended up with a draft that day, we had a bombing-halt proposal. I thought that meeting turned the speech around."[22]

William Bundy shared this view. He saw Clifford as responsible for turning a hard speech into a plea for a peaceful solution. A few days later, he expressed this view by writing Clifford a letter, complimenting him upon the great public service he had performed and the contribution he had made to peace by his action on March 28.[23]

At the end of the meeting, Rusk had Bundy draft a cable notifying Saigon that the president had accepted the proposal to stop the bombing of North Vietnam north of the 20th parallel. Rostow then called the president, informed him that his advisors were working on an alternative draft of the speech, indicated that it might be time to insert a peace proposal, and asked if he would receive them later in the day.[24]

Both McPherson and Clifford departed to prepare alternate draft speeches. Clifford returned to the Pentagon and informed Warnke and Goulding of the tenor of the meeting and asked them to prepare a draft speech containing a bombing-halt proposal. These Defense officials were disappointed that a total bombing halt would not be offered, but Clifford told them it was out of the question, the president had determined that he was not going to halt the bombing completely.[25]

The problem in drafting an alternate speech became, therefore, for Clifford and his Defense officials to describe Rusk's

[22] Personal interview with Clark Clifford, February 15, 1973.

[23] Personal interview with William Bundy, October 11, 1972; personal interview with Clark Clifford, November 16, 1972. Although Clifford let me read this letter, which he has in his files, he declined to allow quotation from it because of its "personal nature."

[24] Personal interview with William Bundy, October 11, 1972; also Johnson, *The Vantage Point*, p. 420.

[25] Personal interview with Paul Warnke, November 17, 1972.

bombing-halt proposal in language that would stress the sincerity of the proposal and emphasize its peaceful nature. Thus, the draft speech prepared in the Defense Department had as its central theme the idea that our actions were designed to lead to talks. It offered Hanoi two alternative routes to follow after the bombing pause; one was a reaffirmation of the San Antonio formula which could lead to a total stopping of the bombing; the other was for Hanoi to match our restraint, thereby reducing the level of violence.[26]

Clifford, Rusk, and Rostow met with the president at the White House that evening and presented the seven-page alternate draft.[27] The president called Rusk into his office alone and authorized him to send his cable to Saigon informing Ambassador Bunker of his plans and instructing him to inform the South Vietnamese and to obtain their approval. Rusk repeated these instructions to Bundy, and the telegram was dispatched. To Bundy, it was only at this point that it was clear the president had made his decision.[28] To Rostow and Rusk, however, this was just "closing out the procedures" for inserting into the speech a peace proposal that had been decided on long before.[29]

Thus, Clifford was not able to change Rusk's proposal for an unconditional bombing pause north of the 20th parallel, but he was able to change the tone of the speech in order to make it conciliatory in nature, deescalatory in emphasis, and easier for North Vietnam to accept as a basis for talks. This was possible because both Rusk and Rostow felt that the president had already decided on such a bombing pause and would not be dissuaded. The language in which it was

[26] Personal interview with Morton Halperin, December 27, 1972.

[27] McPherson's alternate draft came to the White House later that evening. Elements of both the Defense and McPherson draft were used in the final speech. McPherson, *A Political Education*, p. 437.

[28] Personal interview with William Bundy, October 11, 1972. See also State 139439, Secretary of State to American Embassy, Saigon, March 28, 1968.

[29] Personal interview with Walt W. Rostow, December 4, 1972.

couched seemed to be less important. As Rusk saw it: "I did not try to shape the speech in the way I thought it would come out. I didn't roll up my sleeves and hammer away at it. The tone of the speech, given the two major points, had to be adapted to those conclusions."[30]

Thus, as McPherson perceived, it was something more than Clifford's conviction and persuasiveness that caused Rusk and Rostow to acquiesce in changing the tone of the speech. Their knowledge of the president's intentions, more than Clifford's pleading, turned their attention to "what" was to be in the speech as a peace initiative rather than "how" it was expressed.[31] But the "how," the tone in which the peace initiative was stated, was to be significant.

Another drafting session was held on Saturday, March 30. The president was there, coatless, with his tie pulled down, going over every word painstakingly. Clifford, Wheeler, Rostow, Christian, Bundy, and McPherson were present. Nicholas Katzenbach represented Rusk, who had left for Wellington, New Zealand, to attend a previously scheduled meeting of countries that contributed troops to Vietnam. It was in this session that Clifford made sure that what he considered to be the proper emphasis was included in the speech. As McPherson recalled:

> It was unique in my experience. It went on for many hours, with lots of argument about almost every section of the speech. We literally went over it word by word and changed many parts of it. Clifford, in that long drafting session, would question any word that gave the slightest suggestion that we would reinstitute the bombing. The president was quite aware of what he was doing and he would acknowledge it. Nobody ever said, "You will never be able to bomb again once you make this speech." But every message we were trying to convey in the speech was

[30] Personal interview with Dean Rusk, January 22, 1973.
[31] McPherson, *A Political Education*, pp. 436–437.

that we won't resume the bombing, we are dropping the bombing down to the 20th parallel. Clifford again indicated it was a give-and-take process—a winching-down process.[32]

When the meeting concluded, President Johnson, giving the first hint of the political decision that would be announced in this speech, told McPherson that a peroration would not be necessary as he had already written one.[33]

The president had consulted with leading members of Congress during the morning of March 29 concerning his intentions on bombing, and Clifford, at the president's urging, informed others the next day.[34] Also on March 30, Ambassador Bunker reported that he had carried out his instructions and had informed the South Vietnamese. Both Thieu and Ky, the ambassador reported, "immediately and without hesitation said it was satisfactory."[35]

Clifford also consulted with the members of the Joint Chiefs of Staff, whose support the president would need but who, except for General Wheeler, had not been consulted on the bombing pause. They were not difficult to persuade. The pause would be temporary if North Vietnam did not respond, there were few targets worth striking north of the 20th parallel, bad weather would preclude strikes in the area in any case, and some action was needed to rally support from the American public for a continuation of the war. "If this decision had not been made, we wouldn't have had the support of the American people to continue the war in any effective way," General Wheeler later stated.[36]

In a cable to Westmoreland giving him his first notifica-

[32] Personal interview with Harry C. McPherson, Jr., December 21, 1972. Also McPherson, *A Political Education*, p. 437. This session is not mentioned in *The Vantage Point*.

[33] McPherson, *A Political Education*, p. 437.

[34] Johnson, *The Vantage Point*, p. 421; McPherson, *A Political Education*, pp. 437–439; *Congressional Record*, p. 8,570.

[35] Johnson, *The Vantage Point*, p. 422.

[36] Personal interview with General Earle C. Wheeler, November 8, 1972.

tion of the president's decision, the military chiefs stressed these domestic considerations. Wheeler first informed Westmoreland of what he already knew, that the president would announce the deployment of the additional American forces agreed upon for South Vietnam. He stated that the president felt it mandatory that, in order to blunt accusations of escalation from opponents of his policy in Southeast Asia, he must at the same time take another initiative to achieve a peaceful settlement of the conflict. But of the factors "pertinent to the President's decision," public support for the war was stressed, and nothing was said of negotiations:

(a) Since the Tet offensive, support of the American public and the Congress for the war in Southeast Asia has decreased at an accelerating rate. Many of the strongest proponents of forceful action in Vietnam have reversed their positions, have moved to neutral ground, or are wavering. If this trend continues unchecked, public support of our objectives in Southeast Asia will be too frail to sustain the effort.

(b) Weather over the northern portion of North Vietnam will continue unsuitable for air operations during the next 30 days; therefore if a cessation of air operations is to be undertaken, now is the best time from the military viewpoint.

(c) It is hoped that this unilateral initiative to seek peace will reverse the growing dissent and opposition within our society to the war.

(d) The initiative will aid in countering foreign criticism.[37]

The Joint Chiefs of Staff stopped short of enthusiastic endorsement of the president's proposal, on which they had not been actively consulted. It was strictly the president's decision as far as the military chiefs were concerned. Wheeler

[37] JCS 3561, 310232Z March 1968, General Wheeler to Admiral Sharp, General Westmoreland, General Beach, Admiral Hyland, General Ryan.

informed his subordinate commanders: "The Joint Chiefs of Staff have been apprised of the unilateral initiative to be taken, understand the reasons therefore, and they enjoin all commanders to support the decision of the President."[38] In a separate cable, Wheeler informed Westmoreland that, at a White House meeting on March 30, the president pointed out that we had often been accused in the past of accompanying peace initiatives with increased military operations. The field commander was therefore told to conduct operations, especially the planned relief of Khe Sanh, in a low key "as being merely in the usual run of offensive operations against the enemy."[39]

On Saturday, March 30, the State Department dispatched a cable to the United States ambassadors in Australia, New Zealand, Thailand, Laos, the Philippines, and South Korea, instructing them to inform the respective heads of government of the major elements of the president's planned policy announcement. This cable supplied the ambassadors with additional arguments for the new policy for them to use in conversations with foreign leaders and allies:

> a. You should call attention to force increases that would be announced at the same time and would make clear our continued resolve. Also our top priority to re-equipping ARVN forces.
>
> b. You should make clear that Hanoi is most likely to denounce the project and thus free our hand after a short period. Nonetheless, we might wish to continue the limitation even after a formal denunciation, in order to reinforce its sincerity and put the monkey firmly on Hanoi's back for whatever follows. Of course, any major military change could compel full-scale resumption at any time.
>
> c. With or without denunciation, Hanoi might well feel limited in conducting any major offensives at least in the northern areas. If they did so, this could ease the pressure where it is most potentially serious. If they did

[38] Ibid.
[39] JCS 3564, 310431Z March 1968, General Wheeler to General Westmoreland.

not, then this would give us a clear field for whatever actions were then required.

d. In view of weather limitations, bombing north of the 20th parallel will in any event be limited at least the next four weeks or so—which we tentatively envisage as a maximum testing period in any event. Hence, we are not giving up anything really serious in this time frame. Moreover, air power now used north of 20th can probably be used in Laos (where no policy change planned) and in South Vietnam.

e. Insofar as our announcement foreshadows any possibility of a complete bombing stoppage, in the event Hanoi really exercises reciprocal restraints, we regard this as unlikely. But in any case, the period of demonstrated restraint would probably have to continue for a period of several weeks, and we would have time to appraise the situation and to consult carefully with them before we undertook any such action.[40]

Thus, in reassuring our allies of our "continued resolve," the cable clearly indicated that not very much was expected of this initiative. It could possibly reinforce our sincerity and "put the monkey firmly on Hanoi's back for whatever follows." It was not expected that Hanoi would react positively although they might "feel limited in conducting any major offensives at least in the northern areas," which was Clifford's greatest hope but which, the State Department thought, was highly unlikely. The testing period was expected to be four weeks, during a season when the weather would limit bombing in any case. After this period, our "hand would be free," presumably to resume bombing as before, although this was not stated explicitly.

The president's speech to the nation on Sunday, March 31, began with a summary of his efforts to achieve peace in Vietnam over the years.[41]

[40] Department of State 139431, March 30, 1968, quoted in *U.S.-Vietnam Relations*, IVC(7)(c), pp. 78–79.
[41] *Public Papers of Lyndon Johnson, 1968–69*, I, pp. 469–476.

Good evening, my fellow Americans.

Tonight I want to speak to you of peace in Vietnam and Southeast Asia. . . .

For years, representatives of our government and others have travelled the world—seeking to find a basis for peace talks.

Since last September, they have carried the offer that I made public at San Antonio.

That offer was this:

That the United States would stop its bombardment of North Vietnam when that would lead promptly to productive discussions—and that we would assume that North Vietnam would not take military advantage of our restraint.

Hanoi denounced this offer, both privately and publicly. Even while the search for peace was going on, North Vietnam rushed their preparations for a savage assault on the people, the government, and the allies of South Vietnam.

This attack during the Tet holidays, the president indicated, although causing widespread disruption, suffering, and loss of life, did not achieve any of its objectives.

In reiterating the San Antonio formula and dramatically announcing the partial suspension of the bombing of North Vietnam as a new initiative designed to reduce the present level of violence and lead to peace talks, the president did not include any consideration of domestic support for the war nor did he voice any of the doubts of the State Department cable of the previous night that this initiative was not expected to be fruitful. Indeed, the central theme of this portion of the speech was that our unilateral action was designed to lead to early talks. The president even designated the United States representatives for such talks:

There is no need to delay the talks that could bring an end to this long and this bloody war.

Tonight, I renew the offer I made last August—to stop the bombardment of North Vietnam. We ask that talks begin promptly, that they be serious talks on the substance of peace. We assume that during those talks Hanoi will not take advantage of our restraint.

We are prepared to move immediately toward peace through negotiations.

So, tonight, in the hope that this action will lead to early talks, I am taking the first step to deescalate the conflict. We are reducing—substantially reducing—the present level of hostilities.

And we are doing so unilaterally, and at once.

Tonight, I have ordered our aircraft and our naval vessels to make no attacks on North Vietnam, except in the area north of the Demilitarized Zone where the continuing enemy build-up directly threatens allied forward positions and where the movements of their troops and supplies are clearly related to that threat.

The area in which we are stopping our attacks includes almost 90 percent of North Vietnam's population, and most of its territory. Thus there will be no attacks around the principal populated areas, or in the food-producing areas of North Vietnam.

Even this very limited bombing of the North could come to an early end—if our restraint is matched by restraint in Hanoi. But I cannot in good conscience stop all bombing so long as to do so would immediately and directly endanger the lives of our men and our allies. Whether a complete bombing halt becomes possible in the future will be determined by events.

Our purpose in this action is so to bring about a reduction in the level of violence that now exists.

It is to save the lives of brave men—and to save the lives of innocent women and children. It is to permit the contending forces to move closer to a political settlement.

. . .

Now, as in the past, the United States is ready to send its representatives to any forum, at any time, to discuss the means of bringing this ugly war to an end.

I am designating one of our most distinguished Americans, Ambassador Averell Harriman, as my personal representative for such talks. In addition, I have asked Ambassador Llewellyn Thompson, who returned from Moscow for consultation, to be available to join Ambassador Harriman at Geneva or any other suitable place—just as soon as Hanoi agrees to a conference.

I call upon President Ho Chi Minh to respond positively, and favorably, to this new step toward peace.

No conditions were placed upon the bombing pause, and indeed, it was not designated as a "pause" but as a "stopping." Neither was any specific duration mentioned, and the speech contained no threat and listed no conditions under which bombing would be resumed. The president did not discuss what would happen if negotiations failed and indicated only that the South Vietnamese army was becoming stronger, had achieved a great deal, and would be reequipped by the United States in order to be able to make the effort necessary to defend its territory. The announcement of a slight increase in American forces received short mention and seemed almost a footnote to the dramatic statements that had preceded it.

On many occasions I have told the American people that we would send to Vietnam those forces that are required to accomplish our mission there. So, with that as our guide, we have previously authorized a force level of approximately 525,000.

Some weeks ago—to help meet the enemy's new offensive—we sent to Vietnam about 11,000 additional Marine and airborne troops. They were deployed by air in 48 hours, on an emergency basis. But the artillery, tank, aircraft, and other units that were needed to work with and support these infantry troops in combat could not accompany them on that short notice.

In order that these forces may reach maximum combat effectiveness, the Joint Chiefs of Staff have recommended to me that we should prepare to send—during the next five months—support troops totalling approximately 13,500 men.

The next portion of the president's speech listed in detail the costs of the Vietnam war and made a plea for congressional action to reduce the deficit by passing the surtax, which had been requested almost a year before. In summary, the president reiterated the United States' goals and objectives in South Vietnam, explained how these goals were directly related to the future of all of Southeast Asia, and called again on North Vietnam to seek a peaceful solution to the war.

I cannot promise that the initiative that I have announced tonight will be completely successful in achieving peace any more than the 30 others that we have undertaken and agreed to in recent years.

But it is our fervent hope that North Vietnam, after years of fighting that has left the issue unresolved, will now cease its efforts to achieve a military victory and will join with us in moving toward the peace table. . . .

So tonight I reaffirm the pledge that we made at Manila —that we are prepared to withdraw our forces from South Vietnam as the other side withdraws its forces to the North, stops the infiltration and the level of violence thus subsides. . . .

Tonight I have offered the first in what I hope will be a series of mutual moves toward peace.

I pray that it will not be rejected by the leaders of North Vietnam. I pray that they will accept it as a means by which the sacrifices of their own people may be ended. And I ask your help and your support, my fellow citizens, for this effort to reach across the battlefield toward an early peace.

Finally, the president addressed himself in a highly personal manner to his domestic accomplishments and to the issue that had seemed uppermost in his mind throughout the preceding month of deliberation, reassessment, and reappraisal of the nation's Vietnam policy—the issue of domestic unity. He stated:

> The ultimate strength of our country and our cause will lie not in powerful weapons or infinite resources or boundless wealth, but will lie in the unity of our people.
>
> This, I believe very deeply. . . .
>
> For 37 years in the service of our Nation, first as a Congressman, as a Senator and as Vice President and now as your President, I have put the unity of the people first. I have put it ahead of any divisive partisanship. . . .
>
> There is division in the American house now. There is divisiveness among us all tonight. And holding the trust that is mine, as President of all the people, I cannot disregard the peril to the progress of the American people and the hope and the prospect of peace for all peoples.
>
> So, I would ask all Americans, whatever their personal interests or concern, to guard against divisiveness and all its ugly consequences.
>
> Fifty-two months and ten days ago, in a moment of tragedy and trauma, the duties of this office fell upon me. I asked then for your help and God's, that we might continue America on its course, binding up our wounds, healing our history, moving forward in new unity, to clear the American agenda and to keep the American commitment for all of our people.
>
> United we have kept that commitment. United we have enlarged that commitment.
>
> Through all time to come, I think America will be a stronger nation, a more just society, and a land of greater opportunity and fulfillment because of what we have all done together in these years of unparalleled achievement.
>
> Our reward will come in the life of freedom, peace, and hope that our children will enjoy through ages ahead.
>
> What we won when all of our people united just must

not now be lost in suspicion, distrust, selfishness, and politics among any of our people.

Having eloquently stated the need for unity in a divided nation, the president then made the dramatic announcement that electrified the nation and the world, an announcement intended to restore unity to the divided country:

Believing this as I do, I have concluded that I should not permit the Presidency to become involved in the partisan divisions that are developing in this political year.

With America's sons in the fields far away, with America's future under challenge right here at home, with our hopes and the world's hopes for peace in the balance every day, I do not believe that I should devote an hour or a day of my time to any personal partisan causes or to any duties other than the awesome duties of this office—the Presidency of your country.

Accordingly, I shall not seek, and I will not accept, the nomination of my Party for another term as your President.

And let men everywhere know, however, that a strong, a confident, and a vigilant America stands ready tonight to seek an honorable peace—and stands ready tonight to defend an honored cause—whatever the price, whatever the burden, whatever the sacrifices that duty may require.

Thank you for listening.

Good night and God bless all of you.

The president's speech did not state that the 20th parallel would be the limit of American bombing of North Vietnam, although this specific limitation had been in the initial drafts. At the March 30 drafting session, the description had been changed to "the area north of the DMZ." This change had been made at the behest of Acting Secretary of State Katzenbach, who felt that the specific limitation would be meaningless to most people and would decrease Amer-

287

ican flexibility.[42] Although the 20th parallel had been used in describing the American action to the South Vietnamese, to allied governments, to the American military, and to congressional leaders, misunderstanding and controversy quickly arose. On April 1 American aircraft struck Thanh Hoa, an important transfer point just south of the 20th parallel.

News reports indicated that the president's speech had given the impression that the bombing would be limited to an area much closer to the DMZ.[43] Senator Fulbright immediately attacked the President's initiative as "a very limited change in existing policy . . . not calculated to bring a response from North Vietnam."[44] Senator Mansfield and others who had been consulted by the president informed Fulbright that the 20th parallel had been explicitly mentioned to them as the limitation.[45] Nevertheless, instructions were sent to the commanders in the field to "use strict judgment in their choice of targets." A second strike on Thanh Hoa, scheduled for the next day, was cancelled.[46]

On April 4, 1968, the deputy secretary of defense, in a memorandum for the secretaries of the military departments and the chairman of the Joint Chiefs of Staff, established Southeast Asia Deployment Program Number 6. This program added 24,500 personnel to the approved Program Number 5, and placed a new ceiling of 549,500 on United States forces in South Vietnam.[47] None of the 206,000 contingency

[42] Personal interview with William Bundy, October 11, 1972. Also McPherson, *A Political Education*, p. 435; Johnson, *The Vantage Point*, p. 493–494.

[43] "U.S. Jets Hit Deep in North: Bomb Targets 250 Miles Above DMZ"; "Flights Can Go 250 Miles Above DMZ. U.S. Bombs Away in North."

[44] *Congressional Record*, p. 8,569. Johnson, *The Vantage Point*, pp. 493–494.

[45] *Congressional Record*, pp. 4,869–4,877.

[46] Johnson, *The Vantage Point*, p. 494.

[47] Deputy Secretary of Defense, Memorandum for Secretaries of Military Departments, Chairman of the Joint Chiefs of Staff, Assistant Secretaries of Defense, Subject: *Southeast Asia Deployment Program Number 6*, dated April 4, 1968, quoted in *U.S.–Vietnam Relations*, IVC(6)(c), p. 90.

forces requested by General Wheeler on February 27 were to be deployed. The Program 6 figure was to represent the maximum United States deployment to Vietnam. No further request for American troops would be received from the American commander in Vietnam.

Late in the afternoon of April 3, 1968, the White House released the following statement by President Johnson:

> Today the Government of North Vietnam made a statement which included the following paragraph, and I quote:
>
> "However, for its part, the Government of the Democratic Republic of Vietnam declares its readiness to appoint its representatives to contact the United States representative with a view to determining with the American side the unconditional cessation of the United States bombing raids and all other acts of war against the Democratic Republic of Vietnam so that talks may start."
>
> Last Sunday night I expressed the position of the United States with respect to peace in Vietnam and Southeast Asia as follows:
>
> "Now, as in the past, the United States is ready to send its representatives to any forum, at any time, to discuss the means of bringing this war to an end."
>
> Accordingly, we will establish contact with the representatives of North Vietnam. Consultations with the Government of South Vietnam and our other allies are now taking place.[48]

The first step on what was to be a long and tortuous road to peace had been taken.[49] In an unexpectedly prompt and responsive reply to the president's initiative, Hanoi had moved the struggle for South Vietnam onto a new path.

[48] *Public Papers of Lyndon Johnson, 1968–69*, I, p. 492. See also Paul W. Ward, "Hanoi Gives U.S. Reply on Parley Bid."

[49] Peace talks began in Paris on Thursday, May 13, 1968. A cease-fire in South Vietnam was signed on January 27, 1973.

SIXTEEN

✿✿✿

Continuity or Change?

THE PRESIDENT, on March 31, 1968, announced four major decisions that were to have a profound effect on American political life and the conduct of the war in Vietnam. The decisions were: (1) he would make only a token increase in the size of American forces in Vietnam in response to the call of the military for major reinforcements and reconstitution of the strategic reserve; (2) he would make the expansion and improvement of the South Vietnamese armed forces the first priority of the continuing effort in Vietnam; (3) he would stop the bombing of a major portion of North Vietnam in order to move toward peace; and (4) he would not accept his party's nomination for another term.

Many different threads were woven into the making of these decisions, and the results far exceeded the expectations. Why then were these actions taken and these decisions made? What were their ultimate results?

The issue of increased troop deployments to Vietnam and the use to be made of these troops, the first questions that faced the president and his principal advisors in 1968, were problems that had their roots in the initial deployment of American troops to Vietnam in 1965. These troops had been introduced as an emergency measure; there was no unified, coherent, long-range strategy for their use. They were deployed initially to protect our air bases, to prevent the defeat of the South Vietnamese government, and to deny victory to the enemy. This strategy was soon seen by American military commanders as a negative one, yielding the initiative to the enemy and placing primary reliance upon the un-

290

dependable South Vietnamese armed forces. The American military planners preferred to take the war to the enemy, and they soon recommended a more aggressive strategy that would require additional American forces. This new strategy was to allow American forces by aggressive ground action to carry the war to the enemy wherever he might appear in South Vietnam. This major change in strategy was debated heatedly in Washington, but was finally accepted by the president. The participants in this decision knew the choices and understood the consequences. "Now we were committed to major combat in Vietnam," Johnson had stated.

But with this change in strategy came a change in objective as well. Instead of the limited objective of simply denying the enemy victory by convincing him over a period of time that he could not win, the objective of United States policy became that of inflicting casualties upon the enemy in the south to the extent necessary to cause him to change his strategy and cease his aggression. The substitution of the goal of defeating the enemy for that of simply denying him victory left the United States military commitment to Vietnam virtually open-ended. It was not easy to establish what the upper limit to the level of force necessary to accomplish this strategy of attrition would be, and it soon became apparent that there was embarrassingly little knowledge about the amount of force it would take to win the war under these circumstances.

The amount of force required depended almost entirely on the enemy's response, on how much North Vietnam was willing to expend in men and material. As the war progressed, the enemy indicated his stubborn willingness to commit the forces necessary to achieve his objectives. By trying to raise the cost of the war to North Vietnam to the point where it would cease its aggression or agree to negotiations (a strategy that was never made explicit), and with little information as to what was needed militarily to achieve this objective, United States civilian decision makers seemed willing to accept the military field commander's estimate of how much military force was needed and, within certain political and geographical restrictions, how this force should be applied in South Vietnam. Steady progress was promised by the military and, according to its reports, such progress was being achieved as the commitment of American forces steadily increased, although the increase was not as rapid as the military would have liked. As long as troop strength in Vietnam could be increased without large reserve call-ups or domestic economic dislocations, it was accepted by civilian leaders with little questioning of the basic strategy involved. Only Robert McNamara, in November of 1967, finally called for a leveling-off of the United States commitment.

But by March 1968, the choice had become clearer than it ever had been before, and the decisions that had been avoided in past years could no longer be avoided. The price in manpower had now reached the point where it could no longer be met without a large reserve call-up and severe economic adjustments. Further, there was no assurance that the manpower requirement would not grow larger in the future. There were also strong indications that large and growing elements of the American public had begun to believe the cost had already reached unacceptable levels and that these elements would strongly protest a large increase in that cost.

The political reality that faced President Johnson was that more of the same in South Vietnam, with an increased commitment of American lives and money and its consequent impact on the country, accompanied by no guarantee of victory in the near future, had become unacceptable to major elements of the American public. After the shock of the Tet offensive, the military reports of success and progress no longer rang true. The impression grew that progress in many ways had been illusory. The possibility of victory had become remote, and the cost had become too high, in both political and economic terms. Whatever its effects on the enemy in Vietnam, the Tet offensive, in its effects upon the American people, was a psychological victory of great magnitude for the Viet Cong.

The decision not to send American troops was made easier for the president by the continually improving military situation in South Vietnam. Although the press and much of the public had ridiculed early administration claims that Tet represented a military victory for the American and South Vietnamese forces, it soom became apparent that the enemy had indeed suffered severe losses and was in no position to launch a second round of attacks in the immediate future.[1] The troop increase requested by the military, both for Vietnam and for the reconstitution of the strategic reserve, had lost its justification. Further, meeting this request, which would require a widespread mobilization, would have endangered major elements of the domestic programs dear to Johnson's heart and would have resulted in widespread economic dislocation, both at home and abroad.

Thus, in Johnson's own words, four factors led to the denial of the request for a buildup in American troop levels:

First, and most important, it was our collective judgment that another massive Communist attack was increasingly unlikely. Second, the South Vietnamese were clearly improving militarily and getting in shape to carry a heavier combat load. Third, our financial problems remained serious, despite the solution we had found for the gold crisis. The Congress still had not passed a tax bill and we faced a large budgetary deficit. Finally, domestic public opinion continued to be discouraged as a result of the Tet offensive and the way events in Vietnam had been presented to the American people in newspapers and on television. Critics of our policy became more and more vocal as contention for the Presidential nomination heated up.[2]

[1] Institute for Strategic Studies, *Strategic Survey 1969*, pp. 44–45; Westmoreland, *Report on the War in Vietnam*, pp. 161–162.

[2] Johnson, *The Vantage Point*, p. 415.

The second factor, the ability of the South Vietnamese forces to resist the Communist effort and to retain their military capability, was an unexpected but welcome occurrence. Concomitant with the American decision to commit large ground forces to the Vietnam war in 1965 and, in effect, to take over the war effort, was the explicit expression of a total loss of confidence in the RVNAF. In 1965 this lack of confidence was well grounded in the demonstrated inability of the South Vietnamese armed forces to perform effectively against the dedicated Communist cadres. From the beginning of the American ground commitment, then, RVNAF had been relegated to a secondary role. In any case, American commanders, using their vast superiority in mobility and firepower, concentrated on the conventional battle dedicated to destroying enemy main force units and the supply system that supported them, far removed from the centers of population. Lip service was given to the need for developing South Vietnamese political and social institutions and destroying the Viet Cong infrastructure that challenged those institutions. But only the Vietnamese could accomplish this task, it was argued.[3]

Indeed, an overall ground tactical concept was devised to integrate United States and South Vietnamese military tasks to match their different capabilities. American ground forces would form the shield behind which these nation-building activities would take place. American forces would push North Vietnamese and main force Viet Cong units back to the unpopulated mountain, jungle, and border areas, inflict casualties, and interdict the supply system from the North through the sanctuaries of Laos and Cambodia. Behind this shield, the South Vietnamese forces would eliminate local enemy forces in small-scale operations, as the South Vietnamese in this environment were better able to distinguish friend from foe. Also, in these operations, helicopter mobility and massive firepower were less important and, in fact, could

[3] Douglas Pike, *Viet Cong: The Organization and Techniques of the National Liberation Front of South Vietnam*, p. vii.

be disadvantageous. The final element of this tactical concept, the elimination of the political apparatus, would primarily be the job of local police or paramilitary agencies.[4]

But the South Vietnamese army, poorly equipped and poorly motivated, tended to settle into fixed installations from which it ventured on these small-scale operations only during daylight hours. At night, ARVN troops generally withdrew into their static defensive fortifications, leaving the Viet Cong free to influence the great mass of the rural population. It became easier for the American commanders to deal with their own forces than to attempt to motivate the South Vietnamese. Thus, the ARVN was largely ignored as the war became Americanized.[5]

But faced with direct attack by Viet Cong forces during Tet, the South Vietnamese fought for their lives and generally performed well. The South Vietnamese government reacted decisively, at least in the early stages, in declaring martial law and implementing mobilization decrees that had been on the books but dormant for many months. As Johnson recalled: "The reaction in South Vietnam was quite different from what it was in this country. The people there rose up in arms and I think for the first time brought about a degree of unity that never existed before, and brought about a degree of determination that never existed before."[6]

"The heroes of Tet were the South Vietnamese, who really rallied to meet the challenge," Rostow stated.[7]

[4] U.S., Congress, House of Representatives, Committee on Appropriations, *Department of Defense Appropriations for 1969—Hearings, Part I*, pp. 540–543; Draper, *Abuse of Power*, pp. 176–179.

[5] Corson, *The Betrayal*, pp. 95–96; Race, *War Comes to Long An*, pp. 153–155; Bob Considine and Milton Kaplan, "Obsolete Weapons, Supplied by U.S., Hold Viets Back"; Jac Weller, "Our Vietnamese Allies: An Appraisal of Their Fighting Worth"; Brigadier General James Lawton Collins, Jr., *Vietnam Studies: The Development and Training of the South Vietnamese Army, 1950–1972*, p. 48; Joseph B. Treaster, "Paper Army: The Fraud of Vietnamization."

[6] Quoted in Halberstam, "Return to Vietnam," pp. 50–51. Also Carroll Kilpatrick, "LBJ Hails Courage of South Vietnamese."

[7] Personal interview with Walt W. Rostow, December 4, 1972.

For the first time, with the war no longer limited to the border areas and with the population centers directly threatened, it appeared that ARVN could, indeed must, become an efficient partner in the war against the VC/NVA. It quickly became apparent that any increase in American forces would only delay further the long-planned and already long-delayed modernization of the RVNAF. The strategy proposed by General Westmoreland in November, that of having the Vietnamese shoulder more of the burden, had been greeted with enthusiasm, but steps to implement it were to be taken over a period of many months. General Westmoreland himself had relegated this strategy to a secondary position in his post-Tet planning for contingency operations because he felt the war could be ended sooner by increasing American forces. Now, however, making the war the responsibility of the Vietnamese became an important, perhaps the only, means to continue the struggle without massive increases in American forces and with the support of the American people.

The road to ending the war in Vietnam, it finally became clear to American leaders, depended at least as much on South Vietnamese political and military development as it did on American arms. This realization, then, made it possible to return to the original purpose for which American forces were sent to South Vietnam, that of preventing the "defeat" of the South Vietnamese government. American forces, in the numbers now deployed, would continue to provide a shield behind which the South Vietnamese forces could rally, become effective, and win the support of the people. But now, resources would be made available to them, and pressure would be applied to allow, indeed to require, progress in this long-neglected area. Thus, the two decisions, that of limiting the increase in American forces in Vietnam and of improving Vietnamese forces to the point where they could take over more of the effort, were opposite sides of the same coin. They represented a long-overdue rationalization of the American effort in Vietnam and a return to the basic principles that had been used to justify American intervention in Vietnam in the first place.

The decision to announce a pause in the bombing of North Vietnam, except in the area near the DMZ, was compounded of three factors. The first was the apparent military ineffectiveness of the bombing; the second was the growing public disillusionment with the bombing; and the third was the desire to seek a negotiated end to the war.

Although the initial American air strikes in North Vietnam in early 1965 were justified as reprisals for attacks on American installations in South Vietnam, the air campaign quickly and almost imperceptibly evolved into a sustained bombing campaign. The publicly announced rationale for the bombing was to reduce the flow of Communist supplies and men to the South. But there were other unannounced and more complex reasons for the bombing. It was hoped that bombing the North would boost morale in South Vietnam in the face of a deteriorating political situation, demonstrate the determination of the United States to do what was necessary to protect its allies in Southeast Asia, destroy the overall capacity of the North to support the insurgency, punish the North Vietnamese for their actions in the South, compel Hanoi's leadership to stop supporting the Viet Cong, and serve as an important bargaining chip in any future negotiations, something the United States could offer to give up in return for a reduction or cessation of North Vietnam's efforts in the South.

The military, generally speaking, favored a strong, dramatic, and forceful application of air power as the only way to exert significant pressure on the North. A more gradual approach, progressively increasing in intensity, in which the prospect of greater pressure to come was at least as important as the actual damage inflicted, was advocated by civilian leaders. To the distress of the military, the latter approach was adopted. But the bombing campaign did not actually increase greatly in intensity after a certain level had been reached. It quickly came to be recognized that the bombing campaign could not break the will of Hanoi and make it abandon its efforts in South Vietnam. "Even if severely damaged," a CIA assessment indicated, "the DRV was quite likely to be willing to suffer such damage in the course of a test of will with the United States over the course of events in South Vietnam."[8]

The North Vietnamese showed signs of adjusting to a long bombing siege. It became clear, even to the most ardent advocates of air power, that there was no way of interrupting the flow of North Vietnamese supplies to the South to an extent that would seriously hamper the enemy. The bombing of the North leveled off, was relegated to a secondary role in the United States military strategy for dealing with the war, and became, in effect, a punitive measure against the North for its efforts in South Vietnam. The carrot of stopping the bombing was deemed almost as important an element of our strategy as the stick of continuing it, and bombing pauses were instituted periodically in an attempt to elicit matching restraint from the other side.

But punitive bombing of military targets in a small agricultural country by the world's greatest power seemed to many to be insupportable on either moral or policy grounds. Condemnation of the bombing spread to the campuses in the United States and to a widening circle of congressmen. In some cases, the bombing affected the friendly relations of the United States with foreign powers, who found it increasingly difficult to justify to their own people their support of American policy.

The Tet offensive should have made clear to both the proponents and critics of bombing that, as a means of stopping the infiltration of men and supplies, it had been a signal failure. Bombing alone, as it was being conducted, could not prevent the enemy from amassing the material and infiltrating into South Vietnam the manpower necessary to carry out operations on a massive scale if he chose to pay the price. Moreover, Tet further demonstrated that the bombing had

[8] *U.S.–Vietnam Relations*, IVC(2)(c), p. 8.

not succeeded in breaking Hanoi's will to undergo the sacrifices and hardships required to continue the struggle.[9] Thus, the punitive value of the bombing, as the offensive faded, seemed less important to the president than the potential of a bombing suspension (even partial) for producing serious peace negotiations and providing propaganda that would appease the American public.

The president's advisors all felt that a peace initiative might be successful after the winter/spring campaign had demonstrated to the North Vietnamese the impossibility of a military victory in South Vietnam. Rostow recalled: "We saw the situation in Vietnam improving. We expected the enemy to make a maximum effort in his winter/spring offensive. The consensus was that after this offensive had been expended, we would make a peace effort accompanied by a bombing halt to see if they would be willing to negotiate. We expected this peace initiative to be raised about May."[10]

But Rusk raised the issue early in March and, as the month progressed, the president became convinced that Rusk's proposal would suit his purposes the best. The offer would be unconditional, and it would involve little military risk, as the bombing would continue in the area of the DMZ and would be precluded by weather in other areas of North Vietnam in any case. Further, the offer would placate the United States public and elicit sufficient public support to continue the war. Moreover, as the month wore on and the magnitude of the VC/NVA setback became clear, it seemed possible that this proposal could be the serious peace proposal contemplated for later in the year, that the enemy would also recognize the extent of his defeat and enter into serious negotiations.

The decision not to seek the presidential nomination was made, according to Johnson, long before the Tet offensive

---

[9] Jon M. Van Dyke, *North Vietnam's Strategy for Survival*; also Raymond J. Barrett, "Graduated Response and the Lessons of Vietnam"; Salisbury, *Behind the Lines*, pp. 107–108, 137–147.

[10] Personal interview with Walt W. Rostow, December 4, 1972.

and was not directly related to that incident or to the Vietnam war generally. However, the president saw this decision as an opportunity to restore unity to a divided country that would no longer accept his leadership. Although public support for the American effort in Vietnam remained remarkably level during this period, public confidence in the president's handling of the war eroded sharply.[11] Johnson followed the opinion polls closely. He had commented early in 1967: "I think they [my grandchildren] will be proud of two things. What I did for the Negro and seeing it through in Vietnam for all of Asia. The Negro cost me 15 points in the polls and Vietnam cost me 20."[12]

The Tet offensive had made the war in Vietnam and Johnson's conduct of it a partisan political issue. Johnson, to a great extent, had lost control of his own party and, even with the advantages inherent to an incumbent president, faced the possibility of not winning his party's nomination. Although sincerely dedicated to seeking a negotiated solution to the war, any such negotiating initiative in the climate then prevailing would seem to be a political move. Thus, coupling a peace initiative with the announcement of his withdrawal would accomplish several purposes. It would serve to remove the search for peace in Vietnam from politics, it would restore some measure of unity to the country, and it would emphasize the bombing-pause proposal as a serious initiative toward peace. As Johnson later explained his motives: "I was desperately trying to show that I was reasonable, that our country would prefer to talk rather than fight, that we were determined not to let aggression take over Southeast Asia, but that we would try to negotiate it out rather than fight it out. . . . I wanted to use the announcement that had to come as a predicate and as a basis for

[11] Mueller, "Presidential Popularity from Truman to Johnson," pp. 23–24, 28, 30; Verba et al., "Public Opinion and the War in Vietnam," pp. 321–322; Hahn, "Local Referenda," p. 1,189; Converse et al., "Continuity and Change in American Politics," p. 1,086.

[12] David Wise, "The Twilight of a President"; Rostow, *Diffusion of Power*, p. 477.

getting all the steam I could toward a possible successful peace move."[13]

Did these decisions announced by Johnson on March 31, 1968, constitute a turning point, a "fork-in-the-road" in the Vietnam policy and strategy theretofore pursued by the United States? The answer is "yes," although it was not intended or foreseen by most of the principal participants in the making of those decisions that such a result would occur.

Johnson did not see the decision as a change in policy or as a repudiation of past policies. He saw the decisions made in March 1968 as allowing the United States to see through its commitment in Southeast Asia.[14] In fact, Johnson's basic decision to throw the country's resources behind the expanded and more confident South Vietnamese forces opened the way, in his mind, to accelerate forward movement toward American objectives in Vietnam. The war would be leveled off, insofar as the United States effort was concerned, and the South Vietnamese would share more of the burden. But the United States, to Johnson's mind, had a responsibility to finish what it had started. He stated: "Looking ahead, I could not see a time when the United States could, with safety, withdraw totally from Asia and the Pacific, for we were a Pacific power with a profound interest in the stability, peace, and progress of that vital part of the world."[15] This stability and peace, to Johnson, continued to mean that the United States must honor its treaty commitments and stop Hanoi's aggression against South Vietnam. This view did not change.

But Vietnam had now become an issue of partisan domestic politics which threatened the ability of the nation to see its commitment through. To those who had by and large supported the United States intervention in Vietnam, it appeared after Tet that the policy being pursued was not solving the problem; to those who opposed the Vietnam inter-

[13] CBS interview with Lyndon B. Johnson, p. 36.
[14] Johnson, *The Vantage Point*, pp. 422–423.
[15] Ibid., p. 423.

vention, Tet seemed to prove that our policies were not only wrong but ineffective as well. Thus, Johnson was determined to remove this issue from the political arena so that the American commitment could be seen through. His announcement that he was not a candidate was intended to uncouple the Vietnam issue from the forthcoming election.

Johnson's decisions on troop deployments and a bombing pause represented no great departure from past policies in Vietnam, and they were not intended to be irrevocable decisions made to change the course of United States policy in Vietnam. But although the president did not announce that this would be the final American troop deployment, the decision had an air of finality about it. The limit of force the American military could commit to Vietnam without mobilization had finally been reached. In previous years, the decision had always been made to increase American force levels, although not as quickly or to the extent desired by General Westmoreland and the Joint Chiefs of Staff. But now the decision had been made to level off the American commitment. The strategic reserve could be stretched no further. The American effort would now settle in for the long pull. Financial, political, and public opinion problems had made any other course an unacceptable alternative for the president.

But the forces now allocated were far below those deemed necessary by the military to pursue its optimum strategic concept and defeat the enemy in South Vietnam within a short period. Thus, although it was not a conscious intention, and although no new strategic guidance was provided the new field commander, the limitation on American deployments and the emphasis on increased activity by the RVNAF necessitated a new strategy. More of the war necessarily would be fought by the RVNAF as American forces became "increasingly superfluous." However, the president also wanted to insure that all options remained open to his successor. Thus, he did not announce these troop deployments as the final limit to the American ground commitment to

CONTINUITY OR CHANGE?

Vietnam and later refused, when urged to do so by the South Vietnamese president, to announce any future plans for the withdrawal of American forces.[16]

Similarly, the decision to halt the bombing of North Vietnam north of the 20th parallel was not seen as a change in policy. Bombing pauses had been used before to test Hanoi's willingness to negotiate. A new initiative to begin negotiations had been seen as likely at the end of the winter/spring offensive. But, as the military situation in Vietnam improved after Tet and as political support for the war in the United States deteriorated, a peace initiative became necessary to placate the American public.

Although the conditions under which a possible resumption of the bombing would occur were not made explicit in the president's speech, it was understood by him and his principal advisors that it would, indeed, resume if no acceptable response was received from Hanoi. Rostow recalled: "I would guess it was President Johnson's view that he would and could resume full freedom of action if there were no positive response from Hanoi. . . . It was recognized as probably difficult—and it may well have proven difficult—but it is my impression that the common assumption at the end of March was that bombing throughout North Vietnam would be resumed if there was no diplomatic opening with Hanoi."[17]

Rusk's view was not so definite, but he felt that the bombing pause did not restrict the president's options. He stated: "This was a more dramatic, a more significant instance of what we had tried several times before. It wasn't new. The idea of a partial bombing halt had been around a long time and had been tried before. But if there had been no response from Hanoi, I don't know if we would have resumed. It would have turned largely on the military situation and the reaction of Congress."[18]

[16] Ibid., pp. 511–513; Rostow, *Diffusion of Power*, p. 423; personal interview with Walt W. Rostow, December 4, 1972.

[17] Personal correspondence from Walt W. Rostow, July 11, 1973.

[18] Personal interview with Dean Rusk, January 22, 1973.

Others among the president's advisors felt that the re-institution of the bombing would be difficult in any case and suspected that Johnson was much more serious at this time in seeking a negotiated end to the war. "I believed it would be very difficult to resume, to reincrease the war, to restore the previous level, but it would not have been impossible," recalled William Bundy. But Bundy also thought it significant that the president did not underscore the temporary nature of the bombing halt. As he recalled: "When the president stopped the bombing in October, he extracted a blood pledge, a promise, from everyone to support him if he had to resume. He extracted no such pledges at this time. At this time, he was playing something more indeterminate and much more serious; the possibility of a resumption was left open."[19]

General Wheeler, Rusk, and Rostow did not see the decisions of March 1968 as heralding a new American policy in Vietnam. They all saw the president's announcements as a means to rally public support in order to continue the war much as before. Wheeler, of course, had often stated the military's dissatisfaction and frustration with the limitations, both geographical and numerical, that had been placed on its efforts to defeat the enemy. The Joint Chiefs of Staff saw the Vietnam war as a military problem and, in the absence of specific strategic guidance to the contrary from their civilian superiors, set about to defeat the enemy. They felt that the limits imposed on military operations by the unwillingness to call up reserve forces, to allow an all-out bombing campaign against the North, or to allow attacks on enemy sanctuaries in Laos and Cambodia stretched out the achievement of United States objectives in Vietnam and endangered the ability to meet possible military contingencies elsewhere in the world. The strategic reserve was dangerously weakened in order to support the military effort in Vietnam, yet this military effort was hampered by political restrictions.

[19] Personal interview with William Bundy, October 11, 1972.

As late as November 1967, the Joint Chiefs had indicated to the president that they considered the rate of progress in Vietnam to have been and to continue to be slow largely because American military power had been constrained in a manner that had significantly reduced its effectiveness. The Joint Chiefs had informed the president at that time that progress would continue to be slow as long as limitations on military operations continued.

The military chiefs, although shocked by the unexpected intensity and length of the Tet offensive, saw it as a great opportunity. It appeared to offer the solution to their problems. By stressing the dangers inherent in the Vietnamese battlefield, General Wheeler hoped to persuade the president, who would not endure a defeat, and the new secretary of defense, known for his support of the American strategy in Vietnam, that the time had come for, indeed, the situation necessitated, drastic action. Although the critical underlying issue was mobilization in order to reconstitute the strategic reserve, this aspect of General Wheeler's troop request was subordinated to the field commander's apparent needs. A popular and apparently endangered American field commander's request for troops would justify mobilization. Once the strategic reserve had been reconstituted and the nation put on a virtual war footing, resources would be available for achieving victory in Vietnam. The Joint Chiefs of Staff, therefore, saw Tet not as a repudiation of past efforts in Vietnam but as an opportunity to attain their basic objectives by eliminating the hated restrictions that had hampered previous efforts.

Rusk was sincere in his desire to seek peace through negotiations. He felt, however, that such efforts would be fruitless until the North Vietnamese were convinced by military force that they could not win on the ground in South Vietnam. Only then would they enter into serious negotiations. Indeed, Rusk felt that premature and insistent efforts to convince Hanoi to enter into negotiations could be and had been counterproductive. He has stated: "There was a question whether our anxiety to bring about a peaceful settlement led North Vietnam to believe we wanted peace so badly that we would do anything to achieve it. This view was expressed to me many times by foreign leaders."[20]

But after Tet, Rusk was also worried about the erosion of public support for the war in the United States. He recalled: "The thing that concerned me was that this tumult in Congress and in the press continued to deprive Hanoi of any incentive to negotiate. The home front collapse would give them politically what they could not get militarily. I thought that we ought to make a major effort to bring the war to a negotiated settlement."[21]

Rusk could not recommend a complete cessation of the bombing, which Hanoi had indicated was its condition for entering into negotiations. He felt that, although the bombing of much of North Vietnam produced no compensatory effect on the battlefield compared to its cost and could be stopped with little military risk, we could not deprive our troops on the ground of air support near the DMZ or on the Ho Chi Minh trail. "In the absence of any serious indication that Hanoi would do business, a complete halt would have made it rough on our men in South Vietnam," he felt. "Thus, I was in favor of a partial, not a complete, halt." Rusk foresaw no major change in American policy necessitated by the Tet offensive. "The idea of a partial bombing halt had been around and had been tried before," Rusk stated. "It wasn't new." He saw the initiative of March 1968 as "a more dramatic, more significant instance of what we had tried several times before."[22]

Rostow, too, never wavered in his conviction that the war could be materially shortened only by putting substantial American forces on the ground across the Ho Chi Minh trail in Laos or into the southern part of North Vietnam to cut off North Vietnamese supplies to the South. Without such decisive action, the United States would be committed to a

---

[20] Personal interview with Dean Rusk, January 22, 1973.
[21] Ibid.   [22] Ibid.

long, uncertain struggle. "I regarded as ridiculous the view that you couldn't make the cost too high to the enemy," he stated.[23]

But he also saw the Tet offensive as a massive political as well as military setback for North Vietnam.[24] He saw this setback as offering new opportunities for the United States to achieve its objectives in Vietnam. Initially, he felt that these objectives could be achieved by sending General Westmoreland those forces that were immediately available. But as the American and South Vietnamese military position improved, the case for an increase in troops, and public support for such a policy, diminished. As he saw it: "The military situation was getting better, and the South Vietnamese were doing well. The essential element as far as troops were concerned was what we could round up immediately to give Westmoreland the minimum he needed. Berlin and Korea were also settling down."[25]

With military needs less urgent, Rostow's thoughts turned to a negotiating initiative, an initiative he felt would be necessary at the end of the enemy's winter/spring offensive and which he thought would come around the beginning of May. He recalled: "I knew what this incredible, desperate effort meant in terms of guerrilla warfare. It was a damn desperate thing for them to do. It was obvious that they wouldn't have a Sunday punch for a long time. For those of us who had watched and lived with the situation, after two years of slow improvement, we smelled the desperation of it. I really felt we would get a diplomatic contact when it was clear that they had failed."[26]

Indeed, Rostow was impressed with the series of diplomatic initiatives for peace that had come from third parties during the previous months. He felt that a fundamental military and political turning point had been achieved in South

[23] Personal interview with Walt W. Rostow, December 4, 1972.
[24] Walt W. Rostow, "Losing Big: A Reply."
[25] Personal interview with Walt W. Rostow, December 4, 1972.
[26] Ibid.

Vietnam which might make a talk-and-fight situation possible. "Given the importance I attached (and attach) to the removal of North Vietnamese forces from Laos," he stated, "I knew we were a long way from the end of the road."[27] Thus, he saw negotiations at that point as useful for achieving American objectives, not as a change in United States policy or objectives. As he recalled:

> I wanted to make sure that North Vietnam had made the judgment that the Tet offensive had failed. We had been thinking about a postoffensive peace proposal since autumn. I could now see logic in their entering into a talk-fight stage after Tet. Thus, our minds were well prepared for a peace initiative, and we were comfortable with it. Clifford had the view that he had to overcome Rusk and Rostow. He was fighting a battle for the president's mind that didn't have to be fought. So far as President Johnson, Dean Rusk, and I were concerned, a major peace proposal was contemplated.[28]

But Clifford sought and fought for a more fundamental change in administration policy in Vietnam and in a more fundamental way was indeed fighting for the mind of the president. He was the only one who advocated that the direction and level of our effort be changed, that our objectives be modified, and that different methods be used. He had taken office at the beginning of March with one overriding thought—indeed, as he perceived it, one overriding assignment from the president—that of responding to the military request for additional forces in Vietnam in order to prosecute the war more forcefully. But he had had his doubts about the wisdom of the overgrown American efforts in South Vietnam, and his doubts were fed by his principal advisors who, with Clifford's predecessor, had long before come to the conclusion that our current strategy offered no hope for victory or peace in the immediate future.

[27] Personal correspondence from Walt W. Rostow, July 11, 1973.
[28] Personal interview with Walt W. Rostow, December 4, 1972.

Clifford began to ask questions that had not been asked before. Our involvement in Vietnam had grown, based upon enemy action and the piecemeal commitment of ground troops to Vietnam. But now Clifford asked the hard questions as to just what these troops were to do, what strategy would be pursued, what specific results would be accomplished and in what period of time? These questions had not really been answered in the Defense Department. The Joint Chiefs of Staff, in the absence of any clear strategic guidance, had seen their role as supporters of the field commander. As General Wheeler recalled: "The Joint Chiefs of Staff are good at some things and not good at others. They are good at developing and issuing strategic guidance. But they are not good at developing force levels or guiding the use of forces. These activities must be left to the field commander."[29] But the president did not accept the strategic guidance recommended by his senior military advisors, that of an all-out war against North Vietnam without geographic limitations or sanctuaries. He placed political constraints on the war, in effect determining strategic guidance himself.

The Joint Chiefs of Staff made no independent analyses of what force would be needed to achieve United States objectives within the restrictions placed upon military operations by the president, nor of what actually could be achieved within the constraints of this strategy. They had no desire to second guess General Westmoreland concerning the need for or the employment of American forces in Vietnam. It was Westmoreland, therefore, who developed the strategy, and it was he who calculated the force levels necessary to implement that strategy.

Westmoreland explained his strategy, and the adjustments he made in it to accommodate the political realities he faced, in the following manner:

Within my area of responsibility, I devised a coherent strategy. In 1965 I asked for troops to stave off defeat. In

[29] Personal interview with General Earle G. Wheeler, November 8, 1972.

309

1966 I worked up a rather ambitious plan to go on the offensive. My troop request included a corps force to be in reserve, and to be committed when needed or when I felt it could be utilized to our advantage. This reserve force was tacitly approved but never materialized. And in 1967 I asked for what I considered the optimum force, which I viewed as a final request but did not officially announce it as such. I did not get my optimum force but did essentially get my fallback request which I classified as "minimum essential." My optimum force was designed to accelerate progress by putting more pressure on the enemy and give me enough forces to pursue options, as political authority permitted. The force received (minimum essential) did not provide that flexibility. Every time I submitted my annual troop program, it was scrutinized and cut back. Cuts in my request were made by the secretary of defense and were arbitrary. Experience proved my original requests as militarily justified. The strategy of authorities in Washington was never articulated but deduced to hurt the enemy until he agreed to negotiations. Initially, the enemy was going to be hurt by bombing the North. Later, a strong school of thought developed, encouraged by me, that we also had to hurt him in the South. Civilian authorities tried frequently to "signal" the enemy and thereby maneuver him to the conference table. . . . I frankly was never sanguine about that prospect because I felt that the enemy was not going to negotiate until he thought it would be in his interest. . . . In 1967 I realized that hurting the enemy until he agreed to negotiate was not a viable strategy so I searched for what I considered a practical strategy and brought it to Washington in November 1967. As events evolved, I had two strategies. One was to accept a prolonged war but to phase out U.S. troops over a period of time. The other was to take advantage of a spectacular defeat—the enemy's Tet offensive as it turned out—to apply the necessary force to bring the war to an early end. The two strategies were compatible and depended upon political decisions.[30]

The president and the secretary defense had always consulted the military leaders before making decisions about force levels. But decisions on force levels alone were not a substitute for the development of a coherent, viable strategy for the employment of those forces. And the advice of the military leaders in Washington concerning force levels was always predictable: "Do what General Westmoreland and Admiral Sharp ask, lift the political and geographical restraints under which our forces operate, and increase the size of the strategic reserve in the United States."[31]

Thus, the strategy for which Clifford searched had not been articulated in Washington. The coherent plan he sought for ending the war had not been developed by the Joint Chiefs of Staff. Indeed, that had not been their objective. The military objective had always been to impose casualties on the North Vietnamese and Viet Cong to the extent that they would realize that they could not win in the South and would be forced to enter into negotiations to end the war. But there was no clear idea as to when this elusive psychological objective would be achieved. Thus, the decision as to when to end the war was left in the hands of the North Vietnamese.

Clifford was not satisfied with the answers the military leaders gave to his questions. He became convinced that the United States was pursuing both an endless and a hopeless course in Vietnam. He became convinced that gradual disengagement of American forces was the only feasible way to achieve a negotiated peace in Vietnam, This conviction was reinforced by what he sensed was the attitude of an influential segment of the American people toward the conduct of the war. As Clifford recalled: "What influenced me was

[30] Personal interview with General William C. Westmoreland, September 16, 1973.

[31] Alain C. Enthoven and K. Wayne Smith, *How Much Is Enough? Shaping the Defense Program, 1961–1969*, pp. 299–300.

the attitude of the public. I didn't think the public was willing to support the policy we had been following."[32]

Thus, Clifford could see no way out of the war except by compromise and mutual deescalation, and he risked his friendship with the president by pressing his views within the councils of the administration. He was never apologetic or retiring about the matter. The president was often annoyed with him and sometimes showed his annoyance, but as a practical matter he consulted Clifford and listened to his views, and their friendship at first did not suffer severely.[33] But Clifford did not convince the president nor change his mind prior to March 31. McPherson recalled an incident in April 1968 in which Clifford expounded his views to the president, who patiently heard him out and then replied, "Old friend, I don't agree with a word that you have said."[34]

So it was Clifford who was brought on board. He finally was persuaded to accept Rusk's partial bombing halt as a peace initiative, not because he was convinced that it would be useful but because he was convinced that it was as far as the president would go. He was able to see to it that this proposal was phrased in conciliatory language. This was no insignificant contribution, as the tone of the president's speech and the shock of his political retirement gave Rusk's peace proposal a dramatic aura and an acceptability that it would not otherwise have had. Clifford may not have won this battle, but he was ultimately triumphant in insuring that the president's decisions put the United States on a new road in Vietnam, on a course of disengagement he had helped to chart.

[32] Personal interview with Clark Clifford, November 28, 1972.

[33] Personal interview with Harry C. McPherson, Jr., December 21, 1972; also Christian, *The President Steps Down*, pp. 78, 115. However, the relationship between the two men cooled considerably, and they remained alienated following the publication of Clifford's account of his change of heart in *Foreign Affairs* in July 1969. Personal interview with Harry J. Middleton, October 11, 1973.

[34] Personal interview with Harry C. McPherson, Jr., December 21, 1972.

If an official at a high enough level in government repeats something often enough, it becomes government policy unless the president himself steps in and contradicts or denies that policy. Clifford had already used this technique in modifying the administration's interpretation of the San Antonio formula. Now, in the days and months following the president's speech, Clifford launched a deliberate public campaign, which was to last until he left office, to interpret the president's decisions in the way he felt they should be interpreted. He did not criticize the president's decisions or oppose them publicly. He did not indicate that the president was in error, nor did he attempt to leak or undercut a presidential action or decision. He continually presented the president as a man of peace who had given his all in the quest for peace. But while thus scrupulously refraining from undermining or criticizing the president, Clifford deliberately, skillfully, and consistently moved in public to interpret the president's actions so as to occupy ground that Johnson had not yet reached. In this way, Clifford made the president's decisions of March 31 a turning point in the direction of the United States effort in South Vietnam.[35]

No public statements by Clifford during this period were accidental. As he has stated it: "This was a conscious effort on my part. It was based upon what I believed the president's attitude should be and what I thought our policy should be. During that period of time during which I touched on it repeatedly, at no time did I get a word of criticism or caution from the president."[36]

Clifford moved quickly to insure that the American public saw the president's decision as a turn in American policy. He hoped to generate a mood, both in Washington and in Saigon, that the deployments announced did indeed represent an upper limit on the American troop commitment to Vietnam. At his first press conference, on April 11, the secretary of defense repeated the theme of "troop limitation" which he

[35] Goulding, *Confirm or Deny*, p. 329.
[36] Personal interview with Clark Clifford, February 15, 1973.

had first voiced at a background press briefing the day following the president's speech.[37]

In this press conference, Clifford stressed the "policy decision . . . to turn over gradually the major effort to the South Vietnamese," and indicated that this was "part and parcel . . . of the President's decision to place a limitation at this time upon our troop level at a point not exceeding 550,-000."[38] Clifford, in this same press conference, publicly reiterated the views he had advocated so often in private to the president in the preceding weeks concerning the future course of American action in South Vietnam: "We are starting on a new course of action. The President made an offer to Hanoi to start a planned program of deescalation, the theory being that he would take a step, they might then take a step, he would take another, and over the course of time it could lead to a substantial deescalation of the fighting."[39]

Clifford's tactics worked admirably. The American press was unanimous in interpreting the secretary's statement as an explicit enunciation of a new strategy. The *New York Times* reported the following day:

> Defense Secretary Clark M. Clifford announced today a ceiling of 549,500 on the American troop strength in Vietnam and declared that the Johnson Administration had adopted a policy aimed at the gradual transfer to South Vietnam of the major responsibility for the war effort.
>
> He linked the transfer policy to a decision by President Johnson to treat the level of 549,500 . . . as a ceiling beyond which the Administration does not intend to go at this time.
>
> But Mr. Clifford was careful not to make his remarks sound like an ultimatum to Saigon. . . .
>
> The implications of his remarks, however, were that the United States was telling Saigon for the first time that it

[37] Goulding, *Confirm or Deny,* pp. 329–330.
[38] News conference of Secretary of Defense Clark M. Clifford, April 11, 1968, pp. 6, 10.
[39] Ibid., p. 12.

could not look forward to an unending flow of American reinforcements. If more troops are needed, Mr. Clifford was saying in effect, Saigon must supply them.[40]

In an editorial on the same day, the *Washington Post* also saw a significant shift in strategy by the administration, a shift Clifford intended they should see: "Now another major decision has been made . . . for it shifts us back on the original track—indeed the only track which offers the promise of a secure and stable South Vietnam without a massive, indefinite American military presence. It is a decision, as explained by Secretary Clifford, to move in a much more positive and forceful way toward the day when the South Vietnamese are carrying proportionately more of the load and the United States is becoming . . . 'progressively superfluous.' "[41]

Clifford's message had gotten across clearly to the American public. There is evidence that his interpretation of the president's decisions was clearly perceived in Saigon as well. Ambassador Bunker has stated: "President Johnson's statement of March 31 brought the Vietnamese face-to-face with the fact that our commitment was not open-ended, that one day they would be on their own. This realization had an important and subtle impact on the subsequent development of Vietnamese attitudes and events."[42]

[40] William Beecher, "U.S. Calls 24,500 Reserves; Sets G.I. Ceiling at 549,500, Giving Saigon Major Role"; also Charles W. Corddry, "U.S. Intends to Give Saigon Main War Role"; Mike Miller, "U.S. Hopes South Viets Will Take Over War"; Chalmers W. Roberts, "Saigon Due for Larger Battle Role"; Bernard Gwertzman, "Policy Shifting to Boost Role of Saigon"; "U.S. Seeks to Gradually Turn All Fighting Over to South Vietnamese, Clifford Says."

[41] "Back on the Track."

[42] Address by Ambassador Ellsworth Bunker on acceptance of the Sylvanus Thayer Award, United States Military Academy, West Point, New York, May 8, 1970. General Westmoreland has indicated that the Vietnamese leadership had come to this realization much earlier. He stated: "After I made my speech at the National Press Club in November 1967, I came back to talk to President Thieu and General Vien. They were elated. President Thieu said, 'This is the first time I have been given a strategy that allows us to plan ahead.' He had that

Clifford continued his campaign in the ensuing months. In his first public address as secretary of defense, at the annual luncheon of the Associated Press on April 22, he reported the high-level administration review of the war during March and the results of that review: "We concluded that Americans will not need always to do more and more, but rather that the increased effectiveness of the South Vietnamese Government and its fighting forces will now permit us to level off our effort—and in due time begin the gradual process of reduction."[43]

At his next press conference, on June 20, Clifford again recalled, somewhat inaccurately, that the president had indicated on March 31 that "he was not going to send another massive number of troops to Vietnam."[44] In a press conference on August 15, Clifford associated General Abrams with the limitation on American troops. He stated: "General Abrams informed me that he believes the allies have the ability to cope with the enemy threat. In view of his attitude in this regard, it is our intention to limit American troops in South Vietnam to the total of 549,500."[45]

But it was on September 5, in an address to the National Press Club, that the secretary of defense explicitly cast the troop limit of 549,500 into hard concrete. Indicating that

---

speech printed on his own printing presses and started talking to me that day on how he would accelerate their taking over more of the war. He realized at that time that this strategy visualized our levelling off our commitment. And he accepted it because it was a vote of confidence for him." Personal interview with General William C. Westmoreland, September 16, 1973.

[43] Address by Clark M. Clifford, Secretary of Defense, before annual luncheon of the Associated Press, New York City, April 22, 1968; for press reaction, see Saville R. Davis, "A New Voice: Clark Clifford Puts a Fresh Look on Vietnam Policy Exposition"; Peter Kihss, "Clifford Expects Saigon to Take on More of Fighting"; John Maffre, "Plans Set for Shift in Viet Load"; Charles W. Corddry, "Viet Parley Hope Voiced by Clifford."

[44] News conference by Secretary of Defense Clark M. Clifford, June 20, 1968, p. 17.

[45] News conference by Secretary of Defense Clark M. Clifford, August 15, 1968, p. 1.

the president had decided on March 31 "that US troop strength in Vietnam would be limited to 549,500," Clifford added: "We have been assured by General Abrams, and our commanders in the field told me personally . . . that this strength . . . is sufficient to withstand and defeat any offensive that our enemy can mount. Our effort in South Vietnam can now be seen not to be an unlimited drain on our resources. The so-called 'bottomless pit' has been capped."[46]

Thus, by the time the president left office, the tentative decision he had made in March to send only a few thousand troops to Vietnam at that time had been transformed through the words and statements of his secretary of defense into a definite limit on the American troop commitment to Vietnam. Whether intended or not, the president's decision of March 31, 1968, had signalled the upper limit of American military commitment to the defense of South Vietnam.

As for the other major military decision on the war, the bombing pause, this, too, was not thought of by the president as irrevocable, a new direction for American strategy. There were many times in the remaining months of 1968 that the president and his advisors considered a resumption of the bombing in response to Communist intransigence at the bargaining table or actions on the battlefield.[47] Clifford followed his same technique in these instances, using news conferences and public appearances to interpret the administration's policy according to his own deescalation scenario. Whenever a resumption of the bombing was considered within the administration, Clifford publicly reemphasized why such a move would be both contradictory to the president's position and why such resumption was not warranted. He reemphasized that bombing below the 20th parallel included

---

[46] Address by Clark M. Clifford at the National Press Club, Washington, D.C., September 5, 1968, p. 4. As General Westmoreland points out, it was the defeat suffered by the enemy at Tet that enabled Abrams to be in a position to make this assurance. Personal interview with General William C. Westmoreland, September 16, 1973.

[47] Johnson, *The Vantage Point*, pp. 508–509, 521.

the same number of missions formerly flown throughout North Vietnam and that this redirection of the air effort probably was more effective in causing enemy attrition. Indeed, in one press conference, a questioner accused the secretary of defense of building "a case for further restricting the bombing."[48] By insisting that the limitation on the bombing was not harming our efforts in South Vietnam and did not affect the level of combat there, the secretary of defense was successful in halting any move to resume the bombing north of the 20th parallel, and thus set the stage for the president's decision in October to halt the bombing throughout North Vietnam.[49]

In this manner, the bombing of North Vietnam north of the 20th parallel was suspended during the remaining months of the Johnson administration. Clifford continued to emphasize that it was our bombing limitation that had brought Hanoi to the bargaining table and that the United States should take no escalatory step with the bombing that might break off or even disrupt these peace negotiations. Even if the talks were moving slowly (or not at all), the alternative was a return to a path he considered hopeless. In this view he prevailed, convincing both the president and the public that the Paris negotiations could neither be disrupted nor abandoned.[50]

Thus, the decisions of March 1968 started the United States down a new road in Vietnam. Those decisions marked the limit of United States commitment of its military forces. Notice was served to the South Vietnamese government that its open-ended claim on American resources and manpower had come to an end and that it would be expected to shoulder an increasing share of the war in the future. Although not

---

[48] News conference by Secretary of Defense Clark M. Clifford, August 15, 1968, p. 11; see also Question and Answer Session Following Speech at National Press Club, September 5, 1968, p. 1.

[49] Johnson, *The Vantage Point*, pp. 520–529; Graff, *The Tuesday Cabinet*, pp. 157–165; Christian, *The President Steps Down*, pp. 48–107.

[50] Goulding, *Confirm or Deny*, pp. 341–342.

explicitly stated and not entirely expected, the first steps on the road to American disengagement in Vietnam began on March 31, 1968. As William Bundy stated: "These decisions started the whole process that unravelled our Vietnam commitments. They removed a hopeless weight and changed it to supportable proportions."[51]

[51] Personal interview with William Bundy, October 11, 1972. See also James F. Cairns, *The Eagle and the Lotus: Western Intervention in Vietnam 1847–1971*, p. 167.

SEVENTEEN

✩✩

Explaining the Decision-Making Process

Summary

FOR policy decisions from which so little had been expected, a great deal had been initiated. Whatever the intentions of the president and his advisors, the decisions of March 31, 1968, led the Americans and the North Vietnamese to the conference table in Paris to begin the journey on what was to be a long road to peace. A limit to the United States commitment of ground forces was established, and the South Vietnamese were put on notice that they would be expected to do more in their own defense. The limited United States political objectives in South Vietnam were, for the first time, affirmed. The new American military commander's ground strategy was based on these limited objectives; a ceiling on and eventual reduction of American forces and increased participation of South Vietnamese forces.

It is not difficult to force the rich, chaotic, and confused flow of events and particular conjunction of circumstances of the early months of 1968 into a scheme of decision making that may have significance for many other aspects of the Vietnamese war and of the decision-making process in general. The picture that emerges is of a president dedicated personally and politically to an objective and a course of action, surrounded by advisors who generally had fashioned and continued to support that objective and course of action, but now challenged not only by the press of events but by an advisor who had begun to question both the objectives and the course being pursued.

The Tet offensive showed that the attainment of American objectives in Vietnam, if possible at all, was to be far in the future. The political reality was that more of the same in

320

EXPLAINING THE DECISION-MAKING PROCESS

South Vietnam, with an increased commitment of American lives and money, accompanied by an immense effect on the domestic life of the United States, and with no guarantee of military victory in the near future, had become unacceptable to large elements of the American public. Another alternative had to be found.

Only then were our ultimate national objectives toward Vietnam brought out and reexamined. The Clifford Task Force, while pointing out that new guidance was needed and that new and modified objectives had to be formulated and approved, could not itself clearly develop those objectives. This was a task that required presidential attention. Disagreement over national objectives became critical, and only the president could establish new national objectives.

To some extent, bureaucratic priorities and perceptions were responsible for the inability of these cabinet advisors to formulate new guidance.[1] Rusk provided little opportunity for the State Department bureaucracy to contribute to the decision-making process after Tet. He acted as the president's personal foreign policy advisor and gave his advice directly and confidentially to the president. His views have been previously described.

Unlike Rusk, Clifford represented two bureaucratic structures with widely divergent points of view and interests. His civilian bureaucracy, the Pentagon's State Department, as it has been called, had long since concluded, as the State Department had not, that too little attention was being paid to American political objectives in South Vietnam. Basic to American success in Vietnam, these officials felt, was the development of a Vietnamese political framework that would establish an institutional link between the rural population and its government and that would eliminate the alienation of much of that population from the government. With-

[1] For a discussion of bureaucratic constraints on policy making, see Graham T. Allison, *Essence of Decision: Explaining the Cuban Missile Crisis*, pp. 67–96; Morton H. Halperin, *Bureaucratic Politics and Foreign Policy.*

out such a link, they believed, there was no way to translate military successes into permanent political achievement. These military successes could proceed indefinitely into the future, and the North Vietnamese and the Viet Cong could be made to suffer casualties far in excess of American casualties. But victories would be empty, the Defense civilians felt, if they did not contribute to the development of a South Vietnamese political framework that eventually would provide the basis for American withdrawal. As far as these officials were concerned, the military strategy being pursued in Vietnam by United States forces contained no concept of, and certainly devoted few resources to, the establishment of a South Vietnamese political structure that could relate the Saigon government to the people in the countryside. The arguments of these Defense Department officials previously had raised doubts in the mind of Secretary McNamara concerning the military strategy being pursued in Vietnam, and he had sought to place limitations on the growth of American forces there. But McNamara, in his thinking, never re-examined fundamental American objectives in Vietnam and never questioned these objectives.

The military bureaucracy, on the other hand, had long chafed under the political restraints that it felt prevented it from pursuing the war to a rapid and successful conclusion and that, because of the drain on the strategic reserve, threatened America's defense in other vital areas of the world. As was to be expected, the Joint Chiefs of Staff saw their problem in Vietnam as being primarily military, and the strategy adopted by General Westmoreland followed the classic doctrine that victory depended upon offensive action to defeat the enemy's main forces and inflict casualties substantially greater than our own until Hanoi's losses became unacceptable. In addition, offensive action along the frontiers of Vietnam would stop these enemy forces before they had access to the population of South Vietnam. Thus, civilian casualties would be avoided, the local guerrillas—cut off from outside support—would wither on the vine, and the South Vietnamese government could initiate programs that would contribute to building ties to the rural peasantry (which was not a military responsibility in any case).

But this strategy, the military felt, was thwarted by the availability to enemy troops of sanctuaries in Laos and Cambodia where they could refit, reequip, and escape the destruction of American ground power. Further, the political restraints on the use of air power in North Vietnam allowed the enemy to adjust so that the pressure against him did not become unacceptable. Of equal consequence to the military bureaucracy, however, was the weakening of our ability to meet other possible military contingencies caused by the political decision not to call up reserve forces. As has been indicated, as far as General Wheeler was concerned, it was the reserve problem that was the main cause of his request for additional forces in February 1968.

In the face of these predictable bureaucratic reactions, Clifford was an independent actor in a very real sense. Rusk and Rostow were committed to the policy they had helped to formulate. "Clifford didn't understand the problem. He hadn't lived with it for years, the way we had," Rostow stated.[2] "I knew what the president wanted," Rusk felt.[3] And Clifford recalled, "Rusk and Rostow told me that I didn't understand the problem, that I hadn't lived with it for years the way they had."[4]

But this was Clifford's advantage. He was unique among the president's advisors in not being actively responsible for the current policy and therefore not vitally committed to its defense. Thus, he was convinced by the civilian Defense Department officials that not only should the American military commitment in Vietnam be limited but that to continue on the same road would lead the country to political and military bankruptcy. The military bureaucracy, although unable to persuade him to accept mobilization and a recon-

[2] Personal interview with Walt W. Rostow, December 4, 1972.
[3] Personal interview with Dean Rusk, January 22, 1973.
[4] Personal interview with Clark Clifford, February 15, 1973.

stitution of the strategic reserve, organized its arguments to keep him from straying too far from that path.

However, Clifford was able to point out the need for an alternative route. With the exception of George Ball in 1965, no one close to the president had questioned our basic Vietnam strategy, nor had the president welcomed or sought such questioning. When McNamara in 1967 began to question the validity of our ground strategy in Vietnam and the increasing cost of pursuing that strategy, Clifford had been one of the principal advisors used by the president to "shoot him down," and McNamara's departure from the administration was announced shortly thereafter.

But Clifford was an independent actor in another sense as well. Economically independent and having agreed somewhat reluctantly to serve in the cabinet at a time of crisis, he did not feel that he owed his prominence and success to the president alone. As he has suggested, alone among the presidential advisors, he dealt with Johnson as an equal. Clifford manifested his personal fealty to the president by telling him the way he saw it, rather than by protecting his own cherished government position by telling the president what the president wanted to hear. Also, he was able to go outside the bureaucracy, to consult with friends in Congress and in the business and economic community. He was thus able to get a feel for the mood of the country from which his colleagues who had been in government service longer were somewhat insulated. As McPherson has interpreted his role: "Clifford was political in the Aristotelian sense and not the 'Mayor Daley' sense. He was concerned about the president's ability to lead the country and his ability to stand as a strong and responsible figure in American life. He felt the president was being devastated by the war."[5]

This is, of course, not to say that Rusk and Rostow were sycophants, giving the president the advice they thought he wanted to hear. They had helped establish the policy that the

[5] Personal interview with Harry C. McPherson, Jr., December 21, 1972.

United States was pursuing in Vietnam, and they strongly supported it. Both felt the importance of preventing the loss of Southeast Asia to the Communists, and both felt that military action on the part of the United States was the only way this could be accomplished. Both, at one time or another, had examined alternative strategies and had rejected them. However, as the situation in Vietnam and in the United States changed, Rusk and Rostow never reexamined their original premises either in the light of changing circumstances or in the light of the demonstrated failure or inadequacies of the policies being pursued.

But the question of the ultimate goals of American policy in Vietnam was to be a decision of the president and his decision alone. After the Clifford Task Force made its report, the remainder of the decision-making process became a struggle among the highest advisors to the president to influence him to adopt their particular alternative, to pursue their particular conception of national objectives for the United States in South Vietnam. The bureaucracy participated only peripherally.

Thus, the decision-making process as it operated after Tet demonstrated again that the establishment of overall national objectives, as opposed to the making of decisions to implement those objectives, is ultimately a political decision. The president ultimately has the responsibility for establishing national objectives and priorities, and he is judged by the electorate on his performance in establishing objectives that are in agreement with the desires of the majority of the electorate. "Poor policy is made by leaders who fail to foresee accurately the consequences of their decisions or attempt to maximize values not held by the electorate."[6] And so the decisions of March 1968, involving as they did ultimate questions concerning the direction of American policy, were personal decisions of the president.

Johnson's style, as he moved toward a major decision, has

[6] Stephen D. Krasner, "Are Bureaucracies Important? (Or Allison Wonderland)," p. 161.

been described in detail by his former associates. Desirous of consensus, he investigated all aspects of a problem before he made a decision. He often indicated contrary opinions to his separate advisors in order to help them toward such a consensus. He was not patient with those whose opinions he opposed.[7] The president creates the environment that surrounds him—the advice that he gets—both by his personality and also by who he selects as close advisors. Johnson made it quite clear that he believed it vitally important to the world, the nation, and to himself not to lose Vietnam to communism. The advisors to whom he listened shared this view and reinforced his resolve. Out of a sense of awe, friendship, responsibility, hubris, and even fear, Johnson's advisors did not often cross him. When the president said he wanted "alternatives examined and, if possible, agreed recommendations," his advisors generally took the cue. They came up with agreed recommendations without highlighting the differences and compromises that had led to this agreement.[8]

Policy decisions made at the presidential level, as opposed to those made lower in the bureaucracy, since they are political decisions, are more sensitive to congressional and public opinion. Indeed, it has been said that public support is the "acid test of a foreign policy." Johnson appreciated the necessity of public support for his Vietnam policies. From the very beginning, he realized that solid support at home was a prerequisite for the success of his policy in Vietnam. Throughout United States involvement in Vietnam, the president fought to maintain this public support. He knew that the American people disliked long and interminable wars. He also knew that Hanoi understood this fact and was basing its strategy on the erosion of American will in the face of an indecisive and protracted war. The core of the dilemma was summed up by a North Vietnamese official in

[7] Christian, *The President Steps Down*, pp. 9–10, 15; Kearns, *Lyndon Johnson and the American Dream*, pp. 318–323; Humphrey, *The Education of a Public Man*, p. 325.

[8] Gelb, "The Pentagon Papers and *The Vantage Point*," pp. 39–41.

1962: "Americans do not like long, inconclusive wars—and this is going to be a long, inconclusive war. Thus, we are sure to win in the end."[9]

Thus, American public opinion was always seen to be what has been called "the essential domino."[10] Both sides geared a major element of their strategy to influencing American public opinion. Perceptions as to domestic opinion in the United States put a constraint on the rate of growth of ground forces in Vietnam, prohibited calling up the reserves, and led to continued predictions of progress and success. The British strategist, Basil Liddell Hart, had long before pointed out that in a democracy, the "inconvenient reality" was that military effort "rests on a popular foundation—that for the supply of men and munitions and even for the chance of continuing to fight at all, it depends on the consent of the 'man in the street.'" But there seemed little inclination on the part of the president and his military advisors to modify their objectives in Vietnam so as to tune their strategy, "so far as is rightly possible, to the popular ear."[11]

Johnson found it politically and personally impossible to change publicly the policy he had tenaciously pursued for so long. In his deliberations on a policy for Vietnam in the post-Tet period, the president was made keenly aware of the fact that congressional and public support for the current policy had begun to dissipate. Clifford quickly realized this fact and used it to attempt to persuade the president that a new course in Vietnam had to be found, not only to regain public support but to seek a satisfactory end to American involvement.

The Joint Chiefs of Staff, on the other hand, seemed at this time to have no appreciation of the growing disaffection from

[9] Quoted in Bernard Fall, "Master of the Red Jab," p. 20; also David Halberstam, "Laos and the Old Illusions"; Rostow, *Diffusion of Power*, pp. 435–437.

[10] Leslie H. Gelb, "The Essential Domino: American Politics and Vietnam," p. 459.

[11] Basil H. Liddell Hart, *The Decisive Wars of History: A Study in Strategy*, p. 131.

the war on the part of a large segment of the American public. They saw no need for a new strategy, but instead saw Tet as an opportunity to finally pursue the strategy they had for so long advocated. They seemed totally unbraced for the public reaction to their troop request, a request that could not have been revealed at a worse time psychologically. They continued to press for an increased American effort in Vietnam which, in the existing atmosphere, was politically unacceptable to a large segment of the American public.

There is no doubt that Clifford raised doubts in the president's mind about the policies that continued to be advocated and defended by his other close and trusted advisors. These doubts were reinforced by the president's knowledge of the effects that present policy was having on the public, on the Congress, and on other advisors outside of government. Clifford skillfully used all these allies in his campaign to change the direction of U.S. policy.

As was his way, Johnson sought consensus among his advisors, and he achieved that consensus in a dramatic compromise. He accepted Rusk's suggestion for a peace initiative that would placate public opinion and allow him to continue the war as before if this initiative failed to produce results. But he gave in to Clifford's outlook by broaching this initiative in conciliatory language to make it more acceptable to the enemy and coupling it with his dramatic announcement to emphasize its sincerity.

It was Hanoi's acceptance of this offer that enabled our Vietnam policy to change. Johnson could then allow his secretary of defense to interpret American policy so as to make the talks in Paris the major avenue for achieving United States purposes in Vietnam without abandoning his strongly held objective of not losing South Vietnam to the Communists.

There is no firm indication of the extent to which the president was influenced by public opinion during the period following Tet. Rostow has cautioned against overemphasizing any structural change in American public opinion that would

328

indicate that the American public, after Tet, would have accepted with equanimity the loss of South Vietnam to communism. Insofar as the president's motives were concerned, however, he has stated: "What was on the president's mind was that the country was slipping. He needed to hold public opinion, which had eroded because of our strategy of attrition and the resulting protracted war. Although it is hard to get into the mind of another person, the more we talked, the more I became convinced that the president's decisions were related to public opinion."[12]

William Bundy saw the influence of public opinion on the events of March 1968 in the following manner: "My own impression—for what it is worth—is that the thrust of professional civilian advice would probably have been toward the most limited possible force increases, but that the change in bombing policy was greatly influenced—particularly in Secretary Clifford's actions and recommendations—by a sense of the progressively eroding domestic political support that was so dramatically evident to us all during the month of March."[13]

Only faint echoes of the policy debate within the administration reached the American people or, indeed, most of the government bureaucracy. The president was insulated from the public, who had the most at stake; his decisions were personal decisions. "The public's business—at the highest level of life and death—was being determined as though it were none of the public's business," Reedy has charged.[14]

Even granting the most thorough information and the best of intentions, this is a method of policy making whose grave defects were demonstrated throughout the Vietnam war. It limits meaningful debate to a small and highly selected circle within the government. Indeed, as the importance of the

[12] Personal interview with Walt W. Rostow, December 4, 1972.
[13] Personal interview with William Bundy, October 11, 1972. See also Eugene V. Rostow, "L.B.J. Reconsidered," p. 118; Louis Harris, *The Anguish of Change*, pp. 63–65.
[14] George E. Reedy, "The Personal Touch."

issue becomes greater and has more political significance, the circle becomes even smaller. The president chooses the members of this circle and establishes the limits of their debate. Thus, the nature of the debate and the variety of the viewpoints expressed in this circle are of vital importance. But these individuals most certainly share the values and perspectives of the president and identify with his beliefs. They also must feel some personal loyalty and attachment to the man responsible for their very presence in that inner circle.

This places an almost impossible burden upon the man within that circle who dissents from the apparent trend of the president's views. Such dissent at some point results in ostracism or even dismissal. Once a policy is launched, once an objective and the road to it are accepted by the president and made his own, the government environment is structured to reinforce and carry out that policy. The bureaucracy receives its marching orders and takes over. Flexibility is then limited, and the reformulation and clarification of objectives are no longer important and, indeed, may be looked upon as interfering with the work at hand. This is the task of a competent bureaucracy, which is not intended to make political policy. Once the objectives are determined, the bureaucracy should relieve political leaders of many of the routine decisions of foreign policy. But the decision maker, to the extent that he desires, can reassert control and can cause the bureaucracy to present him with alternatives. After Tet 1968, these alternatives finally were presented to a president who had not indicated in the past that he wanted to hear them.

There are governmental structures that are supposed to guarantee some adversary debate at the highest levels of government. The National Security Council is one such structure. Other forms of multiple advocacy in making foreign policy have been suggested.[15] But these forms are supposed to serve the president's will, and each president has used them

[15] Alexander A. George, "The Case for Multiple Advocacy in Making Foreign Policy."

330

in his own way and to suit his own purposes.[16] The American system provides no institutional procedure for adversary political debate at the highest level in determining national objectives and policy other than the political process itself.

[16] For a detailed description of President Nixon's reorganization of the National Security Council, see U.S., President, *U.S. Foreign Policy for the 1970's: A New Strategy for Peace*, pp. 17–23; U.S., President, *U.S. Foreign Policy for the 1970's: Building for Peace*, pp. 225–232; U.S., President, *U.S. Foreign Policy for the 1970's: The Emerging Structure of Peace*, pp. 208–212; U.S., Congress, Senate, Committee on Government Operations, *The National Security Council: Comment by Henry Kissinger*; "The National Security System: Responsibilities of the Department of State"; Stanley L. Falk, "The Restoration of the National Security Council"; Vincent Davis, "American Military Policy: Decision-Making in the Executive Branch"; Robert H. Johnson, "The NSC: The Relevance of Its Past to Its Future"; E. A. Kolodziej, "The National Security Council: Innovations and Implications"; Frederick C. Thayer, "Presidential Policy Processes and 'New Administration': A Search for Revised Paradigms"; Charles W. Yost, "The Instruments of American Foreign Policy"; Irving M. Destler, *Presidents, Bureaucrats and Foreign Policy: The Politics of Organizational Reform*, pp. 118–153; Irving M. Destler, "The Nixon NSC: Can One Man Do?"; John P. Leacaos, "Kissinger's Apparat"; Brook Nihart, "National Security Council: New Staff System After One Year." For accounts of the historical evolution of the National Security Council, see Ernest R. May, "The Development of Political-Military Consultation in the United States"; Sidney W. Souers, "Policy Formulation for National Security"; Robert Cutler, "The Development of the National Security Council"; U.S., Congress, Senate, Committee on Naval Affairs, *Unification of the War and Navy Departments and Postwar Organization for National Security*; U.S., Congress, Senate, Committee on Government Operations, *Organizing for National Security*; Senator Henry M. Jackson, ed., *The National Security Council: Jackson Subcommittee Papers on Policy-Making at the Presidential Level*; Paul Y. Hammond, "The National Security Council as a Device for Interdepartmental Coordination: An Interpretation and Appraisal"; Keith C. Clark and Lawrence J. Legere, eds., *The President and the Management of National Security*, pp. 55–114; Paul Y. Hammond, *Organizing for Defense: The American Military Establishment in the Twentieth Century*; Stanley L. Falk, "National Security Council Under Truman, Eisenhower, and Kennedy"; Stanley Hoffmann, "Will the Balance Balance at Home?" pp. 63–67; Roger Hilsman, *The Politics of Policy Making in Defense and Foreign Affairs*, pp. 151–171.

Before the bureaucracy can function, it is necessary to know what objectives are being sought. Objectives, in both domestic and foreign policy, ultimately determine the values and beliefs of a society. But once the objectives are determined, the bureaucracy also has an obligation to the president to apprise him of the costs, both political and economic, of attaining those objectives. This function of the bureaucracy is routinely performed in government. For every change in the tax law, the bureaucracy can predict the gain or loss in revenue over time. For every modification in social security taxes or payments, the bureaucracy can predict the ultimate effect on the recipient as well as on the government. Every new weapon system is analyzed to determine the total resources required to deploy it. The ultimate cost to the government of the military retirement system or of veterans' benefits is projected 100 years hence. But when the objectives of the United States were established by the president in Vietnam, the decision-making process failed to address the problem of determining cost, both in resources and time, of attaining the objectives.

United States goals in South Vietnam were clear and remained constant.[17] The major concern remained that of preventing the loss of South Vietnam to communism by force. This goal was primary in Johnson's thinking because of the perceived international and domestic repercussions of such a loss. Internationally, Vietnam was seen as a test of the United States military commitments to its allies around the world. Vietnam was also seen as a vital clash of wills between communism and the system of alliances established by the United States after World War II. Vietnam was the testing ground where the challenge of Communist wars of national liberation would be met by counterinsurgency warfare. The cost of aggression would be shown to be too high for the Communists to pay, and the principle that armed

[17] Colonel John M. Collins, *The Vietnam War in Perspective*, pp. 8–11.

aggression would not be allowed to succeed would be validated.

Domestically, the successful defense of South Vietnam was seen to be essential to the political well-being of the United States. In his memoirs, President Johnson justified American policy in Vietnam in the following manner: "I knew our people well enough to realize that if we walked away from Vietnam and let Southeast Asia fall, there would follow a divisive and destructive debate in our country. . . . A divisive debate about 'who lost Vietnam' would be, in my judgment, even more destructive to our national life than the argument over China had been. . . . Our allies . . . throughout the world would conclude that our word was worth little or nothing. . . . Moscow and Peking could not resist the opportunity to expand their control into the vacuum of power we would leave behind us."[18]

Thus, Johnson felt that the alternative to defending South Vietnam would not be peace but an expanded area of conflict. With the fall of Vietnam, according to the domino concept, communism would spread throughout Southeast Asia, other United States commitments would be called into question, and the nation would be split by a vicious internal debate as to the wisdom of the policy adopted. President Johnson has been quoted as saying as early as 1963, "I am not going to be the President who saw Southeast Asia go the way China went."[19]

In pursuing this objective, President Johnson was not prepared to run the risk of a direct military confrontation with the Soviet Union or China, perhaps with the ultimate possibility of a nuclear war. The avoidance of such a confrontation became, in effect, an equally important objective.

Thus, Johnson's policy objectives translated into doing the minimum amount militarily to prevent a South Vietnamese

[18] Johnson, *The Vantage Point*, pp. 151–152. Also Kearns, *Lyndon Johnson and the American Dream*, pp. 252–253.

[19] Wicker, *JFK & LBJ: The Influence of Personality on Politics*, p. 208.

defeat while convincing Hanoi that it could not succeed in its aggression. The long-term goal was a political settlement that would "allow the South Vietnamese to determine their own future without outside interference." In a speech at Johns Hopkins University in April 1965, the president laid out for the American people what would be done in Vietnam: "We will do everything necessary to reach that objective [that the people of South Vietnam be allowed to guide their own country in their own way]. And we will do only what is absolutely necessary."[20]

These policy objectives were implemented by a gradual step-by-step American military involvement in Vietnam. Johnson had to resist pressures from the military for victory, for doing more, on the one side, and pressures for disengagement or for deescalation and negotiation from those who opposed our military intervention, on the other. These pressures were accommodated by a decision-making process that shied away from decisive action, that failed to develop a cohesive and realistic strategy for attaining these objectives, that failed to examine the ultimate costs, and that attempted to compromise the various pressures for winning and for disengaging by a gradual military escalation that would satisfy the hawks by appearing to be doing more while satisfying the doves by calling for negotiations.

In seeking this middle-of-the-road consensus, the price, as one commentator has stated, was "a middle road of contradictions and no priorities for action."[21] Guided by judgments of domestic reaction, careful not to take actions that would lead to Chinese or Russian intervention, the president made at least eight separate decisions on United States force levels in Vietnam over a four-year period. But as late as May of 1967, the secretary of defense could be told by one of his principal civilian advisors that the " 'philosophy' of the war should be fought out so that everyone would not be

[20] *Public Papers of Lyndon Johnson, 1965*, I, p. 395.
[21] Leslie H. Gelb, "Vietnam: The System Worked," p. 164.

proceeding on their own major premises and getting us in deeper and deeper."[22]

Thus, the issues that were addressed and the decisions that were made were always tactical in nature. The only alternative policies examined were alternative force levels or alternative bombing campaigns. Since the cost of not intervening in Vietnam was deemed to be greater than the cost of intervening, the ultimate military cost of that intervention was not measured. The only cost that had to be considered was continued public support, and, consequently, decisions about additional military resources for Vietnam had to be measured against public support for such actions.

Gradual escalation was therefore the strategy chosen for achieving United States objectives. Domestic politics dictated the minimum necessary disruption in American life. But with each passing year of war, the domestic political position of the president grew weaker. Optimism without results produced, in time, a credibility gap.[23]

To insist that the cost of not intervening to save Vietnam would be far greater than any cost that could be incurred in defending American interests in Southeast Asia was to place an unlimited commitment on American resources and was also to have a stultifying effect upon any serious examination of alternatives. Indeed, the strategy adopted assigned more rationality to the North Vietnamese decision-making process than it did to our own. By the gradual application of

[22] Memorandum for the Secretary of Defense from Assistant Secretary McNaughton, dated May 6, 1967, quoted in *U.S.–Vietnam Relations*, IVC(6)(b), p. 147.

[23] I am indebted to Walt W. Rostow and Leslie H. Gelb for the outlines of this analysis. However, the conclusions stated in the following paragraphs are my own and are opposite to the conclusions of those two scholars. See Gelb, "Vietnam: The System Worked"; Rostow, *The Diffusion of Power*, pp. 435–459, 504–514. Also personal correspondence from Walt W. Rostow, July 11, 1973 and July 24, 1973. See also Russell H. Fifield, *Americans in Southeast Asia: The Roots of Commitment*, pp. 257–290; Leslie H. Gelb, "Today's Lessons from the Pentagon Papers," p. 35.

power, the United States would find that elusive point at which the war would become too costly to the old revolutionaries in North Vietnam, causing them to abandon their goals in the South. But there would be no limit on the effort we would expend in driving them to that point. In the application of this strategy, the nation's leaders repeatedly misjudged the enemy's ability to frustrate American aims and to counterescalate at every stage.

At some point, it should have been clear that the costs, both political and economic, incurred by the United States in defending Vietnam could indeed exceed the costs of disengagement, or, conversely, that the costs we were willing to pay could not guarantee victory. But to state this, or seriously to question Vietnam's place in our international and domestic priorities, was not encouraged in the Johnson administration and was seen as indicating an unacceptable lack of resolve in meeting the Communist challenge. Some few officials foresaw the eventual cost or, at some point, indicated that they felt the cost had become too high, but they either had little influence or were shuffled off the scene.

On the other hand, those who advocated a stronger U.S. effort in and around Vietnam, especially the Joint Chiefs of Staff, were disarmed in a different fashion. Denied a strategic concept and the military freedom they felt was needed to win the war, the military chiefs were pacified by gradual increases in force levels and in bombing targets and, eventually, by the replacement of a secretary of defense who had become anathema to them. But these increases in military authority were always within the president's guidelines. And so the military chiefs, while each sought a larger role for his own service, in effect became sophisticated yes men for the president's policies, assuring the public, as did General Westmoreland, that every request from the field commander had been met, and seldom raising in public their view of the eventual military consequences in Vietnam of the president's restrictions. As General Westmoreland later reflected:

In my press conferences and public appearances both during my service in Vietnam and after my return, I recognized that it was not the job of the military to defend American commitment and policy. Yet it was difficult to differentiate between pursuit of a military task and such related matters as public and congressional support and the morale of the fighting man, who must be convinced that he is risking death for a worthy cause. The military thus was caught in between, and I myself as the man perhaps most on the spot may have veered too far in the direction of supporting in public the government's policy, an instinct born of devotion to an assigned task even more than to a cause and of a loyalty to the President as Commander in Chief. . . . I felt impelled to give support in public to a national policy that I essentially believed in.[24]
Thus, fundamental assumptions concerning objectives were never questioned. The decision-making process was never engaged to determine ultimate costs and to draw up a balance sheet as to when these costs would become excessive. Alternatives were not examined, and decisions concerning the allocation of American resources to Vietnam were made on the basis of what was the minimum additional that could be done while maintaining public support for the war. There was no coherent strategy to win American objectives. The strategy was to persevere so as not to pay the domestic political price of failure and to convince the Communists, with the minimum force necessary, that our will was firm and that they could not win. The consequences of this failure to develop a precise clear aim with necessary limitations, consequences certainly unintended by civilian leaders, at least, were a large-scale bombing campaign against North Vietnam and a commitment of half a million American troops to a ground war in Asia.

Only when the price of attaining United States objectives became so dear in lives, dollars, and public confidence and

[24] Westmoreland, *A Soldier Reports*, p. 417.

the benefits became so intangible, remote, and even im-
plausible did our national leadership match the objectives
that were being pursued with the resources and time needed
to attain them. Only when the cost had *already* become too
high were the objectives that were being pursued and the
strategy being followed to attain them matched to see if they
were in accord. This was the failure of the decision-making
process as it operated at the highest levels of the government.

After Tet 1968 the decision-making process functioned
properly for the first time. Objectives were matched to the
resources required to achieve those objectives, and the
strategy being followed was modified when it was seen that
the costs, political and material, of attaining those results
within a reasonable period of time would be more than the
nation was willing to pay. Afterward the debate became an
issue of policy—how to attain national objectives with limited
resources, how to modify the objectives without abandoning
them completely, how to regain public acceptance for subsequent American actions in South Vietnam.

The existing policy, which had enjoyed public support for
several years, was shown not to be producing the results
expected in a reasonable time or at an acceptable cost.
The public could not see an end to the war. In order to
produce quicker or more decisive results, the commitment of
resources would have to be increased vastly, and the whole
nature of the war and its relationship to the United States
would be changed. There was strong indication that large
and growing elements of the American public had begun to
believe that the cost had already reached unacceptable
levels and that the objective was no longer worth the price.
It was brought home to Johnson finally that the policy being
pursued in Vietnam would no longer be supported by the
American electorate. The political reality—one recognized
by the president—was that, without renouncing the former
policy, a new direction, a new and less costly strategy,
had to be found.

Thus, the president's decisions of March 1968 were based upon two major considerations:

1. The conviction of his advisors, particularly Secretary of Defense Clifford, that an increased American effort would not make the achievement of American objectives more likely or more rapid; and

2. His own deeply felt conviction that unity must be restored to the American nation.

It is conventional wisdom among scholars today, in retrospect, to denounce the involvement of the United States in Vietnam as having been accidental, unnecessary, unfortunate, and a complete failure.[25] But in the climate prevailing in the 1960s, there were few voices raised to argue that Vietnam was not vital to our national security and that it could be allowed to fall into Communist hands without damage to American interests.[26] The domino theory, in such disrepute now, was a plausible way of looking at Southeast Asia. It genuinely seemed to foretell the deterioration of American security around the world. At that time, Communist-inspired and Communist-led insurgencies threatened the internal stability and independence of Malaysia, Indo-

[25] Halberstam, *The Best and the Brightest*; James C. Thomson, Jr., "How Could Vietnam Happen?"; Richard J. Pfeffer, ed., *No More Vietnams? The War and the Future of American Foreign Policy*; Bernard Brodie, "Why Were We So (Strategically) Wrong?"; Daniel Ellsberg, "The Quagmire Myth and the Stalemate Machine," in *Papers on the War*, pp. 42–135; Hannah Arendt, *Crises of the Republic*, pp. 3–47; Eugene Eidenberg, "Americanizing the War in Vietnam"; Seyom Brown, *The Faces of Power: Constancy and Change in United States Foreign Policy from Truman to Johnson*, pp. 330–337; Bernard Brodie, *War and Politics*, pp. 157–227; Godfrey Hodgson, "The Establishment," pp. 17–29; Noam Chomsky, *American Power and the New Mandarins*.

[26] Henry Fairlie, "We Knew What We Were Doing When We Went Into Vietnam"; see also U.S., Congress, Senate, Committee on Foreign Relations, *Causes, Origins, and Lessons of the Vietnam War*; Haynes B. Johnson and Bernard M. Gwertzman, *Fulbright: The Dissenter*, pp. 195–198; Ralph K. White, *Nobody Wanted War: Misperceptions in Vietnam and Other Wars*, pp. 124–127.

nesia, Singapore, Thailand, Burma, and the Philippines. Laos seemed on the verge of falling into Communist hands. Wars of national liberation seemed to be the new, and highly successful, Communist route to power in the developing nations of Southeast Asia.

Thus, despite the final tragic and abysmal failure of American intervention in Indochina, some U.S. foreign policy objectives were indirectly enhanced by that intervention. Time was provided for the nations in proximity to Indochina to organize themselves against internal subversive menaces. These nations presently are governed in large part by self-confident leaders who believe themselves to be fully capable of maintaining internal stability and developing their economies. The dangers of wars of national liberation as a technique for expanding Communist domination have, at the very least, abated in Southeast Asia.

The question, then, it would seem, is not whether or not the United States should have undertaken to support a non-communist government in South Vietnam, but, rather, could its objectives in this region have been met in a different manner and at less cost in lives, time, and prestige, and, further, could those costs have been anticipated? The United States did not stumble into Vietnam. Each step was a deliberate choice by a careful president who weighed the alternatives as he saw them, limited each response insofar as possible, and took into account the opinion of the public. But the effort was piecemeal and misdirected. Politically, there was little realization of the revolutionary dynamics of the situation, the popular appeal of the Viet Cong, the weakness of the half-formed, traditionalist military regimes in Saigon. There was little realization that critical to security was the development of an honest and efficient South Vietnamese government committed to administer justice and to improve the welfare of its people.

Political science provides no clear prescription for the development of a viable democratic political system in a traditional society recently freed from colonial rule, with limited physical and administrative resources, and in the midst of a bitter civil war. Certainly, there is no agency of the United States government charged with such a task. There-fore, there must be some doubt as to what could have been accomplished along such lines by an outside power in an alien society even if a clear realization of the true prob-lem had been present. So it is not surprising that the Amer-ican response was a conventional military one. The military defeat of the enemy seemed an achievable goal, and we escalated and reescalated in order to progress toward that goal. The defeat of the enemy became an end in itself, as it had been in more conventional American wars.

There was some recognition that more was needed in Viet-nam. Lip service was given to a "positive program," to "pacification" or "revolutionary development" programs designed to bring social justice to the countryside in order to win the "hearts and minds" of the people and gain their active support for a government interested in their welfare and responsive to their needs. But comparatively meager re-sources were devoted to this program, and they were devoted too late. Often, such programs as were developed were largely planned, financed, and implemented by Americans with little GVN involvement. And again, there was no agency within the United States government solely responsible for such programs. The State Department certainly abnegated such a role and, after the introduction of large numbers of Amer-ican forces, the U.S. embassy in Saigon limited its roles to the traditional ones of representation and reporting on, rather than trying to influence, political developments.

Thus, the administration of American civil programs in Vietnam was marked by fragmented and inefficient planning and execution. An innovative and unique organization which integrated all U.S. civil and military pacification support and provided a single channel of advice and assistance to the Viet-namese at all levels was finally instituted in Vietnam, under the overall direction of General Westmoreland and not the ambassador, in May 1967. Unfortunately, unification in the field was not paralleled by a similar unification among the many interested agencies in Washington, and these programs remained superficial and achieved few lasting results. Indeed, there was a general shallowness of knowledge and indifference to consideration of South Vietnam as a society with its own structures and history. Even though a constitution was written and democratic elections were held at the national level, the basic structure of South Vietnamese society, government, and power relationships was not disturbed. And so the existence of South Vietnam as a nation continued to be sustained, as it had been at the outset of the American involvement, only by the commitment of American military power.

Military operations were seldom coordinated with or directed toward progress in the pacification program. Military leaders on the ground failed to grasp the causes or the significance of the steady attrition of GVN authority in the countryside, a loss of political authority that was directly linked to the way the war was conducted. Indeed, the effects of military operations—the uprooting of the rural populace, its concentration in refugee camps or in the large cities of South Vietnam, the creation of "free fire zones," the breakdown of government in the rural areas, the demoralization of many aspects of traditional Vietnamese society—worked against the pacification program. As one observer noted: "Instead of the weaknesses within South Vietnam being eliminated they were being aggravated. . . . It was never understood that nation building was the offensive construction programme designed to strengthen the government's assets and eliminate its weaknesses, while the military operations were defensive and destructive, designed to hold the ring for the constructive program and, in so doing, to weaken the enemy's military assets."[27] So the many and spectacular American military victories over VC/NVA forces could not be translated into political gains for the South Vietnamese government. When American forces withdrew from an area,

[27] Sir Robert G. K. Thompson, *No Exit From Vietnam*, pp. 146, 149.

the enemy continued to find shelter, or at least passive acquiescence to his presence, from the rural population of South Vietnam. The two wars, political and military, were pursued as two relatively unrelated activities. But success in the military war could make no lasting difference without corresponding success in the political war.

The American failure in Vietnam up to the time of Tet was not a failure caused by the limitations placed upon military action, as some military leaders and other commentators continue to charge.[28] Indeed, overwhelming American military power was brought to bear. The United States enjoyed complete control of the sea and air and had a striking superiority in materiel on land. The American failure was caused by the lack of realization that military power alone could not solve what was basically a political problem. Overwhelming American military power was never directed toward solving that political problem. Military power was never used in ways that would contribute to the political stability and competence of the Saigon government. As one participant has stated: "In the last analysis, the U.S. effort in Vietnam—at least through 1967—failed largely because it could not sufficiently revamp or adequately substitute for a South Vietnamese leadership, administration, and armed forces inadequate to the task."[29]

As Secretary of State Henry Kissinger has written, we now perhaps have learned this lesson, but we have learned it late: "We have learned important lessons from the tragedy of

---

[28] Westmoreland, *A Soldier Reports*, pp. 410–411; Vernon A. Guidry, Jr., "A Pentagon View: War Fought With One Hand Tied"; Lieutenant General Victor H. Krulak, "The Strategic Limits of Proxy War," pp. 55–56; Drew Middleton, *Can America Win the Next War?*, pp. 5–6.

[29] R. W. Komer, *Bureaucracy Does Its Thing: Institutional Constraints on U.S.–G.V.N. Performance in Vietnam*, p. 18. See also Herbert Y. Schandler, "Vietnam: What Remains Is the Basic Structure of a Feudal Society." Barbara Tuchman recounts the similar frustrations encountered by Stilwell in an earlier time. See Barbara Tuchman, *Stilwell and the American Experience in China, 1911–1945*, pp. 455–457.

Indochina—most importantly that outside effort can only supplement, but not create, local efforts and local will to resist. . . . And there is no question that popular will and social justice are, in the last analysis, the essential underpinning of resistance to subversion and external challenge."[30]

Thus, after Tet 1968, there was no question in the minds of Clifford and his civilian associates in the Pentagon that a different approach had to be pursued in South Vietnam. They realized that the attainment of a satisfactory peace would be dependent upon South Vietnamese political development and not solely on American arms. The American military effort, in effect, had failed. Now the war was to be turned back to the South Vietnamese, who had been seen as incapable of fighting it before. Meanwhile the Americans would seek a negotiated solution to the war, or at least to their participation in it.

American forces would remain in South Vietnam for a time in order to prevent a military defeat of the South Vietnamese government by Communist forces, to stimulate negotiations with the North, and to provide a shield behind which the South Vietnamese government could rally, try to become effective, and win the support of its people. This American commitment gradually would be reduced as the South Vietnamese became capable of meeting their own defense requirements. But there was no evidence that the South Vietnamese government would rise to this challenge and become able to accomplish by itself what it had been unable to accomplish with American prodding and with massive American assistance. Complete American withdrawal from the war and the survival of the South Vietnamese government remained, as they had always been, contradictory objectives. The ultimate tragic result for South Vietnam of future American troop withdrawals might have been predicted as inevitable.

There is another aspect of the decision-making process that has not been studied separately and in detail. That aspect is

[30] U.S., Department of State, *Department of State Bulletin*, vol. 73, pp. 3–4.

the unique constraints on and requirements of presidential decision making during an election year.

Would Johnson's options have been different if 1968 had not been a presidential election year? Quite obviously, they would have been. Divorced from the need of seeking immediate public justification and acceptance for his policies, Johnson might have been more easily persuaded by his advisors to capitalize on the Viet Cong defeat by increasing American forces and removing geographic constraints on military operations, thus going all out in order to seek a rapid and decisive conclusion to the war. This course, then, would have allowed him to seek negotiations at some future time and from a position of demonstrated military and psychological strength. Many of the president's advisors urged this all out course of action. Rostow and the military leaders felt that such action offered the prospect of future success, would capitalize on the enemy's military defeat, and would mobilize the public to greater support for the war.[31]

Thus, if he had not had to face a presidential election, the president could have considered options after Tet that he perceived as unavailable because of that election. He could, of course, have adopted the policy proposed by his military leaders, that of increasing American forces in Vietnam, calling up the reserves, and eliminating geographic restrictions

---

[31] Rostow, *The Diffusion of Power*, pp. 520–522, 481–483. General Westmoreland described his thoughts as follows: "The missing element in the entire equation associated with an escalated strategy which would, in my opinion, greatly shorten the war—would, in the final analysis, reduce casualties—was something that would make it politically feasible for the president to rally public opinion and say, 'In view of this, we have now got to expand our military forces and show the enemy we mean business.' This occurred with the Tet offensive. I felt if it were ever going to be done, we had to take advantage of this situation. I knew we would defeat the enemy, and after we had, he was going to be down psychologically and was going to be weakened. It was like two boxers in a ring. If you have your opponent on the ropes, that's the time to bore in. It is not the time to throw in the towel. That was the time to really move in and we would have had him by the jugular vein. I thought this development was inevitable." Personal interview with General William C. Westmoreland, September 16, 1973.

on the use of American forces. Some presidential advisors felt that a majority of the public would support such decisive action by the president. Johnson initially felt that this option remained open to him, and he was inclined toward this course of action. Rousing the people to punish and defeat the enemy and to preserve the national honor has been historically a successful way for an incumbent wartime president to rally public support. But President Johnson, in his attempt to gain consensus, soon found that the situation was different in 1968. The public was no longer united on the war nor on his conduct of it. To the American people, the danger to the national interests of the United States posed by the Communist threat to South Vietnam had not been made evident, and the cost of meeting that threat had become too high.

There seems to be no doubt that widening the war in March of 1968 would have led to vehement and perhaps violent protest from large segments of the American public, from the media, and from the Congress. There seems to be little doubt that such protest would have torn asunder the Democratic party in the presidential election year of 1968. The adoption of such a policy by the president would have been feasible *only* if great progress and success could have been achieved in the few months remaining before the election. But this the president's advisors could not promise, and so the president found that many of his options were foreclosed because of the upcoming election.

Another astute and veteran politician had seen the handwriting on the wall much earlier. Richard Nixon is quoted as stating prophetically after the elections of 1966: "The peace party always wins. I know my own party. If the war is still going on in 'sixty-eight, there is no power on earth can keep them from trying to outbid the Democrats for the peace vote."[32]

In the post-Tet period, then, disagreement over foreign

[32] Henry Paolucci, *War, Peace, and the Presidency*, p. 21. Also Harris, *The Anguish of Change*, pp. 65–66; Robert B. Semple, Jr., "Nixon Vows to End War With a 'New Leadership'."

policy objectives necessarily spilled into the arena of domestic politics. For one of the few times in American history, foreign policy objectives of the United States, and the means to be devoted to the attainment of those objectives, became legitimate subjects of partisan political debate. In addition, the influence of the press and of television in mobilizing the public in favor of or in opposition to proposed foreign policy decisions became a new factor in the decision-making process.

This is not to say that the motives for Johnson's actions in March 1968 were simply political ones designed to give his party an advantage in the coming elections. On the contrary, President Johnson was prepared to do what was necessary to prevent the defeat of his field commander. Moreover, he desperately wanted to move toward peace, and he sincerely sought a formula that would lead to negotiations. His decisions ultimately were taken with this motive in mind and with the intent of achieving unity within the country, which he accomplished, and unity within his party, which he did not accomplish.

Thus, the president was limited in his decision making by the constraints inherent in meeting a crisis that required not just unpopular measures but public support in the midst of a presidential campaign. Any president at such a time must have certain considerations foremost in his mind that are perhaps less sharply focused at other times in his administration. Among these considerations are his place in history, his role as peacemaker, his role as leader of the nation, and his responsibility to provide assistance to his party and, ultimately, to his successor. Although these might not be conscious motives, they are necessarily present and influence the decision-making process.

Every president, especially near the end of his administration, must be concerned with the judgment of history concerning his accomplishments as president. Johnson had fathered seminal social and civil rights legislation during his presidency. But these historic accomplishments had been overshadowed, and their effectiveness threatened, by a war he could not end. Now, with an election coming up, and with his party threatened by internal dissension over his war policies rather than reacting in triumph over his domestic achievements, the president sincerely sought a policy that would at least constitute a beginning step toward ending this frustrating war.

A presidential candidate, in the American system of government, is the leader of his party. Once he becomes president, however, he must not only exert effective party leadership, he must also represent all the people and preserve national unity from the dangers of unbridled civil dissent. Johnson in March 1968 was faced not only with the disaffection of large blocs of supporters within his party, but also with the disaffection of large elements of the nation because of his conduct of the war. It was essential that he adopt a policy that would restore both party unity and national unity.

It is not discreditable for the chief of government of a democratic state to take into account domestic politics, in the widest sense, in his decision making on foreign policy. Although there is a myth that domestic politics is divorced from foreign policy, that "politics stops at the water's edge," in actuality it is inescapable that a president be aware of and constantly weigh the competing claims of foreign and domestic affairs and assess the effects of decisions in one area upon the other.[33]

Thus, a policy of conciliation, of searching for peace, of not again escalating the war was a necessity for Johnson at this time. No matter how compellingly it was presented by his military leaders, no matter how advantageous it seemed in the conduct of the war, a policy of following the Tet attacks with increased pressure upon a badly damaged enemy could not withstand the stresses inherent in the domestic

[33] Rostow, *The Diffusion of Power*, p. 705; Gelb, "The Essential Domino," pp. 209–210.

political scene and the president's own self-image in an election year.

Perhaps, then, enemies of the United States would be well advised in the future to confine their thrusts against us, thrusts that would ordinarily call for a response involving hard decisions and unpopular, expensive, or controversial actions, to the period prior to an American presidential election. Surely a nation is ill-governed if its chief executive fails or even hesitates to adopt policies essential to the nation's security in the hope of gaining partisan political advantage or out of fear of alienating powerful political supporters, even if his political opponents are taking irresponsible positions. There are times when unpopular actions are required. However, the decision-making process in the United States seems to contain within itself certain constraints to action at times of presidential elections which may be less likely to be compelling between elections.

In fact, just a few years later, the options examined and rejected by Johnson in early 1968 were examined and utilized in a different political context by President Nixon in 1970 when he sent American forces into Cambodia, in 1971 when South Vietnamese forces entered Laos to breach the enemy's sanctuaries and destroy his logistical bases, and in 1972 when air and naval attacks on North Vietnam were resumed and Haiphong harbor was mined. Thus, it appears there was a continuity between President Johnson's decisions of March 1968, and President Nixon's decisions of later years. Nixon's decisions, indeed, gave rise to a great wave of public protest, but this protest had largely died out and become politically ineffective by the time of the next presidential elections, at which time the administration seemed to be on the verge of successfully concluding negotiations that would end direct American participation in the war.

There is another continuity between the Tet offensive and President Nixon's later decisions concerning Vietnam, and another indication that Tet 1968 was indeed a turning point in American strategy in South Vietnam. The Tet offensive was extremely costly to the enemy, and, although it was pyschologically a victory, the Viet Cong forces in South Vietnam never recovered their military capability. This military weakness led to an "accelerated pacification campaign" by the South Vietnamese in 1968 and 1969 which seemed to improve greatly the military and political situation and presented new options to the president. The excess United States military capability in South Vietnam occasioned by the weakness of the Viet Cong and by the apparent strength of the improving and expanding RVNAF allowed the president to counter each politically risky escalation of the war with a politically popular move toward Vietnamization. This led to the withdrawal of American forces from combat and, eventually, over the succeeding three years, from South Vietnam, leaving the Vietnamese to their fate in a "peace with honor."

Tet 1968, then, represented a turning point in American policy toward Vietnam. American objectives in Vietnam remained the same. But, after years of military effort and political anguish, the American government finally, in March of 1968, developed a strategy for attaining those objectives that it hoped would not place an unlimited burden upon national economic and military resources, and that could, over time, hold public acceptance. As Kissinger later pointed out: "The Tet offensive marked the watershed of the American effort. Henceforth, no matter how effective our actions, the prevalent strategy could no longer achieve its objectives within a period or with force levels politically acceptable to the American people. . . . This made inevitable an eventual commitment to a political solution and marked the beginning of the quest for a negotiated settlement."[34]

[34] Henry Kissinger, "The Viet Nam Negotiations," p. 216.

APPENDIXES

Total U.S. Military Personnel in South Vietnam

Date	Army	Navy	Marine Corps	Air Force	Coast Guard	Total
31 Dec. 1960	800	15	2	68	–	About 900
31 Dec. 1961	2,100	100	5	1,000	–	3,205
30 June 1962	5,900	300	700	2,100	–	9,000
31 Dec. 1962	7,900	500	500	2,400	–	11,300
30 June 1963	10,200	600	600	4,000	–	15,400
31 Dec. 1963	10,100	800	800	4,600	–	16,300
30 June 1964	9,900	1,000	600	5,000	–	16,500
31 Dec. 1964	14,700	1,100	900	6,600	–	23,300
30 June 1965	27,300	3,800	18,100	10,700	–	59,900
31 Dec. 1965	116,800	8,400	38,200	20,600	300	184,300
30 June 1966	160,000	17,000	53,700	36,400	400	267,500
31 Dec. 1966	239,400	23,300	69,200	52,900	500	385,300
30 June 1967	285,700	28,500	78,400	55,700	500	448,800
31 Dec. 1967	319,500	31,700	78,000	55,900	500	485,600
30 June 1968	354,300	35,600	83,600	60,700	500	534,700
31 Dec. 1968	359,800	36,100	81,400	58,400	400	536,100
30 Apr. 1969	363,300	36,500	81,800	61,400	400	*543,400
30 June 1969	360,500	35,800	81,500	60,500	400	538,700
31 Dec. 1969	331,100	30,200	55,100	58,400	400	475,200
30 June 1970	298,600	25,700	39,900	50,500	200	414,900
31 Dec. 1970	249,600	16,700	25,100	43,100	100	334,600
30 June 1971	190,500	10,700	500	37,400	100	239,200
31 Dec. 1971	119,700	7,600	600	28,800	100	156,800
30 June 1972	31,800	2,200	1,400	11,500	100	47,000
31 Dec. 1972	13,800	1,500	1,200	7,600	100	24,200
30 June 1973	**	**	**	**	**	**

Source: U.S., Department of Defense, OASD (Comptroller), Directorate for Information Operations, March 19, 1974.

* Peak strength.

** Totals for all five services combined less than 250.

Strength of Free World Military Assistance Forces
in South Vietnam
1964–1970

Country	1964	1965	1966	1967	1968	1969	1970
Australia							
Strength	200	1,557	4,525	6,818	7,661	7,672	6,763
Number of maneuver battalions	–	1	2	2	3	3	3
Korea							
Strength	200	20,620	45,566	47,829	50,003	48,869	48,537
Number of maneuver battalions	–	10	22	22	22	22	22
Thailand							
Strength	0	16	244	2,205	6,005	11,568	11,586
Number of maneuver battalions	–	0	0	1	3	6	6
New Zealand							
Strength	30	119	155	534	516	552	441
The Philippines							
Strength	17	72	2,061	2,020	1,576	189	74
Republic of China							
Strength	20	20	23	31	29	29	31
Spain							
Strength	0	0	13	13	12	10	7
Total strength	467	22,404	52,566	59,450	65,802	68,889	67,444
Total maneuver battalions	0	11	24	25	28	31	31

Source: Larsen and Collins, *Vietnam Studies: Allied Participation in Vietnam*, p. 23.

APPENDIX THREE

U.S. Military Deaths Due to Hostile Action, Vietnam
January–March 1968

Week ending	Number dead
Jan. 6, 1968	184
Jan. 13, 1968	278
Jan. 20, 1968	218
Jan. 27, 1968	203
Feb. 3, 1968	416
Feb. 10, 1968	400
Feb. 17, 1968	543
Feb. 24, 1968	470
Mar. 2, 1968	542
Mar. 9, 1968	509
Mar. 16, 1968	336
Mar. 23, 1968	349
Mar. 30, 1968	330

Source: Directorate for Statistical Services, Office of the Secretary of Defense, 1968.

BIBLIOGRAPHY

INTERVIEWS

The following people were interviewed by the author on the dates indicated and were willing to have their remarks, in whole or in part, attributed by name.

Blackburn, Brigadier General Donald D., March 9, 1976. (Assistant Division Commander, 82d Airborne Division, 1967–68.)

Braestrup, Peter, October 28, 1972. (Reporter, *Washington Post*, 1968–72.)

Bundy, William P., October 11, 1972 and March 5, 1973. (Assistant secretary of state for East Asian and Pacific affairs, 1964–69.)

Cantril, Albert H., January 18, 1973. (Public opinion analyst, Institute for International Social Research, Princeton, New Jersey.)

Clifford, Clark M., November 16 and November 28, 1972 and February 15, 1973. (Secretary of defense, 1968–69.)

Collins, Colonel John M., August 15, 1972. (Chief, Contingency Plans Branch, Military Assistance Command, Vietnam, 1967–68.)

Cooper, John Sherman, January 12, 1973. (United States senator, 1952–55, 1957–73.)

Dale, Edwin L., Jr., October 21, 1975. (Economics reporter, Washington Bureau, *New York Times*, 1963– .)

Davidson, Daniel, March 5, 1973. (Special assistant to William Bundy, 1967–68; special assistant to W. Averell Harriman, 1968–72.)

Fowler, Henry H., December 28, 1972. (Secretary of the treasury, 1965–68.)

Fulbright, J. William, November 2, 1973. (United States senator, 1945–75.)

Gelb, Leslie, January 5, 1973. (Director, Policy Planning Staff, Office of the Assistant Secretary of Defense for International Security Affairs, 1967–69.)

355

Ginsburgh, Major General Robert N., August 25, 1975. (Chairman's Staff Group, Office of the Chairman, Joint Chiefs of Staff and concurrently senior staff member, National Security Council Staff, 1966–69.)

Goldberg, Arthur, January 24, 1973. (United States ambassador to the United Nations, 1967–69.)

Halperin, Morton, December 27, 1972. (Deputy assistant secretary of defense, Policy Planning and Arms Control, Office of the Assistant Secretary of Defense for International Security Affairs, 1967–68.)

Hoopes, Townsend, March 6, 1973. (Undersecretary of the Air Force, 1967–69.)

Jackson, Henry, March 25, 1973. (United States senator, 1953– .)

Komer, Robert, March 6, 1973. (Deputy commander for civil operations and revolutionary development support, United States Military Assistance Command, Vietnam, 1967–69.)

McPherson, Harry C., Jr., December 21, 1972. (Speech writer and special counsel to the president, 1966–69.)

Meritt, J. F., January 5, 1973. (Contracts Division, Office of the Assistant Secretary of the Army, Installations and Logistics, 1966–73.)

Middleton, Harry J., October 11, 1973. (Speech writer for President Johnson 1967–70; director, Lyndon Baines Johnson Library, 1970– .)

Miles, Lieutenant Colonel Paul, September 30, 1972. (Aide and special assistant to General William C. Westmoreland, 1969–72.)

Miller, William G., December 1, 1972 and September 30, 1975. (Administrative assistant to Senator John Sherman Cooper.)

Nitze, Paul, October 6, 1972. (Deputy secretary of defense, 1967–69.)

Rostow, Walt W., December 4, 1972. (Special assistant to the president for national security affairs, 1967–69.)

Rowe, James H., Jr., December 29, 1975. (Campaign consultant to President Johnson, 1968.)

Rusk, Dean, January 22, 1973. (Secretary of state, 1961–69.)

Sheehan, Neil, October 20, 1975. (*New York Times* correspondent, Vietnam, 1965–67; national security affairs reporter, Washington Bureau, *New York Times*, 1967– .)

BIBLIOGRAPHY

Smith, Hedrick, October 13, 1975. (Diplomatic correspondent, Washington Bureau, *New York Times*, 1962–63, 1966–68.)

Taylor, General Maxwell D., December 28, 1972 and January 31, 1973. (Chairman of the Joint Chiefs of Staff, 1962–64; United States ambassador to South Vietnam, 1964–65; consultant to the president, 1965–69.)

Warnke, Paul, November 17, 1972. (Assistant secretary of defense for International Security Affairs, 1967–69.)

Westmoreland, General William C., October 23, 1972 and September 16, 1973. (Commander, United States Military Assistance Command, Vietnam, 1964–68; chief of staff, U. S. Army, 1968–72.)

Weyand, General Fred C., December 27, 1973. (Commanding General, II Field Force, United States Military Assistance Command, Vietnam, 1967–68.)

Wheeler, General Earle G., November 8, 1972. (Chairman, Joint Chiefs of Staff, 1964–70.)

CORRESPONDENCE

Personal correspondence was received from the following, who were willing to have this correspondence attributed by name:

Mansfield, Mike, majority leader of the United States Senate, 1961–76.

Rostow, Walt W., special assistant to the president for national security affairs, 1967–69.

Rusk, Dean, secretary of state, 1961–69.

Smith, Margaret Chase, United States senator, 1948–73.

Ward, Barbara (Lady Jackson), author.

BOOKS

Acheson, Dean. *Present at the Creation*. New York: W. W. Norton and Company, 1969.

Agee, Warren K. *Mass Media in a Free Society*. Lawrence, Kan.: University of Kansas Press, 1969.

Albright, John; Cash, John A.; and Sandstrum, Allan W. *Seven Fire Fights in Vietnam*. Washington, D.C.: Office of the Chief of Military History, Department of the Army, 1970.

357

Allison, Graham T. *Essence of Decision: Explaining the Cuban Missile Crisis*. Boston: Little, Brown and Company, 1971.

Arendt, Hannah. *Crises of the Republic*. New York: Harcourt Brace Jovanovich, 1972.

Arlen, Michael J. *Living Room War*. New York: Viking Press, 1969.

Aronson, James. *The Press and the Cold War*. Indianapolis: Bobbs-Merrill Company, 1970.

Art, Robert J. and Waltz, Kenneth N., eds. *The Use of Force: International Politics and Foreign Policy*. Boston: Little, Brown and Company, 1971.

Austin, Anthony. *The President's War*. Philadelphia: J. B. Lippincott, 1971.

Bach, G. L. *Making Monetary and Fiscal Policy*. Washington, D.C.: The Brookings Institution, 1971.

Bagdikian, Ben H. *The Information Machine*. New York: Harper and Row, 1971.

Baldwin, Hanson W. *Strategy for Tomorrow*. New York: Harper and Row, 1970.

Barnet, Richard J. *The Roots of War*. New York: Atheneum, 1972.

Bauer, Raymond A. and Gergen, Kenneth J., eds. *The Study of Policy Formation*. New York: Free Press, 1968.

Beech, Keyes. *Not Without the Americans: A Personal History*. Garden City, N. Y.: Doubleday and Company, 1971.

Beichman,, Arnold. *The "Other" State Department: The United States Mission to the United Nations—Its Role in the Making of Foreign Policy*. New York: Basic Books, 1968.

Bloodworth, Dennis. *An Eye for the Dragon: Southeast Asia Observed: 1954–1970*. New York: Farrar, Straus, and Giroux, 1970.

Boettiger, John R., comp. *Vietnam and American Foreign Policy*. Boston: Heath and Company, 1968.

Braestrup, Peter. *Big Story: How the American Press and Television Reported and Interpreted the Crisis of Tet 1968 in Viet Nam and Washington*. 2 vols. Boulder, Col.: Westview Press, 1976.

Brandon, Henry. *Anatomy of Error: The Inside Story of the Asian War on the Potomac, 1954–69*. Boston: Gambit, 1969.

Brodie, Bernard. *War and Politics*. New York: The Macmillan Company, 1973.

Brown, Seyom. *The Faces of Power: Constancy and Change in United States Foreign Policy from Truman to Johnson.* New York: Columbia University Press, 1968.

Buhite, Russell, ed. *The Far East,* Vol. IV of *The Dynamics of World Power: A Documentary History of United States Foreign Policy 1945–1973,* edited by Arthur M. Schlesinger, Jr. 5 vols. New York: Chelsea House Publishers and McGraw-Hill, 1973.

Buttinger, Joseph. *The Smaller Dragon: A Political History of Vietnam.* New York: Frederick A. Praeger, 1958.

Cagan, Phillip; Esteg, Marten; Fellner, William; McLure, Charles E, Jr.; and Moore, Thomas Gale, eds. *Economic Policy and Inflation in the Sixties.* Washington, D.C.: American Enterprise Institute for Public Policy Research, 1972.

Cairns, James F. *The Eagle and the Lotus: Western Intervention in Vietnam 1847–1971.* Melbourne: Lansdowne Press, 1971.

Cantril, Albert. *The American People, Viet-Nam and the Presidency.* Princeton, N. J.: Institute for International Social Research, 1970.

Cater, Douglas and Geyelin, Philip L. *American Media: Adequate or Not?* Washington, D.C.: American Enterprise Institute for Public Policy Research, 1970.

Center for Strategic Studies. *Economic Impact of the Vietnam War.* Washington, D.C.: Georgetown University, 1967.

Chen, John H. M. *Vietnam: A Comprehensive Bibliography.* Metuchen, N. J.: The Scarecrow Press, 1973.

Chester, Lewis; Hodgson, Godfrey; and Page, Bruce. *An American Melodrama: The Presidential Campaign of 1968.* New York: Viking Press, 1969.

Chomsky, Noam. *American Power and the New Mandarins.* New York: Pantheon Books, 1969.

———. *At War With Asia.* New York: Pantheon Books, 1969.

Chomsky, Noam and Zinn, Howard, eds. *The Senator Gravel Edition: The Pentagon Papers, Critical Essays.* Vol. 5. Boston: Beacon Press, 1972.

Christian, George. *The President Steps Down: A Personal Memoir of the Transfer of Power.* New York: The Macmillan Company, 1970.

Clark, Keith C. and Legere, Lawrence J., eds. *The President and the Management of National Security.* New York: Frederick A. Praeger, 1969.

Collins, Brigadier General James Lawton, Jr. *Vietnam Studies: The Development and Training of the South Vietnamese Army, 1950–1972.* Washington, D.C.: Department of the Army, 1974.

Collins, Colonel John M. *The Vietnam War in Perspective.* Washington, D.C.: Strategic Research Group, The National War College, 1972.

Cooper, Chester L. *The Lost Crusade: America in Vietnam.* New York: Dodd Mead, 1970.

Corson, William R. *The Betrayal.* New York: W. W. Norton, 1968.

Crawford, Ann Caddell. *Customs and Culture of Vietnam.* Tokyo: Charles E. Tuttle and Company, n.d.

Critchfield, Richard. *The Long Charade: Political Subversion in the Vietnam War.* New York: Harcourt, Brace and World, 1968.

Cummings, Milton C., Jr. *The National Election of 1964.* Washington, D.C.: The Brookings Institution, 1966.

Deakin, James. *LBJ's Credibility Gap.* Washington, D.C.: Public Affairs Press, 1968.

deRivera, Joseph. *The Psychological Dimension of Foreign Policy.* Columbus, Ohio: Charles E. Merrill Publishing Company, 1968.

Destler, Irving M. *Presidents, Bureaucrats and Foreign Policy: The Politics of Organizational Reform.* Princeton, N. J.: Princeton University Press, 1972.

Downs, Anthony. *Inside Bureaucracy.* Boston: Little, Brown and Company, 1967.

Draper, Theodore. *Abuse of Power.* New York: The Viking Press, 1967.

Duncanson, Dennis J. *Government and Revolution in Vietnam.* New York: Oxford University Press, 1968.

Dvorin, Eugene P., ed. *The Senate's War Powers: Debate on Cambodia from the Congressional Record.* Chicago: Markham Publishing Company, 1971.

Efron, Edith. *The News Twisters.* Los Angeles: Nash Publishing, 1971.

Eisenhower, Dwight D. *The White House Years: Waging Peace 1956–1961.* Garden City, N. Y.: Doubleday and Company, 1965.

Ellsberg, Daniel. *Papers on the War.* New York: Simon and Schuster, 1972.

Enthoven, Alain C. and Smith, K. Wayne. *How Much is Enough? Shaping the Defense Program, 1961–1969.* New York: Harper and Row, 1971.

Etzioni, Amitai. *Complex Organizations: A Sociological Reader.* New York: Holt, Rinehart and Winston, 1961.

Fair, Charles M. *From the Jaws of Victory.* New York: Simon and Schuster, 1971.

Fairlie, Henry. *The Kennedy Promise: The Politics of Expectation.* London: Eyre Methuen, 1973.

Falk, Stanley and Bauer, Theodore W. *The National Security Structure.* Washington, D.C.: Industrial College of the Armed Forces, 1972.

Fall, Bernard B. *Hell in a Very Small Place: The Siege of Dien Bien Phu.* Philadelphia: J. B. Lippincott, 1967.

———. *Last Reflections on a War.* Garden City, N. Y.: Doubleday and Company, 1967.

———. *The Two Vietnams: A Political and Military Analysis.* New York: Praeger, 1963.

Fallaci, Oriana. *Nothing and So Be It.* Garden City, N. Y.: Doubleday and Company, 1972.

Fifield, Russell H. *Americans in Southeast Asia: The Roots of Commitment.* New York: Thomas Y. Crowell Company, 1973.

Fishel, Wesley R., ed. *Vietnam: Anatomy of a Conflict.* Itasca, Ill.: F. E. Peacock, 1968.

FitzGerald, Frances. *Fire in the Lake: The Vietnamese and the Americans in Vietnam.* Boston: Atlantic Monthly, Little, Brown and Company, 1972.

Fox, Douglas M. *The Politics of U. S. Foreign Policy Making: A Reader.* Pacific Palisades, Cal.: Goodyear Publishing Company, 1971.

Fulbright, J. William. *The Crippled Giant: American Foreign Policy and Its Domestic Consequences.* New York: Random House, 1972.

Fulton, Major General William B. *Vietnam Studies: Riverine Operations 1966–1969.* Washington, D.C.: Department of the Army, 1973.

Furgurson, Ernest B. *Westmoreland, The Inevitable General.* Boston: Little, Brown and Company, 1968.

Galloway, John. *The Gulf of Tonkin Resolution.* Rutherford, N. J.: Fairleigh Dickinson University Press, 1970.

Gallucci, Robert L. *Neither Peace nor Honor: The Politics of American Military Policy in Vietnam*. Baltimore: The Johns Hopkins University Press, 1975.

George, Alexander L.; Hall, David K.; and Simons, William E. *The Limits of Coercive Diplomacy: Laos, Cuba, Vietnam*. Boston: Little, Brown and Company, 1971.

Gernsheimer, Jacob S. and Potter, Howard M. *Historical Atlas of Indochina: 100 BC to the Present*. West Point, N. Y.: Department of Social Sciences, United States Military Academy, 1970.

Geyelin, Philip L. *Lyndon B. Johnson and the World*. New York: Praeger, 1966.

Giap, General Vo Nguyen. *Big Victory, Great Task*. New York: Frederick A. Praeger, 1967.

———. *People's War, People's Army*. Hanoi: Foreign Languages Publishing House, 1961.

———. *Viet Nam People's War Has Defeated United States War of Destruction*. Hanoi: Foreign Languages Publishing House, 1969.

Girling, J.L.S. *People's War: Conditions and Consequences in China and South East Asia*. New York: Frederick A. Praeger, 1969.

Goldman, Eric F. *The Tragedy of Lyndon Johnson*. New York: Alfred A. Knopf, 1969.

Goodwin, Richard N. *Triumph or Tragedy: Reflections on Vietnam*. New York: Random House, 1966.

Goulden, Joseph C. *The Superlawyers: The Small and Powerful World of the Great Washington Law Firms*. New York: Weybright and Talley, 1972.

———. *Truth is the First Casualty—The Gulf of Tonkin Affair: Illusion and Reality*. Chicago: Rand McNally and Company, 1969.

Goulding, Phil G. *Confirm or Deny: Informing the People on National Security*. New York: Harper and Row, 1970.

Graff, Henry F. *The Tuesday Cabinet: Deliberation and Decision on Peace and War under Lyndon B. Johnson*. Englewood Cliffs, N. J.: Prentice Hall, 1970.

Grauwin, Paul. *Doctor at Dienbienphu*. New York: John Day Company, 1955.

Gravel, Senator Mike, ed. *The Senator Gravel Edition: The*

Pentagon Papers: The Defense Department History of United States Decisionmaking on Vietnam. 4 vols. Boston: Beacon Press, 1971.

Greene, Fred. *United States Policy and the Security of Asia.* New York: McGraw-Hill Book Company, 1968.

Halberstam, David. *The Best and The Brightest.* New York: Random House, 1972.

————. *The Unfinished Odyssey of Robert Kennedy.* New York: Random House, 1968.

Halper, Thomas. *Foreign Policy Crises: Appearance and Reality in Foreign Policy.* Columbus, Ohio: Charles E. Merrill Publishing Company, 1971.

Halperin, Morton H. *Bureaucratic Politics and Foreign Policy.* Washington, D.C.: The Brookings Institution, 1974.

————. *Defense Strategies for the Seventies.* Boston: Little, Brown and Company, 1971.

Hammond, Paul Y. *Organizing for Defense: The American Military Establishment in the Twentieth Century.* Princeton, N. J.: Princeton University Press, 1969.

Harriman, W. Averell. *America and Russia in a Changing World: A Half Century of Personal Observation.* Garden City, N. Y.: Doubleday and Company, 1971.

Harris, Louis. *The Anguish of Change.* New York: W. W. Norton and Company, 1973.

Harvey, Frank. *Air War—Vietnam.* New York: Bantam Books, 1967.

Haskins, James. *The War and the Protest: Vietnam.* Garden City, N. Y.: Doubleday and Company, 1971.

Heiser, Lieutenant General Joseph M., Jr. *Vietnam Studies: Logistic Support.* Washington, D.C.: Department of the Army, 1974.

Heren, Louis. *No Hail, No Farewell.* New York: Harper and Row, 1969.

Herzog, Arthur. *McCarthy for President.* New York: Viking Press, 1969.

Hilsman, Roger. *To Move a Nation: The Politics of Foreign Policy in the Administration of JFK.* Garden City, N.Y.: Doubleday and Company, 1967.

————. *The Politics of Policy Making in Defense and Foreign Affairs.* New York: Harper and Row, 1971.

363

Hobsbawm, Eric J. *Revolutionaries: Contemporary Essays.* London: Weidenfeld and Nicolson, 1973.

Hoffmann, Stanley. *Gulliver's Troubles, or The Setting of American Foreign Policy.* New York: McGraw-Hill Book Company, 1968.

Holmgren, Rod and Norton, William. *The Mass Media Book.* Englewood Cliffs, N. J.: Prentice Hall, 1972.

Hoopes, Townsend. *The Limits of Intervention.* New York: David McKay Company, 1969.

Hosmer, Stephen T. *Viet Cong Repression and Its Implications for the Future.* Lexington, Mass.: D. C. Heath and Company, 1970.

Hughes, Henry Stuart. *History as Art and Science: Twin Vistas on the Past.* New York: Harper and Row, 1964.

Hughes, John Emmet. *The Living Presidency: The Resources and Dilemmas of the American Presidential Office.* New York: Coward, McCann and Geoghegan, 1973.

Humphrey, Hubert H. *The Education of a Public Man: My Life and Politics.* Garden City, N. Y.: Doubleday and Company, 1976.

Institute for Strategic Studies. *Strategic Survey 1969.* London: Institute for Strategic Studies, 1970.

Jackson, Senator Henry M., ed. *The National Security Council: Jackson Subcommittee Papers on Policy-Making at the Presidential Level.* New York: Frederick A. Praeger, 1965.

Janis, Irving L. *Victims of Groupthink: A Psychological Study of Foreign Policy Decisions and Fiascos.* Boston: Houghton Mifflin Company, 1972.

Johnson, Haynes B. and Gwertzman, Bernard M. *Fulbright: The Dissenter.* Garden City, N. Y.: Doubleday and Company, 1968.

Johnson, Lady Bird. *A White House Diary.* New York: Holt, Rinehart and Winston, 1970.

Johnson, Lyndon B. *The Vantage Point: Perspectives of the Presidency, 1963–1969.* New York: Holt, Rinehart and Winston, 1971.

Johnson, Sam Houston. *My Brother, Lyndon.* New York: Cowles Book Company, 1970.

Kalb, Marvin and Abel, Elie. *Roots of Involvement: The United States in Asia 1784–1971.* New York: W. W. Norton and Company, 1971.

Kearns, Doris. *Lyndon Johnson and the American Dream.* New York: Harper and Row, 1976.

Komer, R. W. *Bureaucracy Does Its Thing: Institutional Constraints on U.S.–GVN Performance in Vietnam,* Report R–967, ARPA. Santa Monica, Cal.: The Rand Corporation, 1972.

Kraslow, David and Loory, Stuart H. *The Secret Search for Peace in Vietnam.* New York: Random House, 1968.

Krause, Patricia A., ed. *Anatomy of an Undeclared War: Congressional Conference on the Pentagon Papers.* New York: International Universities Press, 1972.

Krock, Arthur. *The Consent of the Governed.* Boston: Little, Brown and Company, 1971.

Ladd, Bruce. *Crisis in Credibility.* New York: The New American Library, 1968.

Lamb, Helen B. *Vietnam's Will to Live: Resistance to Foreign Aggression From Early Times Through the Nineteenth Century.* New York: Monthly Review Press, 1972.

Landecker, Manfred. *The President and Public Opinion: Leadership in Foreign Affairs.* Washington, D.C.: Public Affairs Press, 1968.

Larner, Jeremy. *Nobody Knows: Reflections on the McCarthy Campaign of 1968.* New York: The Macmillan Company, 1970.

Larsen, Lieutenant General Stanley R. and Collins, Brigadier General James L., Jr. *Vietnam Studies: Allied Participation in Vietnam.* Washington, D.C.: Department of the Army, 1975.

Lee, Richard W., ed. *Politics and the Press.* Washington, D.C.: Acropolis Books, 1970.

Liddell Hart, Basil H. *The Decisive Wars of History: A Study in Strategy.* London: G. Bell and Sons, 1929.

Lifton, Robert L. *America and the Asian Revolutionaries.* Chicago: Aldine Publishing Company, 1970.

Lindblom, Charles E. *The Intelligence of Democracy: Decision-Making Through Mutual Adjustment.* New York: Free Press, 1965.

————. *The Policy Making Process.* Englewood Cliffs, N. J.: Prentice Hall, 1968.

Littauer, Raphael and Uphoff, Norman, eds. *The Air War in Indochina,* rev. ed. Boston: Beacon Press, 1972.

Lodge, Henry Cabot. *The Storm Has Many Eyes: A Personal Narrative.* New York: W. W. Norton and Company, 1973.

Lowenthal, Abraham F. *The Dominican Intervention*. Cambridge, Mass.: Harvard University Press, 1972.

MacNeil, Robert. *The People Machine*. New York: Harper and Row, 1968.

McCarthy, Eugene J. *The Year of the People*. Garden City, N. Y.: Doubleday and Company, 1969.

McGaffin, William and Knoll, Erwin. *Anything But the Truth: The Credibility Gap—How the News is Managed in Washington*. New York: Putnam, 1968.

McPherson, Harry C., Jr. *A Political Education*. Boston: Atlantic Monthly, Little, Brown and Company, 1971.

Melman, Seymour. *The War Economy of the United States*. New York: St. Martin's Press, 1971.

Meyerhoff, Hans, ed. *The Philosophy of History in Our Time*. Garden City, N. Y.: Doubleday Anchor Books, Doubleday and Company, 1959.

Meyerson, Harvey. *Vinh Long*. Boston: Houghton Mifflin Company, 1970.

Middleton, Drew. *Can America Win the Next War?* New York: Charles Scribner's Sons, 1975.

Miller, Norman and Aya, Roderick, eds. *National Liberation: Revolution in the Third World*. New York: Free Press, 1971.

Mueller, John E. *War, Presidents and Public Opinion*. New York: John Wiley and Sons, 1973.

Nalty, Bernard C. *Air Power and the Fight for Khe Sanh*. Washington, D.C.: Office of Air Force History, United States Air Force, 1973.

Neustadt, Richard E. *Presidential Power: The Politics of Leadership*. New York: John Wiley and Sons, 1960.

Newfield, Jack. *Robert Kennedy: A Memoir*. New York: Dutton, 1969.

Nighswonger, William A. *Rural Pacification in Vietnam*. New York: Praeger Special Studies, Frederick A. Praeger, 1967.

Oberdorfer, Don. *Tet*. Garden City, N. Y.: Doubleday and Company, 1971.

Okun, Arthur M. *The Political Economy of Prosperity*. Washington, D.C.: The Brookings Institution, 1970.

O'Neill, Robert J. *The Strategy of General Giap Since 1964*. Canberra: Australian National University Press, 1969.

366

Osgood, Robert E. *America and The World: From the Truman Doctrine to Vietnam.* Baltimore: Johns Hopkins University Press, 1970.

Palmer, Lieutenant Colonel Dave R. *Readings in Current Military History.* West Point, N. Y.: Department of Military Art and Engineering, United States Military Academy, 1969.

Paolucci, Henry. *War, Peace, and the Presidency.* New York: McGraw-Hill Book Company, 1968.

Paul, Roland A. *American Military Commitments Abroad.* New Brunswick, N. J.: Rutgers University Press, 1973.

Pearson, Lieutenant General Willard. *Vietnam Studies: The War in the Northern Provinces, 1966–1968.* Washington, D.C.: Department of the Army, 1975.

Pfeffer, Richard J., ed. *No More Vietnams? The War and the Future of American Foreign Policy.* New York: Harper and Row for the Adlai Stevenson Institute of International Affairs, 1968.

Pierce, Lawrence C. *The Politics of Fiscal Policy Formation.* Pacific Palisades, Cal.: Goodyear Publishing Company, 1971.

Pike, Douglas. *Viet Cong: The Organization and Techniques of the National Liberation Front of South Vietnam.* Cambridge, Mass.: The M. I. T. Press, 1966.

————. *The Viet-Cong Strategy of Terror.* Saigon: United States Mission, Viet-Nam, 1970.

————. *War, Peace, and the Viet Cong.* Cambridge, Mass.: The M. I. T. Press, 1969.

Plimpton, George. *An American Journey: The Times of Robert Kennedy.* New York: Harcourt Brace Jovanovich, 1970.

Polsby, Nelson. *Congress and the Presidency.* Englewood Cliffs, N. J.: Prentice Hall, 1964.

Race, Jeffrey. *War Comes To Long An.* Berkeley, Cal.: University of California Press, 1972.

Raskin, Marcus G. *The Vietnam Reader: Articles and Documents on American Foreign Policy and the Vietnam Crisis.* New York: Vintage Books, 1967.

Reedy, George E. *The Presidency in Flux.* New York: Columbia University Press, 1973.

————. *The Twilight of the Presidency.* New York: World Publishing Company, 1970.

Reston, James B. *The Artillery of the Press: Its Influence on American Foreign Policy*. New York: Harper and Row, 1967.

Rice, Stuart A. *Methods in Social Science*. Chicago: University of Chicago Press, 1937.

Rivers, William L. *The Adversaries*. Boston: Beacon Press, 1970.

Roberts, Chalmers M. *First Rough Draft: A Journalist's Journal of Our Times*. New York: Praeger, 1973.

Roberts, Charles W. *LBJ's Inner Circle*. New York: Delacorte Press, 1965.

Roberts, Donald F. and Schramm, Wilbur, eds. *The Process and Effects of Mass Communication*, 2d ed. Urbana, Ill.: University of Illinois Press, 1971.

Rosenau, James N. *The Attentive Public and Foreign Policy*. Princeton, N. J.: Center for International Studies, 1968.

————, ed. *Domestic Sources of Foreign Policy*. New York: Free Press, 1967.

————. *International Politics and Foreign Policy: A Reader in Research and Theory*. New York: Free Press of Glencoe, Inc., 1961.

————. *National Leadership and Foreign Policy: A Case Study in the Mobilization of Public Support*. Princeton, N. J.: Princeton University Press, 1963.

————. *Public Opinion and Foreign Policy*. New York: Random House, 1961.

Rosenberg, Milton J.; Verba, Sidney; and Converse, Philip E., eds. *Vietnam and the Silent Majority*. New York: Harper and Row, 1970.

Rostow, Walt W. *The Diffusion of Power: An Essay in Recent History*. New York: The Macmillan Company, 1972.

————. *The United States in the World Arena*. New York: Harper and Brothers, 1961.

Roy, Jules. *La Bataille de Dien Bien Phu*. Paris: René Julliard, 1963.

————. *The Battle of Dien Bien Phu*. New York: Harper and Row, 1965.

Royal United Service Institution. *Lessons from the Vietnam War*. London: Royal United Service Institution, 1969.

Salisbury, Harrison E. *Behind the Lines: Hanoi, December 23, 1966–January 7, 1967*. London: Secker and Warburg, 1967.

Scenes of the General Offensive and Uprising. Hanoi: Foreign Languages Publishing House, 1968.

368

Schlesinger, Arthur M., Jr. *A Thousand Days: John F. Kennedy in the White House.* Boston: Houghton Mifflin Company, 1965.

————. *The Bitter Heritage: Vietnam and American Democracy.* Boston: Houghton Mifflin Company, 1967.

————. *History of American Presidential Elections 1789–1968.* Vol. 4. New York: McGraw-Hill Book Company, 1971.

Schurmann, Franz; Scott, Peter Dale; and Zelnik, Reginald. *The Politics of Escalation in Vietnam.* Boston: Beacon Press, 1966.

Schwartz, Benjamin I. *Communism and China: Ideology in Flux.* Cambridge, Mass.: Harvard University Press, 1968.

Shadegg, Stephen C. *What Happened to Goldwater? The Inside Story of the 1964 Republican Campaign.* New York: Holt, Rinehart and Winston, 1965.

Shaplen, Robert M. *The Lost Revolution.* New York: Harper and Row, 1965.

————. *The Road from War: Vietnam 1965–1970.* New York: Harper and Row, 1970.

————. *Time Out of Hand: Revolution and Reaction in Southeast Asia.* New York: Harper and Row, 1969.

Sharp, Admiral U. S. Grant, USN. *Report on the War in Vietnam: Section I, Report on Air and Naval Campaigns Against North Vietnam and Pacific Command-Wide Support of the War, June 1964–July 1968.* Washington, D.C.: United States Government Printing Office, 1969.

Sheehan, Neil; Smith, Hedrick; Kenworthy, E. W.; and Butterworth, Fox, eds. *The Pentagon Papers as Published by The New York Times.* New York: Quadrangle Books, 1971.

Shepherd, Jack and Wren, Christopher S. *Quotations from Chairman LBJ.* New York: Simon and Schuster, 1968.

Sherrill, Robert. *The Accidental President.* New York: Pyramid Books, 1968.

Shore, Captain Moyers S., USMC. *The Battle for Khe Sanh.* Washington, D.C.: Historical Branch, G–3 Division, United States Marine Corps, 1969.

Sidey, Hugh. *A Very Personal Presidency: LBJ in the White House.* New York: Atheneum, 1968.

Sindler, Allan P., ed. *American Political Institutions and Public Policy.* Boston: Little, Brown and Company, 1969.

Skolnick, Jerome H. *The Politics of Protest.* New York: Ballantine Books, 1969.

Small, William T. *Political Power and the Press.* New York: W. W. Norton, 1972.

————. *To Kill A Messenger.* New York: Hastings House, 1970.

Son, Lieutenant Colonel Pham Van. *The Viet Cong Tet Offensive 1968.* Saigon: Printing & Publications Center, RVNAF, 1968.

Sorensen, Theodore. *Decision-Making in the White House.* New York: Columbia University Press, 1963.

South Viet Nam: A Month of Unprecedented Offensive and Uprising. Hanoi: Giai Phong Publishing House, 1968.

Stavins, Ralph L.; Barnet, Richard J.; and Raskin, Marcus G. *Washington Plans an Aggressive War.* New York: Vintage Books, 1971.

Stebbins, Richard P. and Adam, Elaine P., eds. *Documents on American Foreign Policy 1968–69.* New York: Council on Foreign Relations, 1972.

Stein, Robert. *Media Power: Who Is Shaping Your Picture of the World?* Boston: Houghton Mifflin Company, 1972.

Steinberg, Alfred. *Sam Johnson's Boy: A Close-up of the President from Texas.* New York: Macmillan and Company, 1968.

Stevenson, Charles A. *The End of Nowhere: American Policy Toward Laos Since 1954.* Boston: Beacon Press, 1972.

Stout, Richard C. *People.* New York: Harper and Row, 1970.

Strum, Philippa. *Presidential Power and American Democracy.* Pacific Palisades, Cal.: Goodyear Publishing Company, 1972.

Sullivan, Cornelius D.; Eliot, George Field; Gayle, Gordon D.; and Corson, William R., eds. *The Vietnam War: Its Conduct and Higher Direction.* Washington, D.C.: Center for Strategic Studies, Georgetown University, 1968.

Sweezy, Paul M. *Vietnam: The Endless War.* New York: Monthly Review Press, 1970.

Talese, Gay. *The Kingdom and the Power.* New York: World Publishing Company, 1969.

Tanham, George K. *War Without Guns: American Civilians in Rural Vietnam.* New York: Frederick A. Praeger, 1966.

Tanter, Raymond and Ullman, Richard H., eds. *Theory and Policy in International Relations.* Princeton, N. J.: Princeton University Press, 1972.

Taylor, General Maxwell D. *Swords and Plowshares.* New York: W. W. Norton, 1972.

Thai, Nguyen Van and Mung, Nguyen Van. *A Short History of Vietnam*. Saigon: Times Publishing Company for the Vietnamese-American Association, 1958.

Thompson, Sir Robert G. K. *No Exit from Vietnam*. London: Chatto and Windus, 1969.

Thompson, W. Scott. *Unequal Partners: Philippine and Thai Relations with the United States, 1965–75*. Lexington, Mass.: D. C. Heath and Company, 1975.

Trewhitt, Henry L. *McNamara: His Ordeal in the Pentagon*. New York: Harper and Row, 1971.

Truman, Harry S. *Memoirs*, 2 vols. Garden City, N. Y.: Doubleday and Company, 1955.

Tuchman, Barbara. *Stilwell and the American Experience in China, 1911–1945*. New York: The Macmillan Company, 1970.

Ungar, Sanford J. *The Papers and the Papers; An Account of the Legal and Political Battle Over the Pentagon Papers*. New York: E. P. Dutton and Company, 1972.

Valenti, Jack. *A Very Human President*. New York: W. W. Norton, 1975.

Van Dyke, Jon M. *North Vietnam's Strategy for Survival*. Palo Alto, Cal.: Pacific Books, 1972.

Wakefield, Dan. *Supernation at Peace and War*. Boston: Little, Brown and Company, 1968.

Walt, General Lewis W., USMC. *Strange War, Strange Strategy*. New York: Funk and Wagnalls, 1970.

Wedgwood, C. V. *The Sense of the Past*. London: Cambridge University Press, 1957.

Wells, Alan, ed. *Mass Media and Society*. Palo Alto, Cal.: National Press Book, 1972.

Westmoreland, General William C., USA. *Report on the War in Vietnam: Section II, Report on Operations in South Vietnam, January 1964–June 1968*. Washington, D.C.: United States Government Printing Office, 1969.

————. *A Soldier Reports*. Garden City, N. Y.: Doubleday and Company, 1976.

White, Ralph K. *Nobody Wanted War: Misperceptions in Vietnam and Other Wars*. Garden City, N. Y.: Doubleday and Company, 1968.

White, Theodore H. *The Making of the President, 1964.* New York: The New American Library, 1965.

————. *The Making of the President, 1968.* New York: Atheneum, 1969.

Wicker, Tom. *JFK & LBJ: The Influence of Personality on Politics.* New York: Morrow, 1968.

Wilson, Woodrow. *Constitutional Government in the United States.* New York: Columbia University Press, 1908.

Windchy, Eugene C. *Tonkin Gulf.* Garden City, N. Y.: Doubleday and Company, 1971.

Wise, David. *The Politics of Lying: Government Deception, Secrecy and Power.* New York: Random House, 1973.

Witcover, Jules. *85 Days: The Last Campaign of Robert Kennedy.* New York: G. P. Putnam's Sons, 1969.

Yarmolinsky, Adam. *The Military Establishment: Its Impact on American Society.* New York: Harper and Row, 1971.

Zeiger, Henry A. *Robert F. Kennedy: A Biography.* New York: Meredith Press, 1968.

ARTICLES

Adams, Samuel A. "Vietnam Cover-Up: Playing War With Numbers." *Harper's Magazine,* May 1975, p. 41.

"After the Tet Offensive." *New York Times,* February 8, 1968, p. 42, col. 2.

Allison, Graham T. "Conceptual Models and the Cuban Missile Crisis." *American Political Science Review* 63 (September 1969): 689–718.

Alsop, Joseph. "Captured Documents Indicate a Major Red Strategy Shift." *Washington Post,* December 15, 1967, p. A29, col. 1.

————. "Westmoreland's Replacement Hints Wavering LBJ Support." *Washington Post,* March 25, 1968, p. A15, col. 1.

Anderson, Jack. "Daniel Ellsberg: The Other News Leak." *Washington Post,* September 25, 1975, p. B7, col. 1.

Anderson, Jack and Whitten, Les. "Numbers Game on Tet Offensive." *Washington Post,* October 31, 1975, p. B26, col. 1.

Apple, R. W., Jr. "Vietnam: Signs of Stalemate." *New York Times,* August 7, 1967, p. 1, col. 6.

Arnett, Peter. "Tactics Shift Reduces Hanoi's Losses." *Washington Post*, April 12, 1970, p. A19, col. 4.

————. "Viet Red Drive Challenges U.S. Military Assumptions." *Baltimore Sun*, February 7, 1968, p. A1, col. 6.

Aronson, James. "The Sell-Out of the Pulitzer Prize." *The Washingtonian Monthly*, October 1970, pp. 55–59.

"As Mr. Rusk Has Been Saying. . . ." *New York Post*, March 13, 1968, p. 56, col. 1.

Ashworth, George W. "Westmoreland's Viet Inventory." *Christian Science Monitor*, April 8, 1969, p. 10, col. 1.

"Back on the Track." *Washington Post*, April 13, 1968, p. A10, col. 1.

Baldwin, Hanson. "The Case for Mobilization." *Reporter*, May 19, 1966, pp. 20–23.

————. "Public Opinion in U.S. and South Vietnam is Viewed as Main Target of New Offensive by Vietcong." *New York Times*, February 1, 1968, p. 12, col. 1.

————. "U.S. Manpower Needs for War." *New York Times*, February 3, 1968, p. 10, col. 6.

Barrett, Raymond J. "Graduated Response and the Lessons of Vietnam." *Military Review*, May 1972, pp. 80–91.

Beech, Keyes. "Westmoreland's Image Tarnished by Red Drive." *New York Post*, March 9, 1968, p. 6, col. 1.

Beecher, William. "565,000 Total Is In View: Strategy Change Weighed." *New York Times*, March 23, 1968, p. 1, col. 6.

————. "U.S. Calls 24,500 Reserves, Sets G.I. Ceiling at 549,500, Giving Saigon Major Role." *New York Times*, April 12, 1968, p. 1, col. 6.

————. "Vietnam Assayed by Westmoreland." *New York Times*, April 7, 1969, p. 1, col. 7.

Beisner, Robert L. "1898 and 1969: The Anti-Imperialists and the Doves." *Political Science Quarterly* 85 (June 1970): 187–216.

Bell, Jack. "Dissenters Unmoved by General." *Washington Post*, November 24, 1967, p. 5, col. 1.

Beveridge, George. "The Army's-Conning-of-LBJ Story." *Washington Star*, March 29, 1976, p. A15, col. 5.

Bickel, Alexander M. "The Constitution and the War." *Commentary* 54 (July 1972): 49–55.

"Blood on the Screen." *St. Louis Post-Dispatch*, February 6, 1968, p. 2B, col. 2.

Boatner, Mark M. III. "The Unheeded History of Counterinsurgency." *Army*, September 1966, pp. 31–36.

Bradford, Lieutenant Colonel Zeb B., Jr. "U.S. Tactics in Vietnam." *Military Review*, February 1972, pp. 63–76.

Braestrup, Peter. "Khesanh Waits and Probes Strategy." *Washington Post*, February 19, 1968, p. A19, col. 1.

————. "Pentagon Report on Vietnam War Stresses Restraints." *Washington Post*, April 7, 1969, p. A1, col. 1.

Broder, David S. "Ford Urges Balanced Tet View." *Washington Post*, September 21, 1974, p. A4, col. 1.

————. "Young House Members Seek Over-All Viet Strategy Review." *Washington Post*, November 7, 1967, p. A17, col. 6.

Brodie, Bernard. "Why Were We So (Strategically) Wrong?" *Foreign Policy*, no. 5 (Winter 1971–72), pp. 151–162.

Brower, Brock. "McNamara Now Seen Full Length." *Life*, May 10, 1968, p. 76.

Bruen, Lieutenant Colonel John D. "Repercussions from the Vietnam Mobilization Decision." *Parameters, the Journal of the Army War College*, Spring-Summer 1972, pp. 30–39.

Buchwald, Art. " 'We Have Enemy on the Run,' Says Gen. Custer at Big Horn." *Washington Post*, February 6, 1968, p. A15, col. 3.

Buckley, Tom. "Generals Ponder Foe's DacTo Aims." *New York Times*, November 20, 1967, p. 3, col. 1.

————. "Hope Says Some Performers Refused Vietnam Trip." *New York Times*, December 22, 1966, p. 3, col. 1.

————. "Offensive is Said to Pinpoint Enemy's Strengths." *New York Times*, February 2, 1968, p. 12, col. 5.

Bundy, William P. "The Path to Vietnam: Ten Decisions." *Orbis*, Fall 1967, pp. 647–663.

Buttinger, Joseph. "How We Sank Into Vietnam." *Dissent*, Spring 1972, pp. 407–441.

Cahill, Jerome S. "Scott Opposes A-Weapon Use in Vietnam War." *Philadelphia Inquirer*, February 19, 1968, p. 3, col. 3.

Cameron, Juan. "The Armed Forces' Reluctant Retrenchment." *Fortune* 82 (November 1970): 68.

Cannon, Lou. " '67 Viet Data Said Concealed." *Washington Post*, April 24, 1975, p. A13, col. 1.

Cash, John A. "Battle of Lang Vei." In *Seven Fire Fights in Vietnam*, edited by John Albright, John A. Cash, and Allan

W. Sandstrum, pp. 109–138. Washington, D.C.: Office of the Chief of Military History, Department of the Army, 1970.

"Change of Command." *Washington Star*, March 25, 1968, p. A12, col. 1.

Childs, Marquis W. "A-Bombs Reported Stockpiled in Vietnam." *St. Louis Post-Dispatch*, February 9, 1968, p. 1A, col. 6.

Chomsky, Noam. "The Pentagon Papers as Propaganda and History." In *The Senator Gravel Edition: The Pentagon Papers, Critical Essays*, edited by Noam Chomsky and Howard Zinn, vol. 5, pp. 179–201. Boston: Beacon Press, 1972.

Clark, Blair. "Westmoreland Appraised: Questions and Answers." *Harper's Magazine*, November 1970, pp. 96–101.

Claymore, John. "Vietnamization of the Foreign Service." *Foreign Service Journal* 48 (December 1971): 14.

Clifford, Clark M. "A Viet Nam Reappraisal: The Personal History of One Man's View and How it Evolved." *Foreign Affairs* 47 (July 1969): 601–622.

"Clifford Won't Testify on the War." *Washington News*, March 14, 1968, p. 2, col. 1.

Cohen, Bernard C. "Foreign Policy Makers and the Press." In *International Politics and Foreign Policy: A Reader in Research and Theory*, edited by James N. Rosenau, pp. 220–227. New York: Free Press of Glencoe, 1961.

Considine, Bob and Kaplan, Milton. "Obsolete Weapons, Supplied by U.S., Hold Viets Back." *San Francisco Chronicle*, November 5, 1967, p. 2, Sect. A, col. 4.

"Contribution of the Hearings." *Washington Post*, March 13, 1968, p. A20, col. 1.

Converse, Philip E.; Miller, Warren E.; Rusk, Jerold G.; and Wolfe, Arthur C. "Continuity and Change in American Politics: Parties and Issues in the 1968 Election." *American Political Science Review* 63 (December 1969): 1,083–1,105.

Converse, Philip E., and Schuman, Howard. "Silent Majorities and the Vietnam War." *Scientific American*, June 1970, pp. 17–26.

Cooper, Chester. "Fateful Day in Vietnam–10 Years Ago." *Washington Post*, February 11, 1975, p. A14, col. 3.

Corddry, Charles W. "A-Bomb Use Never Urged, Officers Say." *Baltimore Sun*, February 13, 1968, p. A2, col. 8.

Corddry, Charles W. "End to War in Sight for Commander." *Baltimore Sun*, November 22, 1967, p. A1, col. 8.

————. "Johnson to Recall Westmoreland from Vietnam Command in July to Be New Army Chief of Staff—Westmoreland Attains No. 1 Goal." *Baltimore Sun*, March 23, 1968, p. A1, col. 5.

————. "McNamara Will Take World Bank Job When Defense Budget is Set." *Baltimore Sun*, November 30, 1967, p. A1, col. 8.

————. "More Viet Aid Being Studied." *Baltimore Sun*, March 9, 1968, p. A1, col. 2.

————. "Time, Not Price, Was Guide in Rifle Pacts, Army Says." *Baltimore Sun*, May 9, 1968, p. A7, col. 2.

————. "U.S. Intends to Give Saigon Main War Role." *Baltimore Sun*, April 12, 1968, p. A1, col. 6.

————. "Viet Parley Hope Voiced by Clifford." *Baltimore Sun*, April 23, 1968, p. A1, col. 8.

————. "Viet 'Phase-Down' Defined as Long-Term, Gradual Step." *Baltimore Sun*, November 18, 1967, p. A1, col. 6.

Cormier, Frank. "Johnson Sees Eisenhower, Troops in Tour." *Washington Star*, February 19, 1968, p. A1, col. 3.

Crewdson, John M. "False Troop Data in Vietnam Cited." *New York Times*, September 19, 1975, p. 7, col. 1.

Cutler, Robert. "The Development of the National Security Council." *Foreign Affairs* 34 (April 1956): 441–458.

Darling, Frank C. "American Policy in Vietnam: Its Role in the Quakeland Theory and International Peace." *Asian Survey* 11 (August 1971): 818–839.

Davis, Saville. "A New Voice: Clark Clifford Puts a Fresh Look on Vietnam Policy Exposition." *Christian Science Monitor*, April 23, 1968, p. 6, col. 1.

Davis, Vincent. "American Military Policy: Decision-making in the Executive Branch." *Naval War College Review*, May 1970, pp. 4–23.

Day, Robin. "Troubled Reflections of a TV Journalist." *Encounter* 34 (May 1970): pp. 78–88.

"Dean Rusk Looks Back on Vietnam." *Washington Sunday Star*, July 11, 1971, p. E2, col. 1.

"Debate in a Vacuum." *Time*, March 15, 1968, pp. 13–15.

Deepe, Beverly. "Khe Sanh: Legacy of Westmoreland." *Christian Science Monitor*, March 27, 1968, p. 1, col. 4.

————. "South Vietnam Shaken: Hardly a Hamlet Feels Safe." *Christian Science Monitor*, February 7, 1968, p. 1, col. 3.

————. "U.S. Shushes Viet Drive." *Christian Science Monitor*, April 18, 1968, p. 1, col. 2.

Denniston, Lyle. "Senators Demand Voice in Viet Troop Build-up." *Washington Star*, March 8, 1968, p. A1, col. 7.

Destler, Irving M. "The Nixon NSC: Can One Man Do?" *Foreign Policy*, no. 5 (Winter 1971–72), pp. 28–40.

Dodd, Philip. "Lyndon Calls Parley on Viet Nam Policy." *Chicago Tribune*, November 21, 1967, Sect. 1A, p. 1, col. 2.

Doty, Robert C. "Fanfani Saw 2 Hanoi Aides." *New York Times*, February 15, 1968, p. 2, col. 3.

Dudman, Richard. "Moving Westmoreland May Not Alter Strategy." *St. Louis Post-Dispatch*, March 24, 1968, p. 2A, col. 1.

Eidenberg, Eugene. "Americanizing the War in Vietnam." In *American Political Institutions and Public Policy*, edited by Allan P. Sindler, pp. 104–121. Boston: Little, Brown and Company, 1969. Also in *The Politics of U.S. Foreign Policy Making: A Reader*, edited by Douglas M. Fox, pp. 310–323. Pacific Palisades, Cal.: Goodyear Publishing Company, 1971.

Erskine, Hazel. "The Polls: Is War a Mistake?" *Public Opinion Quarterly*, Spring 1970, pp. 134–150.

Evans, Roland and Novak, Robert. "Johnson's Decision on Men, Money Could Add Third to Viet War Budget." *Washington Post*, February 29, 1968, p. A25, col. 1.

————. "Policy Makers and Generals Worry Over Massive Buildup at Khe Sanh." *Washington Post*, January 31, 1968, p. A21, col. 3.

————. "A Tet Memo from Ellsberg." *Washington Post*, July 7, 1971, p. A19, col. 3.

"Exit McNamara." *The Nation*, December 11, 1967, p. 8.

Fairlie, Henry. "We Knew What We Were Doing When We Went Into Vietnam." *The Washingtonian Monthly*, May 1973, pp. 7–26.

Falk, Stanley L. "National Security Council Under Truman, Eisenhower, and Kennedy." *Political Science Quarterly* 79 (September 1964): 403–434.

————. "The Restoration of the National Security Council." *Perspectives in Defense Management*, Winter 1972–73, pp. 69–73.

Fall, Bernard. "Master of the Red Jab." *Saturday Evening Post*, November 24, 1962, pp. 18–21.

Fallaci, Oriana. "North Vietnam Commander Admits 500,000 Men Lost, Vows to Win." *Washington Post*, April 6, 1969, p. B1, col. 3.

Farrar, Fred. "Enemy Fails in War Goals, Westy Says." *Chicago Tribune*, April 7, 1969, p. 10, Sect. 1, col. 1.

Feinsilber, Mike. "Ambassador Bunker Reports: Irony of Vietnam." *Philadelphia Bulletin*, February 19, 1968, p. 13, col. 7.

Feis, Herbert. "The Shackled Historian." *Foreign Affairs* 45 (January 1967): 332–343.

———. "Speaking of Books: Unpublic Public Papers." *New York Times Book Review*, April 21, 1968, p. 2, col. 1.

Fenton, John W. "Switches by Press on War Reported." *New York Times*, February 18, 1968, p. 9, col. 1.

Finney, John W. "Anonymous Call Set Off Rumors of Nuclear Arms for Vietnam." *New York Times*, February 13, 1968, p. 1, col. 2.

———. "Criticism of War Widens in Senate on Build-Up Issue." *New York Times*, March 8, 1968, p. 1, col. 8.

———. "139 in House Support Drive for a Review of Policy in Vietnam." *New York Times*, March 19, 1968, p. 32, col. 4.

———. "Senate Panel to Press Rusk for a Debate on War." *New York Times,* November 1, 1967, p. 3, col. 5.

———. "War Doubts in Senate." *New York Times,* February 12, 1968, p. 6, col. 3.

———. "Wheeler Doubts Khesanh Will Need Atom Weapons." *New York Times*, February 15, 1968, p. 1, col. 5.

"The First Amendment on Trial." *Columbia Journalism Review*, September/October 1971, pp. 7–50.

"Flights Can Go 250 Miles Above DMZ: U.S. Bombs Away in North." *Washington Daily News*, April 2, 1968, p. 2, col. 2.

Frankel, Max. "Johnson Confers with Eisenhower; Briefs Him on War." *New York Times*, February 19, 1968, p. 1, col. 4.

———. "Johnson Pullout Conceived in '65." *New York Times*, April 2, 1968, p. 1, col. 7.

———. "McNamara Takes World Bank Post: War Shift Denied." *New York Times*, November 30, 1967, p. 1, col. 8.

———. "U.S. Girding at Khesanh to Avoid a 'Dienbienphu': Johnson Holds Reins." *New York Times*, February 10, 1975, p. 1, col. 3.

Fritchey, Clayton. "A Cabinet Lesson Seen in McNamara's Case." *Washington Star*, December 4, 1967, p. A13, col. 5.

————. "Mansfield's Warnings on Asia Date Far Back." *Washington Star*, March 4, 1968, p. A9, col. 5.

————. "Rusk Commitment Thesis Lambasted." *Washington Star*, March 15, 1968, p. A9, col. 1.

————. "Westmoreland's Vietnam Strategy." *Washington Star*, February 9, 1968, p. A15, col. 1.

Fulbright, J. William. "Reflections: In Thrall to Fear." *New Yorker*, January 8, 1972, p. 41.

Gallagher, Wes. "Foe Can't Stand Long War." *Chicago Tribune*, February 26, 1968, p. 1, col. 7.

Gallup, George. "Johnson Rating in Poll Hits Low." *Washington Post*, March 31, 1968, p. A2, col. 1.

Gallup Opinion Index. "Johnson's Popularity." Report no. 34, April 1968, p. 2.

————. "New Wave of Pessimism on Vietnam Conflict Found Throughout Nation." Report no. 33, March 9, 1968, p. 6.

————. "Sharp Increase Found in Number of Doves." Report no. 34, May 1, 1968, p. 15.

Galvin, John R. "The Relief of Khe Sanh." *Military Review* 50 (January 1970): 88–94.

Gelb, Leslie H. "The Essential Domino: American Politics and Vietnam." *Foreign Affairs* 50 (April 1972): 459–475.

————. "The Pentagon Papers and *The Vantage Point*." *Foreign Policy*, no. 6 (Spring 1972), pp. 25–41.

————. "Six Lessons We Should Have Learned in Vietnam." *Washington Post*, June 14, 1972, p. A26, col. 3.

————. "Today's Lessons from the Pentagon Papers." *Life*, September 17, 1971, pp. 34–36.

————. "Vietnam: The System Worked." *Foreign Policy*, no. 3 (Summer 1971), pp. 140–167.

Gelb, Leslie H. and Halperin, Morton H. "Diplomatic Notes." *Harper's Magazine*, June 1972, p. 28.

————. "The Bureaucrat's Ten Commandments." *Washington Post*, August 6, 1972, p. B3, col. 1.

George, Alexander A. "The Case for Multiple Advocacy in Making Foreign Policy." *American Political Science Review* 66 (September 1972): 751–785.

Goodman, Walter. "Liberals vs. Radicals—War in the Peace Camp." *New York Times Magazine*, December 3, 1967, p. 48, col. 1.

Goulden, Joseph C. "Foe's Hit and Run Raids are Hard to Counter." *Philadelphia Inquirer*, February 2, 1968, p. 19, col. 1.

————. "Johnson Strategists Ponder Crisis Over War Escalation." *Philadelphia Inquirer*, March 8, 1968, p. 3, col. 1.

Gray, Colin. "What RAND Hath Wrought." *Foreign Policy*, no. 4 (Fall 1971), pp. 111–129.

Greene, Jerry. "Westy Briefing Gives Johnson a Jaunty Airing." *New York News*, November 18, 1967, p. 4, col. 4.

Grose, Peter. "War of Attrition Called Effective by Westmoreland." *New York Times*, November 20, 1967, p. 1, col. 5.

"Ground War in Asia." *New York Times*, June 9, 1965, p. 46, col. 1.

Guidry, Vernon A., Jr. "A Pentagon View: War Fought With One Hand Tied." *Washington Star*, April 30, 1975, p. A12, col. 1.

"Guns and Butter: Failure of a Policy." *U.S. News and World Report*, February 12, 1968, pp. 27–30.

Gwertzman, Bernard. "Policy Shifting to Boost Role of Saigon." *Washington Star*, April 11, 1968, p. A1, col. 8.

————. "War Again Strains U.S.–Press Ties." *Washington Star*, February 11, 1968, p. A13, col. 1.

Hahn, Harlan. "Correlates of Public Sentiment About War: Local Referenda on the Vietnam Issue." *American Political Science Review* 64 (December 1970): 1,186–1,198.

Halberstam, David. "Laos and the Old Illusions." *New York Times*, February 25, 1971, p. 37, col. 4.

————. "McCarthy and the Divided Left." *Harper's Magazine*, March 1968, pp. 32–44.

————. "Return to Vietnam." *Harper's Magazine*, December 1967, pp. 47–58.

Halperin, Morton H. "The Decision to Deploy the ABM: Bureaucratic and Domestic Politics in the Johnson Administration," *World Politics* 25 (October 1972): 62–95.

————. "The President and the Military." *Foreign Affairs* 50 (January 1972): 310–324.

————. "Why Bureaucrats Play Games." *Foreign Policy*, no. 2 (May 1971), pp. 70–90.

Halperin, Morton H. and Allison, Graham T. "Bureaucratic Politics: A Paradigm and Some Policy Implications." In *Theory and Policy in International Relations*, edited by Raymond Tanter and Richard H. Ullman, pp. 40–79. Princeton, N. J.: Princeton University Press, 1972.

Hamilton, William A. "The Decline and Fall of the Joint Chiefs of Staff." *Naval War College Review* 24 (April 1972): 36–58.

Hammond, Paul Y. "The National Security Council as a Device for Interdepartmental Coordination: An Interpretation and Appraisal." *American Political Science Review* 54 (December 1960): 899–910.

Handleman, Howard. "The Coin Has Flipped Over to Our Side." *U.S. News and World Report*, November 27, 1967, pp. 52–53.

"Hanoi Attacks and Scores a Major Psychological Blow." *Newsweek*, February 12, 1968, pp. 23–24.

Harris, Louis. "Confidence Shaken But Majority Rejects Vietnam Pullout." *Philadelphia Inquirer*, March 28, 1968, p. 3, col. 1.

———. "Johnson Regains Popularity." *Philadelphia Inquirer*, December 4, 1967, p. 3, col. 2.

———. "U.S. Reacts With Sober Determination to Step-Up of War." *Philadelphia Inquirer*, February 15, 1968, p. 3, col. 1.

———. "Viet War Support Declines to 54%." *Washington Post*, March 25, 1968, p. A16, col. 1.

———. "War Support Spurts After Tet Attacks." *Washington Post*, February 12, 1968, p. A1, col. 4.

Harwood, Richard. "Power of the Press: Myth or Reality?" *Washington Post*, January 28, 1971, p. A14, col. 3.

———. "Will Leave Pentagon in Early '68." *Washington Post*, November 30, 1967, p. A1, col. 1.

Henry, John B. "February, 1968." *Foreign Policy*, no. 4 (Fall 1971), pp. 3–34.

Henry, John B. and Espinosa, William. "The Tragedy of Dean Rusk." *Foreign Policy*, no. 8 (Fall 1972), pp. 166–189.

Herbers, John. "Johnson Rejects Primary Contests." *New York Times*, March 7, 1968, p. 1, col. 7.

Hirst, Don. "Was LBJ Bilked at Bragg?" *Army Times*, March 15, 1976, p. 6, col. 1.

"His Finest Hour." *Atlanta Constitution*, April 1, 1968, p. 4, col. 1.

Hodgson, Godfrey. "The Establishment." *Foreign Policy*, no. 10 (Spring 1973), pp. 3–40.

Hoffman, Fred S. "LBJ Was Not Hoodwinked at Ft. Bragg." *The Pentagram News*, March 11, 1976, p. 6, col. 1.

————. "U.S. Strategic Reserve Lacks Major Equipment." *Washington Star*, January 11, 1968, p. A6, col. 1.

Hoffmann, Stanley. "Will the Balance Balance at Home?" *Foreign Policy*, no. 7 (Summer 1972), pp. 60–87.

Holmberg, David. "Westy Had Headline Words." *Washington News*, November 22, 1967, p. 3, col. 2.

Hoopes, Townsend. "LBJ's Account of March, 1968." *The New Republic*, March 14, 1970, pp. 17–19.

————. "Legacy of the Cold War in Indochina." *Foreign Affairs* 48 (July 1970): 601–618.

Huntington, Samuel. "The Bases of Accommodation." *Foreign Affairs* 46 (July 1968): 642–656.

"Impervious to Reality." *St. Louis Post-Dispatch*, March 13, 1968, p. 2C, col. 2.

"Interview with Senator Henry M. Jackson." *Washington Post*, November 21, 1971, p. C1, col. 1.

Ions, Edmund. "Dissent in America: The Constraints on Foreign Policy." *Conflict Studies*, no. 18 (December 1971), pp. 1–14.

Jameson, Colonel John G., Jr. "A Letter to the Editor: AFJ's Bum Dope on LBJ's Farewell." *Armed Forces Journal International*, April 1976, pp. 20–21.

"Johnson Bars Bid in Massachusetts." *New York Times*, March 6, 1968, p. 1, col. 4.

Johnson, Robert H. "The NSC: The Relevance of Its Past to Its Future." *Orbis* 13 (Fall 1969): 709–735.

"Johnson's Rating on Vietnam Drops." *New York Times*, February 14, 1968, p. 4, col. 4.

"Joint Chiefs Endorse Defense of Khesanh." *Washington Post*, February 5, 1968, p. A6, col. 1.

Just, Ward. "The Heart-Mind Gap in the Vietnam War." *Washington Post*, November 19, 1967, p. B1, col. 1.

————. "KheSanh: Holding the End of the Line." *Washington Post*, January 31, 1968, p. A20, col. 3.

————. "LBJ Musters Aides to Show Gains in War." *Washington Post*, November 26, 1967, p. A10, col. 1.

————. "Vietnam Notebook." *Harper's Magazine*, April 1968, p. 75.

Kahin, George McT. "The Pentagon Papers: A Critical Evaluation." *American Political Science Review* 69 (June 1975): 675–684.

Kann, Peter R. "Saigon Takes Stock." *Wall Street Journal*, February 7, 1968, p. 1, col. 6.

Karnow, Stanley. "Tremendous Blow Struck at Allies, Vietcong Claims." *Washington Post*, February 8, 1968, p. A6, col. 1.

———. "VC Aim Seen to Boost Its Role in Settlement." *Washington Post*, February 7, 1968, p. A16, col. 1.

———. "What Are the Vietcong Trying to Prove?" *Washington Post*, February 2, 1968, p. A18, col. 3.

Kelly, Harry. "Reveal 8-Day Lag in Army's Viet Spy File." *Chicago Tribune*, September 21, 1975, p. 2, col. 1.

Kelly, Orr. "4 Divisions Threatening Marine Post." *Washington Star*, January 21, 1968, p. A1, col. 8.

———. "Loc Ninh Fight Significant." *Washington Star*, November 21, 1967, p. A4, col. 1.

———. "U.S. Caught Off Guard by Intensity of Attacks." *Washington Star*, January 31, 1968, p. A6, col. 1.

———. "War Just About Won—In a Military Sense." *Washington Star*, November 7, 1967, p. A1, col. 2.

———. "Westmoreland, Sharp Write Book on Viet War." *Washington Star*, April 7, 1969, p. A6, col. 1.

———. "Westmoreland To Head Army—Regrets Leaving Vietnam Before Battle Is Over." *Washington Star*, March 23, 1968, p. A1, col. 8.

———. "What Can U.S. Win at Khesanh?" *Washington Star*, February 29, 1968, p. A10, col. 3.

Kempster, Norman. "Former CIA Aide Disputes Charges on Tet Offensive." *Washington Star*, September 22, 1975, p. A1, col. 5.

"Kennedy's Secret Ultimatum." *Time*, March 22, 1968, p. 18.

Kihss, Peter. "Clifford Expects Saigon to Take on More of Fighting." *New York Times*, April 23, 1968, p. 1, col. 8.

Kilpatrick, Carroll. "LBJ Hails Courage of South Vietnamese." *Washington Post*, March 22, 1968, p. A1, col. 6.

———. "President Plans Short Notice for Trips." *Washington Post*, February 20, 1968, p. A8, col. 4.

———. "Westmoreland Sees U.S. Phaseout in '69." *Washington Post*, November 17, 1967, p. A1, col. 3.

Kirk, Donald. "Red Drive Likely During Tet." *Washington Star*, January 19, 1968, p. A1, col. 1.

————. "U.S. Colonel in Delta Denies Getting a Warning on Raids." *Washington Star*, February 8, 1968, p. A4, col. 3.

Kissinger, Henry. "Domestic Structure and Foreign Policy." *Daedalus*, Spring 1966, pp. 503–529.

————. "The Viet Nam Negotiations." *Foreign Affairs* 47 (January 1969): 211–234.

Kolodziej, E. A. "The National Security Council: Innovations and Implications." *Public Administration Review* 29 (November-December 1969): 573–585.

Kraft, Joseph. "The Dean Rusk Show." *New York Times Magazine*, March 24, 1968, p. 34.

————. "Washington Insight: The Enigma of Dean Rusk." *Harper's Magazine*, July 1965, pp. 100–103.

————. "Khesanh Situation Shows Viet Foe Makes Strategy Work." *Washington Post*, February 1, 1968, p. A21, col. 1.

————. "LBJ a Happening President Whether By News Break or Invention." *Washington Post*, November 28, 1967, p. A13, col. 1.

————. "New Strategy, Redeployment Seen U.S. Need, Not More Men." *Washington Post*, February 29, 1968, p. A25, col. 1.

————. "Short-Term Swings of Opinion Blind LBJ to Basic U.S. Mood." *Washington Post*, February 15, 1968, p. A25, col. 1.

Krasner, Stephen D. "Are Bureaucracies Important? (Or Allison Wonderland)." *Foreign Policy*, no. 7 (Summer 1972), pp. 159–179.

Kristol, Irving. "American Intellectuals and Foreign Policy." *Foreign Affairs* 45 (July 1967): 594–609.

Krulak, Lieutenant General Victor H. "The Strategic Limits of Proxy War." *Strategic Review* 2 (Winter 1974): 52–57.

Lardner, George, Jr. "False Data Blamed in '68 Tet Surprise." *Washington Post*, September 19, 1975, p. A1, col. 7.

Laurent, Lawrence. "Walter Cronkite Speaks Out on Vietnam." *Washington Post*, March 8, 1968, p. B9, col. 3.

Lawrence, David. "Implications in Quizzing Rusk." *Washington Star*, March 12, 1968, p. A7, col. 1.

————. "Viet War Under 'Intensive Review'." *Washington Star*, March 26, 1968, p. A13, col. 1.

"LBJ's Story: Five Critical Decisions on Vietnam." *U.S. News and World Report*, November 8, 1971, pp. 77–80.

Leacaos, John P. "Kissinger's Apparat." *Foreign Policy*, no. 5 (Winter 1971/1972), pp. 3–27.

Lederberg, Joshua. "A-Weapons Must Be Limited If Used in South Vietnam." *Washington Post*, February 17, 1968, p. A13, col. 1.

Lescaze, Lee. "Hearts of Vietnamese Not in War." *Washington Post*, January 2, 1968, p. A1, col. 1.

———. "Khe Sanh: A U.S. Obsession?" *Washington Post*, March 3, 1968, p. A1, col. 1.

———. " '68 Push for Viet Gains." *Washington Post*, November 12, 1967, p. A14, col. 5.

"Letters: The Cult of Misintelligence." *Harper's Magazine*, July 1975, pp. 14–16.

Lewis, Ted. "Mr. Anonymous Loses His Cool in Viet Briefing." *New York News*, February 14, 1968, p. 5, col. 4.

Lippmann, Walter. "Walter Lippmann on Defeat." *Newsweek*, March 11, 1968, p. 25.

Lipset, Seymour. "The President, The Polls, and Vietnam." *Transaction* 3 (September/October 1966): 19–24.

"The List Grows." *The Nation*, November 6, 1967, p. 450.

"Living Room War—Impact of TV." *U.S. News and World Report*, March 4, 1968, pp. 28–32.

"The Logic of the Battlefield." *Wall Street Journal*, February 23, 1968, p. 14, col. 1.

Loory, Stuart H. "Hawk's Shift Precipitated Bombing Halt." *Washington Post*, May 31, 1968, p. A2, col. 1.

Lucas, Jim. "Allies to Beef Viet Force." *Washington News*, March 20, 1968, p. 3, col. 1.

———. "Partial Mobilization?" *Washington News*, June 23, 1967, p. 2, col. 1.

Maffre, John. "Clifford Denies He's Only a Caretaker." *Washington Post*, March 9, 1968, p. A4, col. 3.

———. "Plans Set for Shift in Viet Load." *Washington Post*, April 23, 1968, p. A1, col. 7.

Mailer, Norman. "The Steps of the Pentagon." *Harper's Magazine*, March 1968, pp. 47–142.

"Man on the Spot." *Newsweek*, February 19, 1968, pp. 33–42.

"Mansfield Acts to End Row on Rusk Refusal." *Washington Star*, December 19, 1967, p. A8, col. 1.

"Mansfield Backs Rusk on Secrecy." *Washington Post*, February 9, 1968, p. A13, col. 1.

Marder, Murray. "A-Arms in Vietnam Seen Barred by Pact." *Washington Post*, March 20, 1968, p. A24, col. 1.

————. "General Abrams, LBJ Confer on Vietnam." *Washington Post*, March 27, 1968, p. A1, col. 7.

————. "Strain of Tension Is Showing at Top." *Washington Post*, February 11, 1968, p. A1, col. 1.

————. "U.S. Experts Concede Gain by VC." *Washington Post*, February 3, 1968, p. A1, col. 7.

Marder, Murray and Roberts, Chalmers M. "Reds' Offensive Leaves U.S. With Maze of Uncertainties." *Washington Post*, February 26, 1968, p. A1, col. 1.

Markel, Lester. "Public Opinion and the War in Vietnam." *New York Times Magazine*, August 8, 1965, p. 9, col. 1.

Marshall, Brigadier General S.L.A. "New Defense Secretary's Flexibility Lights Up the Senate." *Philadelphia Inquirer*, March 10, 1968, p. 5, col. 3.

Martin, Everett G. "The Devastating Effect on the People." *Newsweek*, February 12, 1968, p. 32.

May, Ernest R. "The Development of Political-Military Consultation in the United States." *Political Science Quarterly* 79 (June 1955): 161–179.

McGaffin, William. "Khe Sanh Battle Near—No Dien Bien Phu in Sight: Pentagon." *Chicago Daily News*, February 3, 1968, p. 9, col. 1.

Mehta, Ved. "The Flight of Crook-Taloned Birds." *New Yorker*, December 8, 1962, p. 59; December 15, 1962, p. 47.

Middleton, Drew. "General Assails Curbs in Vietnam." *New York Times*, December 7, 1975, p. 23, col. 1.

Miller, Mike. "U.S. Hopes South Viets Will Take Over War." *Washington News*, April 12, 1968, p. 10, col. 1.

Mohr, Charles. "Allied Post Falls to Tank Assault Near Buffer Zone." *New York Times*, February 8, 1968, p. 1, col. 8.

————. "G.I.'s Enter Saigon to Help Eliminate Enemy Hold-outs." *New York Times*, February 10, 1968, p. 1, col. 1.

————. "War-Ending Victory Seen as Aim of Enemy Drive." *New York Times*, February 9, 1968, p. 1, col. 2.

————. "Westmoreland Departure Could Spur War Changes." *New York Times*, March 24, 1968, p. 1, col. 6.

Morgenthau, Hans J. "Bundy's Doctrine of War Without End." *The New Republic*, November 2, 1968, pp. 18–20.

Mortimer, Edward. "Vets of Dienbienphu Appraise Khesanh." *Washington Post*, February 14, 1968, p. A18, col. 1.

Mueller, John E. "Presidential Popularity from Truman to Johnson." *American Political Science Review* 64 (March 1970): 18–32.

————. "Trends in Popular Support for the Wars in Vietnam and Korea." *American Political Science Review* 65 (June 1971): 358–375.

"The National Security System: Responsibilities of the Department of State." *Department of State Bulletin* 60 (February 24, 1969): 163–166.

"Needed: A Vietnam Strategy." *New York Times*, March 24, 1968, p. 16E, col. 1.

"A New Policy for Vietnam." *Business Week*, March 30, 1968, p. 174.

Nihart, Brook. "National Security Council: New Staff System After One Year." *Armed Forces Journal*, April 4, 1970, pp. 25–29.

Norman, Lloyd. "The '206,000 Plan'—The Inside Story." *Army*, April 1971, pp. 30–35.

Noyes, Crosby S. "Views of Rusk, Fulbright Panel Irreconcilable." *Washington Star*, March 16, 1968, p. A5, col. 1.

Noyes, Newbold. "Offensive Poses Challenge to the People of America and South Vietnam." *Washington Star*, February 7, 1968, p. A1, col. 1.

"The Nuclear Ramble." *Time*, February 23, 1968, pp. 16–17.

Oberdorfer, Don. "Intelligence in Tet Fight Held Success." *Washington Post*, December 4, 1975, p. A2, col. 1.

————. "The 'Wobble' in the War on Capitol Hill." *New York Times Magazine*, December 17, 1967, p. 30.

"Outlook Assessed by Westmoreland." *New York Times*, February 26, 1968, p. 1, col. 7.

Packard, George R. "U.S. Aides Predict All-Out Red Drive as Prelude to Talks." *Philadelphia Bulletin*, January 11, 1968, p. 1, col. 8.

Pearson, Drew. "Gen. Westmoreland Ouster is Urged." *Washington Post*, February 10, 1968, p. B11, col. 1.

————. "Westy Likely to Keep Viet Post." *Washington Post*, February 5, 1968, p. C7, col. 1.

Pike, Douglas. "The Tet Offensive: A Setback for Giap, But Just How Big?" *Army*, April 1968, pp. 57–61.

Pirenne, Henri. "What Are Historians Trying to Do?" In *Methods in Social Science*, edited by Stuart A. Rice, pp. 435–445. Chicago: University of Chicago Press, 1931.

"Poll Finds Rise in War Support From 61% to 74% in 2 Months." *New York Times*, February 13, 1968, p. 5, col. 3.

Porter, D. Gareth. "People as the Enemy." *The New Republic*, February 10, 1968, pp. 17–19.

"Possible Viet A-Bomb Use Studied, McCarthy Suspects." *Baltimore Sun*, February 12, 1968, p. A2, col. 6.

"The President Bows Out." *Washington Star*, April 1, 1968, p. A16, col. 1.

"President Wary of G.I.'s Fighting China's Millions." *New York Times*, September 29, 1964, p. 1, col. 3.

Puckett, Robert H. "American Foreign Policy Planning." *Foreign Policy Journal* 49 (July 1972): 12.

Raymont, Henry. "Harper's and Atlantic Put Out 'Vietnam' Issues." *New York Times*, February 19, 1968, p. 14, col. 6.

Reed, Roy. "Bunker Sees the President: Predicts Saigon Gain in '68." *New York Times*, November 14, 1967, p. 1, col. 3.

Reedy, George E. "The Personal Touch." *New York Times*, June 30, 1971, p. 41, col. 2.

Reston, James. "Washington: The Flies That Captured the Flypaper." *New York Times*, February 7, 1968, p. 46, col. 3.

————. "Washington: Why Westmoreland and Bunker Are Optimistic." *New York Times*, November 22, 1967, p. 46, col. 3.

Ridgway, General Matthew B., U.S.A. "Indo-China: Disengaging." *Foreign Affairs* 49 (July 1971): 583–592.

Roberts, Chalmers M. "Clifford Formula on Lull Defined." *Washington Post*, January 28, 1968, p. A18, col. 5.

————. "General's Timetable Calls for Victory After '68 Elections." *Washington Post*, November 22, 1967, p. A8, col. 3.

————. "Saigon Due for Larger Battle Role." *Washington Post*, April 12, 1968, p. A1, col. 5.

————. "Vietnam Doubts, Misgivings, Persist." *Washington Post*, March 13, 1968, p. A11, col. 1.

————. "War Is Undergoing Searching Scrutiny." *Washington Post*, March 11, 1968, p. A1, col. 2.

Roberts, Charles. "Inside Story: L.B.J.'s Switch on Vietnam." *Newsweek*, March 10, 1969, pp. 31–33.

Roberts, Gene. "U.S. Command Sees Hue, Not Khe Sanh, as Foe's Main Goal." *New York Times*, March 7, 1968, p. 1, col. 1.

Roberts, Steven V. "McCarthy Appeal Wide in Wisconsin." *New York Times*, March 24, 1968, p. 31, col. 1.

Roche, John P. "The Jigsaw Puzzle of History." *New York Times Magazine*, January 24, 1971, p. F14, col. 1.

————. "Recollections of Ellsberg." *Washington Post*, July 24, 1971, p. A19, col. 7.

Roper, Burns. "The Public Looks at Presidents." *The Public Pulse*, January 1969, pp. 1–3.

Rostow, Eugene V. "L.B.J. Reconsidered." *Esquire* 75 (April 1971): 118.

Rostow, Walt W. "Aftermath, Losing Big: A Reply." *Esquire* 78 (December 1972): 10–12.

————. "Dangers That Remain in the Vietnam War." *U.S. News and World Report*, November 8, 1971, pp. 80–85.

"Rusk Turns Bear." *Atlanta Constitution*, March 13, 1968, p. 4, col. 1.

"Rusk's Statement of February 15, 1968 on Probability of Peace Talks." *Department of State Bulletin* 58 (March 4, 1968): 305.

"Rusk's TV Appearance Provokes Senate Panel." *New York Times*, February 7, 1968, p. 15, col. 2.

"Saigon Slated for Larger DMZ Role." *Washington Star*, November 22, 1967, p. A1, col. 8.

Schandler, Herbert Y. "Vietnam: What Remains Is the Basic Structure of a Feudal Society." *Washington Post*, February 11, 1974, p. A23, col. 2.

Schemmer, Benjamin F. "The Day the President got Conned." *Armed Forces Journal International*, February 1976, pp. 26–28.

Scott-Barnet, Major General D.W. "The Media and the Armed Services." *Military Review*, April 1972, pp. 62–76.

Semple, Robert B., Jr. "Nixon Vows to End War With a 'New Leadership'." *New York Times*, March 6, 1968, p. 1, col. 2.

Shackford, R. H. "Hanoi Launches Big Political Push." *Washington News*, February 20, 1968, p. 23, col. 2.

Shaplen, Robert. "Letters from Saigon." *New Yorker*, March 2, 1968, p. 44.

Sheehan, Neil. "Conflicts Over Asia: Within the Administration, a 'Kind of Malaise' Over Vietnam." *New York Times*, March 24, 1968, p. E3, col. 1.

―――. "General Abrams in Capitol, Sees President and Aides." *New York Times*, March 27, 1968, p. 1, col. 6.

―――. "Joint Chiefs Back Troop Rise Asked by Westmoreland." *New York Times*, July 3, 1967, p. 1, col. 4.

―――. "Khesanh: Why U.S. is Making a Stand." *New York Times,* February 23, 1968, p. 1, col. 5.

―――. " '68 Gain Was Seen by Westmoreland." *New York Times*, March 21, 1968, p. 1, col. 3.

Sheehan, Neil and Smith, Hedrick. "Westmoreland Requests 206,000 More Men, Stirring Debate in Administration." *New York Times*, March 10, 1968, p. 1, col. 6.

Sidey, Hugh. "Shaken Assumptions About the War." *Life*, February 16, 1968, p. 32B.

Singer, Benjamin D. "Violence, Protest, and War in Television News: The U.S. and Canada Compared." *Public Opinion Quarterly*, Winter 1970–71, pp. 611–616.

"Sizing Up the Public on the War." *Business Week*, February 24, 1968, p. 37.

Smith, Hedrick. "Rusk Says Hanoi Spurns U.S. Terms for Negotiation." *New York Times*, February 15, 1968, p. 1, col. 8.

―――. "U.S. Girding at Khesanh to Avoid a 'Dienbienphu': Washington Mood Tense." *New York Times*, February 10, 1968, p. 1, col. 2.

―――. "Wilson Cautions on A-Arms in War." *New York Times*, February 12, 1968, p. 4, col. 5.

Smith, Terence. "Student Leaders Warn President on Doubts on War." *New York Times*, December 30, 1966, p. 1, col. 1.

Souers, Sidney W. "Policy Formulation for National Security." *American Political Science Review* 63 (June 1949): 534–543.

"Standoff." *Time*, March 22, 1968, p. 20.

Stern, Laurence. "Humphrey Early Critic of Viet War." *Washington Post*, May 9, 1976, p. A1, col. 4.

————. "McNamara, Rusk: A Mood Contrast." *Washington Post*, February 5, 1968, p. A8, col. 1.

Stevens, Phil. "Troop Switch? Baloney!" *Army Times*, March 15, 1976, p. 6, col. 5.

Stilwell, Lieutenant General Richard. "Evolution in Tactics— The Vietnam Experience." *Army*, February 1970, pp. 14–23.

Stone, I.F. "The Best Kept Secret of the Vietnam War." *I.F. Stone's Weekly*, April 21, 1969, pp. 1–4.

Tanham, George K. and Duncanson, Dennis J. "Some Dilemmas of Counterinsurgency." *Foreign Affairs* 48 (October 1969): 113–122.

Tanner, Henry. "Thant Confers with Hanoi Representative." *New York Times*, February 15, 1968, p. 2, col. 4.

Taylor, Frederick. "Request for More Vietnam Troops Studied by White House; Some Oppose Any Buildup." *Wall Street Journal*, March 11, 1968, p. 2, col. 3.

Taylor, General Maxwell D. "The Lessons of Vietnam." *U.S. News and World Report*, November 27, 1972, pp. 22–26.

Thayer, Frederick C. "Presidential Policy Processes and 'New Administration': A Search for Revised Paradigms." *Public Administration Review* 31 (September-October 1971): 552–561.

Thompson, Sir Robert. "Squaring the Error." *Foreign Affairs* 46 (April 1968): 442–453.

————. "Viet Reds' Drive was Giap Masterstroke." *Washington Post*, February 11, 1968, p. A8, col. 1.

Thomson, James C., Jr. "How Could Vietnam Happen?" *Atlantic Monthly* April 1968, pp. 47–53.

Tolson, Lieutenant General John J. "Pegasus." *Army*, December 1971, pp. 9–19.

Treaster, Joseph B. "Paper Army: The Fraud of Vietnamization." *Harper's Magazine*, July 1975, pp. 61–65.

"Troop Issue Still Open, Clifford Says." *Washington Star*, March 8, 1968, p. A3, col. 7.

Tuchman, Barbara. "Can History Be Served Up Hot?" *New York Times Book Review*, March 8, 1964, p. 1.

————. "The Historian's Opportunity." *Saturday Review*, February 25, 1967, p. 27.

Tuchman, Barbara. "History by the Ounce." *Harper's Magazine,* July 1965, p. 6.

Tuohy, William. "Newsmen's View of Viet War Fails to Match U.S. Optimism." *Los Angeles Times,* October 29, 1967, p. 1A, col. 5.

Ullman, Richard H. "The Pentagon's History as 'History'." *Foreign Policy,* no. 4 (Fall 1971), pp. 150–156.

"Unseasoned Men Bolster 7th Army." *Philadelphia Inquirer,* November 2, 1967, p. 2, col. 3.

"U.S. Army Staff Chief Finds 'Smell of Success'." *New York Times,* August 7, 1967, p. 14, col. 8.

"U.S. Bombed Viet Town to 'Save' It." *Baltimore Sun,* February 8, 1968, p. A1, col. 4.

"U.S. Jets Hit Deep in North: Bomb Targets 250 Miles Above DMZ." *Washington Post,* April 2, 1968, p. A1, col. 1.

"U.S. Seeks to Gradually Turn All Fighting Over to South Vietnamese, Clifford Says." *Wall Street Journal,* April 12, 1968, p. 2, col. 3.

Verba, Sidney and Brady, Richard A. "Participation, Policy Preferences, and the War in Vietnam." *Public Opinion Quarterly* 34 (Fall 1970): 325–332.

Verba, Sidney; Brady, Richard A.; Parker, Edwin E.; Nil, Norman H.; Polsby, Nelson W.; Ekman, Paul; and Black, Gordon J. "Public Opinion and the War in Vietnam." *American Political Science Review* 61 (June 1967): 317–333.

Wakefield, Dan. "Supernation at Peace and War." *Atlantic Monthly,* March 1968, pp. 39–105.

Walker, Lannon. "Our Foreign Affairs Machinery: Time For An Overhaul." *Foreign Affairs* 47 (January 1969): 309–320.

"The War." *Time,* March 15, 1968, pp. 21–24.

Ward, Paul W. "Hanoi Gives U.S. Reply on Parley Bid." *Baltimore Sun,* April 9, 1968, p. A1, col. 1.

Warner, Denis. "The Defense of Saigon." *Reporter,* April 4, 1968, pp. 15–19.

———. "Gains and Losses in Saigon," *Reporter,* March 7, 1968, pp. 21–24.

———. "Khe Sanh and Dien Bien Phu." *Reporter,* February 22, 1968, pp. 16–19.

———. "Report from Khe Sanh," *Reporter,* March 21, 1968, pp. 22–30.

Weinraub, Bernard. "56 Marines Die in Battles in Tense Northern Sector." *New York Times*, February 9, 1968, p. 1, col. 2.

———. "Survivors Hunt Dead of Bentre, Turned to Rubble in Allied Raids." *New York Times*, February 8, 1968, p. 14, col. 6.

———. "U.S. Aides Pleased by Thieu's Speech." *New York Times*, March 22, 1968, p. 1, col. 2.

Weller, Jac. "Our Vietnamese Allies: An Appraisal of Their Fighting Worth." *National Guardsman* 22 (April 1968): 2–10.

Westerfield, H. Bradford. "What Use Are Three Versions of the Pentagon Papers?" *American Political Science Review* 69 (June 1975): 685–696.

"Westmoreland Here, Cites Vietnam Gains." *Washington Star*, November 15, 1967, p. A1, col. 7.

"Westmoreland's Nomination as Army Chief Could Portend Shift in U.S. Viet Policy." *Wall Street Journal*, March 25, 1968, p. 2, col. 3.

"Westmoreland's Strategy: Will It Pass the Acid Test." *U.S. News and World Report*, February 12, 1968, p. 13.

"Westmoreland's Transfer." *New York Times*, March 23, 1968, p. 30, col. 1.

Wicker, Tom. "Agonizing Reappraisal." *New York Times*, March 10, 1968, p. E15, col. 5.

———. "In the Nation: Peace, It's Wonderful." *New York Times*, July 4, 1967, p. 18, col. 3.

———. "Vietcong's Attacks Shock Washington." *New York Times*, February 2, 1968, p. 1, col. 7.

Will, George. "Does TV Bias Matter?" *Washington Post*, February 9, 1973, p. A18, col. 3.

Wilson, George C. "General on Master Plan: South Vietnam Troops to Join DMZ Fighting." *Washington Post*, November 22, 1967, p. A1, col. 7.

———. "No A-Arms Requested for Vietnam, U.S. Says." *Washington Post*, February 10, 1968, p. A1, col. 6.

Wilson, Richard. "Hanoi Sure It Can Force a Political Solution." *Washington Star*, February 7, 1968, p. A19, col. 1.

———. "Rostow's Influence and How He Views the War." *Washington Star*, April 29, 1968, p. A13, col. 1.

Wise, David. "The Twilight of a President." *New York Times Magazine*, November 3, 1968, p. 27, col. 1.

Wu, Edward K. "U.S. 'Failure' Is Charged by Hanoi Paper." *Baltimore Sun*, February 12, 1968, p. A2, col. 1.

Yarmolinsky, Adam. "Picking Up the Pieces: The Impact of Vietnam on the Military Establishment." *The Yale Review* 61 (June 1972): 489–490.

Yee, Min S. "The U.S. Press and Its Agony of Appraisal." *Boston Globe*, February 18, 1968, p. 2A, col. 1.

Yost, Charles W. "The Instruments of American Foreign Policy." *Foreign Affairs* 50 (October 1971): 63–66.

————. "Some Conclusions on Vietnam." *Washington Post*, May 23, 1971, p. B6, col. 3.

PUBLIC DOCUMENTS

U. S., Board of Governors of the Federal Reserve System, *Fifty-fifth Annual Report of the Board of Governors of the Federal Reserve System, 1968*. Washington, D.C.: United States Government Printing Office, 1968.

U. S., Bureau of the Budget. *Budget of the United States Government for the Fiscal Year Ending June 30, 1967*. Washington, D.C.: United States Government Printing Office, 1967.

U. S., Congress, *Congressional Record*, Vol. 114, 90th Cong., 2d sess.

U. S., Congress, House of Representatives, Committee on Appropriations. *Department of Defense Appropriations for 1969, Part I, Hearings*. 90th Cong., 2d sess., February–March 1968.

U. S., Congress, House of Representatives, Committee on Armed Services. *Hearings Before the Special Subcommittee on the M–16 Rifle Program*. 90th Cong., 1st sess., May 15–August 22, 1967.

U. S., Congress, House of Representatives, Committee on Armed Services. *Report of the Special Subcommittee on the M–16 Rifle Program*. 90th Cong., 1st sess., October 19, 1967.

U. S., Congress, House of Representatives, Committee on Armed Services. *Selected Aspects of M–16 Rifle Program Contracts*. 90th Cong., 2d sess., October 11, 1968.

U. S., Congress, House of Representatives, Committee on Foreign Affairs. *The Future United States Role in Asia and the Pacific*. Hearings before the Subcommittee on Asian and Pacific Affairs, 90th Cong., 2d sess., February 29–April 4, 1968.

U. S., Congress, House of Representatives, Committee on Foreign Affairs. *National Security and The Changing World Power Alignment*. Hearing–Symposium Before the Subcommittee on National Security Policy and Scientific Developments, 92d Cong., 2d sess., May, June, August 1972.

U. S., Congress, House of Representatives, Committee on Foreign Affairs. *War Powers Legislation*. Hearings before the Subcommittee on National Security Policy and Scientific Developments, 92d Cong., 1st sess., June 1 and 2, 1971.

U. S., Congress, House of Representatives, Committee on Ways and Means. *President's 1967 Surtax Proposal: Continuation of Hearings to Receive Further Administration Proposal Concerning Expenditure Cuts*. 90th Cong., 1st sess., November 29–30, 1967.

U. S., Congress, House of Representatives, Committee on Ways and Means. *President's 1967 Surtax Proposal, Hearings*. 90th Cong., 1st sess., August 1967.

U. S., Congress, Joint Economic Committee. *Economic Effect of Vietnam Spending, Hearings*. 90th Cong., 1st sess., April 1967. 2 vols.

U. S., Congress, Senate. *Two Reports on Vietnam and Southeast Asia to the President of the United States by Senator Mike Mansfield*. April 1973, Document Number 93–11.

U. S., Congress, Senate, Committee on Appropriations. *Supplemental Defense Appropriations Bill, 1967*. H. R. 13546, Senate Report no. 1074, 89th Cong., 2d sess., March 17, 1966.

U. S., Congress, Senate, Committee on Armed Services. *Additional Procurement of M–16 Rifles*. Hearings before the Special M–16 Rifle Subcommittee of the Preparedness Investigating Subcommittee, 90th Cong., 2d sess., June 19–20, 1968.

U. S., Congress, Senate, Committee on Armed Services. *Air War Against North Vietnam, Parts 1–5*. Hearings before the Preparedness Investigating Subcommittee, 90th Cong., 1st sess., August 1967.

U. S., Congress, Senate, Committee on Armed Services. *Nomination of Clark M. Clifford to be Secretary of Defense*. Hearings. 90th Cong., 2d sess., January 25, 1968.

U. S., Congress, Senate, Committee on Armed Services. *United States Army Combat Readiness*. Hearings before the Preparedness Investigating Subcommittee, 89th Cong., 2d sess., May 3–4, 1966.

U. S., Congress, Senate, Committee on Foreign Relations. *Background Information Relating to Southeast Asia and Vietnam.* 7th rev. ed. Committee Print, 93rd Cong., 2d sess., December 1974.

U. S., Congress, Senate, Committee on Foreign Relations. *Bombing as a Policy Tool in Vietnam: Effectiveness.* Committee Print, 92d Cong., 2d sess., October 12, 1972.

U. S., Congress, Senate, Committee on Foreign Relations. *Causes, Origins, and Lessons of the Vietnam War.* Hearings, 92d Cong., 2d sess., May 9–11, 1972.

U. S., Congress, Senate, Committee on Foreign Relations. *Changing American Attitudes Toward Foreign Policy.* Hearings, 90th Cong., 1st sess., with Henry Steele Commager, Professor, Amherst College, February 20, 1967.

U. S., Congress, Senate, Committee on Foreign Relations. *Conflicts Between United States Capabilities and Foreign Commitments.* Hearings, 90th Cong., 1st sess., with Lieutenant General James M. Gavin (U. S. Army, Retired), February 21, 1967.

U. S., Congress, Senate, Committee on Foreign Relations. *The Formulation and Administration of United States Foreign Policy.* Study prepared by the Brookings Institution. 86th Cong., 2d sess., January 13, 1960.

U. S., Congress, Senate, Committee on Foreign Relations. *The Gulf of Tonkin, the 1964 Incidents.* Hearings with the Honorable Robert S. McNamara, Secretary of Defense, 90th Cong., 2d sess., February 20, 1968.

U. S., Congress, Senate, Committee on Foreign Relations. *The Gulf of Tonkin, the 1964 Incidents, Part II.* 90th Cong., 2d sess., December 16, 1968.

U. S., Congress, Senate, Committee on Foreign Relations. *Hearings, Foreign Assistance Act of 1968, Part I–Vietnam.* 90th Cong., 2d sess., March 11–12, 1968.

U. S., Congress, Senate, Committee on Foreign Relations. *Impact of the War in Southeast Asia on the United States Economy.* Hearings, Parts I and II, 91st Cong., 2d sess., April 1970.

U. S., Congress, Senate, Committee on Foreign Relations. *Present Situation in Vietnam.* Hearings, with General David M. Shoup, USMC, 90th Cong., 2d sess., March 20, 1968.

U. S., Congress, Senate, Committee on Foreign Relations. *Stalemate in Vietnam: Report by Senator Joseph S. Clark on a Study Mission to South Vietnam.* 90th Cong., 2d sess., Committee Print, February 1968.

U. S., Congress, Senate, Committee on Foreign Relations. *United States Involvement in the Overthrow of Diem, 1963: A Staff Study Based on the Pentagon Papers.* 92d Cong., 2d sess., Committee Print, July 20, 1972.

U. S., Congress, Senate, Committee on Foreign Relations. *The United States and Vietnam: 1944–47: A Staff Study Based on the Pentagon Papers.* 92d Cong., 2d sess., Committee Print, April 3, 1972.

U. S., Congress, Senate, Committee on Foreign Relations. *Vietnam and Southeast Asia, Report of Mike Mansfield, J. Caleb Boggs, Claiborne Pell and Benjamin A. Smith.* 88th Cong., 1st sess., Committee Print, 1963.

U. S., Congress, Senate, Committee on Foreign Relations. *Vietnam Commitments, 1961: A Staff Study Based on the Pentagon Papers.* 92d Cong., 2d sess., Committee Print, March 20, 1972.

U. S., Congress, Senate, Committee on Foreign Relations. *The Vietnam Conflict: The Substance and The Shadow. Report of Senator Mike Mansfield and Others.* 89th Cong., 2d sess., Committee Print, January 6, 1966.

U. S., Congress, Senate, Committee on Foreign Relations. *Vietnam: May 1972: A Staff Report.* 92d Cong., 2d sess., Committee Print, June 29, 1972.

U. S., Congress, Senate, Committee on Foreign Relations. *Vietnam, December 1969.* James G. Lowenstein, ed. 91st Cong., 2d sess., 1970.

U. S., Congress, Senate, Committee on Foreign Relations. *Vietnam Policy Proposals.* Hearings, 91st Cong., 2d sess., February 3–March 16, 1970.

U. S., Congress, Senate, Committee on Government Operations. *Organizing for National Security, Parts I–VII.* Hearings before the Subcommittee on National Policy Machinery, 86th Cong., 2d sess., February–July 1960.

U. S., Congress, Senate, Committee on Government Operations. Subcommittee on National Security and International Operations. *The National Security Council: Comment by Henry Kissinger, March 30, 1970.* 91st Cong., 2d sess., 1970.

U. S., Congress, Senate, Committee on the Judiciary. *Testimony of Jim G. Lucas.* Hearing before the Subcommittee to Investigate the Administration of the Internal Security Act and Other Internal Security Laws, 90th Cong., 2d sess., March 14, 1968.

U. S., Congress, Senate, Committee on Naval Affairs. *Unification of the War and Navy Departments and Postwar Organization for National Security.* Report to the Honorable James Forrestal, Secretary of the Navy, by Ferdinand Eberstadt. 79th Cong., 1st sess., October 22, 1945.

U. S., Department of Defense, Directorate for Armed Forces Information and Education. *Know Your Enemy: The Viet Cong.* DOD Pamphlet Gen–20, 1966.

U. S., Department of Defense. *United States–Vietnam Relations, 1945–1967.* 12 vols. Washington, D.C.: United States Government Printing Office, 1971.

U. S., Department of State. *Department of State Bulletin,* Vols. 52, 58, 60, 73.

U. S., Military Assistance Command, Vietnam. *Command History, 1968.* 3 vols. Saigon: United States Military Assistance Command, Vietnam, 1969.

U. S., Military Assistance Command, Vietnam. *Command Information Topic Number 5–65, Vietnamese Tet.* Saigon: United States Military Assistance Command, Vietnam, 1965.

U. S., Military Assistance Command, Vietnam. *1967 Wrap-up: A Year of Progress.* Saigon: United States Military Assistance Command, Vietnam, 1968.

U. S., Mission in Vietnam. *Captured Document Indicates Final Phase of Revolution at Hand.* Press release, January 5, 1968.

U. S., President. *Economic Report of the President Transmitted to the Congress, January 1967.* Washington, D.C.: United States Government Printing Office, 1967.

U. S., President. *Economic Report of the President Transmitted to the Congress, February 1968.* Washington, D.C.: United States Government Printing Office, 1968.

U. S., President. *Public Papers of the Presidents of the United States: Lyndon B. Johnson, 1965.* 2 vols. Washington, D.C.: United States Government Printing Office, 1966.

U. S., President. *Public Papers of the Presidents of the United States: Lyndon B. Johnson, 1967.* 2 vols. Washington, D.C.: United States Government Printing Office, 1968.

BIBLIOGRAPHY

U. S., President. *Public Papers of the Presidents of the United States: Lyndon B. Johnson, 1968–69.* 2 vols. Washington, D.C.: United States Government Printing Office, 1970.

U. S., President. *U. S. Foreign Policy for the 1970's: Building for Peace.* A Report to the Congress by Richard Nixon, President of the United States, February 25, 1971. Washington, D.C.: United States Government Printing Office, 1971.

U. S., President. *U. S. Foreign Policy for the 1970's: The Emerging Structure of Peace.* A Report to the Congress by Richard Nixon, President of the United States, February 9, 1972. Washington, D.C.: United States Government Printing Office, 1972.

U. S., President. *U. S. Foreign Policy for the 1970's: A New Strategy for Peace.* A Report to the Congress by Richard Nixon, President of the United States, February 18, 1970. Washington, D.C.: United States Government Printing Office, 1970.

OTHER SOURCES

Adams, Samuel A. Statement before the House Select Committee on Intelligence. September 18, 1975.

Bundy, McGeorge. "American Policy and Politics: Reflections from Southeast Asia." Speeches to the Council on Foreign Relations, New York City. Three parts. May 1971.

Bunker, Ellsworth. Address on acceptance of the Sylvanus Thayer Award, United States Military Academy, West Point, New York. May 8, 1970.

Cantril, Albert H. "The American People, Viet-Nam and the Presidency." Paper delivered at the sixty-sixth annual meeting of the American Political Science Association, Los Angeles, California, September 8–12, 1970.

Clifford, Clark M. Address at the National Press Club, Washington, D.C. September 5, 1968. (OASD/PA News Release No. 824–68).

———. Address before annual luncheon of the Associated Press, New York City. April 22, 1968.

———. News conference at Pentagon, 10:00 A.M. (E.S.T.). April 11, 1968.

Clifford, Clark M. News conference at Pentagon, 10:30 A.M. (E.S.T.). June 20, 1968.

————. News conference at Pentagon, 10:30 A.M. (E.D.T.). August 15, 1968.

Colby, William E. Statement before the House Select Committee on Intelligence. December 3, 1975.

Columbia Broadcasting System. "LBJ: The Decision to Halt the Bombing." Interview with President Johnson by Walter Cronkite. February 6, 1970.

Columbia Broadcasting System Television Network. *Face the Nation, September 21, 1975–Guest–James R. Schlesinger.* New York: CBS News Information Services, 1975.

Graham, Lieutenant General Daniel O. Statement before the House Select Committee on Intelligence. December 3, 1975.

Henry, John B. "March 1968: Continuity or Change?" Honors thesis, Harvard College, 1971.

Library of Congress, Congressional Research Service. "Defense Trends in the United States, 1952–1973." Washington, D.C.: Library of Congress, September 18, 1973.

Library of Congress, Congressional Research Service. "The Pentagon Papers as Described by the American Press: Summaries of Major Newspaper Articles." Washington, D.C.: Library of Congress, August 6, 1971.

Library of Congress, Congressional Research Service. "United States Policy Toward Vietnam: A Summary Review of Its History." Washington, D.C.: Library of Congress, June 9, 1970.

Library of Congress, Congressional Research Service. "Vietnam: A Bibliography." Washington, D.C.: Library of Congress, October 1, 1970.

Library of Congress, Legislative Reference Service. "Southeast Asia: A Survey of Political and Economic Problems." Washington, D.C.: Library of Congress, January 14, 1969.

May, Ernest R.; Williamson, Samuel R., Jr.; and Woodside, Alexander B. "The Pentagon Papers: An Assessment." Paper presented before a panel of the American Historical Association, December 29, 1971.

Memorandum for The President. "Peace with Honor in Vietnam." March 19, 1968, signed James Rowe.

BIBLIOGRAPHY

National Broadcasting Company, *Meet the Press, Sunday, November 19, 1967*. Washington, D.C.: Merkle Press, 1967.

Palmer, Lieutenant Colonel Dave R. "The Summons of the Trumpet: A Soldier's View of Vietnam." Unpublished manuscript.

Westmoreland, General William C. Address to the National Press Club, Washington, D.C. November 21, 1967.

————. Press conference at Joint U.S. Public Affairs Office (JUSPAO), Saigon. February 1, 1968.

INDEX

☆☆☆

INDEX

Navy, U.S., 6, 25, 115, 126. *See also* forces, U.S.
negotiations: bombing seen as bargaining chip in, 37, 38, 188, 297, 298, 303; Mc-Namara recommendations to increase prospects for, 43; attempts to involve North Vietnamese in, 47, 209, 291; options discussed by Clifford Task Force, 172, 181; committee formed to develop U.S. positions, 181; U.S. indicates willingness for, 181–182; Rusk's views on, 184, 209, 305–306, 308; proposals received, pursued, 266–267; seen as necessary for public opinion purposes, 303; Rostow's view of, 307–308
New Hampshire primary, 202, 219–224, 258
Newsweek Magazine, 199
New York Times, 48, 53, 54, 198, 200–201, 202, 203, 207, 213, 230, 314
New Zealand, 53, 277, 280
Nguyen Hue (Quang Trung), 72
Nha Trang, 24
Niagara, Operation, 69
Nitze, Paul, 124–127, 132, 133, 157, 162, 181, 214–215, 241, 259
Nixon, Richard M., 269, 346, 349
NLF, *see* Viet Cong
North Korea, 85, 109
North Vietnam: air war against, 4, 5, 6, 7–8, 9, 10, 12, 13, 14, 15, 16, 24, 34–35, 37, 51, 54–55, 57, 58, 60, 92, 118, 161, 164, 166, 172–173, 237, 279, 349; actions in South Vietnam, 7, 18, 35, 36, 68, 74, 291; U.S. strategy, objectives toward, 10, 18, 43, 46, 144, 152, 297, 311; adjusts to bombing, 18, 298, 323; reaction to bombing pauses, 18–19, 38,

188, 191, 241, 250, 253, 267, 280–281; bombing seen as bargaining chip against, 37, 282; peace initiatives toward, 47, 209, 266, 276, 285; morality of air campaign against, 48; implements new strategy, 66–68, 77–78; celebrates Tet early, 73; success in achieving objectives, 78–79; U.S. proposals to stop bombing of, 130, 276–277, 286, 290, 318; seen as accepting San Antonio formula, 242; Clifford seeks reciprocal steps from, 247–248; willingness to negotiate, 289, 305–306, 328
North Vietnamese forces, 45, 50, 68, 78, 71, 93–94, 112, 154, 155, 159, 160
nuclear weapons, 89–90
NVA, *see* North Vietnamese forces
NVN, *see* North Vietnam

objectives, U.S.: debate over, 28–30, 47, 152, 156, 337; as seen by President Johnson, 30, 33; Joint Chiefs of Staff view of, 50, 161, 309; defended by McNamara, 55; president seeks acceleration in achieving, 57; in Vietnam, 144–145, 285, 291, 296, 301, 332–334, 340; recommendations for change in, 263, 308; Rostow sees U.S. as achieving, 307; effect of Tet offensive on, 320–321, 338, 350; not developed by Clifford Task Force, 321; as seen by Pentagon, 321–322; not modified to gain public support, 327; as set by bureaucracy, 330, 332
Okinawa, 23
One Hundred First (101st) Airborne Division, 94, 159
One Hundred Seventy Third (173d) Airborne Brigade, 23

411

pacification, 38, 43, 112, 118, 146, 185, 259, 341, 342, 350
Pacific Command, U.S., *see* CINCPAC
Papal delegate, 266
Paris, France, 320
Park, President Chung Hee, 85, *see also* Korea
peace proposals, *see* negotiations
Pearl Harbor, 75
Peking, *see* China
Phan Thiet, 153
Phase I, *see* air war; forces, U.S.
Phase II, *see* air war; forces, U.S.
Phase III, *see* forces, U.S.
Philippines, 53, 236, 280, 340
Phu Bai, 20, 21, 94
Phuc Tuy, 153
planning process, 37, 39, 40, 44, 51–52, 54, 63, 136–138, 309, 311, 335
Pleiku, 11, 108
Pope, 80
Preparedness Investigating Sub-committee, *see* Armed Services Committee, Senate
Presidential Palace, 74
press, U.S.: McNamara, Rusk meet with, 49; effects of reporting on Tet offensive, 80–81, 83, 198, 256, 293; President Johnson meets with, 84, 234, 235–236; Rusk meets with, 85; Westmoreland meets with, 85–86; dispute as to objectivity of, 196; Clifford meets with, 313–314, 316; interprets president's decisions, 314–315
Program 3, 40, 42
Program 4, 45, 137
Program 5, 54, 115, 137, 142, 288
Program 6, 288, 289
public opinion: bombing pauses as a way of influencing, 38, 187, 251, 267, 299, 328; Wise Men see problems with,

November 1967, 64; influence on the president, 83, 300, 326–329; role of president in forming, 178; effects of Tet offensive on, 178, 194–196, 220–221, 229, 257, 292, 293, 300, 338, 346; as formed by television coverage, 197; effect of *New York Times* story on, 201–202; effect on president's decisions, 266, 279, 304, 327, 335, 337; Rusk concerned with erosion in, 306; influence on Clifford, 311–312; Joint Chiefs of Staff fail to recognize effects of Tet offensive on, 327–328
Pueblo, USS, 85, 102
Pursley, Colonel Robert, 157

Quang Ngai, 24, 25
Quang Tri, 68, 71, 72, 84, 86, 96, 108, 112, 153, 159
Quang Trung, *see* Nguyen Hue
Qui Nhon, 14, 24

rally-round-the-flag effect, *see* public opinion
Rangoon, Burma, 253. *See also* Burma
Reedy, George B., 22, 329
reserve call-up, *see* mobilization
reserve components, *see* mobilization
reserve forces, *see* mobilization
Reston, James, 198, 201
Revolutionary Development, *see* pacification
Ridgeway, General Matthew, 257, 259, 262
Rivers, Congressman Mendel, 48
Rolling Thunder, 15, 16, 17–18, 37, 43, 166
Roosevelt, President Franklin D., 269
Rostow, Walt W.: view of McNamara's proposals, 60; anticipated Tet, 79; views as to effects of Tet offensive, 81,

Library of Congress Cataloging in Publication Data

Schandler, Herbert Y   1928–
  The unmaking of a president.

  Bibliography: p.
  Includes index.
    1.   Vietnamese Conflict, 1961–1975—United States.
2.   United States—Politics and government—1936–1969.
3.   Johnson, Lyndon Baines, Pres. U.S., 1908–1973.
I. Title.
DS558.S33   959.704'3373   76–24297
ISBN 0–691–07586–7

also Johnson, President
  Lyndon B.
White House Situation Room,
  69
winter/spring offensive, 64, 70,
  299, 303, 307
Wisconsin primary, 225, 249
Wise Men: meet with president,
November 1967, 64–65, 129;
  meet March 1968, 255, 259–
  265, 267, 272–273
World Bank, 60
World War II, 178, 259, 332

Yale University, 203
Young, Senator Stephen M., 211